AP® ENGLISH LANGUAGE AND COMPOSITION

PREMIUM PREP

19th Edition

The Staff of The Princeton Review

PrincetonReview.com

Penguin
Random
House

The Princeton Review
110 East 42nd St, 7th Floor
New York, NY 10017

ISBN: 978-0-593-51761-1
eBook ISBN: 978-0-593-51762-8
ISSN: 2690-5361

AP is a trademark registered and owned by the College Board, which is not affiliated with, and does not endorse, this product.

The Princeton Review is not affiliated with Princeton University.

The Princeton Review Publishing Team

Rob Franek, Editor-in-Chief
David Soto, Senior Director, Data Operations
Stephen Koch, Senior Manager, Data Operations
Deborah Weber, Director of Production
Jason Ullmeyer, Production Design Manager
Jennifer Chapman, Senior Production Artist
Selena Coppock, Director of Editorial
Orion McBean, Senior Editor
Aaron Riccio, Senior Editor
Meave Shelton, Senior Editor
Chris Chimera, Editor
Patricia Murphy, Editor
Laura Rose, Editor
Isabelle Appleton, Editorial Assistant

Penguin Random House Publishing Team

Tom Russell, VP, Publisher
Alison Stoltzfus, Senior Director, Publishing
Emily Hoffman, Associate Managing Editor
Patty Collins, Executive Director of Production
Mary Ellen Owens, Assistant Director of Production
Alice Rahaeuser, Associate Production Manager
Maggie Gibson, Associate Production Manager
Suzanne Lee, Senior Designer
Eugenia Lo, Publishing Assistant

Editor: Patricia Murphy
Production Editors: Becky Radway and Wendy Rosen
Production Artist: Jennifer Chapman
Content Contributor: Corinne Dolci

For customer service, please contact **editorialsupport@review.com**, and be sure to include:

- full title of the book
- ISBN
- page number

Printed in the United States of America.

10 9 8 7 6 5 4 3 2 1

19th Edition

Acknowledgments

The Princeton Review would like to thank Corinne Dolci for her thorough review of this title and useful updates to the 19th edition. The editor of this edition would like to thank Becky Radway, Wendy Rosen, and Jennifer Chapman for their hard work on this edition as well.

Contents

Get More (Free) Content

at PrincetonReview.com/prep

As easy as 1·2·3

1 Go to PrincetonReview.com/prep or scan the **QR code** and enter the following ISBN to register your book:
9780593517611

2 Answer a few simple questions to set up an exclusive Princeton Review account. *(If you already have one, you can just log in.)*

3 Enjoy access to your **FREE** content!

Access Your Online Test Practice

Your AP Prep book comes with new interactive practice exams to help you prepare for digital test-taking! Find these tests in your online Student Tools, provided in two different formats:

- Fully digital versions with a timer option to simulate the exam experience
- Downloadable interactive PDFs with digital features like clicking your answer and typing your free-responses

Check back often as we continue to update the included AP Student Tools.

PLUS, IN YOUR ACCOUNT YOU CAN:

- Get valuable advice about the college application process, tips for essay writing, and financial aid info
- Use our searchable rankings to learn more about your dream school

- Access comprehensive study guides, digital flashcards, and a vocab list
- Check to see if there have been any updates or corrections to this edition

Need to report a potential **content** issue?

Contact **EditorialSupport@review.com** and include:
- full title of the book
- ISBN
- page number

Need to report a **technical** issue?

Contact **TPRStudentTech@review.com** and provide:
- your full name
- email address used to register the book
- full book title and ISBN
- Operating system (Mac/PC) and browser (Chrome, Firefox, Safari, etc.)

Look For These Icons Throughout The Book

 ONLINE ARTICLES

 OTHER REFERENCES

 APPLIED STRATEGIES

 PROVEN TECHNIQUES

 GOING DEEPER

 CRITICAL CONNECTION

 STUDY BREAK

Download our app at www.princetonreview.com/mobile/ apps/highschool or scan the QR Code.

Part I
Using This Book to Improve Your AP Score

- Preview: Your Knowledge, Your Expectations
- Your Guide to Using This Book
- How to Begin

PREVIEW: YOUR KNOWLEDGE, YOUR EXPECTATIONS

Your route to a high score on the AP English Language and Composition Exam depends a lot on how you plan to use this book. Respond to the following questions.

1. Rate your level of confidence about your knowledge of the content tested by the AP English Language and Composition Exam.

   A. Very confident—I know it all
   B. I'm pretty confident, but there are topics for which I could use help
   C. Not confident—I need quite a bit of support
   D. I'm not sure

2. Circle your goal score for the AP English Language and Composition Exam.

   5   4   3   2   1   I'm not sure yet

3. What do you expect to learn from this book? Circle all that apply to you.

   A. A general overview of the test and what to expect
   B. Strategies for how to approach the test
   C. The content tested by this exam
   D. I'm not sure yet

Not Sure Yet?
If you answered these three questions with "I'm not sure," you may need more time before you take the AP exam. But don't be discouraged! Review the content chapters before you take the practice tests in this book and you'll see improvement in your confidence and even your test scores.

YOUR GUIDE TO USING THIS BOOK

This book is organized to provide as much—or as little—support as you need, so you can use this book in whatever way will be most helpful to improve your score on the AP English Language and Composition Exam.

- The remainder of **Part I** provides guidance on how to use this book and helps you determine your strengths and weaknesses.

- **Part II** of this book contains your first practice test, a Diagnostic Answer Key, detailed answers and explanations for each question, and a scoring guide. (A bubble sheet is included after the last test and additional ones can be printed from your online Student Tools.) This is where you should begin your test preparation in order to realistically determine:
   ○ your starting point right now
   ○ which question types you're ready for and which you might need to practice
   ○ which content topics you are familiar with and which you will want to carefully review

   Once you have nailed down your strengths and weaknesses with regard to this exam, you can focus your test preparation, build a study plan, and be efficient with your time. Our Diagnostic Answer Key will assist you with this process.

- **Part III** of this book:
   ○ provides information about the structure, scoring, and content of the AP English Language and Composition Exam
   ○ will help you to make a study plan
   ○ points you toward additional resources

- **Part IV** explores various strategies, including:
  - how to tackle multiple-choice questions
  - how to write effective essays
  - how to manage your time to maximize the number of points available to you

- **Part V** of this book is a review of the academic content and skills that will give you an edge on the AP English Language and Composition Exam.

- **Parts VI and VII** contain Practice Tests 2–5, and their answers and explanations. (Bubble sheets can be found in the very back of the book for easy tear-out.) If you skipped Practice Test 1, we recommend that you do all the tests (with at least a day or two between each of them) so that you can track your progress. Additionally, this will help to identify any external issues: if you get a certain type of question wrong each time, you probably need to review it. If you got it wrong only once, you may have run out of time or been distracted by something. In either case, this will allow you to focus on the factors that caused the discrepancy in scores and to be as prepared as possible on the day of the test.

- **Online Resources** contain three additional practice tests. Follow the study guide based on the amount of time you have to study for your exam. Use the key terms to improve your vocabulary by creating flashcards to help you learn words you might see on the test.

You may choose to use some parts of this book over others, or you may work through the entire book. Your approach will depend on your needs and how much time you have. Let's now look at how to make this determination.

Once you register your book online, you can print the bubble sheets and scoring worksheets for your practice tests! Remember that these worksheets are meant to serve as a rough guideline only. AP exam scores are weighted according to a statistical process that varies slightly every year based on how students perform on the exam, but you can use the worksheets to approximate your score.

HOW TO BEGIN

1. **Take Practice Test 1**

   Before you can decide how to use this book, you need to take a practice test. Doing so will give you insight into your strengths and weaknesses, and the test will also help you create an effective study plan. If you're feeling test-phobic, remind yourself that a practice test is a tool for diagnosing yourself—it's not how well you do that matters, but how you use information gleaned from your performance to guide your preparation.

   So, before you read further, take Practice Test 1 starting at page 7 of this book. Be sure to do so in one sitting, following the instructions that appear before the test.

2. **Check Your Answers**

   Using the Diagnostic Answer Key on page 34, follow our three-step process to identify your strengths and weaknesses with regard to the tested topics. This will help you determine which content review chapters to prioritize when studying this book. Don't worry about the explanations for now, and don't worry about why you missed questions. We'll get to that soon.

3. Reflect on the Test

After you take your first test, respond to the following questions:

- How much time did you spend on the multiple-choice questions?
- How much time did you spend on each essay?
- How many multiple-choice questions did you miss?
- Do you feel you had the knowledge to address the subject matter of the essays?
- Do you feel you wrote well-organized, thoughtful essays?

4. Read Part III and Complete the Self-Evaluation

Part III provides information on how the test is structured and scored. As you read Part III, re-evaluate your answers to the questions above. At the end of Part III, you will revisit and refine the questions you answered above. You will then be able to make a study plan, based on your needs and time available, that will allow you to use this book most effectively.

5. Engage with Parts IV and V as Needed

Notice the word *engage*. You'll get more out of this book if you use it intentionally than if you read it passively, hoping for an improved score through osmosis.

The Strategy chapters will help you think about your approach to the question types on this exam. Part IV opens with a reminder to think about how you approach questions now, and closes with a reflection section asking you to think about how or whether you will change your approach in the future.

The Terms and Modes chapters in Part V are designed to provide a review of the terminology you are likely to encounter on the exam, and will help you to identify the rhetorical fallacies and modes used in both test passages and student essays. You will have the opportunity to assess your knowledge of the content of each chapter through test-appropriate questions and a Reflection section.

6. Take More Practice Tests and Assess Your Performance

Once you feel you have developed the strategies you need and gained the knowledge you lacked, you should take Practice Test 2, which starts at page 233. You should do so in one sitting, following the instructions at the beginning of the test.

When you complete the test, check your answers to the multiple-choice sections against the answer key on page 260. If possible, find a teacher to read your essays and provide feedback.

Once you have taken the test, reflect on what areas you still need to work on, and revisit the chapters in this book that address them. Through this type of reflection and engagement, you will continue to improve. Then, take Practice Tests 3, 4, and 5 in this book and Practice Tests A, B, and C online.

7. Keep Working

As we will discuss in Part III, there are other resources available to you, including a wealth of information on **AP Students:** apstudent.collegeboard.org/apcourse/ap-english-language-and-composition. You can continue to explore and engage in areas needing improvement right up to the day of the test.

Go Online!

Check us out on YouTube for test-taking tips and techniques to help you ace your next exam at www.youtube.com/ThePrincetonReview.

Part II
Practice Test 1

Practice Test 1

AP® English Language and Composition Exam

SECTION I: Multiple-Choice Questions

DO NOT BEGIN THE EXAM UNTIL YOU ARE TOLD TO DO SO.

DISCLAIMER: The official AP English Language and Composition Exam will be administered digitally. Instructions for the digital exam may differ from this practice test.

At a Glance

Total Time
1 hour
Number of Questions
45
Percent of Total Grade
45%

Instructions

Section I of this examination contains 45 multiple-choice questions. Choose the best answer to each question. Note: Pay particular attention to the requirements of questions that contain the words "NOT," "LEAST," or "EXCEPT."

Indicate all of your answers to the multiple-choice questions on the answer sheet. No credit will be given for anything written in this exam booklet, but you may use the booklet for notes or scratch work. After you have decided which of the suggested answers is best, completely fill in the corresponding oval on the answer sheet. Give only one answer to each question. If you change an answer, be sure that the previous mark is erased completely. Here is a sample question and answer.

Sample Question   Sample Answer

Chicago is a   Ⓐ ● Ⓒ Ⓓ
(A) state
(B) city
(C) country
(D) continent

Use your time effectively, working as quickly as you can without losing accuracy. Do not spend too much time on any one question. Go on to other questions and come back to the ones you have not answered if you have time.

About Guessing

Many candidates wonder whether or not to guess the answers to questions about which they are not certain. Multiple-choice scores are based on the number of questions answered correctly. Points are not deducted for incorrect answers, and no points are awarded for unanswered questions. Because points are not deducted for incorrect answers, you are encouraged to answer all multiple-choice questions. On any questions you do not know the answer to, you should eliminate as many choices as you can, and then select the best answer among the remaining choices.

GO ON TO THE NEXT PAGE.

This page intentionally left blank.

ENGLISH LANGUAGE AND COMPOSITION
SECTION I
Time—1 hour

Directions: This part consists of selections from prose works and questions on their content, form, and style. After reading each passage, choose the best answer to each question and completely fill in the corresponding oval on the answer sheet.

Note: Pay particular attention to the requirements of questions that contain the words NOT, LEAST, or EXCEPT.

Questions 1–12. Read the following passage carefully before you choose your answers.

The following is excerpted from a political leader's 1836 address to the British Parliament's House of Commons.

It appears to me impossible to suppose that the House will consider me presumptuous in wishing to be heard for a short time on this question….one in the highest degree
Line interesting to the people of Ireland. It is, whether we mean to
5 do justice to that country—whether we mean to continue the injustice which has been already done to it, or to hold out the hope that it will be treated in the same manner as England and Scotland. That is the question.

England never did do justice to Ireland—she never
10 did. What we have got of it we have extorted from men opposed to us on principle—against which principle they have made us such concessions as we have obtained from them. Years are coming over me, but my heart is as young and as ready as ever in the service of my country, of which
15 I glory in being the pensionary and the hired advocate. I stand in a situation in which no man ever stood yet—the faithful friend of my country—its servant—its stave, if you will—I speak its sentiments by turns to you and to itself. I require no £20,000,000 on behalf of Ireland[1]—I ask you
20 only for justice: will you—can you—I will not say dare you refuse, because that would make you turn the other way. I implore you, as English gentlemen, to take this matter into consideration now, because you never had such an opportunity of conciliating.
25 Experience makes fools wise; you are not fools, but you have yet to be convinced. I cannot forget the year 1825[2]. We begged then as we would for a beggar's boon; we asked for emancipation by all that is sacred amongst us, and I remember how my speech and person were treated, when I
30 had no opportunity of reply. The other place turned us out

and sent us back again, but we showed that justice was with us. The noble lord says the other place has declared the same sentiments with himself; but he could not use a worse argument. It is the very reason why we should acquiesce
35 in the measure of reform, for we have no hope from that House—all our hopes are centered in this; and I am the living representative of those hopes.

I have not fatigued myself, but the House, in coming forward upon this occasion. I may be laughed and sneered
40 at by those who talk of my power; but what has created it but the injustice that has been done in Ireland? If you refuse justice to that country, it is a melancholy consideration to me to think that you are adding substantially to that power and influence, while you are wounding my country to its
45 very heart's core; weakening that throne, the monarch who sits upon which, you say you respect; severing that union which, you say, is bound together by the tightest links, and withholding that justice from Ireland which she will not cease to seek till it is obtained; every man must admit
50 that the course I am taking is the legitimate and proper course—I defy any man to say it is not.

Condemn me elsewhere as much as you please, but this you must admit. You may taunt the ministry with having coalesced me, you may raise the vulgar cry of "Irishman
55 and Papist[3]" against me, you may send out men called ministers of God to slander and calumniate me; they may assume whatever garb they please, but the question comes into this narrow compass. I demand, I respectfully insist: on equal justice for Ireland, on the same principle by which it
60 has been administered to Scotland and England. I will not take less. Refuse me that if you can.

---

1. The author is petitioning for famine relief in the form of an immediate government loan. £20,000,000 was the exact amount the Treasury gave to slave owners when the British government outlawed slavery in the Caribbean.

2. In 1825, the British House passed a bill abolishing the author's Catholic Association.

---

3. This is a derogatory term for a Catholic.

GO ON TO THE NEXT PAGE.

1. Which of the following best describes the writer's exigence in the passage?

   (A) The lack of interest among members of the British Parliament to consider the rights of Irish people under common law
   (B) A growing Irish nationalism in rebellion to British rule
   (C) The need for equal justice for the citizens of Ireland under British rule
   (D) Widening disparities between the wealthy and the poor in Ireland

2. In the opening paragraph (lines 1–8), the writer provides two possible outcomes to the problems in Ireland primarily to

   (A) suggest to his audience that one of those outcomes is more fair-minded than the other
   (B) explain why the British are reluctant to extend equal treatment to Ireland
   (C) emphasize the influence of Irish nationalism on his political thinking
   (D) suggest that the rights of the Irish people had been steadily eroding over time

3. In the second paragraph (lines 9–24), which of the following best characterizes the writer's position on the relationship between Ireland and Britain?

   (A) Because the British aristocracy is so disconnected from the needs of ordinary people, political equality can only be achieved through extortion.
   (B) Because the British Parliament refuses to give any money to the Irish people, the author will settle for merely equal justice on behalf of his countrymen.
   (C) By adopting the methods suggested by the author, the Irish people have managed to secure most of their basic liberties.
   (D) Although Ireland has made some progress toward greater equality, the author believes there is more action needed.

4. In context, lines 9–15 ("England never . . . hired advocate") show that the writer's tone is

   (A) patronizing, yet stalwart
   (B) ingratiating, yet proud
   (C) somewhat bitter, yet resolute
   (D) sympathetic, yet irreverent

5. In the third paragraph, the writer mentions "the year 1825" (line 26) in order to

   (A) remind the audience of a prior attempt at reform that was resisted by the British Parliament
   (B) show that, since emancipation had failed, he must settle for reform
   (C) point out the key distinction between being foolish and being convinced
   (D) champion his own efforts at political reform

6. Based on the overall context of this passage, the "emancipation" described in the third paragraph was most likely

   (A) an Act of Parliament which allowed Roman Catholics to become members of the British House of Commons
   (B) an Irish law which forbade the keeping of slaves or indentured servants
   (C) a law which forbade Catholics in Ireland to be represented by members of their own faith in Parliament
   (D) a law which gave all Irish people the right to vote

7. In the fourth paragraph (lines 38–51), the writer mentions his own power primarily to

   (A) question the motives of those who are hearing his speech
   (B) highlight the irony of the Parliament's resistance to meeting the needs of the Irish people
   (C) defend his own political influence in the face of criticism
   (D) challenge the listeners to accept his role as primary spokesperson for the Irish people

8. In the context of the passage, all of the following phrases refer to similar ideas EXCEPT

   (A) "justice" (line 5)
   (B) "emancipation" (line 28)
   (C) "reform" (line 35)
   (D) "power and influence" (lines 43–44)

GO ON TO THE NEXT PAGE.

9. In the last paragraph, the speaker implores his listeners to

   (A) provide an explanation for why the Irish people have not yet received equal justice under the law
   (B) explore two distasteful alternatives and choose one of them over the other
   (C) accept that conflict is inevitable when negotiating political compromise
   (D) set aside their personal aversion to his character in favor of equal justice for the people of Ireland

10. Elsewhere, in a letter written to a friend, the author is quoted as saying:

    "The Protestants of Ireland...are political Protestants, that is, Protestants by reason of their participation in political power."

    This quote best supports the arguments made in which of the following paragraphs?

    (A) Paragraph 2
    (B) Paragraph 3
    (C) Paragraph 4
    (D) Paragraph 5

11. Each of the following political actions or opinions would be consistent with the sentiments expressed in this speech EXCEPT

    (A) opposition to slavery in other countries
    (B) promoting freedom of religion
    (C) the use of violence in political activism
    (D) allowing the use of both Irish Gaelic and English in public schools

12. Throughout the passage, the writer's tone suggests that he

    (A) acknowledges past failures, but believes in the possibility of future success
    (B) is triumphant about past successes, but is hungry for more advances
    (C) is bitter about the British aristocracy, but determined to win over their approval
    (D) is eager for advancement, but fatigued from failure

GO ON TO THE NEXT PAGE.

Questions 13–24. Read the following passage carefully before you choose your answers.

This passage is excerpted from a speech delivered to the United Nations in Paris, France, on September 28, 1948.

I have come this evening to talk with you on one of the greatest issues of our time—that is the preservation of human freedom. I have chosen to discuss it here in France,
Line at the Sorbonne, because here in this soil the roots of human
5 freedom have long ago struck deep and here they have been richly nourished. It was here the Declaration of the Rights of Man was proclaimed, and the great slogans of the French Revolution—liberty, equality, fraternity—fired the imagination of men. I have chosen to discuss this issue
10 in Europe because this has been the scene of the greatest historic battles between freedom and tyranny…

We must not be confused about what freedom is. Basic human rights are simple and easily understood: freedom of speech and a free press; freedom of religion and worship;
15 freedom of assembly and the right of petition; the right of men to be secure in their homes and free from unreasonable search and seizure and from arbitrary arrest and punishment.

We must not be deluded by the efforts of the forces of reaction to [corrupt] the great words of our free tradition and
20 thereby to confuse the struggle…

There are basic differences that show up even in the use of words between a democratic and a totalitarian country. For instance, "democracy" means one thing to the U.S.S.R. and another the U.S.A. and, I know, in France. I have served
25 since the first meeting of the nuclear commission on the Human Rights Commission, and I think this point stands out clearly.

The U.S.S.R. Representatives assert that they already have achieved many things which we, in what they call
30 the "bourgeois democracies" cannot achieve because their government controls the accomplishment of these things. Our government seems powerless to them because, in the last analysis, it is controlled by the people. They would not put it that way—they would say that the people in the U.S.S.R.
35 control their government by allowing their government to have certain absolute rights. We, on the other hand, feel that certain rights can never be granted to the government, but must be kept in the hands of the people…I think the best example one can give of this basic difference of the use of
40 terms is "the right to work." The Soviet Union insists that this is a basic right which it alone can guarantee because it alone provides full employment by the government. But the right to work in the Soviet Union means the assignment of workers to do whatever task is given to them by the
45 government without an opportunity for the people to participate in the decision that the government should do this. A society in which everyone works is not necessarily a free society and may indeed be a slave society; on the other hand, a society in which there is widespread economic
50 insecurity can turn freedom into a barren and vapid right for millions of people.

We in the United States have come to realize it means freedom to choose one's job, to work or not to work as one desires. We, in the United States, have come to
55 realize, however, that people have a right to demand that their government will not allow them to starve because, as individuals, they cannot find work of the kind they are accustomed to doing, and this is a decision brought about by public opinion which came as a result of the great depression
60 in which many people were out of work, but we would not consider in the United States that we had gained any freedom if we were compelled to follow a dictatorial assignment to work where and when we were told. The right of choice would seem to us an important, fundamental freedom.
65 The place to discuss the issue of human rights is in the forum of the United Nations. The United Nations has been set up as the common meeting ground for nations, where we can consider together our mutual problems and take advantage of our differences in experience…It is now as
70 always our hope that despite the wide differences in approach we face in the world today, we can with mutual good faith in the principles of the United Nations Charter, arrive at a common basis of understanding.

13. Which of the following is most likely the reason why the author delivered this speech to the United Nations?

   (A) She was advocating for the creation of universal standards of human rights by the members of the United Nations.
   (B) She wished to affirm the United Nations continuing commitment to the defense of human rights in all its member nations.
   (C) As the only female member of the United States delegation, she wished to assert her power to influence the United Nations in all its endeavors.
   (D) She wished to counteract the Soviet influence on standards of human rights in the United States.

14. The speaker's overall purpose in the first paragraph is to

   (A) capture the listeners' attention
   (B) demonstrate acknowledgment of her listeners' diverse backgrounds
   (C) express satisfaction for the advancements already made for human rights
   (D) inspire faith in a better future for the world

GO ON TO THE NEXT PAGE.

15. In the first paragraph, the author makes references to the "Declaration of the Rights of Man" and the "French Revolution" for all of the following reasons EXCEPT

(A) to refer to important historical events with which most in her audience would be familiar
(B) to establish herself as educated about the subject matter at hand
(C) to cite examples of very different interpretations of democracy and human rights
(D) to explain why she has chosen to deliver her speech in France

16. Throughout the passage, the writer equates "human rights" with all of the following EXCEPT

(A) employment for all
(B) freedom
(C) the United States Bill of Rights
(D) democracy

17. In line 50, "vapid" most nearly means

(A) meaningless
(B) boring
(C) lively
(D) interesting

18. In the context of the speech, the author cites the "right to work" in line 40 as an example of

(A) a basic human right which must be protected
(B) the assignment of workers to certain tasks by government force or coercion
(C) a term which may have different interpretations in different societies
(D) a euphemism for a slave society

19. In the final paragraph, how does the author imply that her audience may reach a consensus on the issue of human rights?

(A) She suggests that nations in disagreement with her stance should acquiesce to the wishes of the majority.
(B) She warns of the danger of persistent differences of opinion on the matters at hand.
(C) She acknowledges the difficulty of agreeing on core principles, but remains confident in the possibility of compromise.
(D) She asserts that the United Nations is the only place where real agreement between the nations involved can be had.

20. In a different excerpt from this speech is the following:

"People who have glimpsed freedom will never be content until they have secured it for themselves.... People who continue to be denied the respect to which they are entitled as human beings will not acquiesce forever in such denial."

The above quote is most related to which of the ideas expressed in this speech?

(A) "the scene of the greatest historic battles between freedom and tyranny," (lines 10–11)
(B) "We must not be confused about what freedom is." (line 12)
(C) "'democracy' means one thing to the U.S.S.R. and another the U.S.A. and, I know, in France." (lines 23–24)
(D) "a decision brought about by public opinion which came as a result of the great depression" (lines 58–59)

GO ON TO THE NEXT PAGE.

21. World War II ended in 1945 just before the creation of the United Nations, and the author delivered this speech in 1948. In keeping with these themes, all of the following are possible reasons for the timing of these events EXCEPT

    (A) The United Nations wished to prevent a future war by addressing the issue of global human rights.
    (B) The author wanted to prevent a future war by addressing the issue of human rights at the United Nations.
    (C) After their defeat in World War II, the Soviet Union embraced democracy by joining the United Nations and adopting its tenets on human rights.
    (D) Despite their alliance during World War II, the United States and the Soviet Union had divergent views on freedom and human rights, a challenge for the United Nations to reconcile.

22. Suppose that an American politician wished to cite principles outlined in this speech to further domestic civil rights legislation. Which assertion would be most consistent with its sentiments?

    (A) Civil rights legislation has been successfully implemented in other countries; therefore, it should be implemented in the United States.
    (B) With proper dialogue and consent, civil rights can be implemented successfully in both foreign countries and in the United States.
    (C) The United States has learned valuable civil rights lessons from studying the practices of other countries.
    (D) The United States has civil rights policies that should be adopted by other countries.

23. All of the following quotes by famous Americans are consistent with the themes of this speech EXCEPT

    (A) "The battle for human rights—at home and abroad—is far from over."
    (B) "We owe it to ourselves and to those who sacrificed so much for our liberty to keep America in the forefront of this battle [for human rights]."
    (C) "Freedom means the supremacy of human rights everywhere."
    (D) "Knowledge makes a man unfit to be a slave."

24. Which of the following most accurately represents the author's views on freedom as expressed in the speech?

    (A) With great freedom comes great responsibility.
    (B) Freedom is essential to the preservation of human rights.
    (C) Even though freedom may lead to hunger and unemployment, it is an essential component of human rights.
    (D) When freedom and human rights conflict, freedom should prevail.

GO ON TO THE NEXT PAGE.

Questions 25–31 are based on the following passage.

The passage below is a draft.

(1) Instantly, almost 50 years since her death, her hard work and fabulous novels still have much to teach the modern audience. (2) She bravely overcame the challenges she faced and demonstrated that perseverance makes anything possible.

(3) Hurston ascribed much of her deeply individualistic personality to the experience of growing up in Eatonville, Florida. (4) The town was unique in that it was particularly hot in the summer, but mild at other times of the year. (5) Hurston always said growing up in a community totally separate from the larger white society allowed her a freedom and independence not available to everyone in the south.

(6) Hurston began her undergraduate studies at Howard University, but her obvious intelligence and talent soon earned her a scholarship to Barnard College in New York City. (7) Moving north in the 1920s thrust her into the midst of the Harlem Renaissance, a Black cultural movement that spawned exceptional achievements in literature, art, and music. (8) Interacting with the likes of Langston Hughes, W.E.B. Du Bois, Billie Holiday, and Duke Ellington, Hurston developed her skills as a writer and published numerous short stories and poems. (9) The most influential work that came to define her career grew out of her attempt to capture the Black experience. (10) That novel, called *Their Eyes Were Watching God*, traced three generations of a family living in Eatonville. (11) Her authentic representation of the southern dialect caused her Harlem Renaissance contemporaries to belittle the work for what they saw as its propagation of inaccurate stereotypes. (12) Hurston, however, remained true to her project, convinced that the accuracy of her representation would ultimately prevail over the political pressures her peers sought to inflict upon her.

(13) History has shown that Hurston was right. (14) Modern critics admire her authentic and skillful representation of the language as well as her realistic portrayal of daily life in the early twentieth century. (15) She is universally applauded as one of the best writers of her era and ranked with Toni Morrison, Maya Angelou, and Alice Walker as one of the most important African American writers of all time.

25. Which of the following sentences, if placed before sentence 1, would both convey the complexity of Zora Neale Hurston's career and provide the most effective introduction to the essay?

(A) The granddaughter of a Baptist preacher, Black writer Zora Neale Hurston was born on January 7, 1891 in Notasulga, Alabama.

(B) Zora Neale Hurston proves to be a study in contrasts: a Black writer reaching a white audience, a woman struggling in a man's profession, and an independent thinker living in a conformist era.

(C) Although Zora Neale Hurston was largely ignored and marginalized during her lifetime, academics have recently begun to pay closer attention to this writer who has so influenced subsequent generations of Black writers.

(D) In 1918, Zora Neale Hurston was admitted to Howard University, a historically Black college in Washington, DC, was one of the original members of the Zeta Phi Beta Black sorority, and later founded *The Hilltop*, the university's student newspaper.

26. The writer wants to change the beginning of sentence 1 (reproduced below) to better set up a comparison within the paragraph and also wishes to create a more objective tone in harmony with the rest of the essay.

Instantly, almost 50 years since her death, her hard work and fabulous novels still have much to teach the modern audience.

Which version best accomplishes this goal?

(A) Presently, almost 50 years since her death, her hard work and fabulous novels still have much to teach the modern audience.

(B) Currently, almost 50 years since her death, her tireless advocacy for civil rights and her renowned novels still have much to teach the modern audience.

(C) Now, almost 50 years since her death, her novels' insights into the African-American experience still have resonance with modern audiences.

(D) At the present, almost 50 years since her death, her novels are beloved by some and scorned by others.

GO ON TO THE NEXT PAGE.

27. In sentence 4 (reproduced below), the writer wants to support the main idea about Hurston conveyed in this paragraph.

    The town was unique in that it was particularly hot in the summer, but mild at other times of the year.

    Which version of the underlined text best accomplishes this goal?

    (A) (as it is now)
    (B) a fairly typical Florida small town, founded in the mid-19ᵗʰ century.
    (C) the first all-black town to be incorporated in the country.
    (D) racially integrated, even at a time when Jim Crow laws reigned in the South.

28. The writer wants to add the following sentence to the third paragraph to provide additional explanation.

    Billie Holiday's music evokes such feeling and melancholy that it's no wonder she became so popular.

    Where would the sentence best be placed?

    (A) After sentence 6
    (B) After sentence 7
    (C) After sentence 8
    (D) Do not add the sentence.

29. Which sentence best exemplifies how Hurston's work was viewed by her contemporaries?

    (A) Sentence 1
    (B) Sentence 6
    (C) Sentence 11
    (D) Sentence 14

30. The writer has decided to divide the third paragraph into two parts. The best place to add the new paragraph break would be at the beginning of sentence

    (A) 9, because it would indicate that Hurston's writing was most strongly influenced by Langston Hughes.
    (B) 9, because it would signal the essay's shift in focus to one of Hurston's novels.
    (C) 10, because all the remaining sentences in the paragraph provide a detailed summary of the plot of Hurston's novel.
    (D) 10, because it would indicate that the essay is now going to focus on social conditions in Eatonville.

31. The writer wants to add a phrase at the beginning of sentence 14 (reproduced below), adjusting the capitalization as needed, to set up a comparison with the idea discussed in sentence 13.

    Modern critics admire her authentic and skillful representation of the language as well as her realistic portrayal of daily life in the early twentieth century.

    Which of the following choices best accomplishes this goal?

    (A) However,
    (B) Today,
    (C) Thus,
    (D) In addition,

GO ON TO THE NEXT PAGE.

Questions 32–38 are based on the following passage.

The passage below is a draft.

(1) Most everyone has heard of Jimmy Carter. (2) As president of the United States from 1977 to 1981, he oversaw a particularly turbulent time in American history.

(3) Yet even though Carter held America's most powerful office, he is also renowned for the work he has done since he left the White House. (4) His record on humanitarian issues around the world sets him apart as a caring, dedicated person who wants to see the underprivileged benefit from the great wealth, power, and generosity of this country.

(5) Some of the major issues Carter has focused on throughout his career revolved around relations with the Middle East. (6) He questioned a national energy policy designed to reduce American dependence long before it was popular to do so on foreign oil and brokered a peace treaty between Israel and Egypt. (7) Likewise, he was among the first to insist publicly on basic human rights for everyone around the world, founding a non-profit organization, The Carter Center, to work toward that end. (8) Among other activities, The Carter Center works to expand modern health care to developing nations in order to contain disease and improve quality of life around the world, in many different countries.

(9) Carter works actively to improve the standard of living at home here in the United States as well. (10) He and his wife Roslyn are enthusiastic supporters of Habitat for Humanity. (11) This volunteer-based organization devotes itself to building affordable but quality housing for those who otherwise might not be able to buy a home. (12) Community workers come together on their own free time to construct, paint, and landscape simple homes, working side-by-side with the families that will occupy the residences.

(13) For all these reasons, Carter deserves respect for dedicating his career to public service. (14) Everyone can agree with his impressive philanthropy and acknowledge his obvious devotion to all of humanity.

32. The writer wants to add more information to the first paragraph to support the assertion made in sentence 2. All of the following pieces of evidence help achieve this purpose EXCEPT

(A) a description of the Iran hostage crisis of November 1979 when 52 United States diplomats and citizens were held by militarized Iranian college students who had taken over the U.S. Embassy in Tehran

(B) a description of the "stagflation" that plagued the 1970s U.S. economy, a situation in which the inflation rate is high, economic growth slows, and unemployment is high

(C) a reference to the sudden shortage of gasoline during the summer of 1979 which led to rationing, hoarding, and higher prices for consumers

(D) an enumeration of Carter's pursuit of Israeli/Egyptian peace accords, Strategic Arms Limitation Talks (SALT II), and the return of the Panama Canal to Panama

33. In sentence 4 (reproduced below), which of the following versions of the underlined text would best convey its main idea while also making the tone of the passage more objective?

His record on humanitarian issues around the world sets him apart as a caring, dedicated person who wants to see the underprivileged benefit from the great wealth, power, and generosity of this country.

(A) (as it is now)

(B) culminated in his creation of the Carter Center to promote and expand human rights for which he was awarded the Nobel Peace Prize in 2002.

(C) proves his commitment to the needs of average Americans.

(D) is best illustrated by his peace-making efforts in the ongoing Israeli-Palestinian conflict.

GO ON TO THE NEXT PAGE.

34. In sentence 6 (reproduced below), the writer wants to provide more detail to expand on the ideas mentioned in sentence 5.

    He *questioned a national energy policy designed to reduce American dependence long before it was popular to do so on foreign oil* and brokered a peace treaty between Israel and Egypt.

    Which version of the underlined text best accomplishes this goal?

    (A) (as it is now)
    (B) promoted a national energy policy designed to reduce American dependence on foreign oil long before it was popular to do so
    (C) purchased foreign oil as part of a national energy policy designed to reduce American dependence on the Middle East long before it was popular to do so
    (D) long before it was popular to do so rejected a national energy policy designed for foreign oil to reduce American dependence on it

35. The writer wants to add the following sentence to the fourth paragraph to provide additional explanation.

    However, Carter does not focus all his efforts abroad.

    Where would the sentence best be placed?

    (A) Before sentence 9
    (B) After sentence 9
    (C) After sentence 10
    (D) After sentence 11

36. In sentence 14 (reproduced below), the writer wants to summarize key points made in the essay while maintaining an objective tone.

    Everyone can agree *with President Carter's impressive philanthropy and acknowledge his obvious devotion to all of humanity.*

    Which version of the underlined text best accomplishes this goal?

    (A) (as it is now)
    (B) that the country made a grave mistake by not electing Carter to a second term.
    (C) that President Carter exemplifies the values expressed in the First Amendment to the Constitution as much as any American ever could.
    (D) that President Carter has spent the majority of his life devoted to the service of others.

37. The writer wants to add the following sentence to the essay to provide additional explanation.

    By doing so, they do more than build houses: they build communities.

    Where would the sentence best be placed?

    (A) After sentence 8
    (B) After sentence 9
    (C) After sentence 10
    (D) After sentence 12

38. The writer wishes to add a paragraph to the essay to further expand on its major theme. What would be the best topic for this paragraph?

    (A) Carter's tenure as governor of Georgia from 1971 to 1975, enumerating both his successes and failures
    (B) Carter's experience as a young man when, after the death of his father, he assumed control of the family's Georgia peanut farm
    (C) Carter's decision to pardon draft evaders after the end of the Vietnam War
    (D) Carter's leadership in assisting victims of major hurricanes throughout the last twenty years

GO ON TO THE NEXT PAGE.

Questions 39–45 are based on the following passage.

The passage below is a draft.

(1) Many people believe that language is the domain of human beings. (2) However, cats have developed an intricate language not for each other, but for the human beings who have adopted them as pets. (3) When communicating with each other, cats' "talk" is a complex system of nonverbal signals. (4) In particular, their tails, rather than any kind of "speech," provide cats' chief means of expression. (5) They also use physical contact to express their feelings. (6) With other cats, cats will use their voices only to express pain. (7) Next, incredibly, all of that changes when a human walks into the room. (8) Cats use a wide range of vocal expressions when they communicate with a person, from affectionate meows to menacing hisses. (9) Since cats' verbal expressions are not used to communicate with other cats, it is logical to conclude that cats developed this "language" expressly to communicate with their human owners.

(10) This fact is demonstrated more clearly when observing households that have only one cat. (11) An only cat is usually very vocal, since the only creature around with whom the cat can communicate is its owner. (12) Cats with other feline companions, though, are much quieter. (13) If they want to have a conversation, they need only go to their fellow cats and communicate in their natural way.

(14) Since cats learned to meow for the sole purpose of communicating with human beings, owners should take the time to learn what their different meows mean. (15) If an owner knows, to name just a few examples, which meow means the cat is hungry, which means the cat wants to be petted, and which means the cat wants to have a little "conversation," the bond between cat and owner will grow deeper. (16) Certainly, after a time, owners will see that communicating with their pets, not just cats, is every bit as important to forging good relationships as communicating with other humans. (17) Once, as an owner, one knows that the cat is not just making senseless noises but is making an attempt to communicate, one can make an effort to communicate in return. (18) After all, a cat isn't meowing just for the sake of making noise; however, cats are less communicative than many other animals.

39. In sentence 2 (reproduced below), the writer wants to clearly and effectively express the ownership relationship between humans and cats.

However, cats have developed an intricate language not for each other, but for the human beings who <u>have adopted them as pets.</u>

Which of the following versions of the sentence best achieves this purpose?

(A) (as it is now)
(B) enjoy having cats in their lives.
(C) often have dogs and other pets as well.
(D) are naturally inclined to prefer cats to the company of dogs.

40. In sentence 3 (reproduced below), which of the following versions of the underlined text most clearly expresses the main idea of the sentence?

When communicating with each other, <u>cats' "talk" is a complex system of nonverbal signals.</u>

(A) (as it is now)
(B) a complicated system of nonverbal signals is used by cats to "talk."
(C) cats "talk" with a complex system of nonverbal signals.
(D) "talking" is done by cats with a system of complex nonverbal signals.

41. The writer wants to delete sentence 6. Should the writer make this change?

(A) Yes, because it expresses an idea already mentioned elsewhere in the essay.
(B) Yes, because it is only another repetitive description of the ways in which cats communicate nonverbally.
(C) No, because it provides an important exception to the general trend described in this paragraph.
(D) No, because it is the only time that pain is mentioned in this essay.

GO ON TO THE NEXT PAGE.

42. The writer is considering the possibility of dividing up the second paragraph into two parts and possibly adding or deleting words in order to aid the overall flow of the text, adjusting capitalization as necessary.

Should the writer make this change, and what alterations might be necessary?

(A) Do not divide up the paragraph or make any changes to the wording.
(B) Begin a new paragraph after sentence 6 and eliminate the word "Next" in sentence 7.
(C) Do not begin a new paragraph, but eliminate the word "Next" in sentence 7.
(D) Begin a new paragraph after sentence 6 and replace the word "Next" with "At this time."

43. The writer wants to add the following sentence after sentence 13 to provide additional explanation.

On the other hand, the natural way for most birds to communicate is vocally, by way of the "bird song."

Should the writer add this sentence here?

(A) Yes, because it shows that cats are truly unique in communicating nonverbally.
(B) Yes, because it adds a relevant and enlightening detail about another animal.
(C) No, because it merely repeats information given earlier in the essay.
(D) No, because it does not contribute to the development of this paragraph and the essay as a whole.

44. Which of the following sentences, if placed after sentence 15, would emphasize that cats communicate vocally with their owners to express a large number of different emotions in addition to those listed in the previous sentence?

(A) Cats will tell their owners when they feel pain, sadness, irritation, or love.
(B) Cats communicate these emotions differently if they are communicating with other cats.
(C) Humans have an easier time communicating with mammals rather than other species of animals.
(D) The range of emotions that a cat may experience is as rich and varied as that of any living animal.

45. In sentence 18 (reproduced below), which of the following versions of the underlined text best establishes the writer's position on the main argument of the passage?

After all, a cat isn't meowing just for the sake of making noise; <u>however, cats are less communicative than many other animals.</u>

(A) (as it is now)
(B) rather, there's a good chance that that cat is trying to communicate with a nearby human friend.
(C) instead, that cat is probably trying to communicate with other cats by meowing.
(D) on the other hand, it is better to have more than one cat so they can better experience a natural development.

END OF SECTION I

AP® English Language and Composition Exam

DO NOT BEGIN THE EXAM UNTIL YOU ARE TOLD TO DO SO.

DISCLAIMER: The official AP English Language and Composition Exam will be administered digitally. Instructions for the digital exam may differ from this practice test.

At a Glance

Total Time
2 hours, plus a 15-minute reading period

Number of Questions
3

Percent of Total Grade
55%

Instructions

Section II of this examination requires answers in essay form. To help you use your time well, the coordinator will announce the time at which each question should be completed. If you finish any question before time is announced, you may go on to the following question. If you finish the examination in less than the time allotted, you may go back and work on any essay question you want.

Each essay will be judged on its clarity and effectiveness in dealing with the requirements of the topic assigned and on the quality of the writing. After completing each question, you should check your essay for accuracy of punctuation, spelling, and diction; you are advised, however, not to attempt many longer corrections. Remember that quality is far more important than quantity.

Write your essays with a pen, preferably in black or dark blue ink. Be sure to write CLEARLY and LEGIBLY. Cross out any errors you make.

GO ON TO THE NEXT PAGE.

**ENGLISH LANGUAGE AND COMPOSITION
SECTION II
Total Time—2 hours, 15 minutes**

Question 1

**Suggested reading and writing time—55 minutes.
It is suggested that you spend 15 minutes reading the question, analyzing and evaluating the sources,
and 40 minutes writing your response.
Note: You may begin writing your response before the reading period is over.**

(This question counts for one-third of the total essay section score.)

The exploration of space has been dreamt of and implemented in the United States and in other countries for over 60 years. The National Aeronautics and Space Administration (NASA) was established in 1958 to plan and oversee all American space projects, including the Apollo Moon landing missions, the Skylab space station, and the Space Shuttle. Ever since its inception, space exploration has been controversial, with some saying it is an essential part of human progress and others saying that it is too expensive and dangerous to continue.

Carefully read the following six sources, including the introductory information for each source. Write an essay that synthesizes material from at least three of the sources and develops your position on the notion that continued space exploration is productive and beneficial.

Your argument should be the focus of your essay. Use the sources to develop your argument and explain the reasoning for it. Avoid merely summarizing the sources. Indicate clearly which sources you are drawing from, whether through direct quotation, paraphrase, or summary. You may cite the sources as Source A, Source B, and so forth, or by using the descriptions in parentheses.

Source A (Kennedy)
Source B (Logsdon)
Source C (Federal Funding)
Source D (Highfield)
Source E (Gallup)
Source F (Koren)

In your response you should do the following:

- Respond to the prompt with a thesis that presents a defensible position.

- Select and use evidence from at least 3 of the provided sources to support your line of reasoning. Indicate clearly the sources used through direct quotation, paraphrase, or summary. Sources may be cited as Source A, Source B, etc., or by using the description in parentheses.

- Explain how the evidence supports your line of reasoning.

- Use appropriate grammar and punctuation in communicating your argument.

GO ON TO THE NEXT PAGE.

Source A

Speech from President John F. Kennedy at the Rice
Stadium in Texas on September 12, 1962.

We set sail on this new sea because there is new knowledge to be gained, and new rights to be won, and they must be won and used for the progress of all people. For space science, like nuclear science and all technology, has no conscience of its own. Whether it will become a force for good or ill depends on man, and only if the United States occupies a position of pre-eminence can we help decide whether this new ocean will be a sea of peace or a new terrifying theater of war. I do not say that we should or will go unprotected against the hostile misuse of space any more than we go unprotected against the hostile use of land or sea, but I do say that space can be explored and mastered without feeding the fires of war, without repeating the mistakes that man has made in extending his writ around this globe of ours.

There is no strife, no prejudice, no national conflict in outer space as yet. Its hazards are hostile to us all. Its conquest deserves the best of all mankind, and its opportunity for peaceful cooperation may never come again. But why, some say, the Moon? Why choose this as our goal? And they may well ask, why climb the highest mountain? Why, 35 years ago, fly the Atlantic? Why does Rice play Texas?

We choose to go to the Moon. We choose to go to the Moon...We choose to go to the Moon in this decade and do the other things, not because they are easy, but because they are hard; because that goal will serve to organize and measure the best of our energies and skills, because that challenge is one that we are willing to accept, one we are unwilling to postpone, and one we intend to win, and the others, too.

GO ON TO THE NEXT PAGE.

Source B

Excerpt from "Issues in Science and Technology." By
John M. Logsdon, 2011.

No one aware of today's government deficits and the overall economic situation can suggest that the United States in 2011 commit the type of financial support to future space efforts that Kennedy made available to carry out Apollo. Kennedy made and sustained his commitment to developing the capabilities needed to reach the Moon before the Soviet Union because doing so was clearly linked to enhancing U.S. global power and national pride in the Cold War setting of the 1960s. Today, there most certainly is no pressing national security question, the answer to which the answer is "go to an asteroid," or indeed anywhere else beyond Earth orbit. Space exploration is now a discretionary activity, not a national imperative. This country's leaders need to decide, under very difficult circumstances, whether their image of the U.S. future includes continued leadership in space exploration, and then make the even harder choice to provide on a continuing basis resources adequate to achieving that leading position.

What faces the country today with respect to the future in space is in many ways a more challenging decision than that which faced Kennedy a half-century ago. In his final months in the White House, Kennedy was prescient enough to discern one path toward a sustainable space future: making space exploration a cooperative global undertaking. In the September 1963 UN speech, Kennedy observed that "Surely we should explore whether the scientists and astronauts … of all the world cannot work together in the conquest of space, sending some day … to the Moon not representatives of a single nation, but representatives of all our countries." That admonition remains relevant today.

GO ON TO THE NEXT PAGE.

Source C

Federal Research and Development Funding by
Agency, FY2020–FY2022.

Table I. Federal Research and Development Funding by Agency, FY2020–FY2022
(budget authority, dollar amounts in millions)

Department/Agency	FY2020 Actual	FY2021 Estimate	FY2022 Request	FY2021–FY2022	
				Dollar Change	Percentage Change
Department of Defense	62,438	63,350	62,800	-550	-0.9%
Dept. of Health & Human Services	44,455	43,494	51,232	7,738	17.8%
Department of Energy	19,476	19,312	21,452	2,140	11.1%
NASA	14,801	13,226	14,565	1,339	10.1%
National Science Foundation	6,800	7,408	8,173	765	10.3%
Department of Agriculture	2,989	2,965	3,609	644	21.7%
Department of Commerce	1,953	2,122	2,743	621	29.3%
Department of Veterans Affairs	1,366	1,420	1,498	78	5.5%
Department of Transportation	1,043	1,024	1,339	315	30.8%
Department of the Interior	1,094	1,033	1,221	188	18.2%
Department of Homeland Security	532	590	627	37	6.3%
Smithsonian Institution	516	524	585	61	11.6%
Environmental Protection Agency	237	445	473	28	6.3%
Department of Education	344	322	346	24	7.5%
Other	582	563	597	34	6.0%
Total	**158,626**	**157,798**	**171,260**	**13,462**	**8.5%**

Source: CRS analysis of data form EOP, OMB, *Analytical Perspectives, Budget of the United States Government, Fiscal Year 2022, Research and Development*, May 28, 2021. https://www.whitehouse.gov/wp-content/uploads/2021/05/ap_14_research_fy22.pdf.

GO ON TO THE NEXT PAGE.

> ### Source D
>
> "Colonies in space may be only hope, says Hawking."
> By Roger Highfield. *The Telegraph*. October 16,
> 2001.

The human race is likely to be wiped out by a doomsday virus before the Millennium is out, unless we set up colonies in space, Prof Stephen Hawking warns today.

In an interview with The Telegraph, Prof Hawking, the world's best-known cosmologist, says that biology, rather than physics, presents the biggest challenge to human survival.

"Although September 11 was horrible, it didn't threaten the survival of the human race, like nuclear weapons do," said the Cambridge University scientist.

"In the long term, I am more worried about biology. Nuclear weapons need large facilities, but genetic engineering can be done in a small lab. You can't regulate every lab in the world. The danger is that either by accident or design, we create a virus that destroys us.

"I don't think the human race will survive the next thousand years, unless we spread into space. There are too many accidents that can befall life on a single planet. But I'm an optimist. We will reach out to the stars."

Current theories suggest that space travel will be tedious, using spaceships travelling slower than light.

But Prof Hawking, Lucasian professor of mathematics at Cambridge, says that a warp drive, of the kind seen in Star Trek, cannot be ruled out.

This method of space exploration and colonisation, apparently the stuff of science fiction, could be one possible escape from the human predicament.

Prof Hawking believes that genetic engineering could be used to "improve" human beings to meet the challenges of long duration space travel.

Cyborgs, humans with computers linked to their brains, will be needed to prevent intelligent computers taking over. "I think humans will have to learn to live in space," he said.

GO ON TO THE NEXT PAGE.

> **Source E**
>
> CNN/USA Today/Gallup Poll. Feb. 2, 2003.

Poll questions asked on February 2nd, 2003:

"As you may know, the space shuttle Columbia broke apart and was lost as it attempted to return to Earth yesterday...In light of the space shuttle disaster yesterday in which the seven astronauts were killed do you feel the U.S. should or should not continue the manned space shuttle program?"

Should Continue	Should Not	Unsure
82%	15%	3%

"How much confidence do you have that NASA, the U.S. space agency, will be able to prevent accidents like this from happening in the future: a great deal of confidence, a fair amount, not very much, or none at all?"

A Great Deal	A Fair Amount	Not Very Much	None At All	Unsure
38%	44%	11%	6%	1%

"Looking beyond the tragedy, how would you rate the job being done by NASA? Would you say it is doing an excellent, good, only fair, or poor job?"

Excellent	Good	Only Fair	Poor	Unsure
45%	37%	13%	2%	3%

"Should the amount of money being spent on the U.S. space program be increased, kept at current levels, decreased or ended altogether?"

Increased	Current Levels	Decreased	Ended	Unsure
24%	56%	9%	7%	4%

"Some people say the United States should concentrate on unmanned missions like the Voyager probe. Others say it is important to maintain a manned space program, as well. Which comes closer to your view?"

Unmanned Missions	Manned Missions	Unsure
22%	73%	5%

"Which comes closer to your view? Yesterday's tragedy was regrettable, but you thought something like this would happen again sooner or later. OR, yesterday's tragedy was regrettable and you didn't think something like this would ever happen in your lifetime."

Thought it would happen again	Didn't think it would happen again	Unsure
71%	28%	1%

"Based on what you have heard or read, how likely do you think it is that the loss of the Space Shuttle was a terrorist act? Do you think it was definitely an act of terrorism, probably an act of terrorism, probably not an act of terrorism, or definitely not an act of terrorism?"

Definitely an act of terrorism	Probably an act of terrorism	Probably not an act of terrorism	Definitely not an act of terrorism	Unsure
2%	10%	33%	53%	2%

GO ON TO THE NEXT PAGE.

Source F

"Risks of space colonization." By Marko Kovic,
Futures, Volume 126, February 2021. July 2020.

"Space colonization, the establishment of permanent human habitats beyond Earth, has an enormous potential moral value because successful space colonization is the necessary condition for trillions of future people to come into existence. At the same time, however, space colonization is not risk-free. The risks of space colonization are so grave that, in a bad-case scenario, successful space colonization could create more moral disvalue than value: possibly even orders of magnitude more.

[There are] three types of risks that are created by space colonization: Prioritization risks, aberration risks, and conflict risks. Prioritization risks are risks whereby existing catastrophic and existential risks are exacerbated because of colonization efforts. Aberration risks are newly created risks due to space colonization which expand the moral circle beyond humankind and which can potentially create disvalue orders of magnitude greater than all of humankind's potential positive future value. Conflict risks are risks related to violent conflicts caused by hostile intelligence, human or otherwise. These risk types and the specific risks within them are not an exhaustive list of all risks that are created by space colonization, but they are illustrative of the fact that the risks of space colonization is a priority that warrants scientific and public attention. In an only slightly poetically exaggerated way, space colonization can be considered the single most important juncture of human history — so much is at stake that all suffering and all happiness that has ever existed on Earth simply pales in comparison.

The issue of space colonization risks should spill over from academia into public life as soon as possible. Academic research and debate is certainly necessary in order to further map out the problem, but ultimately, our collective goal, I believe, is to establish empirically and philosophically sensible real-world governance in order to make space colonization as safe as possible. Reducing the risks of space colonization even by a tiny fraction means an enormous increase in expected moral value, or an even greater decrease in expected moral disvalue.

The future in which humankind colonizes space is vast, and so are both the potential happiness as well as the potential suffering we can fill that future with."

GO ON TO THE NEXT PAGE.

Question 2

Suggested time—40 minutes.

(This question counts for one-third of the total essay section score.)

In 2015, then President Barack Obama delivered a speech at Le Bourget in Paris, France at the First Session of COP21, the United Nations Climate Change conference. Read the passage carefully. Then, in a well-developed essay, analyze the rhetorical choices Obama makes to advocate for world efforts to combat climate change.

In your response, you should do the following:

- Respond to the prompt with a thesis that analyzes the writer's rhetorical choices.
- Select and use evidence to support your line of reasoning.
- Explain how the evidence supports your line of reasoning.
- Demonstrate an understanding of the rhetorical situation.
- Use appropriate grammar and punctuation in communicating your argument.

GO ON TO THE NEXT PAGE.

President Hollande, Mr. Secretary General, fellow leaders. We have come to Paris to show our resolve...

Nearly 200 nations have assembled here this week—a declaration that for all the challenges we face, the growing threat of climate change could define the contours of this century more dramatically than any other. What should give us hope that this is a turning point, that this is the moment we finally determined we would save our planet, is the fact that our nations share a sense of urgency about this challenge and a growing realization that it is within our power to do something about it.

Our understanding of the ways human beings disrupt the climate advances by the day. Fourteen of the fifteen warmest years on record have occurred since the year 2000—and 2015 is on pace to be the warmest year of all. No nation—large or small, wealthy or poor—is immune to what this means.

This summer, I saw the effects of climate change firsthand in our northernmost state, Alaska, where the sea is already swallowing villages and eroding shorelines; where permafrost thaws and the tundra burns; where glaciers are melting at a pace unprecedented in modern times. And it was a preview of one possible future—a glimpse of our children's fate if the climate keeps changing faster than our efforts to address it. Submerged countries. Abandoned cities. Fields that no longer grow. Political disruptions that trigger new conflict, and even more floods of desperate peoples seeking the sanctuary of nations not their own.

That future is not one of strong economies, nor is it one where fragile states can find their footing. That future is one that we have the power to change. Right here. Right now. But only if we rise to this moment. As one of America's governors has said, "We are the first generation to feel the impact of climate change, and the last generation that can do something about it."

I've come here personally, as the leader of the world's largest economy and the second largest emitter, to say that the United States of America not only recognizes our role in creating this problem, we embrace our responsibility to do something about it.

Over the last seven years, we've made ambitious investments in clean energy, and ambitious reductions in our carbon emissions. We've multiplied wind power threefold, and solar power more than twentyfold, helping create parts of America where these clean power sources are finally cheaper than dirtier, conventional power. We've invested in energy efficiency in every way imaginable. We've said no to infrastructure that would pull high-carbon fossil fuels from the ground, and we've said yes to the first-ever set of national standards limiting the amount of carbon pollution our power plants can release into the sky.

The advances we've made have helped drive our economic output to all-time highs, and drive our carbon pollution to its lowest levels in nearly two decades....

And, my fellow leaders, accepting this challenge will not reward us with moments of victory that are clear or quick. Our progress will be measured differently—in the suffering that is averted, and a planet that's preserved. And that's what's always made this so hard. Our generation may not even live to see the full realization of what we do here. But the knowledge that the next generation will be better off for what we do here—can we imagine a more worthy reward than that? Passing that on to our children and our grandchildren, so that when they look back and they see what we did here in Paris, they can take pride in our achievement.

Let that be the common purpose here in Paris. A world that is worthy of our children. A world that is marked not by conflict, but by cooperation; and not by human suffering, but by human progress. A world that's safer, and more prosperous, and more secure, and more free than the one that we inherited.

Let's get to work. Thank you very much.

GO ON TO THE NEXT PAGE.

Question 3

Suggested time—40 minutes.

(This question counts for one-third of the total essay section score.)

American essayist and philosopher Ralph Waldo Emerson once said: "It was high counsel that I once heard given to a young person, 'always do what you are afraid to do.'"

Write a carefully reasoned persuasive essay that defends, challenges, or qualifies Emerson's stance. Use evidence from your observation, experience, or reading to develop your position on the value of doing what you are afraid to do.

In your response, you should do the following:

- Respond to the prompt with a thesis that may establish a line of reasoning.
- Select and use evidence to develop and support your line of reasoning.
- Explain the relationship between the evidence and your thesis.
- Demonstrate an understanding of the rhetorical situation.
- Use appropriate grammar and punctuation in communicating your argument.

STOP

END OF EXAM

Practice Test 1: Diagnostic Answer Key and Explanations

PRACTICE TEST 1: DIAGNOSTIC ANSWER KEY

Let's take a look at how you did on Practice Test 1. Follow the three-step process in the diagnostic answer key below and read the explanations for any questions you got wrong, or struggled with but got correct. Once you finish working through the answer key and the explanations, devise a study plan that helps you improve any areas that you may be struggling with.

 STEP 1 >> **Check your answers and mark any correct answers with a ✔ in the appropriate column.**

Q #	Ans.	✔	Content Tested	Q #	Ans.	✔	Content Tested
			Section I: Multiple Choice				
1	C		Rhetorical Situations	24	B		Claims and Evidence
2	A		Claims and Evidence	25	B		Rhetorical Situations
3	D		Claims and Evidence	26	C		Reasoning and Organization
4	C		Style	27	C		Claims and Evidence
5	A		Reasoning and Organization	28	D		Claims and Evidence
6	A		Reasoning and Organization	29	C		Claims and Evidence
7	B		Reasoning and Organization	30	B		Reasoning and Organization
8	D		Claims and Evidence	31	B		Reasoning and Organization
9	D		Claims and Evidence	32	D		Claims and Evidence
10	D		Rhetorical Situations	33	B		Style
11	C		Reasoning and Organization	34	B		Style
12	A		Style	35	A		Reasoning and Organization
13	A		Rhetorical Situations	36	D		Style
14	A		Reasoning and Organization	37	D		Reasoning and Organization
15	C		Reasoning and Organization	38	D		Rhetorical Situations
16	A		Claims and Evidence	39	A		Claims and Evidence
17	A		Style	40	C		Style
18	C		Claims and Evidence	41	C		Reasoning and Organization
19	C		Rhetorical Situations	42	B		Reasoning and Organization
20	A		Reasoning and Organization	43	D		Claims and Evidence
21	C		Rhetorical Situations	44	B		Rhetorical Situations
22	B		Claims and Evidence	45	B		Claims and Evidence
23	D		Claims and Evidence				

Tally your correct answers from Step 1 by objective. For each, write the number of correct answers in the appropriate box. Then, divide your correct answers by the number of total questions (which we've provided) to identify your strongest and weakest areas.

RHETORICAL SITUATIONS
SELF-EVALUATION

STYLE
SELF-EVALUATION

CLAIMS AND EVIDENCE
SELF-EVALUATION

REASONING AND ORGANIZATION
SELF-EVALUATION

 Use the results above to customize your study plan. You may want to start with, or give more attention to, the topics with the lowest percents correct.

PRACTICE TEST 1 EXPLANATIONS

SECTION I: MULTIPLE CHOICE

1. **C**   The "exigence" of a speech or piece of writing is the need or demand that prompted the author to write it. Here, the author is pleading with the members of Parliament to provide equal rights and justice for the Irish people under their control. We cannot prove that there is a "lack of interest," (A). If there was, the author would likely not bother to address them. Choice (B) is probably too extreme and not supported by the text. Choice (D) might be true but is not specifically addressed here. That leaves (C), the one most consistent with the sentiments expressed.

2. **A**   The first paragraph asks the audience to choose between two options: "whether we mean to continue the injustice which has been already done to [Ireland], or to hold out the hope that it will be treated in the same manner as England and Scotland." In context, we can assume that England is being treated fairly (with "justice") by its own Parliament. There is no explanation as to why the British have not already extended such justice to Ireland, (B). The author does not explicitly identify himself as a nationalist, (C). Choice (D) may seem close, but we don't actually know if the rights had been steadily eroding or were simply never there to begin with. Choice (A) is the most consistent with the overall theme.

3. **D**   The second paragraph states that "England never did do justice to Ireland," but then admits that "What we have got of it we have extorted from men opposed to us on principle." So, the Irish people have gotten some concessions from the British, but only through struggle. Choice (A) seems close to this, but the word "only" makes this far too extreme and is likely using the word "extortion" too literally. Choice (B) is incorrect since the author seems to care more about "equal justice" than "money." Choice (C) cannot be right, since the author is pleading for more rights, implying that not all of them have been won. That leaves us with (D). The paragraph acknowledges that some progress has been made in the past, but more is being demanded.

4. **C**   The writer sounds somewhat bitter when he says "England never did do justice to Ireland—she never did." But he sounds more hopeful and resolute, (C), when he pledges "my heart is as young and as ready as ever in the service of my country." There is no evidence of a "patronizing" tone, as in (A), an "ingratiating" tone, (B), nor "sympathy," (D). Choice (C) is the best answer.

5. **A**   The third paragraph states that "I cannot forget the year 1825. We begged then as we would for a beggar's boon; we asked for emancipation by all that is sacred amongst us, and I remember how my speech and person were treated, when I had no opportunity of reply. The other place turned us out and sent us back again, but we showed that justice was with us." According to the footnote, 1825 was the year that the author's Catholic Association was abolished. So, although we do not know all the details, 1825 was a year in which the author requested something that was important to him and his followers, and they were rebuffed. This is most consistent with (A). Choice (B) is partly right, since "emancipation" failed, but he does not establish that "reform" is a disappointing alternative. Choice (C) is unrelated to "1825." Choice (D) may have some truth, but it is not his primary purpose in this paragraph.

6. **A**   Though emancipation can refer to a great many things, you must go by what is present in the speech. There is nothing here about actual slavery, though it is metaphorically mentioned, so eliminate (B). It does not discuss the representation of faith, so rule out (C). Voting is not mentioned, which removes (D) from consideration. Choice (A) makes the most sense in context.

7. **B**   The fourth paragraph states, "I may be laughed and sneered at by those who talk of my power; but what has created it but the injustice that has been done in Ireland? If you refuse justice to that country, it is a melancholy consideration to me to think that you are adding substantially to that power and influence." The author is pointing out the irony of the fact that Britain's oppression of Ireland has enhanced his leadership power, despite their "laughing and sneering" at it. This matches (B). The author is not explicitly questioning motives, (A), nor demanding acceptance, (D). Choice (C) is close, but overlooks what has "created" the speaker's power: the British injustice against Ireland. Choice (B) is the best answer.

8. **D**   "Justice," (A), "emancipation," (B), and "reform," (C), are all presented as things the author wants or wanted in the past for his people. The concept that is not like the others is "power and influence," (D). The writer has "power and influence"; he is not demanding them from Parliament.

9. **D**   In the last paragraph, the author starts off by saying "Condemn me elsewhere as much as you please," and finishes the paragraph by saying "I demand, I respectfully insist: on equal justice for Ireland, on the same principle by which it has been administered to Scotland and England. I will not take less. Refuse me that if you can." He is not looking for any explanations, (A), nor does he provide two alternatives, (B). Choice (C) sounds rather extreme. Choice (D) is the best answer.

10. **D**   Since Protestantism is a religious category, we are looking for a paragraph that mentions religion. If you look at the footnote for paragraph 5, "Papist" is a reference to the Catholic faith. The speaker also claims that someone is sending out "men called ministers of God to slander and calumniate me." This is consistent with the quote. Choice (D) is the best answer.

11. **C**   The speech's overall theme is one of advocacy for equal justice and fairness for the Irish people. Therefore, the author would likely oppose slavery, (A). As a member of the Catholic minority, he would likely approve of freedom of religion, (B). Although languages, (D), are not mentioned in his speech, he is delivering the speech in English, yet is a champion of the Irish people and culture. Choice (C) is the best answer, since nowhere does the author advocate for political violence. Instead, he is trying to further his political goals through speech and persuasion.

12. **A**   In paragraphs 2 and 3, the writer acknowledges that Ireland has not gotten just treatment from Britain nor have certain considerations been granted. But in the last paragraph, he is still asking for the Parliament to cooperate with him. This is most consistent with (A). Choice (C) is too extreme, and (D) is outright incorrect, as the author states that he is *not* fatigued.

13. **A**   This speech explores the issues of freedom and human rights and acknowledges that different countries may have different notions of what these things are. In the final paragraph, the author urges her listeners to use the forum of the United Nations to work out these differences. Choice (B) is incorrect, since it makes it sound as though human rights are being upheld in all nations already. Choice (C) is unsupportable and too extreme. Choice (D) may seem close, but the writer's focus is on international standards for human rights, not those in the United States.

14. **A**   By referring to human freedom as "one of the greatest issues of our time," the author is clearly trying to capture the listeners' attention, (A). All of the other choices are more relevant to other parts of the speech.

15. **C**   The Declaration of the Rights of Man and the French Revolution are both relevant to France, (D), but also are examples of documents and events that made human rights and freedom a central concern. Eliminate (A). Another reason to make these historical allusions might be to establish herself as educated about the topic at hand, (B). Choice (C) is the exception, since the Declaration of the Rights of Man and the French Revolution are similar in approach, not different.

16. **A**   The opening paragraph explicitly equates human rights with freedom, (B). The rights enumerated in paragraph 2 are drawn directly from the American Bill of Rights, (C). Democracy, (D), is mentioned in the fourth paragraph. Although the "right to work" is mentioned as a Soviet value, the author explicitly says that forced employment for everyone is a form of slavery. Choice (A) is the best choice.

17. **A**   In paragraph 5, the author states that "A society in which everyone works is not necessarily a free society and may indeed be a slave society; on the other hand, a society in which there is widespread economic insecurity can turn freedom into a barren and vapid right for millions of people." "Barren" is a good clue here, since land that is barren does not yield anything useful. Since she is talking about an idea like "freedom," (A) is the closest choice.

18. **C**   Choices (B) and (D) may look tempting, but, in the overall context of the speech, the point is that terms such as "right to work" may be interpreted differently by the different nations who use them. The U.S.S.R. may think of the right to work in a positive way, while an American such as the author may consider it a form of slavery. Choice (C) is the best choice.

19. **C**   The final paragraph states that "The place to discuss the issue of human rights is in the forum of the United Nations…we can consider together our mutual problems and take advantage of our differences in experience…we can with mutual good faith in the principles of the United Nations Charter, arrive at a common basis of understanding." This is most consistent with (C). Choice (D) is too extreme, since the United Nations may not be the *only* place where these discussions can be had.

20. **A**   In the quote provided, the author strongly suggests that a failure to secure freedoms for the average person may lead to war—the people "will not acquiesce forever." Choice (A) is a reference to wars about freedom versus tyranny.

21. **C**   This question asks us to consider why the writer's speech was delivered in the immediate aftermath of World War II. Choices (A) and (B) both provide logical explanations for this. Since (C) and (D) both mention the Soviet Union (U.S.S.R.), we must consider the facts as they are presented in her speech. According to her speech, the U.S.S.R. may have notions of human rights that do not square with those of other nations such as the United States, which matches (D). Choice (C) is backwards, since the Soviet Union did not adopt Western standards of human rights after the War (nor were they defeated!).

22. **B**   The overall thrust of this speech is to urge member states of the U.N. to engage in productive dialogue regarding the issues at hand. It does not claim that human rights have been successfully implemented in any particular countries, so eliminate (A), (C), and (D). Choice (B) is the best answer.

23. **D**   All of the quotes are pertinent to human rights concerns except for (D). Although slavery is mentioned once, there is no focus on "knowledge."

24. **B**   Paragraphs 1 and 2 explicitly draw a connection between human rights and human freedom. There is no mention of "responsibility," (A), nor does the author attach freedom to the loss of food or employment, (C). The writer does not weigh one of these values more heavily than the other, (D). Choice (B) is the most consistent with the text.

25. **B**   This question asks us to choose a sentence that conveys the *complexity* of Hurston's career and provide the most effective *introduction* to the essay. While (A) gives some detail about Hurston's early life, it does not indicate that her career was "complex." Choice (C) may convey more complexity than (A), but merely shows that Hurston was overlooked. Choice (D) is out of place since paragraph 1 is not about her college years. Choice (B) is the best answer, since it mentions that she was a "study in contrasts" and is general enough to provide a good introduction to the essay.

26. **C**   This question asks us to provide a logical transition into a comparison and create a more objective tone. Eliminate (A) because it is not objective in its tone. Choice (B) is unsupported: advocacy for civil rights is not a focus of this essay. Choice (D) is likewise unprovable based on the text. Choice (C) is the best answer, because the word "Now" provides a good time transition, while "resonance" is a neutral way to communicate Hurston's impact.

27. **C**   Paragraph 2 states that Hurston had a "deeply individualistic personality" and grew up "in a community totally separate from the larger white society." Choices (A) and (B) are not related to these ideas. Choice (D) may seem close, but is actually the opposite of the notion that her town was "totally separate from the larger white society." That leaves (C), which is consistent with this idea.

28. **D**   Choice (C) may be tempting, since sentence 8 mentions Billie Holiday, but, since the paragraph is focused on Hurston's life, adding more about her would be a needless distraction from the focus of the essay. Choice (D) is the best answer.

29. **C**   Crucially, this question is asking how Hurston's work was viewed by her *contemporaries*, not by modern audiences. Choice (B) does not communicate anything regarding the opinions of her critics, while (A) and (D) are more relevant to modern audiences. Only (C) tells us how she was viewed by people in her time.

30. **B**   To find a place to divide the paragraph, look for two distinct ideas. Sentences 6, 7, and 8 focus on Hurston's early life, while the remainder of the paragraph focuses on her first novel. This means the answer is either (A) or (B). Because (A) is not supported by the paragraph, (B) is the best choice.

31. **B** Sentence 12 states that Hurston believed "that the accuracy of her representation would ultimately prevail over the political pressures her peers sought to inflict upon her." Sentence 13 states that "Hurston was right." So, if modern critics "admire" her (sentence 14), this idea is not a shift in meaning. Eliminate (A). Choice (C) is incorrect, since there is no conclusion being drawn from evidence. Choice (D) may seem close, but sentence 14 is not adding merely an additional detail. Choice (B) is the best choice, as it provides a good transition from the past to the present.

32. **D** In sentence 2, we are told that Jimmy Carter was president during a "particularly turbulent time in American history." Choices (A), (B), and (C) all mention events that are troubling or difficult. Choice (D) does not appear to involve troublesome events; if anything, they seem to represent positive or neutral changes during Carter's administration.

33. **B** Since the goal is to make the tone more objective, eliminate (A). Choice (C) is less opinionated, but does not match up with the beginning of the sentence, which is focused on humanitarian issues "around the world." Choice (D) is close, but does not necessarily indicate a global focus. Choice (B) is the best answer, because it demonstrates Carter's broad support for humanitarian causes in a sufficiently objective manner.

34. **B** The best answer to this question must provide a clear and logical meaning by placing phrases next to the nouns they are modifying. Choice (A) puts the phrase "on foreign oil" in the wrong place and creates confusion. Choice (C) is illogical, since purchasing foreign oil would not make America less dependent on the Middle East or reduce demand. Choice (D) is similar to (A), putting phrases in an illogical order. Only (B) provides a logical account of what Carter may have been trying to do in regard to foreign oil.

35. **A** Since sentence 8 was focused on Carter's international efforts and sentence 9 states that "Carter works actively to improve the standard of living at home here in the United States," it makes sense to mention that he does not focus all of his efforts abroad *before* sentence 9. Choice (A) is the best answer.

36. **D** Since the question asks for an option that would maintain an objective tone, any answers with a positive or negative slant should be eliminated. Only (D) is neutral in its tone, while encompassing most of the activities Carter engaged in throughout his lifetime.

37. **D** In order to place this sentence, we must determine who "they" is, related to building homes. Sentence 10 mentions Habitat for Humanity, while sentence 11 tells us that they build "quality housing." Only (D) would allow us to place the sentence after these.

38. **D** Since the theme of the essay was primarily focused on Carter's humanitarian work, we need an answer that continues with these ideas. Choice (A) is too much about his political career. Choice (B) is about his early life. Choice (C) is not obviously humanitarian. Choice (D) is the best answer, since it harmonizes with Carter's other activities as outlined in the essay.

39. **A** Since the question asks about an "ownership" relationship between humans and cats, (A) is the best choice. Choices (B) and (D) are not explicitly about ownership, while (C) is irrelevant to cats.

40. **C**   The best choice here will convey the main idea in the clearest manner possible. Since the opening modifying phrase is "When communicating with each other," the best answer should start with the word "cats," (C). All of the other choices create some confusion about who or what is "communicating."

41. **C**   Use Process of Elimination. Choice (A) is not true. Neither is (B), as sentence 6 is a different facet of communication than those mentioned elsewhere. Choice (D) is not quite right, since it is unclear why pain would be an essential detail in this essay. Choice (C) is the best answer.

42. **B**   The third paragraph should be divided into two parts if it conveys two different ideas. Indeed, sentences 3–6 are focused on cats' communication with each other, while sentences 7–9 are focused on cats' communication with humans. This means the most logical place to divide the paragraph would be after sentence 6. Eliminate (A) and (C). Choice (D) can also be eliminated on the grounds that "incredibly" is descriptive enough on its own; time references are distracting in this transition. Choice (B) is the best answer.

43. **D**   Since the essay is about cats, any reference to other animals would be a distraction. Choice (D) is the best answer.

44. **B**   Only (B) and (D) are relevant to the question task, which asks about a "large number of emotions." Of the two, (B) is the better choice, since it pertains to communicating "vocally with their owners," another feature of the question.

45. **B**   The main argument of this essay is that cats do communicate with each other and with humans in verbal and nonverbal ways. Choice (A) seems to contradict this idea. Choice (C) is contradicted by information in the essay. Choice (D) is not provable based on the passage and seems to deviate from the main argument. Choice (B) is the best answer and most in harmony with the overall argument in the essay.

SECTION II: FREE RESPONSE

Rubric—1 + 4 + 1 = 6 pts

   A.   Thesis (0–1 pts)
- Responds to the prompt with a thesis that presents a defensible interpretation of the selected work.

   B.   Evidence and Commentary (0–4 pts)
- Evidence: Provides specific evidence to support all claims in a line of reasoning.
- Commentary: Consistently explains how the evidence supports a line of reasoning.
- Explains how multiple literary elements or techniques in the poem contribute to its meaning.

   C.   Sophistication (0–1 pts)
- Demonstrates sophistication of thought and/or develops a complex literary argument.

Question 1—Synthesis Essay

How to Score 6 Points
- Address the prompt with a defensible thesis.
- Present specific evidence from at least three sources and consistently explain how the evidence supports your thesis statement.
- Use style and rhetoric to persuade the reader.

Source Overview

Source A: President Kennedy explains that the U.S. seeks to go to the Moon to ensure that the benefits of space exploration are used for the betterment of all people.

Source B: Space exploration has lost the primacy it had during the Cold War and is now politically discretionary. However, exploring space still offers an opportunity for international cooperation as it did in the past.

Source C: NASA ranks fourth in federal research and development funding, after the Departments of Defense, Health and Human Services, and Energy, and ahead of the Environmental Protection Agency and the Department of Education.

Source D: *The Telegraph* reports that Stephen Hawking believes a biological threat from humans, in the form of an engineered virus, will eliminate humanity unless we extend our species into space colonies.

Source E: A 2003 popular poll found that 82% of those questioned supported continuing a manned space shuttle program in the wake of the Columbia accident. Further, a majority of those polled want to maintain current levels of NASA funding and maintain manned missions.

Source F: Marko Kovic considers the moral risks of space exploration, arguing for the establishment of evidenced-based, ethically responsible governance to ensure the safety of space colonization.

Sample First Paragraph

For as long as there has been space exploration, there have been those questioning its legitimacy as a science and worth as a public investment. While space exploration is certainly productive and beneficial, one would be justified in questioning whether or not NASA merits being the fourth highest funded research and development agency in the United States today.

Question 2—Rhetorical Analysis Essay

How to Score 6 Points

Use the Rhetorical Diamond! While you're reading the prompt and the passage, imagine—and try to flesh out—a baseball diamond with the following six points:

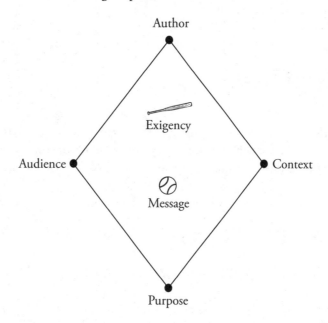

Author: President Barack Obama
Audience: Attendees of the First Session of COP21 in Paris, France
Purpose: To inspire the audience to work toward solutions for climate change
Context: A president from the U.S. gives a public address to the United Nations Climate Change Conference.
Exigency: The imminent dangers climate change poses to the international community
Message: International leaders must act now to avert the worst effects of climate change.

Sample Rhetorical Modes and Devices

- **First-person plural pronouns:** "What should give us hope that this is a turning point, that this is the moment we finally determined we would save our planet, is the fact that our nations share a sense of urgency about this challenge and a growing realization that it is within our power to do something about it."
- **Personification:** "Alaska, where the sea is already swallowing villages and eroding shorelines..."
- **Oxymoron:** "...where permafrost thaws and the tundra burns..."
- **Parallelism:** "Submerged countries. Abandoned cities. Fields that no longer grow. Political disruptions that trigger new conflict..."
- **Hypothetical situation:** "Our generation may not even live to see the full realization of what we do here. But the knowledge that the next generation will be better off for what we do here—can we imagine a more worthy reward than that? Passing that on to our children and our grandchildren, so that when they look back and they see what we did here in Paris, they can take pride in our achievement."

Sample First Paragraph

World leaders today face a threat the likes of which none before have known: climate change, and the environmental threats that face populations across all national borders. In opening the First Session of the COP21 summit in 2015, President Barack Obama sought to acknowledge the challenges posed by climate change and call the international leaders gathered to action. To do so, President Obama acknowledges the fear and challenges associated with climate change and uses first-person plural pronouns, poetic devices, and hypothetical scenarios to inspire his audience to take action against climate change.

Question 3—Argument Essay

How to Score 6 Points

- Take a definite position, so no one will question where you stand on the topic of the prompt.
- Develop an argument that builds and moves forward instead of simply repeating the same point several times in different ways.
- Support the points in your argument with evidence drawn from your own knowledge, reading, experiences, and observations.
- Explain how your evidence supports your argument.

Sample Evidence

- I'm afraid to ride in a car exceeding 80 miles per hour or otherwise driving recklessly.
- Many use cognitive behavioral therapy to address irrational fears, like the fear of flying or the fear of dogs.
- Jerry Seinfeld has a bit about more people being afraid of public speaking than being afraid of dying, meaning most people would rather be lying in the casket than giving the eulogy at a funeral.
- Taking on a new challenge, like more responsibility or introducing one's self to a new friend, can feel scary.
- Some fears are instinctive, such as fire, enclosed spaces, heights, extreme weather, and earthquakes.

Sample First Paragraph

Fear is a primal human emotion, an instinct that safeguards us against the dangers inherent to being human in the world. While our fear can keep us alive, acknowledging our fears can also be a powerful tool for individual growth. While we should always consider doing what we are afraid to do, we should also consider whether or not our fear is keeping us safe.

HOW TO SCORE PRACTICE TEST 1

Section I: Multiple Choice

_____ × 1.5000 = _____
Number Correct   Weighted
(out of 45)   Section I Score
                               (Do not round)

Section II: Free Response

(See whether you can find a teacher or classmate to score your essays using the guidelines in Chapter 4.)

Question 1 _____ × 4.5833 = _____
           (out of 6)   (Do not round)

Question 2 _____ × 4.5833 = _____
           (out of 6)   (Do not round)

Question 3 _____ × 4.5833 = _____
           (out of 6)   (Do not round)

Sum = _____
      Weighted Section II
      Score (Do not round)

The official range used to score the AP changes each year, so use these numbers only as a baseline for your own progress through this book and to get an estimate of where you may need to grow.

AP Score Conversion Chart English Language and Composition

Composite Score Range	AP Score
112–150	5
98–111	4
80–97	3
55–79	2
0–54	1

Composite Score

_____ + _____ = _____
Weighted   Weighted   Composite Score
Section I Score   Section II Score   (Round to nearest
                                      whole number)

Part III
About the AP English Language and Composition Exam

- The Structure of the AP English Language and Composition Exam
- AP English Language and Composition Goes Fully Digital
- How the AP English Language and Composition Exam Is Scored
- Overview of Content Topics
- How AP Exams Are Used
- Other Resources
- Designing Your Study Plan

THE STRUCTURE OF THE AP ENGLISH LANGUAGE AND COMPOSITION EXAM

Below is a helpful outline that describes the basic format for the exam. The total time allotted for the completion of this exam is 3 hours and 15 minutes, or 195 minutes.

Section I: Multiple Choice (1 hour)—counts for 45 percent of your score

Total number of questions: 45

Section II: Free Response (2 hours, 15 minutes; includes a 15-minute reading period)—counts for 55 percent of your score

Composed of three essay questions, which the College Board describes as follows:

1. **Synthesis essay:** You will read several sources on a topic and create an argument that integrates information from at least three of the sources to support your thesis.
2. **Rhetorical Analysis essay:** You will analyze a nonfiction text and discuss how the author's language choices contribute to the purpose and intended meaning.
3. **Argument essay:** You will create an evidence-based argument in response to a given topic.

AP ENGLISH LANGUAGE AND COMPOSITION GOES FULLY DIGITAL

Interactive Practice Tests
Register your book at PrincetonReview.com/prep to access Practice Tests A, B, and C. These online tests are designed to give you a sense of the digital features of the May 2025 AP English Language and Composition Exam, such as clicking your answer and typing your free responses.

The College Board announced that beginning in May 2025 the AP English Language and Composition exam will be conducted digitally. To take the exam, students must have access to the College Board's Bluebook testing app, available for Windows, Apple, tablets, and Chromebooks. If your computer or tablet is owned or managed by your school, then a school official will likely have to install this app for you if it is not already on it. The test cannot be taken on a smartphone.

The testing app will allow you to annotate and highlight texts, eliminate answers, and flag questions for review later. You will also have access to scratch paper to plan responses to essay questions. Unlike other digital exams like the SAT, the digital AP exam will NOT be adaptive: this means that the difficulty of questions will not change depending on how well you do on earlier sections of the test.

With this change, it is important to note that the digital exam includes the same number of sections, number and types of questions, and timing as the paper exam. This means the strategies used for success on paper versions of the AP English Language and Composition exam are just as applicable to the digital version. So don't worry, the practice tests in this book will still prepare you for test day.

1 ⬚ Mark for Review

The authors' main purpose in this excerpt is to

- Ⓐ encourage professionals to adopt a monitoring approach that is similar to the Forestry Service's approach

- Ⓑ influence habitat monitoring professionals to monitor populations too

- Ⓒ concentrate wildlife monitoring efforts on bird populations

- Ⓓ educate readers about how to monitor wildlife habitats

For the latest information regarding the digital AP exams and testing accommodations, visit the College Board website at apcentral.collegeboard.org/ exam-administration-ordering-scores/digital-ap-exams.

HOW THE AP ENGLISH LANGUAGE AND COMPOSITION EXAM IS SCORED

Your Multiple-Choice Score

In the multiple-choice section of the test, you are awarded 1 point for each question that you answer correctly, and you receive no points for each question that you leave blank or answer incorrectly. So, even if you are completely unsure, guess. In Part IV, Chapter 1, we'll show you how to narrow down your choices and make educated guesses.

Your Free-Response Score

Each AP essay is scored on a scale from 0 to 6, with 6 being the best score. Essay readers (who are high school or university English instructors) will grade your three essays, and the scores for your three essays will be added together. The resulting total (which ranges from 0 to 18) constitutes your free-response score.

We will go into the details of essay scoring in Part IV, Chapter 4, but, in general, an essay that receives a 6 answers all facets of the question completely, making good use of specific examples to support its points, and is "well-written," which is a catch-all phrase that means its sentences are complete, properly punctuated, clear in meaning, and varied (that is, they exhibit a variety of structure and use a large academic vocabulary). Lower-scoring essays are considered to be deficient in these qualities to a greater or lesser degree, and students who receive a "0" have basically written gibberish. If you write an essay that is not on the topic, you will receive a blank ("—"). This is equivalent to a zero.

The essay readers do not award points according to a standardized, predetermined checklist. The essays are scored individually by individual readers, each of whom scores essays for only one prompt. Thus, you will have three different readers, and each reader will be able to see only the single essay that they read. The readers do not know how you did on the other essays or what score you received on the multiple-choice section.

Your Final Score

Your final score of 1 to 5 is a combination of your scores from the two sections. Remember that the multiple-choice section counts for 45 percent of the total and the essay section counts for 55 percent. This makes them almost equal, and you must concentrate on doing your best on both parts.

You will have the opportunity to calculate your final score for each Practice Test in this book. The Answers and Explanations chapters include a worksheet to guide you through the scoring formula step by step. (Remember, this worksheet is meant to serve as a guideline only!)

What Your Final Score Means

After taking the test in early May, you will receive your scores sometime around the first week of July, which is probably when you'll have just started to forget about the entire harrowing experience. Your score will be, simply enough, a single number from 1 to 5. Here is what those numbers mean:

Score meaning	Percentage of all test-takers receiving this score*	Roughly equivalent first-year college course grade	Will a student with this score receive credit?
5—Extremely qualified	10.3%	A	Usually
4—Well qualified	19.7%	A–, B+, B	Usually
3—Qualified	26.1%	B–, C+, C	Maybe
2—Possibly qualified	29.5%	N/A	Very Rarely
1—Not qualified	14.4%	N/A	No

*Percentages are based on the May 2023 administration of the exam.

OVERVIEW OF CONTENT TOPICS

The AP English Language and Composition Exam tests your abilities to understand how authors use rhetoric and language to convey their purpose. Students are also expected to apply these techniques to their own writing and research projects. Some of the major skills tested include the ability to:

- identify an author's purpose and intended audience

- recognize rhetorical devices and strategies in an author's work

- demonstrate understanding of citations in research papers

- apply these skills and techniques to their own writing

- create and organize an argument defended with evidence and reasoning

- plan, write, and revise cogent, well-written essays

HOW AP EXAMS ARE USED

Colleges make their own decisions about the minimum AP score required to earn credit (points that count toward your college degree), the number of credit hours awarded, and whether advanced placement (the opportunity to skip introductory courses and enter higher-level courses) is offered.

Policies differ widely. Some colleges require a score of 3, while others require a 4, for instance. Some offer both credit and placement; some offer only credit, and some only placement.

Go Online!
Check us out on YouTube for test-taking tips and techniques to help you ace your next exam at www.youtube.com/ThePrincetonReview.

For more information on colleges, you might want to check out some of our guide books, which include *The Best 390 Colleges, The Complete Guide to College Applications, Paying for College,* and many more!

The AP exam administrators have created a helpful tool that lets you check the AP credit policy for most colleges. Go to apstudent.collegeboard.org/creditandplacement/search-credit-policies and enter the names of the colleges that interest you. The tool will give you the minimum score required for credit and/or placement. It will also give you a link to the college's website so you can check the most up-to-date policy information.

OTHER RESOURCES

There are many resources available to help you improve your score on the AP English Language and Composition Exam, not the least of which are your teachers. If you are taking an AP class, you may be able to get extra help from your teacher, such as obtaining feedback on your essays. If you are not in an AP course, reach out to an English teacher and ask whether they will review your essays or otherwise help you review.

Another wonderful resource is **AP Students,** the official student site for the AP exams. The scope of the information at this site is quite broad and includes:

- the course description, which provides details on what content is covered and sample questions

- the AP English Language and Composition Exam free-response and scoring guidelines

- access to AP Classroom if you are enrolled in a course (teacher assistance required)

- free-response prompts from previous years and exam tips

The AP Students web page is apstudent.collegeboard.org.

The AP English Language and Composition Course home page address is apcentral.collegeboard.org/courses/ap-english-language-and-composition/course.

Finally, The Princeton Review offers tutoring and small group instruction for the AP English Language and Composition Exam. Our expert instructors can help you refine your strategic approach and add to your content knowledge. For more information, call 1-800-2REVIEW or visit princetonreview.com/academic-tutoring/subjects/ap-english-language for AP English Language Homework Help.

Online Student Tools

Our online portal for the AP exams, Student Tools, contains a bunch of helpful resources, including a study guide, printable bubble sheets, admissions advice, additional practice tests, and more. Follow the instructions on the Get More (Free) Content page at the front of this book to access this great content!

Looking to Guarantee a 5?

We now offer one-on-one tutoring for a guaranteed 5 on the AP English Language and Composition Exam. For information on rates and availability, visit PrincetonReview.com/college/ap-test-prep.

Read as much as you can to prepare for the AP exam. While the following texts may or may not appear on the exam itself, they can help you practice identifying and analyzing the rhetorical strategies and modes discussed in this book.

- "The Ones Who Walk Away from Omelas" by Ursula Le Guin

- *The Jungle* by Upton Sinclair

- *Animal Farm* by George Orwell

- Marc Antony's "I Come to Bury Caesar" from *Julius Caesar* by William Shakespeare

- Newspaper columns and cartoons from reputable newspapers

- TED Talks

Also consider political and literary speeches and essays from the following writers:

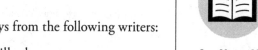

- Samuel Johnson
- Thomas Paine
- Ralph Waldo Emerson
- John Muir
- Virginia Woolf
- Martin Luther King, Jr.
- Malcolm X
- Scott Russel Sanders
- Frederick Douglass
- Joyce Carol Oates
- Mary Wollstonecraft
- Alice Walker
- David Sedaris
- Wendell Berry
- Henry David Thoreau
- Charles Darwin
- Rachel Carson

- Annie Dillard
- John McPhee
- Susan Sontag
- Charles Lamb
- Thomas De Quincey
- Richard Rodriguez
- Oscar Wilde
- Abraham Lincoln
- Sojourner Truth
- Chief Joseph
- King George IV of England
- Franklin D. Roosevelt
- Robert Kennedy
- Indira Gandhi
- Hillary Clinton
- Barack Obama

Are You a Visual Learner?
If you're getting overwhelmed by all of the concepts for an AP course, consider looking at our *Fast Track* or *ASAP* books, available for some AP subjects. These handy guides focus on the most-tested content and present it in a friendly, illustrated fashion.

If you're struggling with the fundamental mechanics of analytical and persuasive writing, this book has been hugely helpful for many AP and college students:

- *They Say, I Say* by Gerald Graff and Cathy Birkenstein

Need More Help on Essays?
We've got just the book for that! *How to Write Essays for Standardized Tests* contains advice and examples of best practices on an assortment of AP exams, plus ACT, and others!

Break up your review into manageable portions. Download our helpful study guide for this book once you register online.

DESIGNING YOUR STUDY PLAN

In Part I, you identified some areas of potential improvement. Now let's delve further into your performance on Practice Test 1, with the goal of developing a study plan appropriate to your needs and time commitment.

Read the answers and explanations associated with the multiple-choice questions (starting on page 36). After you have done so, respond to the following questions:

- Review the Overview of Content Topics on page 51 and, next to each skill listed, indicate your rank as follows: "1" means "I need a lot of work on this," "2" means "I need some review of this," and "3" means "I have sufficiently mastered this."

- How many days/weeks/months away is your exam day?

- What time of day is your best, most focused study time?

- How much time per day/week/month will you devote to preparing for your exam?

- When will you do this preparation? (Be as specific as possible: Mondays and Wednesdays from 3:00 to 4:00 P.M., for example.)

- Based on the answers above, will you focus on strategy (Part IV) or the content and skills review (Part V) or both?

- What are your overall goals in using this book?

Based on your answers to these questions, you should now have a better understanding of how to study for the exam. Use your answers to tailor the online study guide available for download when you register your book online.

Part IV
Test-Taking Strategies for the AP English Language and Composition Exam

PREVIEW

Review your responses to the questions on page 2 of Part I and then answer the following questions about Practice Test 1:

- How many multiple-choice questions did you miss even though you knew the answer?

- On how many multiple-choice questions did you guess randomly?

- How many multiple-choice questions did you miss after eliminating some answers and guessing based on the remaining answers?

- Did you create an outline before you wrote each essay?

- Did you find any of the essays easier or harder than the others—and, if so, why?

Those answers will give you an idea of what you're doing now and where you could improve your performance on the multiple-choice section and the three essays.

- Did you miss too many multiple-choice questions when you knew (or think you should have known) the answer? Perhaps you're not working carefully enough, or you're letting test anxiety get the better of you.

- Did you guess randomly on more than a few questions? Making more educated guesses will help to improve your odds.

Got a Question?

For answers to test-prep questions for all your tests and additional test-taking tips, subscribe to our YouTube channel at www.youtube.com/ ThePrincetonReview.

- Did you use POE (Process of Elimination) to get rid of the obviously wrong answers, and still miss the correct response when you took a guess from the remaining answers? The "Letter of the Day" approach can help. You'll learn about this approach shortly.

- Did you simply start writing your essay without planning what you were going to say and organizing your points? A few minutes spent on an outline will save you from getting half an hour into your essay time and realizing you're seriously off track.

- If you found one essay more difficult than the others (students tend to find the rhetorical analysis essay the most challenging), you know where to focus your efforts. The techniques and practice you'll find in the essay chapters will help you gain confidence in tackling all three of the essays on the exam.

HOW TO USE THE CHAPTERS IN THIS PART

Before you read the following strategy chapters, think about the previous strategies you learned and used for Practice Test 1. As you read on you'll start to recognize ways you can change your current approach in order to be more successful on each section of the exam. At the end of Part IV, you'll have the opportunity to reflect on the changes you plan to make.

Chapter 1
How to Approach Multiple-Choice Questions

WHAT TO EXPECT IN THE MULTIPLE-CHOICE SECTION

The multiple-choice section counts for 45 percent of your total score, but you're given only 31 percent (1 hour) of the total exam time to earn that large chunk of points. How you spend that hour is extremely important.

The multiple-choice portion of the exam consists of five passages and 45 questions. There will be 23–25 Reading questions and 20–22 Writing questions. All multiple-choice questions will be scored by computer. All five passages will be nonfiction. Two of them will be publication-quality passages and associated with Reading questions. These passages will range from the 19th, 20th, and 21st centuries. Three of the readings will be student-level passages and associated with Writing questions. These passages will be examples of contemporary, persuasive writing. Our practice tests include examples of each type of passage and style of question, just like the real exam, so that you will be ready by the time you get to the test.

"Nonfiction" is a very broad term, so you could find Reading passages taken from all sorts of works—essays, biographies, diary entries, speeches, letters, literary criticism, science and nature writing, and writings about politics or history. The passages will also run the gamut as far as types of diction (word choice), syntax (how words are combined into phrases and sentences), imagery, tone, style, point of view, and purpose.

The Reading questions emphasize not just *what* the author is saying, but especially *how* the author says it. The idea is to get you to focus on rhetorical devices, figures of speech, and intended purposes, under rigid time constraints and with material you haven't seen before. You'll need to identify rhetorical devices and structures in a passage, and understand why and how the author used them. (Review Chapters 8–11 to learn more about rhetorical strategies. You'll find this helpful for the rhetorical analysis essay too.) The Reading questions are a challenging opportunity to demonstrate your ability to analyze how writers use language to achieve their purposes.

In the Reading passages, you may also find some questions about citations, which are usually presented as footnotes to the passage. Citations often give credit to sources from which the passage author drew ideas or information. The citation could state a source's date and place of publication, which might be important in evaluating that source. (For example, a very old source might be questionable if there have been more recent discoveries about a topic.) Citations can also supplement information in the passage without cluttering up the main text with details that might distract readers.

The Writing questions will ask you to evaluate passages of student-level persuasive writing. The questions are likely similar to peer-review exercises you've done in English classes over the course of your high school experience. Questions might ask you to select an ideal introductory sentence, revised thesis statement, or a piece of evidence that would enhance the writer's argument. Questions will also ask you to consider concessions, counterarguments, and rebuttals. Though the writing in these passages is simpler than in the Reading passages, you'll have to think critically about the argument being presented and any potential flaws therein.

Bonus Tips and Tricks…

Check us out on YouTube for additional test-taking tips and must-know strategies at www.youtube.com/ThePrincetonReview.

So where do you start preparing to get that much done in such a short time? In this chapter, you'll find techniques for reading the passages and answering multiple-choice questions that will allow you to confront the conditions of the exam head-on.

Active Reading

The passages on the exam are often heavy reading; older nonfiction passages can contain long sentences and obscure words that were common at the time. Read quickly but with understanding. If you just skim through the passage, you will likely have to keep rereading parts to gain a sense of what the author is talking about. You want to thoroughly comprehend the material from the start.

The solution? Active reading. That means you take control of the passage instead of simply letting it pour sentences and paragraphs into your head. Engage with it.

As you read each paragraph, ask yourself these questions:

- What is the author's main point in this paragraph?

- How does it connect to the paragraph that came before it?

- Where is it likely to lead in the next paragraph?

At the end of the passage, ask yourself the following questions:

- What is the author's "big picture" purpose and main point in this passage as a whole?

- Did the author convince me? Interest me? Lead me to disagree strongly? How did the author achieve that effect on me as a reader?

- What impact would this passage likely have had on readers who lived when it was written? What techniques did the author use to achieve that effect?

Active Reading

Look for the main point of the passage, the author's purpose, and the rhetorical strategies used to achieve that purpose.

You can practice this type of active reading with any written material—textbooks, printed ads, or product descriptions, for example. Once you get into the habit, you'll find that your reading comprehension increases considerably, along with your critical thinking skills. With enough practice, active reading will be second nature to you by the time you encounter the AP English Language and Composition Exam passages, where it's a necessity if you're to wade through most, if not all, of the questions and answer them successfully.

Words in Context

Guess the meaning of an unfamiliar word from its context.

Words in Context

Chances are you'll encounter some unfamiliar words on the exam, particularly in the nonfiction Reading passages. Another active reading technique can take you over that hurdle too: guessing the meaning of a word from its context. For example, let's say the passage is describing a politician who is trying to sell an unpopular new law to the voters in his constituency.

> The speaker's passion and ebullience began to cut through the dour mood of the audience that confronted him.

If you have no idea what "ebullience" and "dour" mean, you can still figure them out from the context. The speaker is passionate about this law he's trying to promote, so—paired with "passion"—"ebullience" must have something to do with enthusiasm and excitement. The voters, on the other hand, don't like it at all, so "dour" must signify something opposite—gloomy, unreceptive. The word even sounds dark and unfriendly.

Guessing a word's meaning from its context is something you can practice on material you encounter in your daily life. Then you can check a dictionary or thesaurus to see how your skill is improving.

Tackle the Questions and Go Back to the Passage

Each question is setting a specific task for you. Make sure you understand exactly what it's telling you to do. Read the question stem carefully, word for word.

When a question refers to specific lines in the passage, always go back to the passage and reread them. You should also read a few lines before and after the specified lines; context is often critical in determining the correct answer.

Don't Play Mind Games

Your memory will fool you. Always go back to the passage.

Relying on your memory—particularly in the dense nonfiction works you'll encounter on the exam—can easily lead you astray. Sometimes a sneaky answer choice will start out partly correct, but then make a U-turn into something that is not supported by the passage. Don't let your memory lead you into the trap of picking an answer that starts out right but is ultimately incorrect. Remember, half wrong is all wrong.

POE—Process of Elimination

After you understand the question task and have gone back to the passage to review the lines it specifies, look at the answer choices. Your active reading, careful analysis of the question task, and rereading of specific lines will most likely show you at least a couple of answer choices that are clearly wrong. Now instead of four possible answers, you have only three or perhaps two, and your chances of choosing—or even guessing at—the correct answer just went up substantially.

So start there—by quickly getting rid of choices that are obviously wrong—instead of starting by puzzling through four possible answers looking for the one right choice. That's the Process of Elimination approach, and it will increase your success rate on multiple-choice questions significantly.

> **Main Steps of POE**
> First, eliminate the answers you know are wrong.
> Then, look for the right answer within the remaining choices.

Guessing and the Letter of the Day

So you've tossed out two clearly wrong answers using POE, and narrowed four possible choices down to two. Suppose you still can't tell *which of* those three is the correct answer, though.

What do you do? Two things: guess and use the Letter of the Day.

Guessing

You get no points for a question that you don't answer. The good news with this exam, though, is that you don't lose any points for incorrect answers. So answer every single question, even if your answer is a guess. By using POE, you've raised your chances of guessing correctly within a smaller number of possible answers. There's another technique you can add that will increase your guessing success rate even more.

Letter of the Day

If you make a random guess for each question you can't answer—(A) for one and (D) for another and maybe (E) for this one—you're doing very little to improve your odds. The solution? Pick one letter—any letter—and use it for every single guess. That's the Letter of the Day approach.

Let's say there are 10 questions you can't answer. If you pick, for example, (B) as your Letter of the Day and answer (B) on every one of those 10 questions, what are the chances that (B) really is the correct answer to at least one of them, possibly more? Pretty good.

Proven Techniques
Use POE, Letter of the Day, and the Two-Pass System to help boost your score.

The Two-Pass System

With around 45 questions and 5 passages, you have roughly 1 minute and 20 seconds to answer each question, which is about 12 minutes for each passage and accompanying set of questions. The Two-Pass System will help you use that time most efficiently. Here are the steps to take:

The Two-Pass System

Pass 1: Answer the easy questions and guess at the hard ones, using the Letter of the Day.

Pass 2: Tackle as many of the hard ones as you can during the time left for that passage.

On your first pass through the questions:

- Answer all the easy questions first. If you can answer a question as you come to it, do so.

- Each time you come to a hard question that you can't answer, fill in a "guess" answer using your Letter of the Day and circle the question.

On your second pass through:

- Look at your watch to see how much time you have left for this passage. Go back to the hard questions you circled and tackle as many as you can before the time you allotted for that passage is over.

This system works well since all the questions are worth the same number of points, regardless of difficulty or the order in which you answer them.

Now let's examine a sample passage.

SAMPLE READING PASSAGE—HERE'S HOW IT'S DONE

The following passage is excerpted from *A Technical Guide for Monitoring Wildlife Habitat* by the United States Department of Agriculture Forest Service.

The publication that includes this excerpt is intended as a guide for professionals involved in forest planning and wildlife habitat monitoring. It was published in 2013 by the USDA Forest Service, which aims to balance the use of public resources with the protection of those resources. The authors are professionals in such fields as ecology, biology, and forestry.

Management Considerations

Management objectives will differ substantially among species and, thus, influence habitat monitoring objectives. Emphasis species for which habitat may be monitored
Line may come from a wide spectrum of conservation cat-
5 egories from taxa listed under the Federal Endangered Species Act to ubiquitous species that may be hunted or trapped.

The process of identifying monitoring priorities begins with a review of pertinent laws, regulations, policies,
10 regional and forest management objectives, and priorities set through partnerships and agreements to determine those emphasis species for which monitoring of populations is required. Recovery plans for threatened or endangered species often require that cooperating
15 agencies monitor population parameters for the species.[1] Others commit the Forest Service to monitor habitat.[2] Memoranda of understanding with State wildlife agencies obligate the Forest Service to assist with monitoring populations of important game species.[3]
20 Regional and forest management objectives also influence whether habitat is monitored for an emphasis species. If a land and resource management plan specifies management activities in ecological systems that also provide habitat for an emphasis species, it may be advis-
25 able to monitor habitat for that species.[4] Conversely, an emphasis species associated with habitat that is not likely to be influenced by planned management actions may be a poor candidate for habitat monitoring.[5]

Biological Considerations

Habitat monitoring should focus primarily on species
30 that are most likely to respond to changes in habitat condition because of management actions, disturbances, or climate change. In particular, management actions may impact systems in ways that are detrimental or positive but remain uncertain and require monitoring. Thus,
35 selecting emphasis species should include not only those that are associated with forest plan objectives or desired conditions, but also those that have the potential to be affected by management actions that modify habitat.

In addition, developing a successful habitat monitor-
40 ing program requires making a clear distinction between
habitat and population monitoring.[6] In some cases, the
monitoring objective for a species at risk will specify the
detection of relatively small changes in population size
(especially decreases) or occupancy. Depending on the
45 management concern, monitoring objective, detectability,
demography, and ecological relationships of a species, it
may be prudent to monitor only populations, rather than
to also track habitat. Under some limited circumstances,
behavioral and spatial relationships may exist that allow
50 populations to be closely linked to specific habitat attributes.[7] If strong evidence indicates that habitat features
are directly associated with population size of an emphasis species, then habitat monitoring, with the objective of
indirectly monitoring populations may be an acceptable
55 approach under a limited range of management circumstances.[8] Species that are difficult to detect and, therefore,
difficult to monitor for population abundance are good
candidates for habitat monitoring if strong habitat relationships have been documented and if information on an-
60 nual population fluctuations are not needed. Under these
circumstances, compare habitat monitoring results period-
ically with population data to ensure that the assumed
relationship between habitat and population remains.[9]
The indirect nature of the monitoring program relative to
65 the link between habitat and populations must always be
considered when the resulting monitoring data are used.

---

1 e.g., red-cockaded woodpecker *[Picoides borealis]* USDI USFWS. 2003. Recovery plan for the red-cockaded woodpecker (Picoides borealis). 2nd rev. Atlanta, GA: U.S. Department of the Interior, U.S. Fish and Wildlife Service, Southeast Region. 296 p.

2 e.g., Mexican spotted owl *[Strix occidentalis lucida]* USDI U.S. Fish and Wildlife Service (USFWS). 1995. Recovery plan for the Mexican spotted owl (Strix occidentalis lucida). Albuquerque, NM: U.S. Department of the Interior, U.S. Fish and Wildlife Service, Southwest Region. 172 p.

3 e.g., Sitka black-tailed deer *[Odocoileus hemionus sitkensis]* in the Alaska Region.

4 e.g., woodland caribou *[Rangifer tarandus caribou]* USDA Forest Service. 1987. Forest plan Idaho Panhandle National Forests. Missoula, MT: U.S. Department of Agriculture, Forest Service, Northern Region. Irregular pagination.

5 e.g., gray-crowned rosy finch *[Leucosticte tephrocotis]* in alpine habitats relative to timber management activities.

6 i.e., habitat monitoring should not be confused with population monitoring (see chapter 1).

7 e.g., amount of recently burned conifer forest is directly related to populations of black-backed woodpeckers *[Picoides arcticus]*. Hutto, R.L. 1995. Composition of bird communities following stand-replacement fires in northern Rocky Mountain (U.S.A.) conifer forests. Conservation Biology. 9: 1041–1058.

8 Haufler, J.B.; Mehl, C.A.; Roloff, G.J. 1999. Conserving biological diversity using a coarse-filter approach with a species assessment. In: Baydack, R.K.; Campa, H., III; Haufler, J.B., eds. Practical approaches to the conservation of biological diversity. Washington DC: Island Press: 107–125. Molina, R.; Marcot, B.G.; Lesher, R. 2006. Protecting rare, old-growth, forest-associated species under the survey and manage program guidelines of the Northwest Forest Plan. Conservation Biology. 20: 306–318.

9 See chapter 1.

Approaching Reading Questions

In active reading mode, you should be looking for and writing down the main point of each paragraph in the margins before you move on to the next. From those building blocks, you can identify the main point of the excerpt and the author's purpose.

The first section focuses on forest or other environment management programs. The first paragraph stresses flexibility: objectives and species can encompass a broad range. The authors are providing guidance that can be applied to just about any situation readers face. The second paragraph outlines a framework of requirements and partnerships for undertaking the monitoring of programs—again, within a broad range of situations. The third paragraph positions habitat monitoring within larger management programs, and gives examples of when it may or may not be appropriate to monitor habitats.

The excerpt then looks at selecting species for habitat monitoring. The fourth paragraph specifies that species likely to be affected by a change in habitat should be selected. The fifth paragraph then makes a point the authors want to emphasize: habitat monitoring should be distinguished from population monitoring. The paragraph gives examples of when both types of information could be considered, or when population monitoring could be carried out on its own. However, the two types of monitoring are always considered as distinct activities.

The introductory comments provide context that helps identify the authors' purpose and the rhetorical strategies they use. The excerpt is part of a guide written by nature management professionals for professionals. In order to influence readers to follow their recommendations and practices, the authors need to gain trust and build credibility. Rhetorical techniques they use include formal language, drawing on authorities, and providing examples. The authors do have a clear bias for distinguishing habitat monitoring from population monitoring; however, their tone is neutral and unemotional. They allow for exceptions, and they use qualified language such as "may be prudent" and "may be an acceptable approach." They avoid complex industry jargon, making their information accessible to readers from a broad spectrum of disciplines and with varying degrees of expertise. As a result of these techniques, the authors sound like trustworthy, experienced scientists who are making sound recommendations without alienating readers by being authoritarian.

Let's look at a typical "big-picture" question.

1. The authors' main purpose in this excerpt is to

    (A) encourage professionals to adopt a monitoring approach that is similar to the Forestry Service's approach

    (B) influence habitat monitoring professionals to monitor populations too

    (C) concentrate wildlife monitoring efforts on bird populations

    (D) educate readers about how to monitor wildlife habitats

Through active reading, you will have identified not only the main point of each paragraph, but also the authors' overall purpose. The correct answer is (A). The excerpt outlines the Forestry Service's approach and, through the frequent use of "should," encourages readers to follow a similar approach. The guide specifies that habitat and population monitoring should be distinct activities, and that they should be combined in only limited circumstances, so (B) is clearly wrong and could have been eliminated right away using POE. Although the footnote comments give several examples of birds, they also mention deer and caribou, eliminating (C). The intended audience is made up of professionals in the field, so they would not need to be educated about how to monitor wildlife habitats, eliminating (D).

Here's another "big picture" question, focused on only one paragraph this time.

2. Paragraph 4 implies that
    (A) resources available for habitat monitoring are limited
    (B) forest management programs focus only on the physical environment
    (C) forest management programs include climate change
    (D) habitat monitoring should not be confined to species that are part of forest management programs

The answer is (D). The authors recommend also monitoring species that aren't part of the forest plan, but which could be affected by any resulting changes to their habitat. This recommendation makes (A) incorrect; resources do not appear to be limited when the scope of the monitoring could be expanded beyond the original plan. The paragraph discusses both the physical environment and the species that inhabit it, so (B) is incorrect. Also note that (B) is too extreme ("focus only on"). On the AP exam, it's unusual for an "all or nothing" response such as this to be correct. Extreme choices can usually be eliminated right away using POE. Forest management programs are planned and run by humans; climate change is not, so (C) is incorrect.

Here's another question in which you're asked to make an inference from something stated in the passage.

3. The last sentence of paragraph 2 suggests that
    (A) readers must consult the Forest Service if they want to monitor habitats for endangered species
    (B) the Forest Service requires State wildlife agencies to include it in monitoring game species populations
    (C) the Forest Service must be involved in population monitoring programs for certain game species
    (D) permission must be obtained from the Forest Service before game populations are monitored

A set of relatively close answers such as this one demonstrates the importance of going back to the passage instead of relying on your memory. Review exactly what the sentence says to avoid being tripped up by a choice that sounds close but has something wrong with it. Reread only as much as you need to, though. If you can't answer a question without spending too much time rereading, then guess at the answer (using your Letter of the Day) and, if you have time, return to it on your second pass through the questions for that passage.

The correct answer is (C). As you found when you identified the main point of paragraph 2, the authors are cautioning that a framework of requirements governs monitoring programs. Readers can't necessarily just set off on their own. In the last sentence of paragraph 2, the authors state—in a gentle, non-threatening way —that the Forest Service is "obligated" to "assist" with population monitoring programs for important game species. Choice (A) can be eliminated immediately because the sentence mentions game species, not endangered species. The authors don't specify which organization initiated the agreements with State wildlife agencies, so we can't say for sure whether (B) is true. Choice (D) would suggest getting permission and then going off and conducting the monitoring program without any further involvement by the Forest Services, which is incorrect.

Here are a couple of questions dealing with rhetorical strategies—*how* the authors say what they say in order to achieve their purpose with a specific audience in a particular context.

4. In the rhetorical strategies they use, the authors are trying to convince readers that they are

    (A) expert authorities in the field
    (B) a trustworthy source
    (C) a benign enforcement mechanism
    (D) independent thinkers

The correct answer is (B). Through their formal language, objective tone, supporting citations, and flexibility in acknowledging exceptions, the authors position themselves as a source whose recommendations can be trusted by professionals in the field. While the authors do cite some other U.S. environmental agencies in the footnotes, they also give references to nongovernment research results. They position themselves as experienced guides, not as expert authorities, (A). The authors do not suggest that they can or will enforce compliance with the monitoring practices they describe, so (C) is incorrect. Even when they outline "laws, regulations, policies," they don't specify penalties for noncompliance. There is no suggestion that the authors are advocating an approach that differs markedly from established monitoring practices, (D).

5. One rhetorical strategy the authors use in order to
    achieve their purpose with their professional audience is

    (A) examples of the negative results of combining
         population and habitat monitoring
    (B) appeals to authority
    (C) specialized technical language
    (D) appeals to logical reasoning

Choice (B) is the correct answer. In several of the footnotes, the authors draw on
published works and authorities in the field to support their points. The citations
in the footnotes become part of the authors' rhetorical strategy. Choice (A) can be
eliminated: the authors actually acknowledge that the two types of monitoring can
be combined in certain circumstances. They do not give any examples of negative
results from combining them in the wrong circumstances. The authors do give the
correct scientific classification for certain species, and they use the term "emphasis
species" to signify a monitoring target. However, their use of technical language is
not extensive. The authors are aiming at a diverse range of industry participants,
so in general they use formal language to signify their professionalism while not
excluding readers by using highly technical language from one specific field, so
(C) is incorrect. The authors' tone is objective and neutral. The authors don't rely
on logical arguments, (D), such as "X and Y are the case; therefore, you should do
Z or else *this* will happen because of *this*."

This next question shows the type of detail some questions can cover.

6. The term "taxa" in paragraph 1 refers to

    (A) characteristics of a group of organisms that
         distinguish them from other groups
    (B) criteria used to determine whether a species is
         endangered
    (C) a grouping of certain species of organism
    (D) any group of widespread and thriving organisms

This question demonstrates the importance of context in guessing the meaning
of an unfamiliar word, and the need to go back to the passage to find the answer.
Always read a line or two above and below the word specified, too, so you won't
miss any important information from the context.

Here, the correct answer is (C). The paragraph states that habitat monitoring is
appropriate for a full range of organisms, from those on the endangered species
list to those that are so numerous and widespread ("ubiquitous") that they can be
hunted. It sets up a contrast between species on both extreme ends of the range.
Using the technical term "taxa" allows the authors to avoid repeating the word
"species" three times in the same sentence. However, "taxa" could accurately
be replaced by "species" in this sentence. Choice (A) is incorrect because "taxa"
(the plural of "taxon," which would indicate a single species) refers to the groups
themselves, not to the characteristics of those groups. Both (B) and (D) are
incorrect as meanings for "taxa" because species could be either endangered or
thriving.

Here are some typical questions about citations, which are shown as footnotes. That means you'll need to read the footnote as well as go back to the corresponding place in the passage (indicated by the superscript number of the footnote). Read a couple of lines above and below the footnote number so you understand the context in which the authors cite a particular source or make a supplementary comment.

7. The primary function of footnote 9 is most likely to

   (A) give readers a method for carrying out a procedure
   (B) explain the reason for the authors' recommendation
   (C) provide an additional source for readers who are interested in more information
   (D) convince readers that they need more information before they can follow the authors' recommendations successfully

Choice (A) is correct. The excerpt doesn't say what is in Chapter 1, so you'll need to guess at the most likely primary reason for referring readers to it. Since the footnote occurs at the end of a sentence that describes a procedure (comparing habitat monitoring results with population data to confirm an assumed relationship between the two), (A) is the best choice. The footnote is simply a side comment, not an integral part of the text, where the authors would likely have explained their reasoning, (B), or made a convincing case, (D), if they felt the need to do so. Choice (C) is too vague when the footnote follows the description of a specific procedure.

8. The most unique aspect of footnote 8 in paragraph 5 is its

   (A) support for the separation of habitat and population monitoring
   (B) seven-year time span of support for the program objective of monitoring populations
   (C) geographical diversity of the resources cited
   (D) additional support for the authors' acknowledgment of a situation that would favor incorporating some population monitoring into a habitat monitoring program

The answer is (D). Footnote 8 is the only one that cites two sources of support for the same point (indirect population monitoring as an objective of habitat monitoring). The sources are cited as support for a condition in which habitat and population monitoring could be combined, not separated. Going back to the passage should have allowed you to eliminate (A) immediately using POE. While there is a seven-year time span between the two references, the two sources are not cited as support for only monitoring populations. Choice (B) is half wrong; therefore, it's all wrong. Although the second study in the footnote specifies the northwest, the first study doesn't indicate which geographical area it covers; eliminate (C).

9. The main effect of footnote 7 is to

(A) support the authors' point

(B) convince readers who might be skeptical about the authors' point

(C) illustrate and support the authors' point

(D) support and qualify the authors' point

Choice (C) is correct. The example of the impact of forest fires on woodpecker populations illustrates the authors' point, and the citation from published research supports it. While this footnote supports the authors' point with a reference to published research, that's not the only thing it does, eliminating (A). It's possible that an example and citation might convince skeptical readers, but the question asks for the *main* effect. The footnote is not worded as if its main objective were to convince skeptical readers, so you can get rid of (B). This footnote does support the authors' point. However, they already qualified their point in the main text ("Under some limited circumstances..."), not in the footnote. Remember, half wrong is all wrong. Eliminate (D).

Incidentally, if you had guessed at every one of these answers and had chosen (C) as your Letter of the Day, you would have gotten three correct answers on this passage. No, of course you can't know in advance which letter is best, but this example shows the results that are possible with the Letter of the Day technique.

SAMPLE WRITING PASSAGE—HERE'S HOW IT'S DONE

This is an example of the student-quality persuasive writing that will be associated with Writing questions on the exam. Begin by reading the passage carefully and using the same active reading techniques you used on Reading passages. Look for and write down the main point of each paragraph in the margins as you go. Remember that this passage will be imperfect; many of the Writing questions will provide you options to make it better.

The passage below is a draft.

(1) Bottled water comprises 67.3% of plastic bottle use in the United States, a leading cause of waste that threatens our oceans and our air quality. (2) Many cities, venues, colleges, and recreational areas have decided to ban single-use plastic water bottles.

(3) Upwards of 70% of plastic water bottles in the U.S. never see the inside of a recycling bin, which is why many Americans are upset. (4) Plastic bottle production takes a dramatic toll on the environment, and the Pacific Institute estimates that it took 17 million barrels of oil to produce single-use plastic bottles consumed in the U.S. in 2006. (5) Those numbers have only increased since: bottled water consumption in the U.S. increased 65% between 2006 and 2017, necessitating 13.7 billion barrels of oil that year.

(6) Concord, Massachusetts, San Francisco, California, the Detroit Zoo, the University of Vermont, and the Grand Canyon National Park have all banned single-use water bottles. (7) Not only will banning water bottles protect the environment, it will also be good for our health. (8) This is because bottled water isn't well regulated. (9) Banning single-use plastic bottles will also reduce pollution associated with plastic bottle creation; communities living near plastic bottle manufacturers report higher levels of chronic illness and birth defects than those that don't.

(10) Banning single-use plastic water bottles may seem like an unpopular idea, but tap water is less expensive than you might realize, particularly considering that bottled water costs between 400 and 2,000 times as much as tap water. (11) It's time for the United States to make the choice that is best for the environment and our pocket books and ban single-use plastic water bottles.

Approaching Writing Questions

The first paragraph acts as an introduction. The introduction has a few different goals: to hook the reader's attention, to introduce the topic of the essay, and, perhaps, to state the writer's thesis (though be careful: in some essays, the thesis will develop over the course of the essay).

The introduction is followed by body paragraphs. Though there's no set formula for the construction of the body paragraphs, most will start with a clearly stated claim that will be developed in the paragraph. Usually, that claim is substantiated through the use of evidence. Evidence could consist of concrete data, expert opinion, or personal anecdotes. Body paragraphs may also include a concession, an acknowledgment of a plausible argument held by the opposing view. Similarly, body paragraphs may rebut that concession, providing an explanation as to why the writer's argument remains the better viewpoint, despite the concession.

Because Writing paragraphs are drafts, they may or may not contain a formal conclusion. In a conclusion, the writer usually summarizes their main points and/or restates their thesis. In more complex examples, the conclusion may include the fully-realized form of a thesis that has developed over the course of the essay.

Let's take a look at questions that commonly pertain to the introductory segment of the passage:

1. Which of the following sentences, if placed before sentence 1, would both engage the audience's attention and introduce the topic of the paragraph?

   (A) In 2017, Americans consumed nearly 17 billion gallons of bottled water.

   (B) Every second, 20,000 plastic bottles are bought around the world, most of which contain only drinking water.

   (C) Bottled water manufacturers have been known to deplete water supplies in local communities.

   (D) Cities that have already banned single-use plastic bottles are planning to increase the number of public drinking fountains.

Active reading should help you identify the subject matter of this essay: the effects of bottled water consumption and the need to ban it. Reading the question closely, you know that you're looking for a response that is both interesting and relevant to the passage. Using POE, you can eliminate (B) and (D). Choice (B) pertains to water consumption around the world, whereas the information provided pertaining to water consumption is limited to the United States. Choice (D) describes drinking fountain access, which is irrelevant to the rest of the paragraph as well. Choice (C) is plausible but reads as a random factoid as opposed to an engaging introductory sentence. Choice (A) is the best answer, as many readers will be surprised by the quantity of bottled water Americans consume. It also introduces the topic of the paragraph: bottled water consumption.

Here's another question that addresses the use of transitions in an introductory paragraph:

2. In sentence 2 (reproduced below) the author wants a more fluid transition between the introductory sentences and the thesis of the passage:

   Many cities, venues, colleges, and recreational areas have decided to ban single-use plastic water bottles.

   Which of the following versions of the underlined text achieves this purpose?

   (A) (as it is now)
   (B) In order to reduce waste and protect the environment, many cities
   (C) Angering corporate interests, many cities
   (D) Seeing it as an ethical imperative, many cities

The goal of transitional phrases is to bridge ideas between sentences, so look for a phrase that captures, or even summarizes, the content of the previous sentences and explains the relationship between it and the subsequent sentence. Also note the task given in the question: to connect these sentences to the thesis of the passage (it's time for the United States to make the choice that is best for the environment and our pocket books and ban single-use plastic water bottles). As it is, the sentences are two independent ideas in sequence: the waste produced and environmental consequences of plastic water bottle consumption, and the fact that certain entities have already banned their use. No transition is made, so eliminate (A). Choice (C) can be eliminated because the idea it uses to transition—angry corporate interests— is irrelevant to the sentence that precedes it. While (D) is a plausible response, (B) is significantly more connected to the thesis of the passage. As such, (B) creates a better transition than leaving the text as is. Therefore, (B) is the best answer.

This question focuses on the thesis of the passage:

3. In sentence 3 (reproduced below), which version of the underlined statement most clearly states the author's thesis?

   Upwards of 70% of plastic water bottles in the U.S. never see the inside of a recycling bin, <u>which is why many Americans are upset.</u>

   (A) (as it is now)
   (B) which is just one reason the United States needs to ban single-use plastic bottles.
   (C) which is why consumers need to stop buying bottled water.
   (D) which is why plastic bottles threaten future generations.

This sentence comes at the start of the second paragraph, where the writer begins to develop the argument of the essay. For any questions that pertain to a thesis or the author's argument, it's important to consider the essay as a whole and not just the context of the surrounding sentences. Though the essay is imperfect, each paragraph builds on the idea that banning plastic water bottles has positive effects. Choice (C) presents the idea that consumers need to stop buying plastic water bottles. While this is perhaps a valid point, it is too specific to be described as the thesis of the essay. Choice (D), on the other hand, is too broad, and it is somewhat off topic from the points presented in subsequent paragraphs. The current version, reflected by (A), is weak because it is unsubstantiated; nowhere does the writer present evidence to support the idea that many Americans are upset. Choice (B) is the best answer, because the idea that *the United States needs to ban single-use plastic bottles* is a specific argument that is substantiated over the course of the essay.

The following questions pertain to the body paragraphs of the essay:

4. The writer wants to emphasize the surprising increase in plastic bottle use between 2006 and 2017, described in sentences 4 and 5. Adjusting for capitalization as needed, which phrase best accomplishes this goal at the start of sentence 5 (below)?

    Those numbers have only increased since: bottled water consumption in the U.S. increased 65% between 2006 and 2017, necessitating 13.7 billion barrels of oil that year.

    (A) (as it is now)
    (B) Actually,
    (C) By contrast,
    (D) Shockingly,

This is another question that's asking you to consider the relationship between sequential sentences. However, in this question, you're asked to consider which question emphasizes the surprising relationship between the two ideas. Choice (A) can be eliminated because, as the draft currently stands, there is no transitional phrase. Choice (C) can be eliminated because it is illogical. *By contrast* introduces a different, or even contradictory, piece of information. While the use of water bottles in 2017 does contrast with the use of water bottles in 2006, it is an increasing trend, and not the best use of this transitional phrase. *As a matter of fact* is used to introduce a piece of evidence that substantiates a claim. Choice (B) is plausible, though (D) does more to emphasize the surprising information. Therefore, (D) is the best answer.

5. The writer wants to add evidence to the second paragraph (sentences 3–5) to support the main idea of the paragraph. All of the following sentences accomplish this goal EXCEPT:

    (A) Plastic bottles are usually made from polyethylene terephthalate, a material derived from crude oil.

    (B) Plastic bottle consumption is directly linked to American consumption of crude oil.

    (C) As plastic bottles are rarely recycled, they end up polluting land and oceans.

    (D) Banning plastic bottles could save a family of four up to $5,000 per year.

Note that this question is unique in its structure. You have to select the one answer that doesn't work, as opposed to the one answer that does. The first step to answering this question is identifying the main idea of the passage: the environmental costs of water bottle production. Choices (A) and (B) further develop the relationship between plastic water bottle production and oil consumption. Choice (C) further develops the negative implications of plastic bottles not being recycled. The economic benefits of banning plastic bottles are irrelevant to the topic of the paragraph. Therefore, (D) is the best answer.

6. In sentence 8, the writer wants to provide convincing evidence as to why banning plastic water bottles would be good for Americans' health.

    This is because bottled water isn't well regulated.

    Which sentence below best replaces sentence 8 to achieve this goal?

    (A) (as it is now)

    (B) Tap water is more strictly regulated than bottled water.

    (C) The Environmental Protection Agency monitors tap water (multiple tests per day) more closely than the Food and Drug Administration monitors bottled water (weekly tests).

    (D) Both tap water and bottled water are regulated by government agencies.

This question seeks to assess your understanding of what makes high-quality, persuasive evidence. Good evidence is relevant, specific, and detailed. Choice (A) can be immediately eliminated because it is overly general. The tricky aspect of assessing the remaining options is that they are all accurate and in agreement with each other, so your task is figuring out which evidence is best. Putting them in order of most general to most specific, (D) is the weakest because it is a vague statement stating that both tap water and bottled water are regulated by the government. Choice (B) adds the detail that tap water is more strictly regulated than bottled water. Choice (C) provides the highest quality evidence, naming both the agencies responsible for regulation and the frequency with which the water quality is tested. Therefore, (C) is the best answer.

7. The writer wants to add the following sentence to the third paragraph (sentences 6–9):

This illustrates that there is already public support for banning single-use plastic bottles.

Where is this sentence best placed?

(A) Before sentence 6
(B) After sentence 6
(C) After sentence 7
(D) After sentence 8

Unlock the Text

Think of text that you're adding as a key that has to open the lock of the surrounding sentences. If there's an action word, with which of the given sentences does it best fit?

It is difficult to use POE for this question, because it asks you to insert the sentence in the question into the existing paragraph and assess it for logical flow and clarity. The key to this question is that the sentence starts with *This illustrates*. Therefore, the best strategy is to return to the paragraph in question, asking yourself what illustrates that there is already public support for banning single-use plastic bottles. Placing this sentence after sentence 7 or sentence 8 would not flow logically, since neither sentence gives any indication of public support. Eliminate (C) and (D). It would also create an illogical flow to start the paragraph with this sentence as the sentence's claim is unsubstantiated by the previous paragraph, so eliminate (A). While this sentence could potentially function as a conclusion, it doesn't quite make logical sense for it to follow sentence 9. Sentence 6, however, by describing that water bottles have already been banned in certain places, does suggest that there is already support to ban water bottles. Therefore, (B) is the best answer.

Here are a couple of questions pertaining to the final, or concluding, paragraph of the essay.

8. In the fourth paragraph (sentences 10–11), the writer wants to develop the counterargument that banning plastic water bottles might be unpopular. Which of the following sentences best achieves this goal?

(A) Some argue that banning single-use plastic water bottles limits consumer choice.
(B) Some turn to bottled water when their tap water proves toxic; however, this is often linked to industrial pollution.
(C) Plastic water bottles require fewer crude resources than plastic bottles used for soft drinks.
(D) Residents of some American cities have already voted to ban plastic bottles.

The key to understanding this question is grasping the phrase *develop the counterargument*. This usually means providing reasoning or evidence for the counterargument presented. In this case, the counterargument is that banning plastic water bottles might be unpopular. Choice (D) can be eliminated. Choice (D) supports the original argument and refutes the counterargument. Choice (C) can be eliminated because it supports an environmental argument that describes water bottles as less harmful than soft drink bottles but doesn't necessarily pertain directly to the popularity of a water bottle ban. Choice (B) begins by developing a counterargument, but also points out that tap water toxicity can be caused by industrial pollution. Choice (A) best develops the counterargument as it describes an argument against a ban, thus directly showing a negative public opinion. Therefore, (A) is the best response to the question.

9. In the fourth paragraph (sentences 10–11), the writer wants to include evidence to counter the claim that banning single-use plastic bottles may be unpopular. Which of the following best achieves this aim?

   (A) Residents of some American cities have already voted to ban plastic bags.

   (B) When tap water is undrinkable, bottled water becomes a necessity.

   (C) Banning bottled water often eliminates a healthy beverage choice at restaurants.

   (D) Citizens of a number of cities in the United States have already chosen to eliminate single-use plastic bottles.

This question asks you to consider a claim—that banning single-use plastic bottles might be unpopular—and consider evidence that refutes this claim. In other words, you're looking for a piece of evidence that supports the idea that banning single-use plastic bottles *is* popular. Choices (B) and (C) can be eliminated because they describe benefits of bottled water. Choice (A) is plausible, but support for banning plastic bags doesn't necessarily translate to support for plastic bottles. Choice (D) is the best answer as it describes the popularity the idea has already had in cities in the United States.

You'll have the opportunity to practice what you've learned in the drills in Chapter 3. Next, let's look a bit more closely at some approaches to two essential aspects of doing well on the multiple-choice questions: timing and pacing.

Summary

o The multiple-choice test consists of five passages and 45 questions. Two passages will be associated with Reading questions; three passages will be associated with Writing questions. You will have 60 minutes to complete this portion of the exam.

o Passages for Reading questions will be publication quality and could be from the 19th, 20th, or 21st centuries.

o Passages for Writing questions will be contemporary, argumentative, student-quality writing.

o Use active reading to identify the main point of each paragraph (or chunk) of the passage; then see how they connect to form the main point of the passage as a whole.

o Concentrate on the author's purpose, tone, and point of view.

o Look for the rhetorical strategies the author uses to achieve that purpose.

o Always go back to the passage when multiple-choice questions refer you to specific lines. Relying on your memory can easily lead you to select a close—but incorrect—answer.

o Read a couple of lines above and below the lines specified in the question. The context of the lines is often critical in determining the correct answer.

o Pace yourself. Divide the multiple-choice section into 12-minute chunks for each passage.

o Use the Two-Pass System. On your first pass, answer the questions you can and guess at the rest, using your Letter of the Day. Circle the questions you guessed on, and go back to them later if time remains in your 12-minute chunk.

o Use POE to eliminate wrong answers instead of looking for the right answer among four alternatives.

Chapter 2
Using Time
Effectively to
Maximize Points

STUDYING ISN'T EVERYTHING

Many students neglect their test-taking skills, assuming that if they study hard, they will get a high score, and if they do not study, they will do poorly.

Have you ever studied really hard for an exam and then blown it on test day? Have you ever aced an exam for which you thought you probably hadn't studied enough? Most students have had one, if not both, of these experiences. The lesson should be clear: factors other than how much you've studied influence your final test score, particularly on a test such as the AP English Language and Composition Exam, where timing and pacing are important aspects of thorough preparation.

This chapter will provide you with some insights that will help you perform better on the multiple-choice section of the AP English Language and Composition Exam, and on other exams as well.

Pacing and Timing

A big part of scoring well on an exam is sharpening your awareness of time. Another is working at a consistent pace.

Don't Waste Your Time

If you can't answer a question, make an educated guess and move on to the next question. Although you don't lose any points for wrong answers in the multiple-choice section, you don't want to waste time on a question you're unsure of because you will take away time from questions you're more likely to get correct.

The worst mistake made by inexperienced test-takers is that when they come to a question that stumps them, rather than just skipping it, they panic and stall. Time stands still when you're working on a question you can't answer, and it is not unusual for students to waste five minutes on a single multiple-choice question (especially a question involving a long selection from the passage or the word EXCEPT) instead of cutting their losses and moving on to questions they *can* answer.

Every question is worth the same one point, whether it's a hard question or an easy one. The computer that scores your responses doesn't know whether you agonized for three minutes over a hard question or breezed through an easy one in a few seconds; it only knows whether your answer is right or wrong.

It is important to be aware of how much time you are spending on a given question or section. There are several ways to improve your pacing and timing for the test.

- **Know your average pace.** While you prepare for your test, gauge how long you take on a passage with 11 or so questions. Knowing how long you spend on average per passage (and per question) will help you identify how many passages you can read (and questions you can answer) effectively in 60 minutes, and how best to pace yourself for the test.

- **Have a watch or clock nearby.** You are permitted to have a watch or clock nearby to help you keep track of time. However, constantly checking the clock can be distracting and stressful. Devise a plan. Try checking the clock after every passage or two to see whether you are keeping the correct pace or need to speed up. This will ensure that you're managing your time but won't permit you to fall into the trap of dwelling on it.

- **Know when to move on.** Because all of the multiple-choice questions are scored equally, and you are not penalized for wrong answers, investing long stretches of time on a single question is inefficient and can potentially deprive you of the chance to answer easier questions later on. If you can eliminate answer choices with POE, do so, but on your first pass through the questions, just guess from among the remaining choices (using your Letter of the Day) and move on if you can't find the correct answer. Remember, tests are like marathons: you do best when you work through them at a steady pace.

- **Be selective.** You don't have to do the multiple-choice questions in order. If you are stumped by a question, guess, and move on to the next one. You might not have to answer every question correctly to achieve the score you want for your first choice college. Select the questions you can answer and work on them first. This will boost your confidence, make you more efficient, and give you the greatest chance of getting the most questions correct.

- **Use Process of Elimination on every question.** Every answer choice that you can eliminate increases the odds that you will answer the question correctly.

Remember, when all the questions are of equal value and you don't lose any points for incorrect answers, no single question is that important. Your overall goal for pacing is to get the most questions correct.

Getting the Score You Need

Depending on the score you need, it may be in your best interest *not* to try to work through every multiple-choice question. Check with the schools to which you are applying. If you're aiming for credit hours and need to score a 5, it's best to find out as early in your preparation as possible. On the other hand, if you're simply aiming for placement and you find out your first choice college sets the cut-off point at a score of 3, that may take some of the pressure off and ease your preparation anxiety.

Reducing Test Anxiety

No matter what score you need, everybody experiences anxiety before and during an exam. To a certain extent, test anxiety *can* be helpful. Some people find that they perform more quickly and efficiently under stress. If you have ever pulled an all-nighter to write a paper and ended up doing good work, you know the feeling.

However, too much stress is definitely a bad thing. If you find that your stress level prevents you from doing your best work during exams, here are a few strategies you can use to keep the stress from getting the better of you.

Lit Lover?
Are you taking AP English Literature and Composition as well? Check out our *AP English Literature & Composition Prep!*

- **Put it in perspective.** Evaluate your situation before the test begins. If you have understood and practiced all of the techniques we give for success on the exam, remind yourself that you are well-prepared. Remember that the scoring is based on how everyone does, so a question that is challenging across the board may still leave you ahead of the game. What matters most is that you make every effort to improve your chances on test day.

- **Don't fixate on how much you don't know.** Your job is to score as high as you can by maximizing the benefits of what you do know. Think of the test as a game. How can you get the most points in the time allotted?

- **Try to relax.** Slow, deep breathing works for almost everyone. Close your eyes, take a few slow, deep breaths, and concentrate on nothing but inhaling and exhaling for a few seconds. This is a basic form of meditation, and it should help clear your mind of stress and, as a result, help you concentrate better on the test. If you have ever taken yoga classes, you probably know some other good relaxation techniques you could use in the test setting.

- **Visualize.** Imagine your favorite park, beach, hiking trail, or room, and visualize yourself sitting there taking the exam—all alone, calm and relaxed, and enjoying your surroundings. You're still taking the test, but in a pleasant place instead of in a stress-filled atmosphere. Most likely you'll need to practice this technique in advance in order to be able to slip into another place mentally while you're taking the test. Try it while you're having breakfast, or riding the bus, or walking down a noisy, chaotic street.

- **Eliminate as many surprises as you can.** Make sure you know the testing location, how long it will take you to get there, and where to park if you're driving. Take a "dry run" trip to the test center before the day of the exam. Know when the exam room will open, when the actual exam starts, what type of questions you will be asked, and how long each section of the test will take. You don't want to be worrying about any of these things on the test day.

- **Plan to reward yourself.** After all, you deserve a reward for all of your hard work. Make a plan for doing something enjoyable right after the test is over. While you're preparing, keep thinking of the reward you've promised yourself.

Remember...
Your purchase of this book comes with access to online Student Tools, a resource hub filled with bonus material like study guides and college advice. Follow the instructions on the Get More (Free) Content page to start using your online Student Tools.

The best way to avoid stress is to become familiar with the test material and practice doing exam questions under actual time constraints. (By reading this book, you are taking a major step toward a stress-free AP English Language and Composition Exam.)

In the next chapter, you'll have an opportunity to practice the strategies you've learned.

Chapter 3
Pacing Drills

READING DRILL 1

Questions 1–8. Read the following passage carefully before you choose your answers.

This passage is excerpted from the British prime minister's 1846 speech about the repeal of the Corn Laws.

Sir, believe me, to conduct the Government of this country is a most arduous duty; I may say it without irreverence, that these ancient institutions, like our physical
Line frames, are "fearfully and wonderfully made." It is no easy
5 task to ensure the united action of an ancient monarchy, a proud aristocracy, and a reformed constituency. I have done everything I could do, and have thought it consistent with true Conservative policy to reconcile these three branches of the State. I have thought it consistent with true
10 Conservative policy to promote so much of happiness and contentment among the people that the voice of disaffection should be no longer heard, and that thoughts of the dissolution of our institutions should be forgotten in the midst of physical enjoyment. These were my attempts,
15 and I thought them not inconsistent with true and enlarged Conservative policy. These were my objects in accepting office—it is a burden too great for my physical, and far beyond my intellectual structure; and to be relieved from it with perfect honour would be the greatest favour that could
20 be conferred on me. But as a feeling of honour and strong sense of duty require me to undertake those responsible functions, I declare, Sir, that I am ready to incur these risks, to bear these burdens, and to front all these honourable dangers. But, Sir, I will not take the step with
25 mutilated power and shackled authority. I will not stand at the helm during such tempestuous nights as I have seen, if the vessel be not allowed fairly to pursue the course which I think she ought to take. I will not, Sir, undertake to direct the course of the vessel by the observations which have
30 been taken in 1842. I will reserve to myself the marking out of that course; and I must, for the public interest, claim for myself the unfettered power of judging of those measures which I conceive will be better for the country to propose.
35 Sir, I do not wish to be the Minister of England; but while I have the high honour of holding that Office, I am determined to hold it by no servile tenure. I will only hold that office upon the condition of being unshackled by any other obligations than those of consulting the public inter-
40 ests, and of providing for the public safety.

1. The opening sentence of the passage contains

   (A) an expression of fear
   (B) an appeal to authority
   (C) a humorous simile
   (D) an irreverent attack

2. The speaker is addressing

   (A) a friend
   (B) a group of his peers
   (C) a king
   (D) a crowd of voters

3. The most significant transition takes place in

   (A) line 9 ("I have thought it consistent...")
   (B) line 16 ("These were my objects...")
   (C) line 20 ("But as a feeling of honour...")
   (D) line 24 ("But, Sir, I will not...")

4. All of the following are part of the same extended metaphor EXCEPT

   (A) "helm" (line 26)
   (B) "vessel" (line 27)
   (C) "fairly" (line 27)
   (D) "unshackled" (line 38)

5. Which term in the first paragraph serves to prepare the dominant point of the final paragraph?

   (A) "disaffection" (lines 11–12)
   (B) "enjoyment" (line 14)
   (C) "dangers" (line 24)
   (D) "unfettered" (line 32)

6. Based on the passage, the speaker's motivation to serve as prime minister is dictated mostly by

   (A) greed
   (B) political ambition
   (C) sense of honor
   (D) political power

7. The tone of the entire passage
   (A) remains consistently cynical
   (B) shifts according to the speaker's mood
   (C) shifts from light to serious
   (D) becomes more frivolous in the final paragraph

8. Which of the following best describes the rhetorical function of lines 17–20 ("it is a burden too great… the greatest favor that could be conferred on me")?

   (A) It makes an appeal to emotion.
   (B) It states the overall thesis of the passage.
   (C) It expresses a causal relationship between events in the past and events in the present.
   (D) It reinforces the author's claim of responsibility in the following sentence.

READING DRILL 2

Questions 9–16. Read the following passage carefully before you choose your answers.

This passage is excerpted from an influential work published in 1839.

This archipelago consists of ten principal islands, of
which five exceed the others in size. They are situated
under the Equator, and between five and six hundred miles
Line westward of the coast of America. They are all formed
5 of volcanic rocks; a few fragments of granite curiously
glazed and altered by the heat, can hardly be considered as
an exception. Some of the craters, surmounting the larger
islands, are of immense size, and they rise to a height of
between three and four thousand feet. Their flanks are
10 studded by innumerable smaller orifices. I scarcely hesitate
to affirm, that there must be in the whole archipelago at
least two thousand craters. These consist either of lava or
scoriae, or of finely-stratified, sandstone-like tuff. Most
of the latter are beautifully symmetrical; they owe their
15 origin to eruptions of volcanic mud without any lava: it is a
remarkable circumstance that every one of the twenty-eight
tuff-craters which were examined had their southern sides
either much lower than the other sides, or quite broken
down and removed. As all these craters apparently have
20 been formed when standing in the sea, and as the waves
from the trade wind and the swell from the open Pacific
here unite their forces on the southern coasts of all the
islands, this singular uniformity in the broken state of the
craters, composed of the soft and yielding tuff, is easily
25 explained.
    The *Beagle* sailed round Chatham Island, and anchored
in several bays. One night I slept on shore on a part of the
island, where black truncated cones were extraordinarily
numerous: from one small eminence I counted sixty of
30 them, all surmounted by craters more or less perfect. The
greater number consisted merely of a ring of red scoriae or
slags, cemented together: and their height above the plain
of lava was not more than from fifty to a hundred feet;
none had been very lately active. The entire surface of this
35 part of the island seems to have been permeated, like a
sieve, by the subterranean vapours: here and there the lava,
whilst soft, has been blown into great bubbles; and in other
parts, the tops of caverns similarly formed have fallen in,
leaving circular pits with steep sides. From the regular
40 form of the many craters, they gave to the country an artificial appearance, which vividly reminded me of those parts
of Staffordshire, where the great iron-foundries are most
numerous. The day was glowing hot, and the scrambling
over the rough surface and through the intricate thickets,

45 was very fatiguing; but I was well repaid by the strange
Cyclopean scene. As I was walking along I met two large
tortoises, each of which must have weighed at least two
hundred pounds: one was eating a piece of cactus, and as
I approached, it stared at me and slowly walked away; the
50 other gave a deep hiss, and drew in its head. These huge
reptiles, surrounded by the black lava, the leafless shrubs,
and large cacti, seemed to my fancy like some antediluvian
animals. The few dull-coloured birds cared no more for me
than they did for the great tortoises.

9. This passage is most notable for its

   (A) meticulous classification
   (B) unusual point of view
   (C) precise description
   (D) resourceful analogies

10. The speaker in the passage can best be described as

    (A) a scientist making entries in a nature journal
    (B) a professional sailor touring a remote island
    (C) a fiction writer on holiday
    (D) a surveyor measuring land for future
        development

11. In context, one can infer that "tuff" (line 13) is

    (A) an alternate spelling for "tough"
    (B) a kind of sand
    (C) made up principally of grass
    (D) volcanic rock

12. In this passage, the speaker is most notably
    impressed by

    (A) the flora on the islands
    (B) the force of the Pacific Ocean
    (C) the fragments of granite
    (D) the symmetrical craters on the islands

13. Which of the following phrases represents a literary allusion?

    (A) "parts of Staffordshire" (lines 41–42)
    (B) "the strange Cyclopean scene" (lines 45–46)
    (C) "situated under the Equator" (lines 2–3)
    (D) "the coast of America" (line 4)

14. Which of the following landscape features are described throughout the entire passage?

    (A) Craters and lava
    (B) Craters and tortoises
    (C) Tortoises and birds
    (D) Islands and bays

15. In line 52, "antediluvian" most nearly means

    (A) artificial
    (B) prehistoric
    (C) volcanic
    (D) enormous

16. Which of the following are virtually synonymous as presented in the author's description?

    (A) "ten principal islands" (line 1) and "two thousand craters" (line 12)
    (B) "tuff" (line 13) and "volcanic mud" (line 15)
    (C) "iron-foundries" (line 42) and "intricate thickets" (line 44)
    (D) "craters" (line 40) and "caverns" (line 38)

READING DRILL 3

Questions 17–25. Read the following passage carefully before you choose your answers.

This passage is excerpted from an essay by a 19th-century British writer.

Art begins with abstract decoration, with purely imaginative and pleasurable work dealing with what is unreal and non-existent. This is the first stage. Then Life becomes
Line
5 fascinated with this new wonder, and asks to be admitted into the charmed circle. Art takes Life as part of her rough material, re-creates it, and refashions it in fresh forms, is absolutely indifferent to fact, invents, imagines, dreams, and keeps between herself and reality the impenetrable barrier of beautiful style, of decorative or ideal treatment.
10 The third stage is when Life gets the upper hand, and drives Art out into the wilderness. That is the true decadence, and it is from this that we are now suffering.

Take the case of the English drama. At first in the hands of the monks Dramatic Art was abstract, decorative and
15 mythological. Then she enlisted Life in her service, and using some of life's external forms, she created an entirely new race of beings, whose sorrows were more terrible than any sorrow man has ever felt, whose joys were keener than lover's joys, who had the rage of the Titans and the
20 calm of the gods, who had monstrous and marvelous sins, monstrous and marvelous virtues. To them she gave a language different from that of actual use, a language full of resonant music and sweet rhythm, made stately by solemn cadence, or made delicate by fanciful rhyme,
25 jeweled with wonderful words, and enriched with lofty diction. She clothed her children in strange raiment and gave them masks, and at her bidding the antique world rose from its marble tomb. A new Caesar stalked through the streets of risen Rome, and with purple sail and flute-
30 led oars another Cleopatra passed up the river to Antioch. Old myth and legend and dream took shape and substance. History was entirely rewritten, and there was hardly one of the dramatists who did not recognize that the object of Art is not simple truth but complex beauty. In this they were
35 perfectly right. Art itself is really a form of exaggeration; and selection, which is the very spirit of art, is nothing more than an intensified mode of over-emphasis.

But Life soon shattered the perfection of the form. Even in Shakespeare we can see the beginning of the end. It
40 shows itself by the gradual breaking-up of the blank-verse in the later plays, by the predominance given to prose, and by the overimportance assigned to characterization. The passages in Shakespeare—and they are many—where the language is uncouth, vulgar, exaggerated, fantastic,
45 obscene even, are entirely due to Life calling for an echo of her own voice, and rejecting the intervention of beautiful style, through which alone should life be suffered to find expression. Shakespeare is not by any means a flawless artist. He is too fond of going directly to Life, and
50 borrowing Life's natural utterance. He forgets that when Art surrenders her imaginative medium she surrenders everything.

17. The author of this passage is most likely

    (A) a poet
    (B) a novelist
    (C) an art critic
    (D) a journalist

18. The author relies principally on which of the following to substantiate his thesis?

    (A) A faulty analogy
    (B) Process analysis
    (C) An accumulation of facts
    (D) Illustration by example

19. "…when Art surrenders her imaginative medium she surrenders everything" (lines 50–52) is in the form of

    (A) a fundamental principle
    (B) an inverted sentence structure
    (C) an antithesis
    (D) an understatement

20. Above all else, the author reveres

    (A) beauty
    (B) life
    (C) Shakespeare
    (D) Caesar

21. In the context of the entire passage, "Life gets the upper hand" (line 10) is best interpreted as having which of the following meanings?

    (A) Art is favored over Life in English drama.
    (B) Life rewrites history.
    (C) Life drives Art out of English drama.
    (D) Life dominates Art in English drama.

22. The quality discussed in lines 22–26 is most directly the antithesis of which of the following?

    (A) "marble tomb" (line 28)
    (B) "The passages in Shakespeare" (line 43)
    (C) "to find expression" (lines 47–48)
    (D) "her imaginative medium" (line 51)

23. The author's observation in the first three sentences (lines 1–5) is best described as an example of which of the following?

    (A) Personification
    (B) Linguistic paradox
    (C) First-person narrative
    (D) Dramatic irony

24. In line 26, "She" refers to which of the following?

    I.   "Dramatic Art" (line 14)
    II. "English drama" (line 13)
    III. "Life" (line 15)

    (A) I only
    (B) II only
    (C) I and III only
    (D) II and III only

25. The author's tone in the passage as a whole is best described as

    (A) harsh and strident
    (B) informal and analytical
    (C) rueful and expository
    (D) enthusiastic and optimistic

WRITING DRILL 1

Questions 1–8 are based on the following passage.

The passage below is a draft.

(1) In 2017, the US Mint put 8.4 billion pennies into circulation, more than the number of quarters, dimes, and nickels combined. (2) While 29% of Americans want to abolish the penny, a recent poll found that 55% of Americans want to keep the penny in circulation.

(3) Proponents of keeping the penny argue that taking the penny out of circulation would have negative impacts. (4) Without the penny, prices for everyday items purchased with cash would have to be rounded, and likely rounded up, to the nickel. (5) Studies show that this rounding would exceed $600 million every year, a cost that would be paid by those who use cash. (6) Cash and coinage are important means of currency for those who don't have access to credit.

(7) Many philanthropies rely on the penny for fundraising. (8) The Leukemia and Lymphoma Society reports that they have been able to raise over $150 million in pennies to support blood cancer research and treatment. (9) Collecting pennies is an easy task, as children can easily ask for them and many people don't mind giving them away for a good cause or leaving them at a cash register for following customers.

(10) Those who want to abolish the penny say that this disposability is exactly why the penny should be abolished. (11) As each penny costs 1.8 cents to make, and many are willing to give them away, some question the value of producing them all together. (12) Due to the negative impact abolishing the penny would have on low-income communities and philanthropies, the penny should stay in circulation.

1. Which of the following sentences best captures the writer's thesis statement?

   (A) While 29% of Americans want to abolish the penny, a recent poll found that 55% of Americans want to keep the penny in circulation. (Sentence 2)
   (B) Proponents of keeping the penny argue that taking the penny out of circulation would have negative impacts. (Sentence 3)
   (C) Without the penny, prices for everyday items purchased with cash would have to be rounded, and likely rounded up, to the nickel. (Sentence 4)
   (D) Those who want to abolish the penny say that this disposability is exactly why the penny should be abolished. (Sentence 10)

2. In sentence 2 (reproduced below), the writer wants an effective transition from the introductory paragraph to the following paragraph in the passage.

   While 29% of Americans want to abolish the penny, a recent poll found that 55% of Americans want to keep the penny in <u>circulation.</u>

   Which of the following versions of the underlined text best achieves the writer's purpose?

   (A) (as it is now)
   (B) circulation, indicating that attitudes toward the penny are rapidly changing.
   (C) circulation; it's important that both groups are heard in the debate about whether or not to abolish the penny.
   (D) circulation—as it reflects the attitudes of the majority of Americans, the penny should stay in circulation.

3. In sentence 3 (reproduced below), which of the following versions of the underlined text best articulates the writer's primary argument in the essay?

Proponents of keeping the penny argue that taking the penny out of circulation would have negative <u>impacts.</u>

(A) (as it is now)
(B) impacts on many people.
(C) impacts on low-income communities and philanthropies.
(D) impacts on individuals who are already struggling.

4. In the second paragraph (sentences 3–6) the author wants to add evidence establishing that low-income individuals will be most impacted by the eradication of the penny. Which of the following best achieves that goal?

(A) According to the US Federal Reserve, low-income individuals are more likely to use cash than credit cards, so the weight of this $600 million would fall on those who are already facing economic struggles.
(B) In America, the divide between the rich and the poor is increasing.
(C) The penny creates invaluable flexibility for individuals who are unable to make purchases with credit cards.
(D) Pennies also allow sellers to be more specific with their pricing, avoiding overpricing or underpricing goods.

5. The writer wants to add the following to the third paragraph (sentences 7–9) to provide additional explanation.

The Ronald McDonald House and the Salvation Army also use penny drives as an important source of revenue.

Where would the sentence best be placed?

(A) Before sentence 7
(B) After sentence 7
(C) After sentence 8
(D) This sentence shouldn't be included.

6. In sentence 10 (reproduced below) the writer wants an effective transition to signal the start of the counterargument.

Those who want to abolish the penny say that this disposability is exactly why the penny should be abolished.

Adjusting for capitalization, which of the following transitions best achieves this goal?

(A) (as it is now)
(B) Similarly,
(C) Therefore,
(D) On the other hand,

7. Sentence 10 is reproduced below.

Those who want to abolish the penny say that this disposability is exactly why the penny should be abolished.

This sentence can best be described as:

(A) the thesis statement
(B) a concession
(C) the hook used to get the reader's attention
(D) evidence

8. The writer wants to add evidence to paragraph 4 (sentences 10–12) to rebut the claim that pennies aren't cost-effective to produce. Which of the following best achieves this goal?

(A) The United States could lose nearly $2 billion over the next ten years if the penny stays in production.
(B) It's ironic that cash and coinage can be expensive to produce.
(C) But the same can be said of the nickel as well.
(D) Coins often stay in circulation for 20 to 30 years, making them worth the investment.

WRITING DRILL 2

Questions 9–14 are based on the following passage.

The passage below is a draft.

(1) Students, parents, and scholars have all questioned the value of homework. (2) In light of such varied opinions, the efficacy and equity of homework remains a controversial subject. (3) Because of this controversy, homework should be banned in U.S. public schools.

(4) Students are often so overwhelmed with homework that their mental and physical health suffers. (5) Today, elementary school students average 2.9 hours of homework per week, and high school students spend over 17.5 hours per week on homework. (6) Even students who achieve at the highest levels report exhaustion, headaches, weight loss, and stomach problems due to excessive homework.

(7) While some studies do reveal advantages to homework, these advantages are skewed toward high-income students. (8) High-income students are more likely to have a parent at home who can help them, resources needed to accomplish homework, and the disposable income to pay for private tutoring. (9) Today, private tutoring is a cash cow, developing into a $6 billion per year industry. (10) Many students report not being able to complete homework because they don't have access to a computer or the Internet while at home.

(11) Studies show that students retain only 50% of in-class instruction and need homework in order to apply classroom content to the real world around them. (12) Homework can also help students develop skills such as time management and goal setting. (13) But is it right for schools to offer these benefits to only a fraction of students? (14) Schools should figure out a way to deliver these lessons to all students and ban homework in the meantime.

9. Which of the following sentences, if placed before sentence 1, would both capture the audience's attention and effectively introduce the topic of the essay?

(A) Every day after school, American students spend hours working on homework.

(B) Homework: Teachers love assigning it, but students hate doing it.

(C) Even though it's imperfect, homework is a valuable tool for providing students the opportunity to practice skills independently.

(D) In the past 100 years, homework has been both banned and deemed necessary to keep American students competitive.

10. In sentence 3 (reproduced below), which of the following versions of the underlined text best establishes the writer's reasoning as to the main argument of the passage?

Because of this controversy, homework should be banned in U.S. public schools.

(A) (as it is now)

(B) Due to students' personal needs and the inequality that homework causes,

(C) Since students are better off without it and it causes frustration for parents,

(D) Because it causes students to cheat and lose sleep,

11. Which of the following sentences captures the argument made in paragraph 2 (sentences 4–6) and makes the best topic sentence for that paragraph? The current topic sentence is reproduced below:

Students are often so overwhelmed with homework that their mental and physical health suffers.

(A) (as it is now)
(B) Sleep, exercise, and socialization rank among the most important developmental needs for students from elementary school through high school.
(C) Students of all ages are being assigned more homework now than ever before.
(D) All across the country, homework is causing students of all ages to suffer.

12. The writer wants to add a phrase at the beginning of sentence 10 (reproduced below), adjusting capitalization as needed, to transition from the idea discussed in sentence 9 to the idea discussed in sentence 10.

Many students report not being able to complete homework because they don't have access to a computer or the Internet while at home.

Which of the following best accomplishes that goal?

(A) In my opinion,
(B) Although,
(C) As a result,
(D) Further,

13. The writer wants to add evidence to paragraph 2 (sentences 4–6) to support the idea that homework is detrimental to students' mental health. Which of the following best achieves that goal?

(A) Many studies reveal that homework increases SAT scores by up to 40 points.
(B) When a Florida district replaced homework with free reading, student success increased.
(C) A poll of high school students in California revealed that 82% reported feeling consistently stressed by schoolwork and homework.
(D) Up to 90% of middle school students report cheating on homework.

14. The writer wants to add the following sentence to the fourth paragraph (sentences 11–14) to provide additional explanation.

Students who are taught to prioritize work independently have better grades and receive more positive comments on their report cards.

Where would the sentence best be placed?

(A) Before sentence 11
(B) After sentence 11
(C) After sentence 12
(D) After sentence 13

WRITING DRILL 3

Questions 15–20 are based on the following passage.

The passage below is a draft.

(1) In the 2014 midterm elections, only 36.7% of eligible citizens voted in the United States. (2) Even though presidential elections routinely see higher voter turnout than midterm and local elections, in the 2016 presidential election, only 60.1% of Americans voted.

(3) In order to increase voter turnout, more people should be allowed to vote. (4) Already, cities in California and Maryland allow 16-year-olds to vote in local elections, allowing younger voters to weigh in on issues that affect them directly, such as gun-control policy and climate change. (5) The 18–29 age group is notorious for not participating in elections, whereas in Takoma Park, Maryland (the first city to lower the voting age), turnout among 16- and 17-year-olds has been double that of voters ages 18 and up in 2014.

(6) Many proponents of lowering the voting age describe the positive effect that lowering the voting age can have on democracy in America. (7) When the voting age was lowered from 21 to 18 in the 1970s, a U.S. Senate report applauded student activism, saying "We must channel these energies into our political system and give young people the real opportunity to influence our society in a peaceful and constructive manner." (8) Without a way to participate legally and peacefully, young activists could turn to violent protests or rioting. (9) When younger people start to vote, others will vote more, too.

(10) Some are concerned that changing the laws will be too difficult, as it requires a constitutional amendment, necessitating approval from two-thirds of both houses in Congress and approval in 38 state legislatures. (11) As the past has proven, this change is possible and would increase voter participation and the strength of American democracy in the future.

15. Which of the following sentences, if placed before sentence 1, would both capture the audience's attention and effectively introduce the topic of the essay?

(A) Despite the fact that the U.S. prides itself on being a successful democracy, its citizens over the age of 18 show up at the polls at lower rates than in most other developed countries.

(B) Despite politics dominating the American news cycle, few Americans are willing to take the time to participate in politics themselves.

(C) Who knows how many people will vote in the future?

(D) Many factors affect a citizen's likelihood to vote: age, income, and geographical location.

16. In sentence 3 (reproduced below), which of the following versions of the underlined text best establishes the writer's position on the main argument of the passage?

In order to increase voter turnout, <u>more people should be allowed to vote.</u>

(A) (as it is now)

(B) the voting age should be lowered to 16.

(C) elected officials should reconsider the voting age.

(D) citizenship rights should be expanded across the U.S.

17. The writer wants to add a phrase at the beginning of sentence 5 (reproduced below), adjusting capitalization as needed, to set up a comparison with the idea discussed in sentence 4.

The 18–29 age group is notorious for not participating in elections, whereas in Takoma Park, Maryland (the first city to lower the voting age), turnout among 16- and 17-year-olds has been double that of voters ages 18 and up.

(A) Similarly,

(B) By contrast,

(C) In fact,

(D) However,

18. The writer wants to add more information to the third paragraph (sentences 6–9) to support the main argument of the paragraph. All of the following help achieve this purpose EXCEPT which one?

    (A) 16- and 17-year-olds are more likely to have support from parents and teachers in the voting process, whereas 18-year-olds are distracted by transitioning into adult responsibilities.
    (B) 16-year-olds often start working, driving, and paying taxes; because their relationship with the law changes at this age, they should have the right to vote.
    (C) People who vote once are 13% more likely to vote in subsequent elections than are people who have never voted; by allowing people to vote when they are younger, they will be more likely to vote over the course of their lives.
    (D) Psychologists say 16-year-olds have cognitive abilities similar to older adults.

19. In sentence 9 (reproduced below), the writer wants to provide a convincing explanation for why lowering the voting age would increase voter participation in the U.S.

    When younger people start to vote, others will vote more, too.

    Which version of sentence 9 best accomplishes this goal?

    (A) (as it is now)
    (B) In the same way that people who are 16 can drive and become legally emancipated from their parents, they should also have the right to vote.
    (C) Many people argue that if 16-year-olds are affected by laws, they should have the power to change them.
    (D) Young voters can have a "trickle up" effect, encouraging the older citizens in their lives to participate in the democratic process alongside them.

20. The writer wants to add evidence to the fourth paragraph that refutes the concession made in sentence 10 (reproduced below). Which sentence best accomplishes this goal?

    Some are concerned that changing the laws will be too difficult, as it requires a constitutional amendment, necessitating approval from two-thirds of both houses in Congress and approval in 38 state legislatures.

    (A) In 1971, officials ratified the 26th Amendment, which lowered the voting age from 21 to 18.
    (B) The Vietnam War prompted officials to ratify the 26th Amendment, which lowered the voting age from 21 to 18 in 1971.
    (C) Lowering the voting age offers elected officials from both political parties the opportunity to work together for a common goal.
    (D) Ratifying the 26th Amendment, which lowered the voting age to 18, required only three months, the most efficient ratification of any amendment in U.S. history.

READING DRILL 1 EXPLANATIONS

1. **C** The simile in this first sentence compares the great and ancient parliamentary institutions with the august, but somewhat ancient, bodies of the members of Parliament. The speaker is warming up his audience with a bit of humor before launching into what amounts to a very serious ultimatum: that the speaker will continue to serve as prime minister, but only if they concede to him much greater authority than before (1842). The answer is (C).

2. **B** The speaker is addressing a group of his peers, (B), who are the other members of Parliament. The tricky part here is, of course, the repetition of *Sir*, a political convention in Great Britain—it is as if the prime minister were addressing each member of Parliament as an individual. There is evidence that he is the British prime minister in the final sentences, and these sentences also reveal definitively that he is speaking to peers: *Sir, I do not wish to be the Minister of England; but while I have the high honour of holding that Office, I am determined to hold it by no servile tenure. I will only hold that office upon the condition of being unshackled by any other obligations than those of consulting the public interests, and of providing for the public safety.*

3. **D** Everything before this line is an introduction to the prime minister's real message; until this point, he has joked, given a general review of his former motivations and actions as the leader of the Conservative party, and explained his reasons for accepting to serve again as prime minister (*feeling of honour*) in spite of his failing health and aged mind (*a burden too great for my physical, and far beyond my intellectual structure*). The transition comes with *But, Sir, I will not take the step with mutilated power and shackled authority.* He will do the country and his peers a favor, but only if he is granted much more authority to rule. Choice (D) is the answer.

4. **D** Eliminate (A) and (B) so you're left with (C) and (D), which do not fit neatly into the nautical terminology. Choice (C) is the one to eliminate. All the other terms fit neatly into the nautical terminology. However, one could stretch a point and claim that *fairly* is related to fair weather, whereas *unshackled* is clearly unrelated to this metaphor. The answer is (D).

5. **D** The first step is to determine the *dominant point* of the final paragraph. Thankfully, the second paragraph is short—it is the rhetorical summation of his ultimatum. The key phrases are *servile tenure* and *unshackled by any other obligations*. The point is something like "I refuse to be prime minister again unless I get to do what I want." A big clue is that *unfettered* and *unshackled* are synonyms, so the best answer is (D), *unfettered*.

6. **C** The prime minister states unequivocally that honor is his motivation, in the following section in particular (lines 18–24): *and to be relieved from it [the position] with perfect honour would be the greatest favour that could be conferred on me. But as a feeling of honour and strong sense of duty require me to undertake those responsible functions, I declare, Sir, that I am ready to incur these risks, to bear these burdens, and to front all these honourable dangers.* The word *honor* comes up numerous times in this excerpt. Choice (C) is correct.

7. **C** You should be able to narrow your options to (B) and (C). The speech was carefully constructed, and the tone was coolly calculated when the author wrote it. The prime minister begins with a light tone because he is looking to set up his audience, not because he starts his speech in a good mood. In fact, his real mood never shifts: he manipulates tone for maximum effect.

8. **D** In lines 17–20, the prime minister describes his time in office as a *burden* and how he wishes to be *relieved of it*. But in the following sentence, lines 20–24, he states that *a strong sense of duty* requires him to *incur these risks, bear these burdens, and to front all these honourable dangers*. So he is burdened but feels a sense of responsibility. This aligns with (D). Although readers may feel sympathy with the prime minister, an appeal to emotion is not the primary goal, so eliminate (A). The overall thesis of the passage has more to do with duty than burden, so (B) can be eliminated as well. The author's sense of burden did not cause anything to happen, which eliminates (C).

READING DRILL 2 EXPLANATIONS

9. **C** This is a scientifically precise description of the Galapagos Islands. Choice (A) is incorrect because nothing is being classified in this passage. Choice (B) is also wrong—no point of view is presented here, just facts. The passage is not dominated by analogies, so (D) is incorrect.

10. **A** You can use POE to answer this question. Choice (C) is the easiest to eliminate; the passage is factual, not fictional. Choices (B) and (D) are somewhat plausible; however, there is no evidence that the author is a *professional* sailor, nor that he has done any formal *surveying*. The passage contains a detailed description of nature, so (A) is the best match.

11. **D** In this case, the answer is made clear from the passage; the craters have a border of soft stone (tuff) that has worn away on the southern side. The specific line from the passage that allows you to answer this question is this: *These consist either of lava or scoriae, or of finely stratified, sandstone-like tuff.* Sandstone is a type of rock. Tuff is actually a rock composed of compacted volcanic ash varying in size from fine sand to coarse gravel. Choice (D) is correct.

12. **D** The author doesn't address (A) so you can eliminate that one and look closely at the remaining three choices. Although the author mentions the Pacific Ocean and the fragments of granite, he incorporates these elements in his overarching discussion of the symmetrical craters, (D).

13. **B** A literary allusion is a reference, usually to a character from art, literature, or mythology, which requires the reader to have some outside knowledge of the topic. Staffordshire, (A), is a place, but not a feature of literature or mythology. The Cyclops, (B), is a character from Greek mythology, so this is the best match. Choices (C) and (D) are geographical references, not literary or mythological.

14. **A** Check BOTH paragraphs. Tortoises are mentioned only toward the end of the passage and are not landscape features, so eliminate (B) and (C). Bays are mentioned only at the beginning of paragraph 2, so eliminate (D). Craters and lava are mentioned throughout the passage, making (A) the best answer.

15.　**B**　If you know the definition of *antediluvian*, then you have a distinct advantage here; if not, you can get clues from the context of the passage. Since the word is describing animals, they would not be *artificial* or *volcanic*, so eliminate (A) and (C). *Enormous*, (D), is tempting, since the tortoises are described as *huge*, but that would ignore the middle phrase in that sentence and create a redundancy. *Black lava*, *leafless shrubs*, and *large cacti* are not features of many modern landscapes, and the tortoises are larger than normal, so *old* or *primordial* is the meaning you're looking for here. Choice (B) is the closest choice.

16.　**D**　Synonymous phrases would represent virtually the same idea. The islands have craters, but they are not, in themselves, actual craters, so eliminate (A). *Tuff* and *volcanic mud*, (B), may be associated together in the first paragraph, but you don't know for sure whether they are the same substance. *Iron-foundries* are more closely aligned to craters, not *thickets*, (C). That leaves you with (D): both *craters* and *caverns* are holes in the landscape.

READING DRILL 3 EXPLANATIONS

17.　**A**　In reality, the author is both a poet and a novelist, but you are asked to make a judgment based on the passage. To answer this question correctly, you need to use POE and your best judgment to eliminate all of the least likely answer choices. The passage is an attack against the intrusion of prosaic life into the realm of art. The panegyric (high praise) of classical language is a key to understanding the author's point of view: *a language different from that of actual use, a language full of resonant music and sweet rhythm, made stately by solemn cadence, or made delicate by fanciful rhyme, jeweled with wonderful words, and enriched with lofty diction.* In a word, this is poetry. Choice (A) is correct. The writing is far too lyrical for the author of the passage to be a journalist, (D). The same may be said for (C). The author capitalizes *art* because he is not discussing painting specifically, but the general realm of artistic creation that encompasses all the arts.

18.　**D**　The example is stated rhetorically—*Take the case of the English drama*—and lasts for most of the passage. *Illustration by example*, (D), is definitely the defining rhetorical mode of this passage.

19.　**A**　The sentence provides a fundamental principle on when Art fails, so (A) is the best answer. POE can help you narrow down your choices. The statement seems to be a type of overstatement (hyperbole), and for that reason (D) can be discarded. For the statement to be an antithesis, the author would have needed to put two things or concepts in opposition, but you have only one element (Art); thus, you can eliminate (C). At this point, your chances are fifty-fifty, so you could guess and move on. But look at (B). There is a parallel structure in the two halves of the sentence, so there is no reversal.

20.　**A**　The author does not revere life above everything else—for example, he clearly states that he doesn't like life as an intrusion on Art, at the very least, or as it appears in certain parts of William Shakespeare's work; eliminate (B) and (C). He includes these examples of Caesar and English drama for rhetorical reasons, and while he admires English drama, he does not appear to revere it, eliminating (D). (By the way, to *revere* something is to regard it with awe, deference, and devotion.) Beauty is held up as an ideal, and this is clear when the author says, *the object of Art is not simple truth but complex beauty.* The answer is (A).

21. **D** The idiom *getting the upper hand* means having an advantage over something or someone. If *Life gets the upper hand*, then (A) is wrong. Choice (B) is likewise irrelevant to *getting the upper hand*. Choices (C) and (D) have very close meanings, but (C) is too extreme, since you can't say for sure that Art is absent from all English drama. Choice (D) is the best choice.

22. **B** The quality in lines 22–26 is *a language full of resonant music and sweet rhythm.* This is the antithesis (direct opposite) of the author's description of Shakespeare's writing in line 43. Choice (B) is the best answer.

23. **A** Throughout the first paragraph, the author refers to Life and Art as though they were people: *Life becomes fascinated* (lines 3–4), *Art takes life as part of her rough material* (lines 5–6). This is known as personification, (A). Although Life and Art are in opposition to each other, there is no inherent confusion or contradiction, (B). The passage is not written in first-person narration ("I," "me," etc.), so eliminate (C). And there is no sense that circumstances are the opposite of how one might anticipate, so eliminate (D).

24. **A** Check the beginning of the paragraph. In line 14, *Dramatic Art* is mentioned. In line 15, *she enlisted Life.* So the *she* used throughout this paragraph is *Dramatic Art*, not *Life*, and certainly not *English drama* as a whole.

25. **C** First, eliminate the extreme answers: (A) and (D). *Informal*, (B), is not a good match, since the passage is written in a rather lofty style. Overall, the author laments the *takeover* of Art by Life. This is especially obvious in the last line of the passage. Thus, he is *rueful*, (C). *Expository* simply means that the author is *exposing* the supposed problem with English drama.

WRITING DRILL 1 EXPLANATIONS

1. **B** Choice (B) best captures the writer's central argument: that the penny should remain in circulation due to the negative effects removing it would have (on low-income individuals and philanthropies). Choices (A) and (C) are facts related to the penny, but don't state arguments. Choice (D) reflects a concession or counterargument.

2. **D** Choice (A) offers no transition into the following idea, and (B) makes an unsubstantiated claim as to how attitudes toward the penny are shifting. Choice (C) generally addresses the debate about abolishing the penny, but (D) specifically introduces the writer's argument. Choice (D) is the best answer.

3. **C** Choices (A) and (B) can be eliminated because they are overly general. Choice (D) can be eliminated because *individuals who are already struggling* may describe low-income individuals, but it ignores the philanthropies discussed in paragraph 3. Choice (C) is best because it captures the entirety of the argument made in the essay.

4. **A**   Choice (D) can be immediately eliminated because it introduces an entirely new line of reasoning. Choice (B) can be eliminated because, though relevant, it doesn't develop the idea that low-income individuals will be most affected by the loss of the penny. Choice (A) is better than (C) because it includes a trustworthy source (the U.S. Federal Reserve) and a specific detail as to how much ($600 million) of a cost burden low-income individuals will face.

5. **C**   Choice (D) can be eliminated because the sentence provides additional examples supporting the primary claim in the paragraph, that philanthropies rely on pennies. Choice (A) can be eliminated because the claim should precede the example. Choice (B) can be eliminated because sentence 8 is a more detailed, specific example. The sentence in the question includes the word *also* and provides additional examples of the ideas presented in sentence 8 and is best placed directly after it. Therefore, (C) is the best answer.

6. **D**   *On the other hand* prepares the reader for information contrasting what has previously been stated. Choice (A) omits a transition entirely, and (B) prepares the reader for information that is aligned with previously stated ideas. Choice (C) prepares the reader for a conclusion. Choice (D) is the best answer.

7. **B**   This sentence introduces an argument contradictory to the writer's thesis: that pennies are so disposable they aren't worth producing. As a result, it is best described as a concession, an acknowledgment of the opposing view.

8. **D**   Choice (A) can be eliminated because it supports the opposing view, that the penny should be eliminated. Choice (B) can be eliminated because it is a general observation, not a concrete piece of evidence. Choice (D) is better than (C) because it includes more specific information and reasoning.

WRITING DRILL 2 EXPLANATIONS

9. **D**   Choices (A) and (B) can be eliminated because, though they capture the audience's interest, they don't effectively introduce the idea as to whether homework should be banned. Choice (C) can be eliminated because it presents the opposing view, that homework is beneficial, while this essay argues that homework should be banned. Choice (D) both presents an interesting fact, that homework has been both banned and deemed necessary in recent history, and introduces the topic, that the essay will be considering a ban on homework. The answer is (D).

10. **B**   Choice (A) can be eliminated because it restates information in sentence 2 instead of capturing the writer's reasoning. Choices (C) and (D) can be eliminated because they inadequately and incorrectly represent the writer's reasoning. Choice (B) best states the arguments and reasoning that the writer develops in the second and third paragraphs, that homework strains students' mental and physical health and that homework creates inequality in the education system. The answer is (B).

11. **A** Paragraph 2 describes the mental and physical health consequences brought on by too much home-work. Choice (B) describes the developmental needs of students, which is slightly off topic and doesn't connect to the quantity of homework students receive. Choice (C) makes a claim that goes unsubstantiated, that more homework is being assigned now than in the past. Choice (D) is overly vague and doesn't introduce the idea that this suffering is mental and physical. The correct answer is (A).

12. **D** Sentences 9 and 10 present separate pieces of evidence that support the paragraph's claim, that home-work creates inequality for students of different income levels. Choice (A) can be eliminated because sentence 10 isn't a personal opinion. Choice (B) can be eliminated because it prepares the reader for information that contrasts with information presented in sentence 9, not information that develops the same line of reasoning. Choice (C) can be eliminated because it suggests a cause-effect relationship between the two sentences. Therefore, the answer is (D).

13. **C** Choice (A) can be eliminated because it provides evidence as to the positive benefits of homework. Choice (B) describes student success but isn't directly related to mental health. Similarly, *feeling consistently stressed* is more indicative of mental health than the fact that students cheat, so (C) is better than (D). Therefore, the correct answer is (C).

14. **C** Choice (D) can be eliminated because it forms the conclusion of the passage, and additional counter-evidence is an ineffective means of concluding the passage. Similarly, (A) can be eliminated because this specific detail doesn't introduce any ideas in the passage. Choice (B) can be eliminated because the idea presented in the passage is disconnected from the idea presented in sentence 11. The sentence presented in the question provides further explanation as to how time-management and goal-setting skills impact student achievement, so the answer is (C).

WRITING DRILL 3 EXPLANATIONS

15. **A** Choice (B) can be eliminated because the reference to the public news cycle is off-topic from the rest of the essay. Choices (C) and (D) are engaging in that they utilize a variety of syntactical structures, but (C) doesn't describe the topic of the essay specifically: voting age. While (D) does, it also addresses other factors that are out of the essay's scope. Choice (A) includes a surprising piece of information, that Americans vote at lower rates than others in developed nations, as well as a specific detail pertaining to the topic of the essay, that citizens over the age of 18 are those who are expected to vote. The answer is (A).

16. **B** Choice (D) can be eliminated because citizenship rights are outside the scope of the essay. Choice (B) is better than (A) and (C) because it captures the thesis of the essay with accuracy and the greatest specificity. The thesis isn't just that voting rights should be expanded or that the voting age reconsidered. Rather, the thesis is the definitive statement that the voting age should be lowered to 16. The answer is (B).

17. **C** Sentence 5 provides a detailed, factual example of the idea presented in sentence 4. Choices (B) and (D) can be eliminated because they prepare the reader for different or contrasting information. While (A) is feasible, (C) is better because it more specifically addresses the relationship between sentences 4 and 5; they are not just similar: sentence 5 is a factual example of sentence 4. The answer is (C).

18. **D** The key to this question is identifying the main argument of the paragraph: that lowering the voting age can have a positive impact on democracy in America. Choices (A), (B) and (C) all add concrete evidence to the paragraph and describe how that evidence will positively impact participation in democracy. Choice (D) describes a fact about 16-year-olds, but it doesn't describe a positive connection between cognitive abilities and democracy or American politics. The answer is (D).

19. **D** Choices (B) and (C) can be eliminated because they don't explain the relationship between lowering the voting age and increasing voter participation: they present new arguments as to why 16-year-olds should be allowed to vote. Though (A) describes an increase in voter turnout, it doesn't describe *how* lowering the voting age will increase participation. Choice (D) does this by describing the "trickle up" effect. The answer is (D).

20. **D** The concession in sentence 10 expresses the idea that changing the voter age will be difficult. Eliminate any choice that doesn't refute this. Choice (C) can be eliminated because it provides reasoning to support lowering the voting age, not specific evidence that refutes the concession. Though both (A) and (B) discuss passing an amendment to lower the voting age, neither includes a factor that describes how easy passing the amendment was. Choice (D) accomplishes the goal by adding that it "required only three months" to pass and was "the most efficient ratification of any amendment in U.S. history." The answer is (D).

Chapter 4
How to Approach
the Essays:
Basic Principles

ESSAY SECTION TASKS

Yes, that's right—tasks. You'll need to write three different essays: synthesis, rhetorical analysis, and argument.

In the **synthesis essay**, you'll be given a scenario and tasked with writing a response using at least three of six or seven short accompanying sources for support. You'll need to cite the sources you use (in a simple format such as "Source A"), and incorporate them into your own position (instead of simply quoting them). At least one of the sources will be a visual (such as a picture, drawing, or graph) rather than text.

The **rhetorical analysis essay** asks you to analyze the techniques (such as choice of language or organization of evidence) an author uses, and discuss how those techniques contribute to the author's purpose. The passage you'll be asked to analyze is typically about one page long.

The **argument essay** presents a claim or assertion in the prompt and then asks you to argue a position based on your own knowledge, experience, or reading. You can choose to agree with the claim, disagree with it, or give it qualified support (for example, arguing that the claim is true only in certain circumstances).

In Chapters 5–7, you'll learn more about the approach and expectations for each type of essay.

For all three essays, you will be writing cold on a prompt or passage you read just two minutes ago for the first time. You have to come up with good ideas and get them written down efficiently—on the very first try.

Writing a clear, effective, well-organized essay under rigid time constraints is a learned skill; writing three consecutive essays under such conditions requires special techniques and lots of practice. Fortunately, this book provides you with both of those.

Three Rules for Successful Essay Preparation

1. Do plenty of TIMED practice on all three essay types.

2. Hand-write your practice essays; don't use a computer.

3. Ask for feedback on your essays from a trusted source (such as an English teacher or Princeton Review tutor).

Time Crunch

You'll have 2 hours to write all three essays, which allows about 40 minutes for each. Before you even start working on the essays, though, you'll have 15 minutes to read all three prompts and the source documents for the synthesis essay. While we suggest you use all 15 minutes, if you finish reading the prompts and the documents early, you may start writing your response.

This 15-minute period is crucial for building a solid foundation in understanding the prompts and the source documents. You'll need to put your active reading skills in high gear to get the best possible head start from the reading time available.

Why *Three* Essays?

The AP English Language and Composition Exam is designed to predict your ability to perform college-level work on such assignments as research papers and on-demand essay questions on tests. The AP exam's three types of essays give you an opportunity to demonstrate the important skills required for those types of college assignments:

- using research sources to support your own position

- examining sources critically in order to assess credible or faulty support

- arguing your own position persuasively

The three essays simply separate—and highlight—these skills. In college work, you'll often be combining them.

HOW ARE THE ESSAYS SCORED?

The essays are scored separately on a scale of 0–6; then the three scores are combined. Each essay has equal weight in that combined score, which is then combined with the result of the multiple-choice section to yield a final AP score of 1–5.

Essays are graded analytically, based on:

- your ability to state a clear thesis

- your ability to present concrete evidence and link it to your thesis

- your skillful use of sophisticated language to develop your argument

Together, the essays count for 55 percent of your final score. However, they take up 69 percent of the exam time, so it's easy to lose perspective and feel as if the essay section is more crucial to your success than it actually is. Doing well on the multiple-choice section is almost as important, even though it's only an hour long.

When awarding essay points, the readers consider three specific elements: the thesis statement, evidence and commentary, as well as the overall sophistication of the essay. Each of these areas has the possibility of earning a specified number of points, with a maximum of six points possible:

- Thesis: 0–1 point

- Evidence and commentary: 0–4 points

- Sophistication: 0–1 point

The thesis statement can earn a maximum of one point if it both responds to the prompt and presents a defensible position. No points are awarded for thesis statements that merely paraphrase the prompt, summarize the issue, are off topic, or are absent.

Evidence and commentary weigh most heavily and can earn up to four points. Readers are looking for evidence that is specific and supports all claims in a line of coherent reasoning. Furthermore, they are looking for consistent commentary that explains *how* the evidence supports the essay's reasoning. Essays lose points when evidence is general or irrelevant. Further point loss occurs when the commentary merely summarizes the evidence or develops a faulty line of reasoning.

Like the thesis, sophistication can also earn an essay up to one point. This point is awarded if the essay presents a complex argument and articulates the implications or limitations of that argument. Readers are also looking for essays that use effective rhetorical techniques to convey that argument throughout the essay. Specifically, the readers award this point for essays that are written in a style that is both persuasive and vivid.

In Chapters 5–7, you'll learn some more details about how these parameters apply to each type of essay.

Who Does the Scoring?

The readers are college English professors and AP course teachers who come together in June for an intense week of scoring. Thousands of readers go through thousands of essays in a few short days. A different person will read each of your essays.

Before the scoring starts, though, readers are trained in assessing that particular year's group of essays. The College Board, the nonprofit organization that develops the exam, combs through the current crop of essays looking for work that represents a top-level 6 synthesis essay, a mediocre 3 rhetorical analysis essay, and so on, from that year's group. These sample essays are used to train the readers so the scoring will be as standardized as possible, given that the readers are still human beings who make subjective decisions.

So what? Well, the readers are your audience—the people you're addressing in your essays—and this scoring process tells you a few important things about them.

- First, they're buried in student essays, most of them mundane and mind-numbingly similar, and are just hoping for that one brilliant piece of writing that breaks the monotony and is a pleasure to read.

- Second, the readers have been trained to score your essays in relation to the work of the other students who took the exam that year. They're not judging your work in relation to some ideal standard of what a "perfect" essay should be.

- Third, these are teachers who guide students through English composition for a living. They know that polished essays require time, draft after draft, revision after revision. They don't expect an essay written in 40 minutes to be polished or perfect—they couldn't produce a flawless essay themselves in 40 minutes.

The essay section is the only place in this exam where your personality—at least to a limited degree—will shine through to test graders. Use it as an opportunity to show off what an exceptional thinker and writer you are.

WHAT ARE THE KEYS TO EARNING POINTS?

Your goal is to rise above the vast middle bulge of essays. You're aiming to earn the most points possible. How do you get there? By familiarizing yourself with the types of essays you'll have to write and by following a few basic tips.

Understand the Prompt

Use your active reading skills to tear the prompt apart.

- What is the prompt *really* asking you to do? Understanding your task and maintaining a laser focus on it will keep you out of the swamp of inappropriate examples and unrelated arguments that populate the lower levels of the scoring scale.

- Does the prompt have broader implications? For example, if a quote in the argument essay prompt states that a government has a duty to protect its citizens, could carrying out that duty lead to undesirable limits on people's freedom? And protect citizens from what? Who says that's a government's duty? The key here is to demonstrate some depth of thought instead of simply taking the prompt at face value. Where does it lead you?

- Does the prompt contain any terms that you should define in order to keep your discussion on target? Broad, "fuzzy" concepts such as "justice" or "education" are prime examples. They mean different things to different people. Giving a precise explanation of how you understand the term *as it's used in the prompt* and how you intend to discuss it will help you avoid producing a vague, rambling essay.

Tip:

Underline the action verbs in the prompt to keep you focused. Common verbs are: "explain," "select and use evidence," "argue your position," and "demonstrate an understanding of the rhetorical situation."

Take a Position

No fence-sitting, no ambiguity, no neutral descriptive essays. The highest scoring essays take a definite position on the prompt topic and argue it convincingly. They use strong, relevant, and specific evidence to support the position and leave no doubt about where the essay writer stands.

Even in the rhetorical analysis essay you're expected to take a position: "This is the author's purpose, these are the three (or four, or five) most important techniques the author uses to achieve that purpose, and (very important) this is *how* each technique makes the purpose more effective." Another student might see a different purpose or highlight other techniques in the passage, but then that student would be taking a different position.

Manage Your Time

No one is going to tell you that your first 40 minutes are up and it's time to move on to the next essay. That's up to you. Since each essay has equal weight in the combined score, you should devote about the same amount of time to each one. A slightly better score on one essay will not make up for a bad score on another. Aim for the following breakdown within each 40-minute period:

- 3–5 minutes to think through the prompt and plan your essay
- 30–35 minutes to write
- 1–2 minutes to proofread

BC UR 2 GOOD 4 THIS

Even though you're under tremendous time pressure, don't use shorthand symbols such as "&" or "w/" or "tho." Get into the habit of using a relatively high level of discourse on AP exam essays. Writing in the style of a casual email or text message won't impress the reader who is scoring your essay.

The more you practice writing each type of essay within 40 minutes, the more you'll gain a sense of how that block of time "feels" and the better you'll get at making occasional time checks to stay on track instead of engaging in distracting clock-watching that might only increase your anxiety.

Your school has likely given you sample essay prompts for practice. You can also find example prompts from several previous years on the AP website at https://apcentral.collegeboard.org/courses/ap-english-language-and-composition/exam.

Plan Your Response

Just getting into the car and starting to drive could land you anywhere, at a great waste of time and fuel. It's the same with just starting to write—you could easily spend 20 minutes and then realize you're seriously off track.

To make the best use of your 30–35 minutes of writing time, you first need to spend a few minutes planning where you want to end up and how you'll get there.

- Exactly what do you want to conclude about the topic of the synthesis prompt? Which three sources best support the points you want to make? In which order should you incorporate them into your discussion? Does one of the sources present a significant opposing argument that you should mention and then refute?

- In the rhetorical analysis passage, what is the writer's purpose? What techniques make that purpose clear and effective to you? In which order should you explain them?

- What position do you want to take about the topic presented for the argument essay? What evidence from your own experiences or reading could you use to support your position? How can you make your argument persuasive?

Organize Your Points

You're likely familiar with the five-paragraph essay model. While it's not the only method of organizing an essay, there's nothing wrong with using it on this exam if it's already a comfortable model for you. It goes like this:

Paragraph 1:

- An introductory sentence or two that captures the reader and announces, "This is going to be a great essay within your pile of boring, mediocre essays."

- The thesis that you intend to argue in your essay. A good thesis is debatable (that is, someone could possibly have a different opinion) and narrow enough to be covered adequately in a short essay.

- A brief list of the three pieces of evidence you'll use in the essay to prove your thesis

- A transition to the body of your essay

Paragraphs 2–4:

- One paragraph for each piece of evidence you listed in the first paragraph, in the same order as you listed them. Each piece of evidence should be as specific as possible: direct quotations from evidence or source texts, and/or detailed descriptions of personal or historical anecdotes. All evidence should be accompanied by commentary that explicitly describes how and why the evidence supports the paragraph's claim and the essay's thesis. One of these paragraphs might describe a conflicting view which you then shoot down, or which supports an "only in certain circumstances" position in your thesis.

Paragraph 5:

- A conclusion that doesn't simply restate your thesis. You've developed your argument throughout the body of your essay, so it's now meatier and more convincing. The conclusion should remind the reader of your now-stronger position.

Of course, there's no rule that says you have to stop at three pieces of evidence; you might have four. Just don't take on more complexity and length than you can handle well in 40 minutes. And if you're familiar with another method of organizing an essay and feel more comfortable with it, then use it, as long as it provides a clear organizational framework for your points.

Get Off to a Strong Start

A great first impression goes a long way. Remember your audience of bored readers mired in stacks of mediocre essays? If you can wow them right off the top, you'll create an expectation that the rest of your essay belongs in the "effective" band too. That initial glow of "finally—*finally*—a good essay!" can diminish the impact of later lapses in greatness.

Suppose the prompt for a rhetorical analysis essay quotes from a speech by Mayor Nellie Smith attributing her election victory to the many volunteers who worked on her campaign. You could clearly announce, "This is going to be a mediocre essay" by starting out with a sentence like, "This essay will describe how Mayor Nellie Smith uses rhetorical strategies to communicate the main point of her speech." Yawn. And do you have any clue what her main point is or what rhetorical strategies she uses? Even if you eventually do get to an insightful point later in the essay, chances are your opening has already caused the reader to tune out and miss it.

On the other hand, you could grab the reader's attention with an opening like, "Dedicated volunteers are the bricks and mortar of successful political campaigns. That's the overriding message of Mayor Nellie Smith's speech thanking them for their passionate support and acknowledging the key role they played. Through the skillful use of parallelism, repetition, and analogy, she makes her listeners feel that the victory is really theirs, likely winning their support after she takes office too."

That stronger start doesn't take a lot of extra effort or time, but it shows the reader that you understand the mayor's purpose and rhetorical strategies, and can express your ideas with style and sophistication. You've just raised the reader's impression of your abilities, even if your essay tapers off to a more routine effort later on.

Express Your Ideas Clearly, Specifically, Concisely, Correctly, Smoothly, Persuasively, and with Flair

Oh yes, you *can* do that.

Be clear. You should know exactly what you want to say as a result of your initial planning and organizing. Imagine yourself on a clear path instead of stumbling around in the underbrush. If you find you're getting tangled up in long sentences or overlapping ideas, pause for a minute and think of *telling* someone right beside you what you mean to say. This strategy usually helps clarify your thoughts and language in your own mind. Now write down what you just "said."

Be specific. Making a vague statement such as, "The demand for subsidized housing increased a lot during the past few years (Source A)" isn't good enough if Source A actually referred to a study that proved demand grew by 65 percent between 2010 and 2020. Being as specific and concrete as possible will add credibility and impact to your words. Your argument will be clearer and more persuasive.

Be concise. That doesn't mean leaving out details that are essential to your argument. It means leaving out pointless repetition and padding. Say it once, precisely and with punch, and then move on.

Say it correctly. Use proper grammar. Essays with so many errors that the reader can't follow the argument are consigned to the bottom of the scoring scale.

Create correct paragraphs too. Have you ever opened a book and seen nothing but very long paragraphs? Your next thought is probably, "Do I *really* have to read all of this?" That's exactly what readers think when they see an essay without paragraphs.

So create proper paragraphs—one main idea per paragraph, beginning with a topic sentence and ending with a smooth transition to the next paragraph—and make them obvious by leaving a space between or indenting them.

> Create a great first impression before the person scoring your essay even reads a word.
>
> - Write legibly.
> - Make sure readers can see the paragraphs at first glance.
> - Don't strike out too many things.
> - Make sure your work looks neat, organized, and clear.

Say it smoothly. Lead the reader through your argument with seamless transitions between your points and paragraphs. Transition words and phrases such as "on the other hand," "in addition," "therefore," and "nevertheless" will do the job.

Say it persuasively. These essays are all evidence-based writing, so you need strong evidence that supports each of your main points. Connect each piece of evidence clearly to the point it supports, and explain exactly how or why the evidence is relevant. Unrelated evidence and vague, weak explanations won't persuade anyone.

> The reader expects you to write like someone who is suffering through a tedious, nerve-wracking exercise. If you write like someone who enjoys writing, the reader will enjoy reading your essay and reward you.

Say it with flair. Is there a punchier, more descriptive word you could use? Perhaps "shack" or "cabin" or "mansion" instead of "house." Can you make the phrasing of a sentence slicker? For example, instead of "The candidate's appearance was neat, and the boss gave him the job right away," let yourself get carried away and say, "The candidate's Armani suit and sleek silk tie captivated the boss, who slipped a contract across the table without comment or hesitation."

It doesn't take long to think of a more forceful word or a stronger way of saying something if you put your mind on that track, and even a few of these sprinkled throughout your essay can impress the reader with your ability to control language and use it to achieve your desired effect.

> Make it easy for the reader to give you a high score.
>
> - Understand the task in the prompt.
> - Think about where the prompt takes you.
> - Stake out a definite position.
> - Plan and organize your points before you start to write.
> - Be clear and specific.
> - Link each piece of evidence directly to your thesis.
> - Use correct grammar and paragraph construction.
> - Vary sentence length and structure.
> - Write legibly.

Proofread

You won't have time to revise, but leaving a couple of minutes to proofread allows you to fix minor errors you probably would not have made if you weren't writing in such a rush. And that, in turn, might just knock your essay up a notch on the scoring scale. You'll have to write your essay in dark blue or black pen—no pencils allowed on this section of the exam. However, you can strike out any errors you want the readers to ignore (they will) and then write in (neatly) your correction.

In Chapters 5–7, you'll get a closer look at the types of prompts on the exam, and find additional suggestions for responding to the three different types.

Summary

General Essay Information

o   There are three essays: synthesis, rhetorical analysis, and argument.

o   You have a total of 2 hours, 15 minutes—40 minutes for each essay plus 15 minutes to read the prompts and the sources for the synthesis essay.

o   The three essays count for 55 percent of your total score. Each essay is worth an equal amount.

Essay Scoring

o   Each essay is scored by a different reader on a scale from 0 to 6.

o   Essays are awarded up to one point for the thesis statement, four points for evidence and commentary, and one point for sophistication.

o   The reader wants good essays that are easy to score.

o   Essays that earn high scores show that the writer has thought deeply about the prompt, taken a clear position, supported that position with appropriate and specific examples, and argued that position persuasively with sophisticated control of the language.

o   Students who misunderstand the prompt, use inappropriate examples, and can't express their ideas clearly can expect low scores.

Presentation

o   Make your essay look neat, clear, and well organized with legible writing, obvious breaks between paragraphs, and few strike-outs, if any.

Expression

o Capture the reader and create a great first impression with your opening paragraph.

o Vary your choice of words and sentence structure. A little extra effort will pay great dividends.

o Use correct grammar and paragraph construction.

Content

o Plan and organize your points before you start writing.

o Address the prompt. If you write a great essay that doesn't address the prompt, you will receive a low score.

o Develop your argument based on strong, relevant, and specific evidence. Connect each piece of evidence directly to the point it supports.

Chapter 5
How to Approach
the Synthesis Essay

SYNTHESIZE WHAT?

By "synthesis," the AP exam writers mean that you, the writer of the essay, bring together evidence from a variety of sources to develop a unique argument in response to the topic at hand.

High-scoring synthesis essays draw clear connections between at least three sources and a defensible thesis statement. The evidence is specific and appropriate; the explanations are thorough and convincing.

Also at the higher score levels, the essay writer cites the specific source being used (with a simple reference such as "Source A"; you're not expected to remember formal citation formats for this exam). Writers who earn lower scores merely summarize a jumbled collection of points they've read in various sources, without citing a specific source and linking it to a particular point in their argument.

Your performance on the synthesis essay will help the readers (and yourself) predict how well you'll be able to handle college research assignments. In particular, your essay will show whether you can:

- judge the best sources to back up your position

- incorporate other writers' claims or explanations into your *own* argument

- draw on sources in the order that develops your argument in the most logical, persuasive way

Steps to Choosing Sources

1. Identify the central question in the prompt your thesis must address.

2. Use active reading—what is the main point of each source?

3. Decide which position you want to take.

4. Select three sources that provide the best support for your position.

Anatomy of the Prompt

The synthesis prompt is structured in the same way every year. There are three paragraphs of instructions, followed by seven sources for you to pull evidence from to use in your essay.

Getting familiar with the structure of the prompt can help you save time on the day of the exam. Let's take a look at the instructions:

- **First paragraph:** The first paragraph provides you with an overview of the topic the central question will deal with. In recent years, topics have included the legal justification for eminent domain, the future of public libraries in the Internet Age, whether or not monolingualism puts English speakers at a disadvantage, and the role of honor codes in high schools.

- **Second paragraph:** The second paragraph begins with standard instructions asking you to read the sources provided and synthesize the material from at least three of the sources into a coherent, well-written essay. Then comes the most important part of the prompt: the central question your thesis must address.

- **Third paragraph:** The third paragraph is also standardized. It reminds you to focus your essay on your argument and tells you how to cite sources.

- **Sources:** The sources can be any variety of things: news articles, political cartoons, graphs, instructional slides, an individual's personal opinion, calendars, or expert reports. It's your job to show that you can evaluate the quality of information you're presented with and use it to build an argument.

How can you use the prompt to help you save time? Underline the central question when you read it, keeping it in mind while you read through the sources. Using keywords from the central question in your thesis will make it clear that you are directly addressing it in your thesis. If you get stuck with writing your introduction, you can model it off the introduction in the first paragraph of the prompt.

The prompt will instruct you to use at least three sources, and in most cases that's a safe choice. Trying to use more than three might lead you into an unnecessarily complicated essay at best, and at worst, a pyramid of similar, superficially treated points piled up on top of one another. Using fewer than three will definitely lose points for evidence and commentary.

Three sources are enough to show progress in your argument (for example, a more general or older source of support followed by increasingly specific or more recent claims, each one building upon the previous one). If you choose to argue a qualified position, three sources will give you, for instance, two authors who argue against something and one who is in favor of it in particular circumstances, supporting your qualified rejection of the claim.

Having a Conversation with Your Sources

Since your aim is synthesis, you need to develop a thesis that addresses the central question and supports it by weaving together evidence from at least three of the provided sources. Importantly, you need to provide your own explanation as to how the evidence you present supports your thesis. The exam writers offer a helpful image of how to do that. They call it having a conversation with your sources.

Imagine the creators of your chosen sources are sitting together in a living room discussing the topic of the prompt. Now you walk in and join the conversation. You wouldn't simply record each author's (or artist's) comments. That's the equivalent of just copying and pasting chunks from each source into your essay and stringing them together.

You would respond to each person's comments, build on them, and use them to enrich your own views about the topic. You would add something to the discussion your three authors are having, and they would add something to your own understanding of the topic. Then, if you had a conversation with each author individually, you would try to understand that author's position and add your own ideas to the discussion. That's what the test writers mean. They call the result a "source-informed" argument.

A very common pitfall for essays to make is to fail to provide a thorough explanation. These essays present a thesis and cite relevant sources, but don't explain how the two connect. In other words, the writer never enters the conversation.

Here are some sentence frames you can use to explain your evidence, making sure you have a voice in the conversation:

- This suggests that…

- This indicates…

- This means…

- It is worth emphasizing that…because…

- This is important because…

- While most agree that…some may argue that…

- While this source acknowledges…they ignore…

Direct Quote vs. Paraphrase

When you're drawing a source into your argument, you have a choice of paraphrasing (summarizing in your own words) what the author says, or quoting some of their words directly (within quotation marks, of course).

In many cases, paraphrasing makes it easier to incorporate someone else's ideas smoothly into your own. Several quotes, too, could make your essay appear to be more of a copy-and-paste exercise than a synthesis. However, if an author uses a particularly striking phrase or unusual wording that would be difficult to paraphrase accurately, then an occasional direct quote could make your essay more vivid.

SAMPLE ESSAY—HERE'S HOW IT'S DONE

Here's an example of a synthesis essay prompt. As you go through it, use your active reading skills to make sure you understand exactly what it's asking you to do.

The Directions

Question 1

Suggested reading and writing time—55 minutes.

It is suggested that you spend 15 minutes reading the question, analyzing and evaluating the sources, and 40 minutes writing your response.

Note: You may begin writing your response before the reading period is over.

(This question counts for one-third of the total essay section score.)

Artificial intelligence (AI) is hyped as the magic bullet for every challenge—from easing traffic congestion to providing medical care in remote locations, from protecting endangered species to rescuing hostages in dangerous settings. The common foundation is a conviction that AI operations will be faster, more effective, more accurate, and sometimes cheaper than human operations, and—critically—will avoid human errors. But with their functional superiority and machine learning capabilities, will AI implementations also be able to evolve beyond human control? And is that necessarily a bad thing?

Carefully read the following seven sources, including the introductory information for each source. Then synthesize information from at least three of the sources and incorporate it into a coherent, well-written essay that addresses this question: Is artificial intelligence to be feared because of its potential independence from human control, or is it to be embraced due to its superior ability to deliver benefits that enhance our lives?

Use the sources to develop and explain your argument. Avoid merely summarizing the sources. Indicate clearly which sources you are drawing from, whether through direct quotation, paraphrase, or summary. You may cite the sources as Source A, Source B, and so forth, or by using the descriptions in parentheses.

Source A (Future)

Source B (Letter)

Source C (Frankenstein)

Source D (slides)

Source E (Third Offset)

Source F (Robots)

Source G (graph)

Check Your Understanding

What is the central question in this prompt?

It's Time to Read

There's quite a lot of reading as you go through the sources for a synthesis essay question. In order to use your 15 minutes of reading time effectively, before you start you should already be clear on what the prompt is asking you to do and have some idea which position you want to take on the question you need to address. Do you want to argue that we should fear artificial intelligence (AI)? Welcome it? Or do you want to give a qualified answer? For example, "we should fear it unless…" or "we should welcome it except when…"

To show the depth of thought that pulls an essay up into the "effective" score band, you also need to consider implications that extend beyond the question in the prompt. In other words, use your active reading skills on the prompt. For instance, are fearing and embracing AI our only choices? Can we modify its current course of development? Stop it entirely? If AI is beyond our control, can we make sure we don't need to fear it?

Now you're ready to read through the sources with a fairly clear idea of what you're looking for. You want three sources that will enrich the position you've chosen, and will help you develop your own argument in a logical way. If two sources say essentially the same thing, you probably don't need both—which one is stronger? Which sources deal with the "beyond the prompt" questions you asked during your active reading? If you've chosen to take a qualified position, which source presents an opposing viewpoint that will support your "only in these circumstances" argument?

Linear Graffiti

Underlining, circling, and making brief notes in the margins of the sources are all good practices, but don't get too carried away. The purpose of marking the passage is to make information easy to retrieve. A good rule of thumb is to underline no more than five words at a time. Anything longer should be marked with simple brackets.

To help you locate supporting points later on while you're writing, underline a few key words and put a stroke through sources you don't want to use.

Then plan your essay: jot down a quick outline of the points you want to make, the order in which you'll explain them as you develop your argument, and the source you'll use (and cite) to support each of your points. A few minutes of planning will keep you on track while you're writing.

Source A

"Preparing for the Future of Artificial Intelligence,"
The National Science and Technology Council.
Office of Science and Technology Policy, October
2016. Web. 21 January 2018.

The following is an excerpt from The Office of Science and Technology Policy's 2016 federal government report on the future of artificial intelligence in the U.S.

One area of great optimism about AI and machine learning is their potential to improve people's lives by helping to solve some of the world's greatest challenges and inefficiencies.... Public- and private-sector investments in basic and applied R&D on AI have already begun reaping major benefits for the public in fields as diverse as health care, transportation, the environment, criminal justice, and economic inclusion.

At Walter Reed Medical Center, the Department of Veteran Affairs is using AI to better predict medical complications and improve treatment of severe combat wounds, leading to better patient outcomes, faster healing, and lower costs.... Given the current transition to electronic health records, predictive analysis of health data may play a key role across many health domains like precision medicine and cancer research.

In transportation, AI-enabled smarter traffic management applications are reducing wait times, energy use, and emissions by as much as 25 percent in some places....

Some researchers are leveraging AI to improve animal migration tracking by using AI image classification software to analyze tourist photos from public social media sites. The software can identify individual animals in the photos and build a database of their migration using the data and location stamps on the photos.... Other speakers described uses of AI to optimize the patrol strategy of anti-poaching agents, and to design habitat preservation strategies to maximize the genetic diversity of endangered populations.

Autonomous sailboats and watercraft are already patrolling the oceans carrying sophisticated sensor instruments, collecting data on changes in Arctic ice and sensitive ocean ecosystems in operations that would be too expensive or dangerous for crewed vessels....

The Administration is exploring how AI can responsibly benefit current initiatives such as Data Driven Justice and the Police Data Initiative that seek to provide law enforcement and the public with data that can better inform decision-making in the criminal justice system, while also taking care to minimize the possibility that AI might introduce bias or inaccuracies due to deficiencies in the available data.

Several U.S. academic institutions have launched initiatives to use AI to tackle economic and social challenges. For example, the University of Chicago created an academic program that uses data science and AI to address public challenges such as unemployment and school dropouts. The University of Southern California launched the Center for Artificial Intelligence in Society, an institute dedicated to studying how computational game theory, machine learning, automated planning and multi-agent reasoning techniques can help to solve socially relevant problems like homelessness. Meanwhile, researchers at Stanford University are using machine learning in efforts to address global poverty by using AI to analyze satellite images of likely poverty zones to identify where help is needed most.

Source B

"An Open Letter: Research Priorities for Robust and
Beneficial Artificial Intelligence." *Future of Life
Institute.* January 2015. Web. 21 January 2018.

*The following open letter is an initiative of the Future of Life Institute in collaboration
with the AI research community.*

Artificial intelligence (AI) research has explored a variety of problems and approaches since
its inception, but for the last 20 years or so has been focused on the problems surrounding
the construction of intelligent agents—systems that perceive and act in some environment.
In this context, "intelligence" is related to statistical and economic notions of rationality—
colloquially, the ability to make good decisions, plans, or inferences. The adoption of prob-
abilistic and decision-theoretic representations and statistical learning methods has led to
a large degree of integration and cross-fertilization among AI, machine learning, statistics, control theory, neuroscience, and other fields. The establishment of shared theoret-
ical frameworks, combined with the availability of data and processing power, has yielded
remarkable successes in various component tasks such as speech recognition, image classification, autonomous vehicles, machine translation, legged locomotion, and question-
answering systems.

As capabilities in these areas and others cross the threshold from laboratory research to
economically valuable technologies, a virtuous cycle takes hold whereby even small
improvements in performance are worth large sums of money, prompting greater investments in research. There is now a broad consensus that AI research is progressing steadily,
and that its impact on society is likely to increase. The potential benefits are huge, since
everything that civilization has to offer is a product of human intelligence; we cannot predict
what we might achieve when this intelligence is magnified by the tools AI may provide, but
the eradication of disease and poverty are not unfathomable. Because of the great potential
of AI, it is important to research how to reap its benefits while avoiding potential pitfalls.

The progress in AI research makes it timely to focus research not only on making AI more
capable, but also on maximizing the societal benefit of AI. Such considerations motivated
the AAAI 2008–09 Presidential Panel on Long-Term AI Futures and other projects on AI
impacts, and constitute a significant expansion of the field of AI itself, which up to now
has focused largely on techniques that are neutral with respect to purpose. We recommend
expanded research aimed at ensuring that increasingly capable AI systems are robust and
beneficial: our AI systems must do what we want them to do. This research is by necessity
interdisciplinary, because it involves both society and AI. It ranges from economics, law
and philosophy to computer security, formal methods and, of course, various branches of
AI itself.

In summary, we believe that research on how to make AI systems robust and beneficial
is both important and timely, and that there are concrete research directions that can be
pursued today.

> **Source C**
>
> Shelley, Mary. *Frankenstein, or, The Modern Prometheus.* 1818.

The following is an excerpt from Mary Shelley's 1818 novel.

I trembled and my heart failed within me, when, on looking up, I saw by the light of the moon the dæmon at the casement. A ghastly grin wrinkled his lips as he gazed on me, where I sat fulfilling the task which he had allotted to me. Yes, he had followed me in my travels; …and he now came to mark my progress and claim the fulfilment of my promise.

As I looked on him, his countenance expressed the utmost extent of malice and treachery. I thought with a sensation of madness on my promise of creating another like to him, and trembling with passion, tore to pieces the thing on which I was engaged. The wretch saw me destroy the creature on whose future existence he depended for happiness, and with a howl of devilish despair and revenge, withdrew.…

Several hours passed, and I remained near my window gazing on the sea;…I felt the silence, although I was hardly conscious of its extreme profundity, until my ear was suddenly arrested by the paddling of oars near the shore, and a person landed close to my house.…

Presently I heard the sound of footsteps along the passage; the door opened, and the wretch whom I dreaded appeared. Shutting the door, he approached me and said in a smothered voice,

"You have destroyed the work which you began; what is it that you intend? Do you dare to break your promise? I have endured toil and misery; I left Switzerland with you;…I have endured incalculable fatigue, and cold, and hunger; do you dare destroy my hopes?"

"Begone! I do break my promise; never will I create another like yourself, equal in deformity and wickedness."

"Slave, I before reasoned with you, but you have proved yourself unworthy of my condescension. Remember that I have power; you believe yourself miserable, but I can make you so wretched that the light of day will be hateful to you. You are my creator, but I am your master; obey!"

"The hour of my irresolution is past, and the period of your power is arrived. Your threats cannot move me to do an act of wickedness; but they confirm me in a determination of not creating you a companion in vice.…"

The monster saw my determination in my face and gnashed his teeth in the impotence of anger. "Shall each man," cried he, "find a wife for his bosom, and each beast have his mate, and I be alone?…Beware, for I am fearless and therefore powerful. I will watch with the wiliness of a snake, that I may sting with its venom. Man, you shall repent of the injuries you inflict."

Source D

"High Profile NITRD Technical Activities." *Federal R&D Agency Workshop.* The Networking and Information Technology Research and Development (NITRD) Program, 29 September 2016. Web. 21 January 2018.

The following slides were used in a workshop presentation about the Networking and Information Technology Research and Development Program's (NITRD's) High Profile Technical Activities.

This is an excerpt from a publication by the U.S. Army Strategic Studies Institute. Note: "Third Offset" refers to "leap-ahead technologies and capabilities" that could give an advantage over an otherwise-equal opponent.

…There is a natural symbiosis between military and civilian innovation that, in the end, is driven by a need to solve problems and gain advantage. The challenges and realities of big data, complex networks and systems, uncertain environments, ubiquitous technology, and intense peer competition are drivers in both the commercial and military spaces and steer each toward a common set of solutions. The separation between self-driving automobiles and autonomous military air and ground systems is thin—and will grow thinner as deep and machine learning increasingly blur the separation between civilian or military applications. Once advanced AI is achieved, it will quickly spiral into almost every area of the commercial, governmental, and military domains.

The allure of science fiction-like capabilities will be a strong incentive for states and nonstates to pursue Third Offset technologies. These leap-ahead capabilities could be so game changing that the difference between finishing first and finishing next could mean years of decisive advantage in every meaningful area of warfare.

…The United States is rightfully concerned about the implications of many of the Third Offset technologies—but current policies and priorities are not reflective of the rapidly evolving technologies or the operational environment. As a result, the United States risks falling dangerously behind potential adversaries who are investing heavily in advanced technologies—and are doing so without self-imposed constraints which limit capabilities and fail to allow full exploitation of these technologies.

The DoD[1] Directive 3000.09, *Autonomy in Weapons Systems*, establishes requirements and parameters for development and use of autonomous weapons systems (AWS). In short, Directive 3000.09 seeks to minimize the risk of unintended lethal engagements by requiring positive human interface for all semi-autonomous and AWS, and prohibiting autonomous lethal force against human targets. While this caution is understandable, the policy is out of step with the evolving battlefield.

Placing a "human in the loop" requirement on the development and employment of future weapons systems may inadvertently induce vulnerability into the system. Swarm technology has already exceeded the capability for any meaningful human control of individual agents and, as the technologies advance, swarms of tens or hundreds of thousands of individual agents will make human control—or even human understanding—of the actions and behaviors of the swarms impossible. In the future vague and uncertain environment, the decision to engage or not engage—to kill or not kill—may not be best made by a human.

…The battlefield of the next 30 years will likely evolve far differently (and much faster) than over the past 30 years. The legacy "big five" combat systems, even with version improvements and upgrades, may well be rendered outmatched and ineffective by AI-enabled unmanned autonomous systems, cyber dominance, and swarms. Continued incremental upgrades to current systems may address current readiness challenges, but could leave the Army ill-prepared to contend on a far different battlefield in the future.

---

1. The Department of Defense

Source F

Yong, Ed. "A Swarm of a Thousand Cooperative Self Organising Robots," *Not Exactly Rocket Science: A Blog* by Ed Yong. Phenomena on National Geographic Magazine, 14 August 2014. Web. 21 January 2018.

The following is an excerpt from a blog post on the growing population of self-organizing "kilorobots."

In a lab at Harvard's Wyss Institute, the world's largest swarm of cooperative robots is building a star…out of themselves. There are 1024 of these inch-wide "Kilobots," and they can arrange themselves into different shapes, from a letter to a wrench. They are slow and comically jerky in their movements, but they are also autonomous. Once they're given a shape, they can recreate it without any further instructions, simply by cooperating with their neighbours and organising themselves.

The Kilobots are the work of Mike Rubenstein, Alejandro Cornejo and Radhika Nagpal, who were inspired by natural swarms, where simple and limited units can cooperate to do great things. Thousands of fire ants can unite into living bridges, rafts and buildings.…

"This is a staggering work," adds Iain Couzin, who studies collective animal behaviour at Princeton University. "It offers a vision of the future where robot groups could form structures on demand as, for example, in search-and-rescue in dangerous environments, or even the formation of miniature swarms within the body to detect and treat disease.…"

The tyranny of cost-efficiency meant that the team had to lose any sensors that might tell the robots their bearings or positions. They can't tell where they are, or if they're going straight.…

Fortunately, they have each other. A stuck Kilobot can't tell if it's stuck on its own, but it can communicate with its neighbors. If it thinks it's moving but the distances from its neighbors change, it can deduce that something is wrong.…

Every Kilobot runs on the same program. The team only has to give them a shape and nominate four of them as seeds. Once that's done, the rest slowly pour into the right pattern, in an endearingly life-like way. It takes them around 12 hours, but they do it all without any human intervention. And although the final shapes are always a little warped, that's life-like too. Fire ants don't have a Platonic ideal of what a bridge or raft should look like; they just work with their neighbours to get the job done.…

The next step will be to build robots that actually self-assemble by attaching to each other, says Marco Dorigo from the Free University of Brussels.…

Eventually, he also wants to get to a position where the robots can sense their environment and react accordingly, rather than just slide into some pre-determined shape. Like fire ants, when they get to a body of water, they wouldn't have to be fed the image of a bridge; they would just self-assemble into one. "That's a whole other level of intelligence, and it's not really understood how to do that in robotics," says Rubenstein. "But nature does it well."

Source G

"America's Wars Fact Sheet" and "American War
and Military Operations Casualties: Lists and
Statistics." *U.S. Department of Veterans Affairs
and Congressional Research Service Report for
Congress.* 13 July 2005 and May 2017. Web.
21 January 2018.

*The following graph comparing battlefield fatalities in various historical conflicts is
derived from reports by the U.S. Department of Veterans Affairs and the Naval History
and Heritage Command. The timeline ends with the 1990–1991 Persian Gulf War.
The graph shows battlefield fatalities as a percentage of the number serving in each
conflict, so it offers an "apples-to-apples" comparison, even though the conflicts
differed in size.*

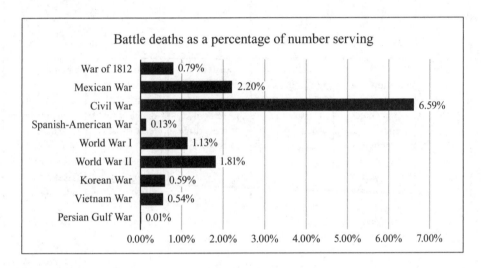

Understanding the Rubric

Luckily for us, we have the rubric that essay graders will be using to judge your essay. By studying it, we can learn how to score the most points possible. Graders will be looking at three different aspects of your essay: the thesis statement (Row A), the evidence and explanation (Row B), and the level of sophistication (Row C). Row B is further divided into two more bullet points: one that considers the quantity of evidence, and one that considers the quality of the explanation.

Synthesis Essay Rubric					
Row A	**0 points:** • Has no defensible thesis • Has thesis that only restates prompt • Has thesis that summarizes the issue with no apparent or coherent claim • Has a thesis that does not respond to the prompt		**1 point:** • Responds to the prompt with a thesis that presents a defensible position		
Row B	**0 points:** • Simply restates thesis (if present), repeats provided information, or references fewer than two of the provided sources	**1 point:** • Provides evidence from at least two of the provided sources AND • Summarizes the evidence but does not explain how the evidence supports the student's argument	**2 points:** • Provides evidence from or references at least three of the provided sources AND • Explains how some of the evidence supports the student's argument, but no line of reasoning is established, or the line of reasoning is faulty	**3 points:** • Provides specific evidence from at least three of the provided sources to support all claims in a line of reasoning AND • Explains how some of the evidence supports a line of reasoning	**4 points:** • Provides specific evidence from at least three of the provided sources to support all claims in a line of reasoning AND • Consistently explains how the evidence supports a line of reasoning
Row C	**0 points:** • Does not meet the criteria for one point		**1 point:** • Demonstrates sophistication of thought and/or a complex understanding of rhetorical sophistication		

As you can see, the essay is scored out of six points total. One point for the thesis, four points for evidence and analysis, and one point for sophistication. Remember: your essay doesn't need to be perfect; it just needs to satisfy the standards on the rubric.

One common mistake is that writers present a complex thesis, but fail to provide enough evidence and explanation to support it. While these essays score the point in Row A, they lose multiple points in Row B. A better strategy is to present a simple thesis that you know you can thoroughly support with the sources in the prompt. This way, the essay earns maximum points in Row A and B, even if it doesn't earn the point in Row C. A five is still a passing score!

Tip:
When in doubt, opt for a thesis you feel confident supporting with evidence and explanation.

You Try It

Now you're ready to begin writing. Remember to plan your essay first and leave a couple of minutes at the end to proofread your work.

After you're finished writing your essay, take a look at the following page. This is a student essay that was written in the allotted 40 minutes. As you read it, evaluate how well it:

- addresses the prompt with a defensible thesis

- ties each source clearly to one of the writer's claims

- integrates the sources smoothly into the progression of the argument

- provides commentary as to how the evidence develops the writer's argument

- uses style and rhetoric to persuade the reader

It's Not Me
Your essay will seem more professional and credible if you use third-person narrative instead of first person ("I think…").

Student Essay: Average Score

The essay below is generally successful. The writing style is strong, and the essay clearly responds to the central question. However, although the writer uses specific evidence from more than three sources, the writer doesn't successfully explain that evidence to develop an argument. In fact, the essay is predominantly just a summary of the seven sources. The essay's organization is also a weakness. The writer waits until the final paragraph to clearly state the central argument. Take a look:

Some people see advances in artificial intelligence as leading to a frightening scenario where we can no longer control AI and therefore can't ensure that it doesn't harm us. Others imagine grand possibilities of AI making our lives easier, safer and less complex.

> Strong introduction to the topic, no indication of the author's positi A delayed thesis can be effective, the explanations in this essay ar strong enough to support it.

We are just now discovering the potential benefits of AI applications. Source A lists several benefits: better medical treatment, less traffic congestion and ways to address social problems. The same source suggests environmental benefits, too: protecting animal habitats and monitoring climate change in the Arctic. In general, Source A is optimistic about how AI can "improve people's lives" and "solve some of the world's greatest challenges and efficiencies."

Source B also mentions social benefits, such as autonomous vehicles and speech recognition. This source is even more ambitious than Source A, predicting that AI might be able to end poverty and disease entirely.

> This is the first analysis in this es explaining one source is "more am tious" than the other.

Many of these benefits depend on AI's ability to collect and analyze vast amounts of data that would be beyond human capability. Others allow us to learn about locations that would be too expensive or dangerous for human agents to enter.

Such characteristics suggest that AI will make us capable of doing more than we could do on our own. We must also consider the other side of the debate, though. By being able to do things we can't do, does AI also have the potential to master us, and will it always use superior capabilities to help us?

> The writer's ideas progress smooth with points building on previc points and smooth transitic between them. For the most pa the writer shows good control of language, expressing thoughts clea and concisely.

Source B, while optimistic about the benefits AI can deliver, does raise this question. AI systems are going to grow more and more capable as research progresses. Therefore, we must focus the different AI research projects on the same goal: "our AI systems must do what we want them to do." AI must enhance and remain a tool of human intelligence, even if its abilities are superior to ours.

Source E raises a frightening scenario of AI research that does not prioritize the social benefits the other two sources describe. AI weapons systems, it says, could become so complex that we wouldn't even be able to understand them, let alone control them. Weapons that don't require a human to make them work should deliver the benefit of reducing war casualties, Source G does

The use of outside knowledge here is a nice touch, but the explanation doesn't go any deeper than saying that AI is frightening.

Here is the essay's thesis: AI might not need to be feared, but it should be viewed with caution. It addresses the question directly so it earns the point on the rubric...

...but this ending makes the thesis confusing. The idea that all scientists working on AI must have the same goal is totally new. It's interesting, but isn't clearly connected to the rest of the essay.

indicate that would be true. From World War II, when radio-controlled bombs were first directed by humans far away from the danger, to the automatic air defense systems of the Gulf War, the percentage of battlefield fatalities has been decreasing. Still, Source E's prospect of an autonomous weapon that can make its own decision to kill is frightening, especially since that same source draws a close connection between military and civilian developments. AI killers could roam our cities as well as our battlefields.

As Source B suggests, it's too late now to stop AI development. Many different disciplines are already collaborating on a vast array of applications. As research results reach commercial success, there is an economic incentive to do more research and develop even more commercially viable applications. The genie can't be put back in the bottle now.

AI, if not to be feared in the light of its potential benefits, must at least be viewed with caution and closely monitored because of its capacity to do harm. If we are to tame AI to do our bidding and to deliver only benefits, then everyone involved in AI research and development must have that same objective. How realistic is that?

How would this essay score?

- Thesis—1: The essay has a thesis that addresses the prompt directly.

- Evidence and explanation—2: The essay provides specific evidence from at least three sources, but the quality of the explanation is unsatisfactory. Evidence is merely summarized and "no line of reasoning is established." The writer doesn't adequately explain how or why AI should be viewed with caution and closely monitored.

- Sophistication—1: The language and rhetoric show style and complexity (though it's unclear if the writer's technique advances the argument of the essay).

Total Score: 4

Student Essay: High Score

Now let's take a look at an essay that scored a six. As you read, pay particular attention to how the writer enters the conversation and explains the evidence within the body paragraphs.

"You are my creator, but I am your master." So says Frankenstein's monster in Mary Shelley's 1818 novel. From Frankenstein to modern worries about artificial intelligence (AI), there have always been fears that technology could develop independence from human control and lead to disastrous consequences. However, due to the measurable humanitarian gains AI has already made and the potential for further benefits, AI should be embraced by society's leaders.

Leaps in technology often cause fear. However, data suggests that these fears are unfounded. Let's consider the impact technology has had on warfare. Despite advances in military technology, battle deaths, as represented by a percentage of numbers of military serving, have actually decreased dramatically over the last 150 years. During the Civil War, military deaths were 6.59%, yet in the Persian Gulf War, military deaths were .01% (Source G). Huge advances in military technology, including AI, were made between these different conflicts, and there has been a concurrent reduction in battlefield deaths. This suggests that technology has been saving lives during military conflict. While the US Army Strategic Studies Institute acknowledges that the government is "rightfully concerned" about life-and-death decisions being made by AI, they point out that such decisions "may not be best made by a human" either. After all, consider the countless atrocities in history that are the result of decisions made by humans. Given the measurable improvement that AI has already made, and humanity's dubious track record, AI ought to be embraced for its potential to reduce death during war.

AI should also be embraced because it offers actual and potential benefits to civilian life as well. In 2016, the Office of Science and Technology reported that AI is already "reaping major benefits for the public in fields as diverse as health care, transportation, the environment, criminal justice, and economic inclusion." This means that anyone who receives health care or education, or anyone who drives, or anyone who lives in Earth's environment—everyone!—has already received benefits from AI. Further, city planners are investing in AI to help doctors improve medical care, teachers improve individualized instruction, and autonomous vehicles reduce traffic deaths (Source D). In the same way that all people have already benefited from technology, the vast majority of the population stands to benefit from future developments in AI. Considering the radical improvements already brought about by AI, it would be negligent and irresponsible not to pursue further benefits AI could bring.

This is the essay's thesis statement. is relatively simple (that technolog should be embraced) but has som complexity because it explains wh (AI has already provided benefi and could provide more). By usir language from the question in th prompt, it's easy for graders to iden tify that the thesis addresses th prompt directly.

Here, the writer is explaining th evidence. The writer compares the da presented to technological advanc over time. Then, the writer suggests cause-effect relationship between th two: that technology could be respon sible for reducing deaths.

This is another example of the writ entering the conversation. The writ points out that human decisio making can be deeply flawed.

Another simple example of analysi the writer paraphrases the evidenc while using sentence structure an punctuation to emphasize the numbe of impacted people—everyone!

This analysis builds on the previou analysis in the paragraph by comparin the people who have benefited fror technology to the people who coul benefit from technology in the future

Technological advances are often controversial. Some resisted electricity, some are opposed to medical innovations that may conflict with their beliefs. While there are valid ethical concerns surrounding AI that warrant oversight and caution, there's no doubt that AI should be embraced as a means of social betterment for the future.

How would this essay score?

- Thesis—1: The essay presents a defensible thesis that addresses the prompt.

- Evidence and explanation—4: The writer presents specific evidence from at least three sources and consistently explains how the evidence supports their thesis statement.

- Sophistication—1: While the thesis isn't particularly complicated, other features of the essay demonstrate a complex understanding of rhetorical sophistication. Look at the engaging hook that grabs the reader's attention, the use of data and examples in the evidence, and the way the writer addresses the opposing view throughout.

Total Score: 6

Next, let's take a look at how to tackle the rhetorical analysis essay.

Chapter 6
How to Approach the Rhetorical Analysis Essay

FIRST THINGS FIRST: WHAT'S A RHETORICAL STRATEGY?

Authors use certain techniques, in both the language and the structure of the piece they're writing, to convey their messages effectively and to achieve the intended effect(s) on their audiences. Speakers use these techniques too. Often they're trying to persuade their audiences to do something or to agree with their points of view.

In Chapters 8–11, you'll find explanations and examples of rhetorical strategies, plus questions so you can practice using them. Once you become familiar with rhetorical strategies and their effects, you'll probably start spotting them in your day-to-day life too—in ads, in interviews given by politicians, or in instructions from your teachers, for instance.

YOUR TASKS IN THE RHETORICAL ANALYSIS ESSAY

The AP readers are looking for three main things in the rhetorical analysis essay:

- an understanding of the author's intended purpose

- the ability to identify the chief rhetorical strategies used to achieve that purpose effectively

- an analysis of *how* those strategies contribute to the development and effectiveness of the writer's argument, *supported by references to the text*

Of course, the graders are also assessing the skillful control of the language, clear expression, and smooth organization that they want to see in all three essays.

Tip:
Your thesis in this essay should identify the author's purpose and describe the rhetorical strategies the author used to achieve that purpose.

In the rhetorical analysis essay, the AP readers don't want a summary of the entire passage, or an argument for or against the author's main point. Your focus is strictly on what the author's purpose is, and what rhetorical strategies the author uses to achieve it effectively. Students typically find this essay the most challenging of the three, and straying from that focus is often where they go wrong.

Another common problem that costs essays points is being too general. An essay might describe the author's purpose right up front, in the first paragraph (a good idea, incidentally), and identify the three or four most important rhetorical strategies, but then fail to link each one to the author's purpose with a specific, thorough explanation of exactly how that strategy makes the message more effective. Direct references to the passage are a must, too, or the explanation runs the risk of being too general and oversimplified.

This additional layer of complexity is reflected in the way the rhetorical analysis essay is scored. In order to earn all four points for evidence and commentary, writers must provide *specific evidence* to support their claims, consistently *explain how* the evidence they've selected supports their argument AND *explain how* the various rhetorical devices in their evidence contribute to the purpose of the passage.

So your first task is to identify the author's purpose, which your active reading skills will enable you to do. After that, your task is to detect the main rhetorical strategies and build a convincing case for why and how each one advances the author's purpose.

Tip:
Take notes as you read. Make two columns. On the left: keep track of rhetorical devices. On the right: describe how the rhetorical device develops the argument.

Anatomy of the Prompt

The rhetorical analysis question presents you with a text and asks you to explain how rhetorical strategies in the text develop the speaker's argument. The text is usually a speech or letter with political, historical, or social significance. Recent texts have included a tribute from then-First Lady Claudia "Lady Bird" Johnson to former First Lady Eleanor Roosevelt, a eulogy given by then-President Barack Obama to Senator Ted Kennedy, and a fundraising speech given by then-President Ronald Reagan for the John F. Kennedy Library.

The prompt itself is formatted as a single paragraph. It provides an introduction to the topic and a central question: How do rhetorical strategies in the text develop the speaker's argument?

The introduction consistently provides important information you need for understanding the rhetorical situation and writing your essay. For a detailed review of these concepts, see Chapter 8.

- **Author:** The prompt will name the speaker and describe their profession and/or what they are known for.

- **Context:** The prompt indicates the year in which the text was written or published, or it may provide the lifespan of the author. It will also describe events or ideas relevant to the text. Reading carefully, you'll likely be able to identify the **exigency** of the passage as well.

- **Audience:** Some prompts state the audience clearly (such as "Abigail Adams wrote a letter to her son"), while other prompts may require you to infer. For example, one previous prompt asked students to analyze an article that was written by Cesar Chavez and published in "the magazine of a religious organization." The audience was composed of that magazine's religious audience, but also likely included other civil rights leaders, union organizers, and politicians who followed Chavez's work.

- **Purpose:** This one is very tricky. The central question may or may not tell you the speaker's argument. Some years, the purpose is clearly stated in the prompt. Other years, the prompt provides the general topic, but not the speaker's specific argument. Other times, the prompt doesn't give you any indication of the speaker's argument at all. In all of these cases, the test will provide the information necessary to write a convincing essay. So read the central question closely and use any information it gives you to help with your essay. As the rhetoric scholar, it will be up to you to determine the **message** that the passage ultimately conveys.

Diamonds Are an AP Student's Best Friend

Think of the four main aspects of a passage (author, context, purpose, and audience) in terms of a diamond. Understanding these main points will help you understand the rhetorical strategies being used in a text.

Using the Rhetorical Diamond

While you're reading the prompt and the passage, imagine—and try to flesh out—a baseball diamond with the following six points:

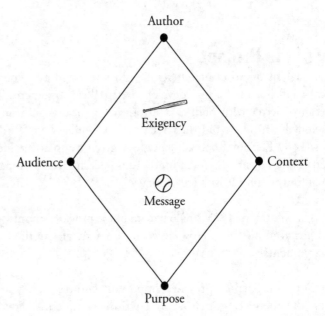

The rhetorical strategies used in the text represent an interaction among these points. Understanding them will help you understand how rhetorical strategies help a speaker achieve their purpose for a specific audience and within a distinct context.

For example, a politician trying to win support from a mass audience at a rally would use different rhetorical techniques than a heart disease specialist describing the findings from a research study for publication in a professional, peer-reviewed journal. The politician, because of the verbal delivery and the diversity of the mass audience, would use simpler language, emotional appeals (pathos), and techniques such as repetition. The heart disease specialist, on the other hand, would use technical language and techniques to inspire respect for her qualifications and the thoroughness of her work (ethos).

This is the task at hand in the rhetorical analysis essay. Identify rhetorical techniques in the text (such as simple language and repetition) and describe how they impact the audience (such as appealing to a diverse audience or helping listeners remember key words).

Once you've identified the author's argument, it will give you some clues about the rhetorical strategies you might find in the passage. Does it deal with a controversial topic, or with a position that would create almost no opposition from anyone? Is it promoting a new, "fuzzy" concept that the audience would find hard to understand, or a topic that would be familiar to most people?

Trying to put yourself in the audience's shoes can also help you uncover rhetorical strategies. If you were part of that audience, at that time and in that context, would this piece of writing influence you? Why? Did it help you understand something through the use of examples, for instance? Did it make you feel the author sympathized with your concerns, perhaps through the use of anecdotes echoing your own experiences? Did it keep bringing you back to one central idea through the skillful use of repetition?

Now that you know your tasks and where you need to focus, let's look at a couple of rhetorical analysis prompts and passages.

A PERSUASIVE SPEECH EXAMPLE

The Directions

Question 2

Suggested time—40 minutes.

(This question counts for one-third of the total essay score.)

Susan B. Anthony delivered the speech below in 1873, after she was arrested for voting in the 1872 presidential election. She spoke throughout the county where her trial was to be held, aiming primarily at potential jurors and other women. Read the passages carefully. Then, in a well-developed essay, analyze the rhetorical strategies Anthony uses to persuade her audience that she did not commit a crime.

Analyzing the Prompt

As you're reading the prompt, look for how much it tells you about the six points on the rhetorical diamond.

- **Author**—Even if you've never heard of Susan B. Anthony (a leading 19th-century advocate for women's rights and co-founder of the National Woman Suffrage Association), the prompt gives you enough information to guess that she was an activist who deliberately defied a current law.

- **Purpose**—Sometimes the prompt will outline the author's purpose; sometimes it won't. In this case, you can guess that since Anthony is in conflict with legal authorities, she is probably giving a speech to present her side of the story in advance of her trial, and to convince her audience that her position is right.

- **Audience**—This prompt provides an unusual amount of information about the audience. Most of the time, you'll need to make inferences based on whatever details about the author and context you can squeeze from the prompt.

In this case, since Anthony has been arrested but not yet tried, you could have guessed (even if the prompt didn't tell you) that the audience would include potential members of the jury pool. And since she felt strongly enough about her cause to risk arrest, you could guess that the audience would include a mix of supporters (who want to hear their champion) and those simply curious about the case.

- **Context**—Anthony is giving a speech, so you can look for rhetorical strategies that you would expect to find in verbal delivery (such as simpler language, shorter sentences, repetition, and rhythm). And since she is facing a trial for following her beliefs, you can expect suggestions of urgency and passion.

- **Exigency**—Anthony wants to harness public interest in her arrest to advance voting rights for women. She further hopes to persuade potential jurors in her upcoming trial.

- **Message**—Anthony asserts that women are people and therefore citizens of the United States. As such, no state can limit the rights guaranteed by the Constitution, specifically the right to vote in order to secure "liberty to ourselves and our posterity."

Armed with the information you've gained from the prompt, you can now put your active reading skills into gear looking for Anthony's rhetorical strategies in the passage. Imagine you're in the audience listening to her speech. Does she convince you to agree with her? If so, how does she do it? If not, what would you need to hear in order to be convinced? As you identify each rhetorical strategy, keep asking yourself, "Why does she use this? How does it help her achieve her purpose?" because you'll need to answer those questions in your essay.

First, try writing your own essay in 40 minutes. Remember to spend a few minutes planning your essay and support your points with direct references to the passage. Then read the sample student essays and assessments that follow the passage.

The Passage

Woman's Rights to the Suffrage
by Susan B. Anthony (1820–1906)
1873
[abridged]

The terms "bill of attainder" and "ex post facto law" in paragraph 5 refer to the power of the legislature to declare someone guilty (often without a trial), and to change, retroactively, the legal status of an action that occurred before the law was passed. The three people mentioned in paragraph 6 all published dictionaries.

Friends and Fellow Citizens: I stand before you tonight
under indictment for the alleged crime of having voted
at the last presidential election, without having a lawful
Line   right to vote. It shall be my work this evening to prove to
5   you that in thus voting, I not only committed no crime,

but, instead, simply exercised my citizen's rights, guaranteed to me and all United States citizens by the National Constitution, beyond the power of any State to deny.

The preamble of the Federal Constitution says:

10 "We, the people of the United States, in order to form a more perfect union, establish justice, insure domestic tranquility, provide for the common defense, promote the general welfare, and secure the blessings of liberty to ourselves and our posterity, do ordain and establish this Constitution

15 for the United States of America."

It was we, the people; not we, the white male citizens; nor yet we, the male citizens; but we, the whole people, who formed the Union. And we formed it, not to give the blessings of liberty, but to secure them; not to the half of

20 ourselves and the half of our posterity, but to the whole people—women as well as men. And it is a downright mockery to talk to women of their enjoyment of the blessings of liberty while they are denied the use of the only means of securing them provided by this democratic-

25 republican government—the ballot.

For any State to make sex a qualification that must ever result in the disfranchisement of one entire half of the people is to pass a bill of attainder, or an ex post facto law, and is therefore a violation of the supreme law of the land. By

30 it the blessings of liberty are for ever withheld from women and their female posterity. To them this government has no just powers derived from the consent of the governed. To them this government is not a democracy. It is not a republic. It is an odious aristocracy; a hateful oligarchy of sex;

35 the most hateful aristocracy ever established on the face of the globe; an oligarchy of wealth, where the right govern the poor... This oligarchy of sex, which makes father, brothers, husband, sons, the oligarchs over the mother and sisters, the wife and daughters of every household—which

40 ordains all men sovereigns, all women subjects, carries dissension, discord and rebellion into every home of the nation.

Webster, Worcester and Bouvier all define a citizen to be a person in the United States, entitled to vote and hold

45 office.

The only question left to be settled now is: Are women persons? And I hardly believe any of our opponents will have the hardihood to say they are not. Being persons, then, women are citizens; and no State has a right to make any

50 law, or to enforce any old law, that shall abridge their privileges or immunities. Hence, every discrimination against women in the constitutions and laws of the several States is today null and void.

Understanding the Rubric

A thorough understanding of the rubric can help you maximize the points your essay scores. Graders will be looking at three different aspects of your essay: the thesis statement (Row A), the evidence and explanation (Row B), and the level of sophistication (Row C).

Rhetorical Analysis Essay Rubric					
Row A	**0 points:** • Has no defensible thesis • Has thesis that only restates prompt • Has thesis that summarizes the issue with no apparent or coherent claim • Has thesis that does not respond to the prompt		**1 point:** • Responds to the prompt with a thesis that analyzes the writer's rhetorical choices		
Row B	**0 points:** • Simply restates thesis (if present), repeats provided information, or offers information irrelevant to the prompt	**1 point:** • Provides evidence that is mostly general AND • Summarizes the evidence but does not explain how the evidence supports the student's argument	**2 points:** • Provides some specific, relevant evidence AND • Explains how some of the evidence supports the student's argument, but no line of reasoning is established, or the line of reasoning is faulty	**3 points:** • Provides specific evidence to support all claims in a line of reasoning AND • Explains how some of the evidence supports a line of reasoning AND • Explains how at least one rhetorical choice in the passage contributes to the writer's argument, purpose, or message	**4 points:** • Provides specific evidence to support all claims in a line of reasoning AND • Consistently explains how the evidence supports a line of reasoning AND • Explains how multiple rhetorical choices in the passage contribute to the writer's argument, purpose, or message
Row C	**0 points:** • Does not meet the criteria for one point		**1 point:** • Demonstrates sophistication of thought and/or a complex understanding of rhetorical sophistication		

Note that Row B has the highest point value and is divided into three different areas. Graders are looking for essays that provide specific evidence, consistently explain how that evidence supports a line of reasoning, and explain how multiple rhetorical choices contribute to the speaker's argument. This means that you must include examples of the rhetorical strategies you discuss in your essay. It also means you will have to identify multiple rhetorical choices. Writing an essay about just one strategy will cost you points.

Understanding how the essay is scored also gives you a clue about how to structure your essay. In your body paragraphs:

- State the author's purpose and which rhetorical device they use. (This is your claim.)

- Provide specific evidence: at least two examples of the rhetorical device.

- Explain how the device develops the author's purpose. How does the device impact the audience? Is the author successful? Why or why not?

You Try It

Now that you understand the prompt, the task at hand, and the rubric, you're ready to begin writing.

After you're finished writing, take a look at the following student essay. This is a student essay that was written in the allotted 40 minutes. As you read it, evaluate how well it:

- identifies rhetorical strategies within the text

- demonstrates an understanding of the text's author, audience, purpose, and context

- provides multiple, specific examples of rhetorical strategies

- consistently explains how those strategies develop the argument

Student Essay: Low Score

This student makes a common mistake in responding to the rhetorical analysis essay question. Look for it as you read: The writer focuses on what the author *says* rather than on how the author says it in order to achieve her purpose. This confusion between *what the author says* and *how the author says it* is one of the main reasons why test-takers typically earn a lower score on the rhetorical analysis essay than on any of the other essay tasks.

> Susan B. Anthony broke the law. For this, she was arrested and about to be tried. Before the trial took place, however, she wanted to prove that she didn't do anything wrong and to gain support for her innocence. So she gave this speech to convince people—potential jurors at her trial, other women and anyone who chose to listen—that it wasn't wrong for her to vote in the presidential election.

> That would have been a radical assertion at the time. Anthony lived in an era when men and women had different rights, and the difference in their status was widely accepted as normal. While the audience likely included people who knew of Anthony and supported her position, others would have been shocked by the fact that she dared to challenge the accepted social order. She would have needed a strong argument to explain her action and win those people over.

> Anthony bases her entire appeal on logos, or logic. "Are women persons?" she asks. If women are people, then they are also citizens and entitled to the "blessings of liberty" that the nation's Constitution guarantees, including the right to vote. She does not try to claim that she didn't break a state law. Instead, she argues that the law she broke is "null and void" because it denies her the status and the rights that the federal Constitution guarantees her.

> In this appeal to reason and logic, Anthony is basically claiming that anyone who thinks she did something wrong by voting is also saying that she—or any woman—is not a person. In addition, anyone who thinks she committed a crime would also have to argue that a state law (which she did break by voting) outweighs the Constitution of the entire nation. Both positions would be hard to defend. By attributing these positions to her opponents, Anthony portrays people who don't agree with her—including everyone connected with her arrest and trial and with passing the law in the first place—as illogical, unreasonable idiots. Such people couldn't possibly be right.

> Not only are her opponents fools; Anthony claims they are more dangerous than that. They have created a "hateful aristocracy" and ensured that every family in the country is plagued by "dissension, discord and rebellion." The government is not a democracy, as the Constitution intended, she claims, but is instead controlled by a privileged few who are depriving her—and

---

Although the first paragraph is simply an uninspiring restatement of the information provided in the prompt, the first sentence is a good attention-getter. It makes the reader want to keep going to uncover more of the story.

The thesis describes Anthony's purpose but not the rhetorical strategies she used in her speech. The writer does touch upon the likely makeup of the audience and the context of an era in which the restricted status of women was the norm. However, the writer connects these two elements only to the content of Anthony's message (the need for a strong argument), not to rhetorical strategies that would help her deliver it. The writer could have discussed strategies such as identifying with the audience and establishing common ground (the wording of the Constitution, the desire for a peaceful home life) to make her action seem less alien to listeners who might initially find it shocking.

This discussion of Anthony's logical argument is accurate, although rather superficial. The trouble is, that's not what the prompt asked. The prompt asks writers to identify and analyze the rhetorical strategies the author uses. That task requires a focus not just on the author's message, but on the interaction among message, purpose, audience, and context. Different elements—for example, if another were creating a written submission to the judge at her trial—would require different rhetorical strategies in order to achieve the author's purpose effectively.

Although the writer correctly identifies Anthony's classical appeal to logic, the student doesn't connect her appeal to the audience's values, to a sense of fairness in this case. The writer also needs to describe how Anthony appeals to logic by considering how key terms (such as "people" and "citizen") are defined in the Constitution and common usage.

e student mentions "passion and perbole" but doesn't connect these etorical devices to Anthony's verbal livery (can't you just hear the rising lume as she goes through that long dious aristocracy" sentence?) or her rpose of inflaming her audience support her right to vote. And nthony injects a bit of humor ("not , the white male citizens") to give ne relief to her impassioned plea support.

all women—of liberty. Her passion and hyperbole come through even more when she describes the government as "the most hateful aristocracy ever established on the face of the globe."

After this tirade, Anthony comes full circle back to her original point: women are citizens too, and therefore no state law (like the one preventing them from voting) can deny them the rights guaranteed by the country's Constitution. Through this passionate appeal to logic, Anthony achieves the purpose she clearly stated at the beginning: "to prove to you that in thus voting, I... committed no crime." It is as if she were a lawyer arguing her case at her upcoming trial, rather than the accused trying to drum up support and influence potential jurors. How could anyone disagree with her after listening to the logic of her argument?

e writer astutely notices that nthony concludes her speech by urning to her starting point. owever, again the writer fails to tie s rhetorical technique to the verbal livery or to the mass audience she's dressing. Her listeners don't have a itten version of her speech in front them. In that context, she can hieve her purpose more effectively reminding them of her main points d wrapping up her speech neatly by urning to the beginning.

How would this essay score?

- Thesis—0: The writer has a defensible thesis that states Anthony's purpose, but not the rhetorical devices she uses to achieve that purpose.

- Evidence and commentary—2: The writer relies on specific evidence from the text but doesn't establish a line of reasoning as to how the rhetorical devices develop Anthony's purpose.

- Sophistication—0: The writer's description of Anthony's purpose is simplistic and the writing lacks style (note particularly the use of "idiot" in the commentary).

Total Score: 2

Student Essay: High Score

The essay that follows earned all six points on the rubric. As you read it, pay particular attention to the writer's explanations. They very clearly accomplish two tasks: explaining how Anthony's rhetorical strategies further her purpose, and expanding on the ideas the writer presented in the essay's thesis statement. This is what the graders are looking for when they want to see evidence and explanations that "support a clear line of reasoning."

After casting a vote in the 1872 presidential election, Susan B. Anthony was arrested for the crime of voting while being a woman. In hopes of persuading her fellow citizens, including potential jurors, of her innocence, Anthony gave a speech in 1873. By appealing to credibility, logic, and emotions, Anthony argues that state governments have no right to discriminate against their citizenry on the basis of sex.

> This introduction is brief: it descri[bes] the context and identifies Anthor[y's] audience. This is the thesis. [It] describes the rhetorical strateg[ies] (developing appeals to credibil[ity,] emotion, and logic) that Antho[ny] uses to convey her argument (t[hat] states can't legally discriminate on [the] basis of sex).

At the very start of her speech, Anthony greets her audience and introduces her topic using familiar language that emphasizes the civic values she shares with her audience. She addresses the crowd as "Friends and Fellow Citizens," a salutation that appeals to the audience's sense of community and shared identity as US citizens. She continues by quoting the Preamble to the Constitution in its entirety, a recital that reaffirms their shared values as US citizens, to guarantee liberty to all citizens. By invoking the preamble, she also develops her ethos as an individual well-versed in the law. She appeals to authority later as well, referencing Webster, Worcester, and Bouvier. These techniques enhance her stature and credibility with listeners who might have regarded her as just some minor figure who was silly enough to challenge the law. Anthony avoids stereotypes that hold women as either ridiculous or hysterical by appealing to her audience's sense of communal history and establishing herself as an authoritative speaker.

> Notice how this concluding senten[ce] refers back to the thesis. "Appealing [to] her audience's sense of communi[ty]" is an appeal to emotions, and "esta[b]lishing herself as an authoritat[ive] speaker" is an appeal to credibility.

As Anthony progresses, she analyzes the language of the Constitution to explain why women are entitled to the rights established therein. She explains the pronoun "we": "It was we, the people; not we the white male citizens." By replacing the word "people" with a false substitution, "white male citizens," Anthony emphasizes the inclusivity of US laws, that they pertain to all citizens regardless of gender or race. She uses false substitution to a similar effect when she reminds her listeners that the Preamble pertains "not to the half of ourselves and the half of our posterity." Altering such familiar lines was likely jarring and uncomfortable for her listeners, inviting them to join her in remembering the correct phrasing: "secure the blessings of liberty to ourselves and our posterity." The repetition of "our" once again emphasizes that she, a woman, is included as a citizen the Constitution was designed to govern and protect. By using repetition and altering lines already familiar to the audience, Anthony caters to her audience of listeners, as opposed to anyone who might read about her trial in a newspaper. This passage exemplifies her balance of logos and pathos: she analyzes diction

> This level of detailed explanation [is] what the graders are looking for. [The] writer refers to Anthony's spec[ific] diction, explaining how it impacts [the] audience and furthers her argumen[t.]

to explain logically why women are included in the law, while also appealing to the audience's sense of justice and fairness.

> This paragraph skillfully weaves a variety of evidence. There are specific examples of both the legal and impassioned language that Anthony uses.

Despite not presenting her argument in writing, Anthony doesn't shy away from technical sophistication. She explains that state laws limiting freedoms guaranteed by the Constitution are "bill[s] of attainder" or "ex post facto law[s]" which are a "violation of the supreme law of the land." This technical terminology would have appealed to any potential jurors in her audience and continues to establish that she—a woman—is capable of understanding and utilizing sophisticated legal theory, thereby proving that women are capable of civic participation. This use of logic juxtaposes the passion she evokes, describing current laws as "downright unnecessary," accusing the government of being a "hateful aristocracy," and suggesting that "all men are sovereigns" and "all women are subjects." Such passionate language conveys Anthony's moral outrage by emphasizing the consequences of women being denied voting rights. By appealing to logos and pathos, Anthony conveys both the illegality of the law for which she is being tried and her own anger at those infringing on her constitutional rights.

> This concluding sentence reinforces the writer's thesis and enhances it by reviewing the rhetorical strategies used to appeal to credibility, logic, and emotion. It's a strong example of a thesis that builds over the course of the essay.

Anthony's purpose is to share both the legal circumstances of her situation and her indignation with her audience. To do so, Anthony establishes herself as an authoritative speaker, and delivers a logical, legal argument alongside language that appeals to emotion: a friendly introduction, recitation of shared cultural doctrine, and an impassioned description of the negative consequences suffered by all when some are denied their rights.

How would this essay score?

- Thesis—1: This essay responds to the prompt with a thesis that analyzes Anthony's rhetorical choices.

- Evidence and explanation—4: The essay successfully develops a line of reasoning by providing a variety of specific evidence, consistent explanation, and a discussion of how the evidence develops Anthony's purpose.

- Sophistication—1: Based upon its vocabulary and organization, this essay demonstrates sophistication of thought and a complex understanding of rhetoric.

Total Score: 6

Here's another example for you to try, this time from a written work.

AN EDUCATIONAL BOOK EXAMPLE

The Directions

Question 2

Suggested time—40 minutes.

(This question counts for one-third of the total essay score.)

In 1880, nine years after he created "The Greatest Show on Earth," circus promoter P.T. Barnum wrote a short book about making money. He became wealthy himself, and believed that anyone could do the same if they would only follow the simple rules he had learned. Read the passage carefully. Then, in a well-developed essay, analyze the rhetorical strategies Barnum uses to convey his point of view.

Analyzing the Prompt

As you're reading the prompt, look for how much it tells you about the four points on the rhetorical diamond.

- **Author**—You may have heard of P.T. Barnum and the Barnum and Bailey Circus. The prompt reveals something about this successful businessman and promoter that you might not expect, though. He wants to share his secrets for making money—to help ordinary people become wealthy too. That suggests a philanthropic quality and empathy for the kind of people who come to see his circus (and who, in the process, have helped him become a millionaire).

- **Purpose**—This prompt reveals a lot of information about the author's purpose. Anyone can get rich, he believes, and he wants to teach them how. And incidentally, he will be able to sell a lot of books to a mass audience if he really does provide helpful information geared to ordinary people. Readers who find his rules useful will tell their friends and relatives, who will buy the book and tell their friends and relatives, and so on.

- **Audience**—Barnum believed that anyone could become wealthy, as he had, by following the rules in his book—so the book is likely directed to anyone who is not already rich and desires to be so—mostly people who don't have much money and might not have a formal education but hope for a better future.

- **Context**—This is a book for the masses, so it has to be useful to ordinary people or it won't sell. Look for rhetorical strategies that make the author's points easy to understand and remember. You can also expect efforts to identify with the audience; they won't listen to someone who thinks he is better than them and who "talks down" to them. He will want to convince his readers that he genuinely wants to help them get rich, and that they really can succeed if they follow his rules.

- **Exigency**—Barnum writes this book after having made his millions. Presumably he wants to share his knowledge and profit from the sale of the book.

- **Message**—To become wealthy one must earn more than one spends. Further, one must spend judiciously and not on frivolous things.

Armed with the information you've gained from the prompt, you can now use your active reading skills to look for Barnum's rhetorical strategies. In this excerpt, does he teach you any lessons that would help you improve your own financial situation? How does he do it? Does he explain his rules in a way that will help you remember them? Does he make you believe that his desire to help you is genuine, and that you, too, can become wealthy? As you identify each rhetorical strategy, keep asking yourself, "Why does he use this? How does it help him achieve his purpose?" because you'll need to answer those questions in your essay.

First, try writing your own essay in 40 minutes. Remember to spend a few minutes planning your essay and support your points with direct references to the passage. Then read the sample student essay and assessment that follow the passage.

Simon Says

Try to use more varied verbs in your essay. Instead of constantly writing "The author says," how about "The author… claims, suggests, implies, states…"?

The Passage

Excerpt from
The Art of Money Getting
or
Golden Rules for Making Money
by P.T. Barnum
1880

In paragraph 2, "Dr. Franklin" refers to Benjamin Franklin, the framer of the Constitution who promoted the virtues of thrift and frugal living. "Mr. Micawber" is the chronic debtor in Charles Dickens' novel, David Copperfield. "Furbelows" signifies showy, basically useless ruffles on women's dresses. In paragraph 4, a "bung-hole" is a hole in a barrel (which might hold beer or whisky) capped with a cork called a bung. "Punch" was a popular satire magazine at the time.

In the United States, where we have more land than
people, it is not at all difficult for persons in good health to
make money. In this comparatively new field there are so
Line   many avenues of success open, so many vocations which
5   are not crowded, that any person of either sex who is willing, at least for the time being, to engage in any respectable
occupation that offers, may find lucrative employment.
    Those who really desire to attain an independence, have
only to set their minds upon it, and adopt the proper means,
10   as they do in regard to any other object which they wish to
accomplish, and the thing is easily done. But however easy
it may be found to make money, I have no doubt many of
my hearers will agree it is the most difficult thing in the
world to keep it. The road to wealth is, as Dr. Franklin truly
15   says, "as plain as the road to the mill." It consists simply in
expending less than we earn; that seems to be a very simple
problem. Mr. Micawber, one of those happy creations of
the genial Dickens, puts the case in a strong light when
he says that to have annual income of twenty pounds per
20   annum, and spend twenty pounds and sixpence, is to be

the most miserable of men; whereas, to have an income of
only twenty pounds, and spend but nineteen pounds and
sixpence is to be the happiest of mortals. Many of my readers may say, "we understand this: this is economy, and we
25 know economy is wealth; we know we can't eat our cake
and keep it also." Yet I beg to say that perhaps more cases
of failure arise from mistakes on this point than almost
any other. The fact is, many people think they understand
economy when they really do not.
30   True economy is misapprehended, and people go
through life without properly comprehending what that
principle is. One says, "I have an income of so much, and
here is my neighbor who has the same; yet every year he
gets something ahead and I fall short; why is it? I know
35 all about economy." He thinks he does, but he does not.
There are men who think that economy consists in saving
cheese-parings and candle-ends, in cutting off two pence
from the laundress' bill and doing all sorts of little, mean,
dirty things. Economy is not meanness. The misfortune
40 is, also, that this class of persons let their economy apply
in only one direction. They fancy they are so wonderfully
economical in saving a half-penny where they ought to
spend twopence, that they think they can afford to squander
in other directions. A few years ago, before kerosene oil
45 was discovered or thought of, one might stop overnight at
almost any farmer's house in the agricultural districts and
get a very good supper, but after supper he might attempt
to read in the sitting-room, and would find it impossible
with the inefficient light of one candle. The hostess, seeing
50 his dilemma, would say: "It is rather difficult to read here
evenings; the proverb says 'you must have a ship at sea in
order to be able to burn two candles at once;' we never have
an extra candle except on extra occasions." These extra
occasions occur, perhaps, twice a year. In this way the good
55 woman saves five, six, or ten dollars in that time: but the
information which might be derived from having the extra
light would, of course, far outweigh a ton of candles.
        But the trouble does not end here. Feeling that she is so
economical in tallow candles, she thinks she can afford to
60 go frequently to the village and spend twenty or thirty dollars for ribbons and furbelows, many of which are not necessary. This false connote may frequently be seen in men of
business, and in those instances it often runs to writing-pa-
per. You find good businessmen who save all the old enve-
65 lopes and scraps, and would not tear a new sheet of paper, if
they could avoid it, for the world. This is all very well; they
may in this way save five or ten dollars a year, but being so
economical (only in note paper), they think they can afford
to waste time; to have expensive parties, and to drive their
70 carriages. This is an illustration of Dr. Franklin's "saving at
the spigot and wasting at the bung-hole;" "penny wise and
pound foolish." Punch in speaking of this "one idea" class
of people says "they are like the man who bought a penny
herring for his family's dinner and then hired a coach and
75 four to take it home." I never knew a man to succeed by
practising this kind of economy.
        True economy consists in always making the income
exceed the out-go.

Student Essay: Average Score

In terms of the task given in the prompt, this student comprehends it to a large extent. Instead of simply rehashing the author's message, the writer focuses on the rhetorical strategies the author uses to help readers understand, remember, and accept his rules for gaining wealth. The writer gives evidence from the passage to support the claims in the essay. It's obvious that the writer planned ahead before she started writing, since the first paragraph contains a laundry list of rhetorical strategies that are discussed in the following paragraphs.

That sense of checking items off a list makes the discussion adequate, landing this essay at a mid-range score. It's the "analyze" part of the task where this student's essay falls short of a top score. The explanations don't have the depth, sophistication, or conviction to elevate the essay into the higher score range. A more effective, thorough analysis would explain how each of the author's rhetorical strategies fits into the interplay among purpose, audience, and context.

One weakness in this essay occurs in the sophistication of expression. No one expects a polished essay from a 40-minute effort. However, there is a choppy, disjointed quality to the way the essay develops, and a weakness in the control of English mechanics (such as some confusion in verb tenses and some unclear pronoun antecedents). As a result, it's difficult to follow the argument in spots. Effective essays demonstrate a smoother, more controlled prose style than this student achieves.

Despite its simplicity, this introduction is still effective in presenting the writer's thesis. It states the rhetorical strategies Barnum used in the text and Barnum's purpose.

The explanations in this essay are consistent throughout. The writer identifies Barnum's rhetorical strategies, then explains how they would have impacted the audience and developed Barnum's argument. This explanation is particularly strong because it compares the rhetorical device Barnum chose to an alternate rhetorical strategy Barnum could have chosen (Barnum could have just told them to save money and not used an anecdote).

Circus promoter P.T. Barnum wanted to do more than entertain people at the Greatest Show on Earth. He wants to teach them how to make money and become wealthy, too. To do this, he uses some effective rhetorical strategies. He tells stories, he gives examples, he uses a comparison/contrast structure, he mentions authorities, he identifies with his readers, he uses the tone of a cheerleader and he uses simple language.

Telling stories is a good way to teach lessons. Barnum's readers are ordinary people, without much formal education. They will remember stories much more easily than if the author ordered them to follow a list of rules. For example, Barnum tells the story of the woman with the candle so vividly that readers could likely see her guest squinting, then finally giving up on trying to read with such inadequate lighting. Then they could imagine the woman dashing around the village buying ribbons with the money she saved by only burning one candle.

Readers would also be more accepting of a lesson told in a story than they would of a rule ordered by a successful businessman. If Barnum just told them not to save money for buying foolish things, but to invest the money instead (in this case, in the knowledge she would gain by reading), readers might resent being ordered around. A story conveys the same rule in a friendlier way to this audience. They are reading Barnum's book because they want to learn, not be ordered around.

The author gives other examples so he can avoid delivering his lessons as rules and so readers will remember them better. He tells the story of the businessman who saves scraps of paper, but wastes the money he saved on parties and carriages. He gives the example of Mr. Micawber, who always spent more than he earned and therefore couldn't become wealthy. The author compares Mr. Micawber's practice with a contrasting habit of spending less than one earns, which leads to the ability to accumulate Wealth.

Citing authorities that would be familiar to readers gives Barnum more credibility with his audience, and also strengthens his position as "one of them" rather than a remote, successful businessman they could never hope to become. Barnum quotes Benjamin Franklin, and Barnum reads Charles Dickens and the satire magazine Punch, too, just like his readers do. His statement, "many of my hearers will agree," reinforces his connection with the audience so they will accept his rules as advice from a friend rather than a route to something they could never achieve (wealth). The author needs to convince his readers that he really wants to help them become wealthy. Making them feel that he is "one of them" helps him achieve that goal.

He cheers them on and encourages them to follow his advice. It's "not at all difficult for persons in good health to make money," he assures them. Anyone can do it, even women (which would have been unusual at the time).

Barnum used simple language to convey simple lessons. There are no complex financial terms or concepts that would make his readers feel the book or Barnum's lessons were beyond their abilities. Spend less than you earn, and invest wisely instead of spending foolishly are his two main messages in this excerpt. The rhetorical strategies he chooses ensure that these important lessons are understood and remembered by ordinary readers.

How would this essay score?

- Thesis—1: The introduction presents a defensible thesis that describes the rhetorical devices Barnum uses to achieve his purpose.

- Evidence and Commentary—3: The essay provides specific evidence and some discussion as to how this evidence supports the thesis. Further, there is some discussion as to how the rhetorical devices contribute to the writer's argument.

- Sophistication—0: The language is simplistic and contains errors that lead to confusion.

Total Score: 4

By following our strategies and using the essays that you've seen as models, you can aim for—and achieve—higher scores.

In the next chapter, we move on to the argument essay.

This evidence needs explanations. Why was Benjamin Franklin a particularly good reference for Barnum to cite? The student doesn't explore what the author gains with a mass audience by drawing on a trusted framer of the Constitution: Barnum gains credibility for his message, legitimacy for his subject (the pursuit of wealth), and a connection to the concept of helping people build something.

The discussion of Barnum's appeal to credibility is overly simplistic. Before he can successfully teach readers how to become wealthy, Barnum needs to convince them that his desire to help them is genuine and that they will benefit from his book. In order to achieve that initial purpose, he first gets his readers on his side with a rousing, encouraging "land of opportunity" opening. It's easy to make money in a country where there is so much land and so many jobs, he claims. An ordinary reader would likely feel, "I can actually do this, too, just like the famous Barnum did, and he really wants me to succeed." Next Barnum identifies with his readers and demonstrates that he understands them: " have no doubt many of my hearers will agree it is the most difficult thing in the world to keep it." Only then does he turn to his main purpose, launching into stories that teach the difference between false economy (which does not lead to wealth) and true economy (which does).

The conclusion reveals the struggle the writer had with organizing this essay. The thesis mentions many (too many) rhetorical strategies, but the conclusion simply refers to "simple language to convey simple lessons." Meanwhile, the content of the essay discusses anecdotes, credibility, and, briefly, tone. Coordinating thesis, content, and conclusion would have made for a more successful essay. Understanding the task and citing evidence from the passage are both important in the rhetorical analysis essay, but so is the ability to express ideas clearly and effectively with smooth transitions to guide the reader through the discussion.

Chapter 7
How to Approach
the Argument Essay

WHERE YOUR OPINION COUNTS

At last—a chance to make your own argument, without being limited by the source documents you're given and without having to focus on rhetorical strategies instead of the merits of what an author says. Here you get to take a stand and present your point of view on the topic in the prompt. This should be an essay you look forward to!

Even better, there is no "right" or "wrong" answer. All that matters is how effectively you argue and back up your position. If you like to debate, this is the part of the essay section where you can really shine.

Anatomy of the Prompt

The argument prompt has three parts. First, the prompt provides you with a direct quotation. It can be from an individual of historical or political importance, or it could be a passage from a novel, short story, or essay. The quotation will contain a provocative claim. In 2018, the prompt included a passage from a novel claiming that unknown experiences are the most enriching. In 2019, it used several brief quotes to show how the word "overrated" had been used to diminish prestige throughout history.

Tip:
Your first step in the argument essay is to identify the claim presented in the prompt.

Second, the prompt will instruct you to write an essay that argues your position relative to the claim presented in the prompt. The concise statement of your position is your essay's thesis statement. It could be as simple as "I agree because..." or "I disagree because...." You can also present a more complex, qualified thesis: "I agree, but...."

The third and final segment of the prompt is a list of bullet-point reminders:

- Respond to the prompt with a thesis that presents a defensible position.

- Provide evidence to support your line of reasoning.

- Explain how the evidence supports your line of reasoning.

- Use appropriate grammar and punctuation in communicating your argument.

Your Task in the Argument Essay

The argument essay isn't a license to ramble on about your own personal views. If you want a high score, you have to do four things.

1. Take a definite position, so no one will question where you stand on the topic of the prompt.

2. Develop an argument that builds and moves forward instead of simply repeating the same point several times in different ways.

3. Support the points in your argument with evidence drawn from your own knowledge, reading, experiences, and observations.

4. Explain how your evidence supports your argument.

Lower-scoring essays tend to simply summarize what the author says in the passage, or wander aimlessly through an impassioned list of the student's own beliefs without giving any evidence to support them. As in the synthesis essay, the concept of a conversation with the author is helpful. If you were talking with this author and either agreeing, disagreeing, or giving a "yes, but" (qualifying) opinion, how would you argue your position? What evidence would you offer to back it up?

Tips for Saving Time

There are a few pre-writing strategies that can save you time. First, brainstorm the evidence you would like to use. The key here is to make your evidence as specific as possible. If you're using a personal anecdote, make it detailed and engaging. Provide specific details, such as dialogue, the scene, and your feelings. If you use an example from history, include as many names, dates, and events as you can.

Then ask yourself: What thesis statement does your evidence support? Based on your evidence, do you agree or disagree with the claim in the prompt? Your thesis may be more sophisticated. You might agree with the claim, but disagree with how the speaker defined a specific idea. Or you may disagree with the claim, except for in certain circumstances. If you can support a sophisticated thesis, go for it! If you're feeling insecure, opt for a simple thesis you know you can support and explain in your essay.

You can also save time by keeping your introductory paragraph simple. State the claim put forward in the prompt and then state your thesis. It can be as simple as that. Save your writing and revising time for making sure your evidence and explanations are thorough and well-crafted.

Argument Essay Checklist

Be sure to accomplish these four tasks in your argument essay!

Tip:

Make sure your evidence is as specific as possible.

Understanding the Rubric

These rubrics should be looking pretty familiar to you by now. Like the synthesis and rhetorical analysis rubrics, the argument rubric considers your essay in terms of your thesis (Row A), your evidence and explanation (Row B), and your sophistication (Row C).

Argument Essay Rubric					
Row A	**0 points:** • Has no defensible thesis • Has thesis that only restates the prompt • Has thesis that summarizes the issue with no apparent or coherent claim • Has a thesis that does not respond to the prompt		**1 point:** • Responds to the prompt with a thesis that presents a defensible position		
Row B	**0 points:** • Simply restates thesis (if present), repeats provided information, or offers information irrelevant to the prompt	**1 point:** • Provides evidence that is mostly general AND • Summarizes the evidence but does not explain how the evidence supports the argument	**2 points:** • Provides some specific, relevant evidence AND • Explains how some of the evidence supports the student's argument, but no line of reasoning is established, or the line of reasoning is faulty	**3 points:** • Provides specific evidence to support all claims in a line of reasoning AND • Explains how some of the evidence supports a line of reasoning	**4 points:** • Provides specific evidence to support all claims in a line of reasoning AND • Consistently explains how the evidence supports a line of reasoning
Row C	**0 points:** • Does not meet the criteria for one point	**1 point:** • Demonstrates sophistication of thought and/or a complex understanding of rhetorical sophistication			

Let's look at an example. We'll work through an analysis of the prompt and passage before you try writing your own essay in 40 minutes. Then read the student essay and evaluation that follow.

SAMPLE ESSAY #1—HERE'S HOW IT'S DONE

Here's a sample argument essay prompt.

The Prompt

Question 3

Suggested time—40 minutes.

(This question counts for one-third of the total essay section score.)

In Utilitarianism, John Stuart Mill promoted a theory of morality that postulated: "The creed which accepts as the foundation of morals, Utility, or the Greatest Happiness Principle, holds that actions are right in proportion as they tend to promote happiness, wrong as they tend to produce the reverse of happiness. By happiness is intended pleasure, and the absence of pain; by unhappiness, pain, and the privation of pleasure."

Mill argues that happiness is the foundation of morality, and that pursuing one's own happiness will necessarily lead to an ethical society for all. Write an essay that argues your position on the extent to which Mill's claims are valid. Use appropriate examples from your reading, experience, or observations to support your argument.

Analyzing the Prompt

If you've taken a lot of history courses, then you may have studied John Stuart Mill, and this would give you some information about context. If not, then the prompt still gives you rich material for a thoughtful argumentative essay.

Whatever you decide to argue, make your position perfectly clear in the first paragraph of your essay.

Your first task is to identify the author's main point, so you can decide what position you want to argue. In this case, the author's main point is clearly stated: "actions are right in proportion as they tend to promote happiness, wrong as they tend to produce the reverse of happiness." In the next sentence, Mill defines happiness ("pleasure") and unhappiness ("pain or the privation of pleasure").

You still have terms to define when you write your own essay, though. Happiness may equal pleasure, but one person's pleasure may be a matter of complete indifference to another person. What does Mill mean by "pleasure"? How will you define it?

You can see why this particular example is tailor-made to take you beyond the prompt. Here you can really demonstrate that you've thought deeply about the topic. Is "pleasure" the same thing for everyone? What are the consequences of individuals pursuing a "pleasure" that doesn't mean the same thing to all of them? If everyone pursued pleasure, what consequences might result for society? Does one person pursuing pleasure mean someone else has to experience pain?

As you think through those questions, what kind of evidence from your own experiences or reading pops into your mind? Which would be the strongest and the easiest to develop? That evidence should determine what stand you take on the argument. Remember that no reader knows or cares what you really think about an issue. You'll want to take the stand that's easiest for you to defend at that particular moment, based on the ideas that come to you. The most important things are that you have clearly decided how you feel about the issue and that you have the examples to back up your position.

> **I Remember When...**
> If you're describing your own experience or observation in the argument essay, you can use first-person narration.

Let's look at an essay that was written by a student under actual testing conditions.

A Student Essay: High Score

The essay on the next page is a successful response to this prompt. As you read it, pay particular attention to the writer's style. The vocabulary, grammar, and use of the quotation in the prompt reflect a high level of sophistication. Though the essay is short and feels as though the writer ran out of time, the examples used in the first body paragraph are highly specific and thus successful.

The introduction is slightly long, but notice how well this student addresses the two tasks set forth. Right away, the student states the author's claim ("the author…with ethical correctness") and takes a firm stand against it: "As history and literature…ethically responsible outcomes." The student's clear definition of pleasure ("humanity's greed, lust, and selfishness") both explains and reinforces this stand.

This is a great example of a clear, concise thesis. The student gives the reader a road map for the rest of the essay by first mentioning history and then literature, and follows that road map in the same order.

This is an excellent example of highly specific evidence drawn from the writer's knowledge of history. Pay attention to how well the writer handles the verb tenses. Importantly, the writer uses the present tense when addressing the author's/text's claim: "the author advances," "it assumes," "achievements often arise," and so on. The student uses the past tense only when presenting historical facts in the second paragraph. One of the common grammatical errors that students make in AP essays is using improper verb tense shifts.

The conclusion is weak and seems tacked on. It would have been stronger if it reminded the reader of the evidence brought in to support the student's stand against Mill's claim.

In John Stuart Mill's work Utilitarianism, the author advances a theory of morality that associates "the promotion of pleasure and the prevention of pain" with ethical correctness. While the pursuit of happiness can sometimes lead to a path of moral righteousness, Mill's claim is flawed in that it assumes hedonism will inherently bring positive results. By championing any action that produces pleasure, Mill condones humanity's greed, lust, and selfishness; three traits that are clearly immoral. As history and literature have demonstrated, pursuing goals motivated purely by self-interest does not lead to ethically responsible outcomes. Furthermore, the greatest achievements often arise when people readily eschew pleasure to attain a nobler end.

During the second half of the nineteenth century, a number of technological advances made the American economy blossom and helped to make the nation a world power. Eager to enjoy the pleasures made possible by great wealth, entrepreneurs and businessmen sought to increase profits and lower costs in any possible way. Workers were paid abysmally low wages, conditions were highly unsafe, and monopolies were commonplace. Though the heads of "Big Business" clearly adhered to Mill's "Greatest Happiness Principle," their actions were highly unethical. Their pleasure came at the expense of the poor and created a polarized society. In contrast, patriots seeking independence from England a century before, gladly relinquished the "absence of pain" afforded by accepting the status quo. Despite the great "privation of pleasure" brought about by the Revolutionary War, the patriots achieved their lofty goal of freedom, a morally desirable outcome. Evidently, seeking happiness does not necessarily entail finding "what is right and good."

F. Scott Fitzgerald's portrait of the Roaring Twenties, The Great Gatsby, examines hedonism and reaches a conclusion much different than Mill's. Jay Gatsby pursues pleasure in the form of rekindling a relationship with a former love, Daisy. Following utilitarian principles, seeking the desirable outcome should be an ethically sound choice. However, it instead leads Gatsby to engage in questionable business and to court a married woman, two clear violations of ethical standards. Clearly, morality based on pleasure is an unsound principle.

How would this essay score?

- Thesis—1: The essay addresses the prompt with a defensible thesis.

- Evidence and Commentary—3: The writer provides specific examples that support the argument and delivers some explanation as to how the evidence supports the argument.

- Sophistication—1: The writing style is formal, persuasive, and crafts a nuanced argument.

Total Score: 5

SAMPLE ESSAY #2—GIVING IT ANOTHER TRY

Let's try another one. Again, now that you're comfortable with the process for writing the argument essay, try writing this one on your own before you look at the student's essay.

The Prompt

Question 3

Suggested time—40 minutes.

(This question counts for one-third of the total essay section score.)

The formerly enslaved abolitionist Frederick Douglass (1818–1895) wrote, "Once you learn to read, you will be forever free."

Write an essay that argues your position on the relationship between literacy and freedom in the world today. Use appropriate examples from your reading, experience, or observations to support your argument.

Student Essay: Low Score

This essay has significant flaws in both content and style and would earn a low score. The most serious problem is the absence of a strong connection between literacy and freedom. The quote in the prompt establishes a cause-effect relationship between literacy and freedom. However, the essay never addresses whether or not that cause-effect relationship is accurate. This is not an easy concept, and many students would struggle to find good, specific examples to bridge a connection between these ideas.

High-scoring essays on the AP English Language and Composition Exam develop specific examples and then carefully connect them to the issue at hand. They also demonstrate a depth of thought and complexity that is mostly absent in this essay. As you write your own essays, be sure to have clear, stable definitions of the essential terms (in this case, "literacy" and "freedom") in mind and don't be afraid to talk about how complex the terms can be.

This introduction would have been strong had the writer taken the time to paraphrase the Douglas quote or define "forever free," a complicated idea. Instead, the writer makes unsubstantiated and uncomfortable assumptions about literacy rates in the United States, India, and China.

This attempted thesis doesn't directly address the relationship between literacy and freedom. While it assumes that increases in literacy are associated with increase in freedom, it's actually about the need for literacy programs in developing nations.

The student makes some awkward errors in style and diction, which detract from the overall effect.

What does this mean? How would literacy have made enslaved people more free"? How did illiteracy help slavers "keep control of them"? While literacy in developing nations and in American enslavement could be excellent examples, they are not made specific or relevant in this essay.

The essay does provide some examples and attempted to address the relationship between literacy and freedom, so it would at least earn some points.

Frederick Douglass once wrote, "Once you learn to read, you will be forever free" and this is true of the modern world. Though everyone in America can read, alot of people in the world can't read today and that's a serious problem for them. There are too many people in places like India and China who can't read and this illiteracy is holding them back. If we would have more programs to teach literacy to people in these developing nations, then we would have more literacy and therefore more freedom for all.

One reason I think there should be more literacy is that you need to educate children early on in their educational experience, otherwise, they will not learn what they need to succeed. Once the children in a given country achieve literacy, then the country can also improve the quality of life and the children can teach there parents how to read when they return home from school. This would help the parents to find better jobs and allow for more financial freedom for the family. Also, if the people in China and India learned English, they could get jobs using their new skills in English.

Another reason why I think literacy increases freedom is because literacy is the key concept to the development of political freedom. When Frederick Douglass was enslaved in America, Black people were held against their will and deprived of literacy. They were not only physically held, but also held back from other freedoms, like if the enslaved people had learned to read, though, they would have been more free and this would have threatened the so-called masters. The deprivation of literacy was a means of control.

In conclusion, literacy is the key to freedom around the world. As the examples of India and enslavement have demonstrated, freedom is possible for people who have a chance to read the way we do.

How would this essay score?

- Thesis—0: The thesis does not address the prompt.

- Evidence and Commentary—2: The writer provides some specific evidence, but doesn't establish a clear line of reasoning.

- Sophistication—0: The essay contains multiple grammatical errors and lacks nuance and persuasion.

Total Score: 2

Now let's take a look at a more successful essay, which was also written by a student under time constraints.

Student Essay: High Score

This essay is an obvious success and would earn a high score on the real AP exam. The student not only provided specific answers to the question at hand but also offered a nuanced assessment of the relationship between literacy and freedom. In fact, the student took pains to define multiple senses of the word *freedom* (intellectual, political, etc.) throughout the paper. The examples were specific, detailed, and relevant to the topic at hand.

The student begins by briefly recounting a personal history of literacy and how literacy empowered the student to develop reading skills. This personal anecdote is successful due to its specificity (it goes so far as to name the exact books the student read) and relevance.

Though written from a first-person perspective, this is a successful thesis that articulates the relationship between reading and freedom.

The first body paragraph explicitly connects increasing literacy with newfound political and religious freedom during the Protestant Reformation. Notice how the student carefully introduces each example and then adds as much relevant, specific information as possible.

The body paragraph discusses another highly specific and relevant example, showing yet another dimension of the complex link between literacy and freedom.

The fluid prose and elegant transitions also yield a high score. The range of vocabulary is good, but not exceptional—it never needs to be to get a high score on this test. Offer the readers as wide a range of vocabulary as you can, but focus on writing a good essay as you execute your response.

Literacy is something we take for granted in America. Most children learn to read at an early age and receive formal education until they are eighteen years old. During this time, they develop a deep understanding of their own language, both in its written and spoken forms. I remember when I first learned to read and how it made me feel so empowered over my younger sister, who hadn't learned yet. As my teachers encouraged me in elementary school I grew to enjoy reading adventure stories and then much harder books. In my AP English class this year, my teacher Mrs. Lasko assigned extremely challenging books, such as Paradise Lost, Gulliver's Travels, and Lord of the Flies. In all these cases, literacy empowered me to feel more and more intellectually free and to explore new ideas through reading.

But literacy does more than just free our minds: it is the key to bringing about political and economic freedom for ordinary people. There are many times in history when increasing literacy allowed people to experience a new kind of political freedom. For example, during the Protestant Reformation, ordinary people began to read because the printing press allowed books to be printed quickly rather than copied by hand. As the people began to read the Bible for themselves, they developed their own interpretations about theology and they challenged the teachings of the Catholic Church. People also read political pamphlets and were empowered to overthrow the leaders in power during that time. These kinds of political pamphlets, which only work when the majority of the population can read, have formed the basis of many political movements in the modern era.

In women's history, too, increasing literacy has brought about an increase in political freedoms. For centuries, few women could read or write and thus they were denied freedoms we now consider basic: the freedom to vote, the freedom to hold political office, the freedom to represent oneself in court. When we think of the movement for women's suffrage a century ago, how could the suffragettes have succeeded if they did not have a largely literate population of women to support them? As women learned to read in large numbers, they began to develop the political tools necessary to fight for their own freedom. In this way, literacy was a prerequisite to real political freedom for millions of women around the world.

When Frederick Douglass wrote of literacy and freedom, he was speaking of real freedom from the bondage of enslavement. For him, the power to read and write played a role in his abolitionist activities. But as I have discussed in this essay, literacy can bring about more than just freedom from enslavement; it can free us to think for ourselves, determine our own theologies, and fight for real political freedom. And whether it is African Americans, children, the poor, or just ordinary people, reading can transform the lives of those with less power. Literacy is thus a direct cause of freedom, both in the distant historical past and in the future of our constantly evolving world.

How would this essay score?

- Thesis—1: The thesis is defensible and relevant, and the argument develops complexity over the course of the essay.

- Evidence and Commentary—4: The writer uses a variety of highly relevant examples and consistently explains how they support the argument.

- Sophistication—1: The writer makes use of fluid prose and elegant transitions.

Total Score: 6

Study Break!
You're about halfway through your review! Before you dive into Part V, be sure to give yourself some downtime to let your brain absorb the information you've been studying.

COMING UP...

In this chapter and the two preceding chapters, you've seen a range of essay examples. In the next part of this book, you'll learn (or review) the important aspects of formal training in rhetoric and composition that will prepare you to craft essays that equal—or exceed—the ones that you've examined so far.

REFLECT

Think about what you've learned in Part IV, and respond to the following questions:

- How long will you spend on multiple-choice questions?

- How will you change your approach to multiple-choice questions?

- What is your multiple-choice guessing strategy?

- How much time will you spend on the first essay? The second? The third?

- What will you do before you begin writing an essay?

- How will you change your approach to the essays?

- Will you seek further help, outside of this book (such as from a teacher, tutor, or the AP Students website), on how to approach multiple-choice questions, the essays, or a pacing strategy?

Go Online!
Check us out on YouTube for test-taking tips and techniques to help you ace your next exam at www.youtube.com/ThePrincetonReview.

Part V
Content and Skill Review for the AP English Language and Composition Exam

HOW TO USE THE CHAPTERS IN THIS PART

You may need to come back to the following chapters more than once. Your goal is to familiarize yourself with the potential content of the exam, and a single reading of a chapter may not be sufficient. At the end of each chapter, you will have an opportunity to reflect on how well you have grasped the content of that chapter.

Chapter 8: Rhetorical Situation

This chapter explores how writers develop an argument within a particular situation, considering the exigence, audience, purpose, and context of their message. This chapter will explain how to use the rhetorical diamond as a short-cut while you're reading passages and preparing to write free-response questions on the exam.

Chapter 9: Claims and Evidence

This chapter considers how writers present claims, counter arguments, and themes within a text. It also describes the relationship between claims and evidence in a reading passage. After reading this chapter, you'll be able to evaluate the efficacy of a writer's argument, and the extent to which they appropriately substantiate their claims.

Chapter 10: Reasoning and Organization

This chapter describes various methods of organizing reasoning and claims within an argument, and how an overall thesis forms over the course of the text. You'll be able to describe a text's overall coherency, and, most importantly, if a text accomplishes its ultimate purpose.

Chapter 11: Style

This chapter includes a nitty-gritty crash course in the mechanics of writing. It reviews the fundamentals of syntax and diction, as well as the more sophisticated elements of figurative language you'll need to ace the AP exam. After reading this chapter, you'll be able to describe how writers use style to develop tone, contributing to the overall efficacy of their argument.

Chapter 8
Rhetorical Situation

THE GOOD NEWS AND THE BAD NEWS ABOUT THE AP ENGLISH LANGUAGE AND COMPOSITION EXAM

The Good News

While the title of this exam allows people to differentiate between this test and the AP English *Literature* & Composition Exam, it's still somewhat misleading. The AP English *Language* & Composition Exam is not a language exam—at least not in the sense that you may think. For example, it is possible not to know the difference between a gerund and a present participle—or even a gerund and a giraffe—and still score a 5 on this exam.

In the multiple-choice section of the exam, test-writers will attempt to evaluate your ability to analyze how writers use language to explain or to argue; in the free-response, or essay, section they will expect *you* to use language to explain or to argue. Naturally, you should avoid making egregious errors in grammar or usage on the test, but don't get hung up on the rules of language as you study. If you're considering taking the AP exam, your language skills are probably sufficient for the task. Now, you may be wondering what *is* tested on the exam. The answer is *composition*, and we'll spend Chapters 9 through 11 of this book reviewing all you need to know about composition to be fully prepared for the test.

The Bad News

Now for the bad news. Despite the test's lack of emphasis on the rules of language, there are some aspects of language that we must examine here to make sure you're ready for test day. We'll start by discussing rhetoric and what rhetorical strategy is. We'll move on to diction, denotation and connotation, and syntax. Then we'll discuss the many types of figurative language, and then circumlocution and euphemism. We will review paradox, rhetorical questions, irony and satire, and style, tone, and mood. Finally, we'll spend a little time on classical appeals and theme.

WHAT IS RHETORIC?

Language does a lot of things: it communicates, it entertains, it preserves information, and it shapes our world view. When we talk about *rhetoric*, we are talking about language as a means of persuasion. More specifically, rhetoric refers to the strategies an author uses to impact an audience and persuade them of a specific idea.

There's a template you can use to help you start to analyze an author's use of rhetoric:

The author uses **X**, which accomplishes **Y** and persuades the **audience** of **Z**.

Tip:
Feel free to use this sentence template in your rhetorical analysis essay! It could be the start of a strong thesis, or it could help you in your explanations.

Let's take a look at what each of these variables represents:

X: This variable represents the specific **rhetorical strategies** an author uses. An author might use a metaphor or a simile, or they might use formal diction or very casual diction. The writer of a published text might use graphics and art. A public speaker might use rhythm, rhyme, or well-known quotations. This chapter reviews the rhetorical strategies you should be able to identify and use yourself on the AP exam.

Y: This variable refers to how the rhetorical strategies in the text **impact the audience**. A catchy title is a rhetorical strategy designed to capture the audience's attention. Verbal irony is often used to make the audience laugh. One metaphor might help illustrate a complex idea; another metaphor might make the audience feel sad. Aristotle thought about audience impact in terms of appeals to credibility, emotion, and logic. (More on that in this chapter too!)

Audience: Audience refers to the **individuals the speaker is trying to persuade**. More generally, it is the people who read (or hear, in the case of a speech) a text. Take this book as an example. Its primary audience is students preparing for the AP Language and Composition Exam. Some students are probably already enrolled and studying for the exam. Other students might be unsure of whether or not they want to take the course and are looking for more general information. The audience may also include AP English Language and Composition teachers and parents curious about what their students are learning. (While you should always consider different groups within the audience, there are times when it is appropriate to use "audience" more generally.)

Z: This variable represents a text's **theme** or **argument**. This is a developed idea an author wants to convey. In other words, the theme is what the author is trying to persuade the audience of. A complex text can contain many themes. For example, themes of this chapter center around the importance of being able to identify rhetorical strategies, the importance of describing how different rhetorical strategies impact an audience, and the importance of identifying themes in a text.

As an example, let's consider this excerpt. Use the template above to analyze the following text:

> *This passage is excerpted from a status update posted to social media upon the loss of a baseball game.*

> Our left fielder couldn't hit the floor if he fell out of bed! After striking out twice (once with the bases loaded!), he grounded into a double-play. My grandmother runs faster than he does! In the eighth inning, he misjudged a routine fly ball, which brought in the winning run. What a jerk! Why didn't the club trade him last week when it was still possible? What's wrong with you guys?

Tip:
Start analyzing by identifying rhetorical strategies in the passage.

There are many different but accurate ways to analyze this excerpt. In the examples below, test yourself by identifying the rhetorical strategy, audience impact, audience, and theme.

- The author uses exclamatory sentences, which creates a sense of alarm and attempts to persuade anyone reading that the left fielder needs to be replaced immediately.

- The author compares the left fielder to his grandmother, which illustrates how slow the left fielder is and attempts to persuade club managers to trade the left fielder.

- The author calls the left fielder a "jerk," which conveys anger to the club managers and attempts to persuade them to trade ineffective players when they can.

So, that's the big picture rhetorical analysis—identifying the choices a speaker makes when crafting an argument and considering the extent to which those choices successfully impact the audience.

It may sound simple, but testing a student's ability to identify and analyze rhetoric, as well as employ it themselves, is not so easy. When designing the AP Language and Composition Exam, the College Board divides rhetoric into four "big ideas":

- rhetorical situation

- claims and evidence

- reasoning and organization

- style

In this and subsequent chapters, we will use these four ideas to guide our review of all you need to know to be prepared for the test.

Understanding the Rhetorical Situation

The **rhetorical situation** refers to the overall context in which an argument is given. Is the text you're assessing a political speech given by a suffragette at the turn of the 20th century? Is it a TV commercial trying to convince you to splurge on a new cell phone? Is it a political cartoon published digitally by a major international newspaper in 2022? All of these are examples of rhetoric, yet they come from wildly different sources, use different stylistic devices, and have different goals.

The big takeaway: Individuals write within a particular situation and make strategic writing choices based on that situation.

- To get a 5 on the AP exam, you are going to need to demonstrate that you can identify how other speakers work within their rhetorical situation. You will also need to demonstrate that you can work within your rhetorical situation, meaning that you will demonstrate your own abilities of persuasion as you respond to the essay questions.

Analyzing the Rhetorical Situation

In many ways, analyzing the rhetorical situation is the easiest part of the exam: most of the information you will need is provided for you on the exam itself, either as part of the prompt of the essay questions or as part of the explanatory text that precedes the written passages that accompany the multiple-choice questions.

To identify and analyze the elements of the rhetorical situation, we are going to use a baseball diamond as an explanatory metaphor.

Diamonds Are an AP Student's Best Friend

Make yourself a worksheet of the rhetorical diamond to fill out for the different texts you work with practicing for the test. Being able to quickly identify these elements of the rhetorical situation will be an enormous help on exam day!

- **Writer:** The writer is the creator of the text in question. Remember that "writer" and "author" are very broad terms. Rhetoric can be applied to all forms of communication, so "writer" can easily refer to a speaker, artist, musician, mathematician, or scientist. The writer can be an individual or a group, such as a newspaper's editorial board. The College Board defaults to the term "writer," but be as specific and accurate as you can when referring to the writers of the texts you address in your essays.

- **Audience:** The audience is composed of the individuals, or groups of individuals, that the argument reaches. Audiences may be very narrow, as in a conversation between an employee asking their boss for a raise, or very broad, as in an international news broadcast or a meme that goes viral online. When identifying the audience of a text, be sure to consider the beliefs, values, needs, and backgrounds of individuals as well as different groups therein. For example, when a politician makes a national address, they will generally face a friendly audience, those of the same political party, and a hostile audience, those of the opposing political party.

- **Context:** The context refers to the time, place, and occasion of the argument.

- **Purpose:** The purpose is what the writer *hopes* to accomplish. A writer who sends an invitation to a charity gala is hoping the recipient will buy a ticket, attend, and donate further. Keep in mind that writers may have more than one purpose.

- **Exigence:** An argument's exigence is that which initially inspired the writer to speak. Why this argument? Why now? What has triggered the argument or motivated the speaker? A legislator may introduce a bill for tighter gun control in response to a mass shooting. A teenager may want to argue for a later curfew in order to attend a formal dance. A technology company wants to run advertisements to sell the new version of its cell phone as soon as it launches.

- **Message:** The message describes that which is actually conveyed by the writer. Theoretically, when a writer is successful, the purpose and the message of the text are the same. Careful reading is important here: A text can have multiple messages that may or may not align with the text's purpose. Messages can be subtle or overt, intended or unintended. As the rhetoric scholar, it's your job to determine exactly what a text's message is and how it is conveyed.

Let's use our previous example of the disgruntled baseball player posting to social media to illustrate these concepts.

- **Writer:** A baseball player frustrated by the left fielder and the management of the baseball team.

- **Audience:** Anyone who has access to technology and follows this player on social media: friends, family, teammates, perhaps the left fielder. The direct address in the final question, "What's wrong with you guys?" suggests that members of the club's management team are among the intended audience.

- **Context:** A status update on social media, posted after the game in question.

- **Purpose:** To blame the left fielder for the loss of the game and encourage management to trade the player.

- **Exigence:** This was posted upon the loss of the game, so management could trade the player before the next game.

- **Message:** This player is angry and blames the left fielder for the loss of the game. This player wants the left fielder traded. The current management choices are ineffective and resulting in losses.

There are a few important things to notice here. First, there might be a lot of over-lapping details. Pay attention to any ideas or circumstances that are popping up over and over again. Second, you may need to make inferences or educated guesses if certain details are unstated. This is fine, but be sure to be clear about this in your writing. Use phrases like "presumably," "likely," or "one might assume that…" on the free-response questions so your reader can easily distinguish your inferences from that which is directly stated in the text or prompt.

Analyzing YOUR Rhetorical Situation

The AP exam is going to assess your ability to analyze the rhetorical situation in which writers are delivering their arguments. The readers of the written portion of the exam are likewise going to be assessing *your* ability to successfully convey an argument within *your* rhetorical situation, the AP exam.

As such, let's use the rhetorical diamond to think through exactly what this means for the three essays you will be writing as part of the AP exam.

- **Writer**—You, a high school student taking the AP Language and Composition Exam. No one will expect you to be an expert, but you will need to demonstrate an effective command of rhetoric and persuasive writing.

- **Audience**—The individuals grading your essays are high school and university English and writing instructors. What can we assume about their beliefs, attitudes, and needs? They value the written word and quality, accurate writing. They are also going to be grading A LOT of essays at once, meaning they will likely appreciate an exciting introduction or an essay that presents a distinctive voice or point of view.

- **Purpose**—You are trying to pass the AP exam, ideally scoring a six on each of the free-response questions. Make sure you're well-versed in the grading rubric to score as many points as possible.

- **Context**—Ideally, you're taking and doing well in AP Language and Composition. Hopefully you've written and read many practice essays and are well-versed in the task at hand.

- **Exigency**—You have 40 minutes to read and respond to the prompt. Take particular care to ensure your introductions and conclusions are appropriate to *your* rhetorical situation. This means taking particular care in your diction, syntax, and making sure the sophistication of your ideas is up to a collegiate level.

Chapter 9
Claims and
Evidence

CLAIMS AND EVIDENCE

Once you've assessed the rhetorical situation of a piece of writing, you're ready to start assessing the nuts and bolts of a writer's argument: the claims and evidence.

What is a claim?

A **claim** is an argument that the writer makes. Claims are thought-provoking, defensible statements that require evidence and explanation, as opposed to statements that are obvious, known facts. Consider the following examples:

- Statement—Monday occurs at the start of the week, and Friday occurs at the end of the week.

- Claim—Friday is a better day of the week than Monday.

The statement is a description of fact: Monday occurs earlier in the week than Friday. It isn't particularly interesting, and assuming that all parties involved are familiar with the same calendar system. There isn't much to argue about. The claim, however, states the writer's opinion, a personal value judgment that prefers Friday to Monday. This is an arguable, thought-provoking statement that necessitates evidence and explanation. Why is Friday better? For whom? There are a variety of explanations and reasonings that could substantiate this claim.

Keep in mind that not all claims are created equally. Some, such as the example above, are relatively simplistic. Others contain more nuance. These are called **qualified claims**. Consider the examples below:

- Students consider Friday to be the best day of the week, while teachers consider Monday to be the best day of the week.

- While Monday may be the most productive day of the week, Friday is the most fun.

While each of these statements present a different perspective, they add complexity to the claim at hand. The first considers different stakeholders, students and teachers, and how they have different attitudes toward the different days of the week. The second example specifies the idea of "better," as meaning either "productive" or "fun."

Tip:
As an exercise, define the thesis and outline the claims that writers make as you read various passages to prepare for the exam.

Most writing samples you'll be reading on the AP exam, and certainly the essays you'll be writing yourself, will have a **thesis statement**. The thesis is the main, overarching claim a writer seeks to defend or prove in a body of writing. Some of the passages will have a thesis statement that is directly stated in the text; others will have a thesis statement that is implied over the course of the text. Sometimes you will get very lucky, and the thesis will be clarified in the explanatory text or prompt that precedes the passage.

Make sure that in all three of the free-response essays, you provide a clear, concise thesis statement that guides the claims in your essay. Most often, your thesis will preview the series of claims you plan to present over the course of your essay. Take care to present nuanced qualified claims. Assuming you substantiate them effectively, they will score higher than simplistic claims.

Take the time to reread the sample essays presented in Chapters 5, 6, and 7. To what extent do you think they are effective? How would you revise the thesis statements that didn't receive full points? How would you add complexity to claims presented in simplistic, low-scoring essays?

What is evidence?

Evidence is that which a writer uses to prove or substantiate their claims. Evidence is a very broad category and includes: facts, data, anecdotes, analogies, statistics, examples, details, illustrations, expert opinions, personal observations, personal experiences, testimonies, and experiments. The AP exam will test your ability to identify and evaluate evidence, and your ability to use it yourself.

Let's consider the following example paragraph:

> Students consider Friday to be the best day of the week. In a recent survey conducted in my science class, 22 of the 30 students present agreed that Friday was the best day of the week. While this isn't an exhaustive study, it does reflect our culture here on campus. Club events, athletic events, and social events such as dances are more likely to occur on Friday than any other day of the week. Our student body president agrees: "I would happily be absent from school on a Wednesday, but I show up on Fridays no matter what!" While teachers might bemoan the lack of productivity from their distracted students, Friday is undoubtedly the most fun day of the week.

Hopefully you easily spotted the claim in this paragraph, that students consider Friday to be the best, most fun day of the week. Can you identify the three types of evidence this writer used to substantiate the claim?

- Data—*In a recent survey conducted in my science class, 22 of the 30 students present agreed that Friday was the best day of the week.*

- Examples—*Club events, athletic events, and social events such as dances are more likely to occur on Friday than any other day of the week.*

- Expert opinion—*Our student body president agrees: "I would happily be absent from school on a Wednesday, but I show up on Fridays no matter what!"*

Perhaps more importantly, how effective is this evidence? Is a survey conducted in a science class accurately reflective of the student body as a whole? Is 30 an adequate sample size? Are club events, athletic events, and social events the only examples of "fun" that the writer needs to consider? Is the student body president an appropriate "expert" in this situation?

On the exam, you're going to need to assess whether an argument contains sufficient evidence, and whether or not the evidence is sufficient in its quality and quantity to substantiate the argument. Further, you're going to need to show that you can effectively use evidence yourself. In fact, this is what the synthesis essay is all about. You will need to cite sources and effectively embed quotations and evidence into your writing. You will need to distinguish the quality of different sources, assessing them for bias and limitations as you go.

Analyzing Evidence

Beyond identifying evidence and assessing its quality, you will need to determine the impact that the evidence has on the audience. In other words, you will need to analyze the extent to which an author creates an effective argument. High-scoring example essays in Chapters 5, 6, and 7 will provide excellent examples of effective analysis.

There's an easy shortcut to use to get yourself started, and it comes to us courtesy of our friend Aristotle. Aristotle, the original rhetorician, described three "classical appeals" used in persuasion. Try not to be thrown off by the word "appeal," in this context, it means "ways to persuade." In other words, Aristotle defined three ways that evidence can impact an audience.

Classical Appeals

Aristotle identified three methods of appealing to an audience in order to persuade them to your point of view: *logos*, *pathos*, and *ethos*.

Logos is an appeal to reason and logic. An argument that uses logos to persuade needs to provide things like objective evidence, hard facts, statistics, or logical strategies such as cause and effect to back up its claim. (*Logos* is the root of our word "logic," which is a good way to remember which of the appeals this is!)

Ethos is an appeal to the speaker's credibility—whether they are to be believed on the basis of their character and expertise. For example, the prosecution in a murder trial might put a renowned psychiatrist on the stand to testify that the defendant is able to identify right and wrong and is thus capable of standing trial. Their argument would be using an appeal to *ethos* to persuade the jury (their audience) that the testimony of this expert is to be trusted. (*Ethos* is related to our word "ethics"— the principles of conduct that govern people and organizations and give them the authority to speak on certain topics.)

Pathos is an appeal to the emotions, values, or desires of the audience. Aristotle felt that, although ideally people would be persuaded by appeals to logic (*logos*, remember?), they would probably most often be persuaded by their emotions and beliefs instead. This is why, in that same murder trial, a defense attorney might tell the jury about the lonely childhood and difficult life of the defendant—he would be appealing to the *pathos* of the audience to convince them that his client should not be convicted. (*Pathos* is also the root of "pathetic," a word we use to describe something that is, shall we say, *suffering* from inferiority.)

Let's take a look at how we might use these appeals to analyze the evidence from our previous example:

- The writer uses both data and examples to appeal to the reader's sense of logic, that based on a survey and examples of extracurricular events, Friday must be the best day of the week.

- The writer further uses a quote from the student body president to appeal to the audience's sense of pathos, a desire to be part of the Friday fun. If the student body president wouldn't miss it, neither should we.

- Unfortunately, the writer fails to establish their ethos as a particularly credible speaker. Neither a survey of 30, nor a casual list of calendar activities, nor the opinion of a single student, provides an adequate representation of the attitudes of the student body as a whole.

A FEW MORE THOUGHTS ON THEME...

Confusingly, when you're dealing with passages presented on the exam, the term "thesis" is often used nearly synonymously with the term "theme." In this case, a **theme** is the overarching argument contained in the text; the theme may be stated explicitly or only suggested. A theme is not just an idea; it is *an idea that is developed,* often over the course of a chapter or an entire book. Usually, one can identify a central theme and several minor ones. Sometimes both are overtly stated, as in the example that follows:

> Many scholars agree that the central theme in *The Adventures of Huckleberry Finn* is the conflict between nature and civilization. But clearly, the book contains other themes, such as the worth of honor and the voyage of self-discovery.

Read the following passage, and see whether you can identify a central theme.

We now touch on civilization's most sensitive spot; it is an unpleasant task to raise one's voice against the folly of the day, against chimeras that have caused a downright epidemic.
Line
5   To speak against the absurdities of trade today means to expose oneself to anathemas, just as much as if one had spoken against the tyranny of the popes and the barons in the twelfth century. If it were a matter of choosing between two dangerous roles, I think it would be less dangerous
10   to offend a sovereign with bitter truths than to offend the mercantile spirit that now rules like a despot over civilization—and even over sovereigns!
And yet a superficial analysis will prove that our commercial systems defile and disorganize civilization and that
15   in trade, as in all other things, we are being led further and further astray.
The controversy on trade is barely half a century old and has already produced thousands of books, and yet the participants in the controversy have not seen that the trade

20 mechanism is organized in such a way that it is a slap in the
    face to all common sense. It has subordinated the whole of
    society to one class of parasitic and unproductive persons:
    the merchants. All the essential classes of society—the
    proprietor, the farmer, the manufacturer, and even the gov-
25 ernment—find themselves dominated by a non-essential,
    contingent class, the merchant, who should be their subor-
    dinate, their employed agent, removable and accountable,
    and who, nevertheless, directs and obstructs at will all the
    avenues of circulation.

It should not surprise you that the title of the essay that this passage is excerpted from is "On Trade." In his essay, the French socialist Charles Fourier develops a central theme: merchants, through trade, have both corrupted society and become its tyrants.

Identifying themes in a text is critical to both the multiple-choice and free-response sections of the text. In the analysis essay, your primary aim is to identify the speaker's theme and analyze how that theme was developed within the text.

Chapter 10
Reasoning and Organization

If Chapter 9 focuses on identifying the nuts and bolts of an argument, claims and evidence, this chapter examines how those nuts and bolts come together to form a fully functioning machine—a well-reasoned argument.

The exam will test your ability to describe the reasoning, organization, and development of an argument. You will be asked to consider questions such as: How are the paragraphs organized? Is there an adequate explanation of how the evidence supports the claims? Is the thesis presented up front, or does it develop over the course of the writing? What flaws may or may not exist in a writer's reasoning?

In the free-response essays, you'll need to demonstrate that you can effectively organize an argument yourself. Essay readers will want to see well-organized paragraphs containing a claim, evidence, and explanation. You'll need to transition fluidly between paragraphs, explaining the relationships between your ideas. You'll score particularly high if you demonstrate an ability to use repetition, synonyms, pronouns, and parallel sentence structure to develop ideas within your argument.

In this chapter, we will cover the most common rhetorical modes, or organization strategies, you're likely to encounter on the exam. Keep in mind that these are strategies you can use in the free-responses essays as well. We will also cover fallacies, or errors in logic, that you're likely to encounter on the exam. Ideally, you'll be able to avoid making these errors yourself.

WHAT ARE RHETORICAL MODES?

The rhetorical modes (or patterns) contained in this chapter are worth studying for two reasons. First, they will provide you with ready-made approaches for writing your essays on the exam, and second, the multiple-choice questions on the test also often include some of the rhetorical mode terminology.

As you prepare for the exam by taking practice tests, you'll see that 40 minutes is not much time in which to write a sophisticated essay, and the shortcuts you'll learn in this chapter will be invaluable in helping you write a great essay in the allotted time. However, you do not need to cram and memorize all the material in this section. If you read and understand the explanations and just make sure you retain the basics, you'll be comfortable enough with the process to do well on the exam.

Another important point to remember is that, more often than not, rhetorical modes are used in combination. Breaking them up into individual components is a somewhat arbitrary process—but for our purposes, it makes the material easier to understand. Let's begin.

CLASSIFICATION

How do you classify things? Well, you probably start by dividing up whatever you have into groups according to certain characteristics. For example, if you wanted to explain "new music" to someone, you might divide the artists into groups by type (female vocalists, male vocalists, and bands) and classify the groups by genre (heavy metal, punk rock, alternative, and so on). This would make the material easier for someone to understand because it would be organized. In other words, *we classify to more easily analyze and explain.*

When you place things into categories on the AP English Language and Composition Exam, avoid creating classifications that overlap. For example, it would not make sense to classify your favorite foods in the following way: sweets, barbecued meats, vegetables, and chocolates; logically, the last group (chocolates) is a smaller subset of the first group (sweets). The huge benefit of using classification is that it creates a clear foundation for other rhetorical modes, such as compare-contrast and cause-effect.

All of this boils down to the following: classification is nearly the same thing as organization. And organization is important. As you know by now, the directions in the free-response section of the AP English Language and Composition Exam request that you write "a well-organized essay." It may seem obvious that the test-writers would request this of you—but then you'd be surprised how poorly organized many of the AP essays that students write are. Classify before you write.

> There is almost always more than one way to classify things. Right now, you may group your teachers as being either cool or uncool. Later, it's more likely that you'll classify them according to what they helped you learn: the new categories may be teachers who inspired you, teachers who taught you the most, teachers who taught you about life, and teachers who should not have been teachers.

Aristotle liked to classify, and he did so quite often. Some of his classifications have stood the test of time, including the one below, which is the beginning of Part 6 of an essay entitled "Categories."

>   Quantity is either discrete or continuous (…). Instances of discrete quantities are number and speech; instances of continuous quantities are lines, surfaces, solids, and, besides these, time and place.
>
> *Line*
> 5   In the case of the parts of a number, there is no common boundary at which they join. For example: two fives make ten, but the two fives have no common boundary, but are separate; the parts three and seven also do not join at any boundary. Nor, to generalize, would it ever be possible in
> 10   the case of number that there should be a common boundary among the parts; they are always separate. Number, therefore, is a discrete quantity.
>   The same is true of speech. That speech is a quantity is evident: for it is measured in long and short syllables.

15 I mean here that speech which is vocal. Moreover, it is a
    discrete quantity for its parts have no common boundary.
    There is no common boundary at which the syllables join,
    but each is separate and distinct from the rest.
        A line, on the other hand, is a continuous quantity, for it
20 is possible to find a common boundary at which its parts
    join. In the case of the line, this common boundary is the
    point; in the case of the plane, it is the line, for the parts of
    the plane have also a common boundary. Similarly you can
    find a common boundary in the case of the parts of a solid,
25 namely either a line or a plane.
        Space and time also belong to this class of quantities.
    Time, past, present, and future, forms a continuous whole.
    Space, likewise, is a continuous quantity; for the parts of
    a solid occupy a certain space, and these have a common
30 boundary; it follows that the parts of space also, which are
    occupied by the parts of the solid, have the same common
    boundary as the parts of the solid. Thus, not only time, but
    space also, is a continuous quantity, for its parts have a
    common boundary.

Here, Aristotle's division of quantity into two categories (discrete and continuous) makes sense. The examples that he uses to illustrate the nature of his categories reveal a great deal about his interests: time, space, language, and mathematics. This is a well-organized passage; the categories are well-defined and Aristotle clearly explains how the members of each category have been classified.

When and How to Use Classification

- When you're asked to analyze and explain something, classification will be very useful.

- Make sure you have a central idea (thesis).

- Sort your information into meaningful groups. Are there enough elements in each group to allow you to write a convincing, useful paragraph? Sometimes you'll find that you need to combine categories.

- Make sure you have a manageable number of categories—three or four. Remember that you have only about 40 minutes to plan and execute each essay.

- Make sure the categories (or the elements in the categories) do not overlap.

- Before writing, make sure the categories and central idea (thesis) are a good fit. Sometimes you'll want to modify your thesis statement based on the categories that you've found.

- As you write, do not justify your classification unless this is somehow necessary to address a very bizarre free-response question. Justify your thesis, not your categories.

Sample Classification Question

Write a short essay in which you analyze the different methods a teacher uses to convey information to their class. In your essay, be sure to use classification to organize your ideas. Once you've written your essay, show it to your AP teacher or tutor. You might want to show it to a fellow AP student for peer review.

Drill: Reflect on How You Could Use Classification to Address the Following Topics

As you read each of the topics, think about how you would organize your essay in terms of classification. Come up with a possible thesis (central idea), and plan how you could categorize the information you have on these topics into three or four meaningful divisions.

TOPIC 1:   Television commercials

TOPIC 2:   Movies

TOPIC 3:   Students

TOPIC 4:   Cars

EXAMPLE OR ILLUSTRATION

Our first rhetorical mode consists of using specific examples to illustrate an idea. Now, this may seem like a pretty simple idea, but one of the most common mistakes students make when writing their AP English Language and Composition essays is to use poor examples. Remember that all examples are not created equal. If you use poor illustrative examples, your ideas will be communicated much less clearly and effectively than if you'd used solid, appropriate ones. In writing these essays, your principal goal is clarity.

Let's take a look at how two speakers used examples to illustrate key points within their speeches. The following excerpt comes from a 2015 speech then-President Barack Obama made to the United Nations Climate Change conference. See if you can spot Obama's claim and the examples he uses to support it.

> I've come here personally, as the leader of the world's largest economy and the second largest emitter, to say that the United States of America not only recognizes our role
> *Line* in creating this problem, we embrace our responsibility to
> 5 do something about it.
> Over the last seven years, we've made ambitious invest-ments in clean energy, and ambitious reductions in our carbon emissions. We've multiplied wind power threefold, and solar power more than twentyfold, helping create parts
> 10 of America where these clean power sources are finally cheaper than dirtier, conventional power. We've invested in energy efficiency in every way imaginable. We've said no

to infrastructure that would pull high-carbon fossil fuels
from the ground, and we've said yes to the first ever set of
15 national standards limiting the amount of carbon pollution
our power plants can release into the sky.

President Obama clearly lays out his claim: America acknowledges its role in climate change and pledges to take action to fight it. The second paragraph provides specific, concrete examples of actions the U.S. government has taken to address climate change. Obama gives his list of evidence more impact by using poetic devices such as anaphora and parallel structure to hold the audience's attention and emphasize the quantity of actions that have already been taken.

Another example comes from a speech by British suffragette Emmeline Pankhurst. In 1913, she gave a speech addressing those who accused her of being overly aggressive in her tactics to forward the women's rights movement. As you read, see if you can spot the claim Pankhurst makes and the example she uses to support it.

We entirely prevented stockbrokers in London from
telegraphing to stockbrokers in Glasgow and vice versa:
for one whole day telegraphic communication was entirely
Line stopped. I am not going to tell you how it was done. I am
5 not going to tell you how the women got to the mains
and cut the wires; but it was done. It was done, and it
was proved to the authorities that weak women, suffrage
women, as we are supposed to be, had enough ingenuity
to create a situation of that kind. Now, I ask you, if women
10 can do that, is there any limit to what we can do except the
limit we put upon ourselves?

Here, Pankhurst argues that women have the ingenuity and capacity to create a situation that threatens international economics. Her evidence? She cites the example of women cutting off communication between London and Glasgow, effectively freezing the stock exchange. She uses other devices as well, such as verbal irony (calling the suffragettes "weak," when she means the exact opposite, that they are strong and dangerous) and a rhetorical question to underscore her point: The suffragettes present a threat to the patriarchal status quo.

Just as it is important to choose relevant, convincing examples to substantiate your own ideas, it is essential to constantly evaluate the examples that others use in their attempts to explain or to convince.

> Tricksters, dogmatists, and charlatans usually illustrate their positions with scanty, inappropriate details. Give critical thought to the nature and perspective of the author of a text.

When and How to Use Example (Illustration)

- Use examples that your reader (the person who reads your essays) will identify with and understand. Do not assume that the AP reader has seen the latest teen cult film or knows any pop culture icons younger than Britney Spears.

- Draw your examples from "real life," "real" culture (literature, art, classical music, and so on), and well-known folklore.

- Make sure the example really does illustrate your point. Don't use a fancy example just to show off your knowledge; find ones that really work!

- Introduce your examples using transitions, such as *for example, for instance, case in point,* and *consider the case of.*

- A single example that is perfectly representative can serve to illustrate your point.

- A series of short, less-perfect (but still relevant) examples can, by their accumulation, serve to illustrate your point.

- The ideal approach is to construct a well-developed, representative example supported by several shorter examples.

- Remember that you are in control of what you write. As you brainstorm, discard examples that may disprove your point. Your AP essays will have little or nothing to do with your beliefs or with a balanced examination of an issue. You will be defending a point of view (synthesis and argument essays) or explaining something (rhetorical analysis essay)—don't feel as if you have to be fair to all sides of an argument; your aim is to get your point across.

- Quality is more important than quantity; poorly chosen examples detract significantly from your presentation. Make sure examples are detailed, specific, and concrete.

When you're drafting free-response essays, use the basic rhetorical modes to guide you. Start by classifying your ideas and organizing them into paragraphs. Then, brainstorm examples and/or analogies to support and illustrate your ideas.

Sample Question for Using Examples

Write a thoughtful and carefully constructed essay in which you use specific examples to defend, challenge, or qualify the assertion that Hollywood movies are a reflection of a decaying society.

Drill: Reflect on How You Could Use Examples to Address the Following Topics

As you read each of the topics listed below, make a list of five examples you could use to support them. Are your examples all relevant? Do they support just this side of the argument? Treat each as the basis for your thesis statement in a practice free-response question.

TOPIC 1: High schools unwittingly encourage students to cheat.

TOPIC 2: Studying the humanities is important.

TOPIC 3: A person's attitude toward diversity reveals much about that person.

ANALOGY

Although analogies are not that useful in argumentative writing, they *are* useful in expository writing—this means that analogies may be useful when you write your rhetorical analysis essay for this test.

Analogies are sometimes used to explain things that are difficult to understand by comparing them with things that are easier to understand. Let's say that you want to explain how a well-run corporation works. You might explain that it functions like a football team. In both cases there are owners or stockholders. In the corporation, there's a CEO, who is similar to the coach of a football team. The CEO directs the managers (or vice presidents), just as the coach directs the assistant coaches; these work directly with the employees—the players. When an employee doesn't heed directions, the success of the enterprise is put at risk, just like when a player fails to execute a block or a tackle. The most important thing about using analogies is that you choose one that will be readily understood by your audience.

> Think of an **analogy** as a comparison used to explain something.

In this case, if the reader knows nothing about football, this analogy may do more harm than good.

You can also use an analogy to explain something that's abstract by comparing it with something that's concrete. Throughout history, people have used analogies to explain their god or gods. Christians explain God, for example, through analogy. They say that God is like a father who loves his children and, thus, both punishes and rewards them. The only difference is that they consider God's judgment to be perfect. They believe that God is like a father in that both are good, but the difference is that God is *perfectly* good.

The most famous philosophical analogy serves as the basis for Plato's "allegory of the cave." The analogy purportedly evolved from a conversation between Socrates and Glaucon.

> Imagine human beings living in an underground cave;
> here they have been from their childhood, and they have
> their legs and necks chained so that they cannot move and
> *Line* can only see before them, being prevented by the chains
> 5 from turning round their heads. Above and behind them,
> a fire is blazing at a distance, and between the fire and the
> prisoners there is a raised way; and there is a low wall built
> along the way, like the screen which marionette players
> have to hide them and over which they show the puppets.
> 10 Men are passing along the wall (and screened by the
> wall) and are carrying all sorts of things and animals made
> of wood and stone and various materials that appear over
> the wall. Some of them are talking, others are silent.
> Like ourselves, they see only their own shadows, or the
> 15 shadows of one another, or the shadows of the things and
> animals, which the fire throws on the opposite wall of the
> cave.
> And if the human beings were able to converse with one
> another, would they not suppose that they were naming
> 20 what was actually before them (even though they were
> seeing only shadows of those things)?
> And suppose further that the prison had an echo which
> came from the other side, would they not be sure to fancy
> when one of the passers-by spoke that the voice which they
> 25 heard came from the passing shadow?
> To them, I said, the truth would be literally nothing but
> the shadows of the images.

This is only part of the analogy, but you probably get the idea. Socrates uses this analogy to explain that we think that we see things just as they really are in our world, but that we are seeing only reflections of a greater truth, an abstraction that we fail to grasp. The cave is our world; the shadows are the objects and people that we "see." We are like the prisoners, for we are not free to see what creates the shadows; the truth, made up of ideal forms, is out in the light.

When and How to Use Analogy

- Use analogy for expository writing (explanation).

- Do not use analogy for argumentative writing (argumentation).

- Use analogy to explain something that is abstract or difficult to understand.

- Make sure your audience will readily understand your "simple" or concrete subject.

Sample Analogy Question

Write an essay in which you explain the process of applying to college. Use analogy when appropriate. Once you've written your essay, show it to your AP teacher or tutor. You might want to show it to a fellow AP student for peer review.

Drill: Reflect on How You Could Use Analogy to Address the Following Topics

As you read each topic, think of it as the basis for the thesis of an expository essay. Come up with a simpler subject that you can use as an analogy for this more complex topic. Write down a basic plan for an essay.

> TOPIC 1: The way your school functions
>
> TOPIC 2: The benefits of honesty

MOVING ON...

In this chapter we discussed three rhetorical modes: example, classification, and analogy. Make sure you are as familiar with these basic types of rhetoric as you are with, say, doing the laundry. If you get into good habits now when using these rhetorical modes, you'll be much better off on test day!

Further proving how useful these modes will be, we guarantee that both your expository and argumentative essay questions will fit into some combination of these modes.

Of course, remember to plan your essay before you begin writing. It often helps to write your thesis statement along with this plan so that you can keep in mind whether the parts of your plan are relevant to your central idea. This will ensure that you write the best organized, most coherent essay you can.

Now that we've covered the three basic rhetorical modes, let's move on to review a few complex modes.

NARRATION

A narrative is a story in which pieces of information are arranged in chronological order. Narration can be an effective expository technique. Decades after her experience in a Japanese internment camp, Jeanne Wakatsuki Houston decided to narrate her experiences before, during, and immediately after imprisonment. She did not want to tell the story just for the story's sake; she wanted to relay her experience to the public to exorcise personal demons and to raise public awareness about this period in history. Here is a passage from this personal narrative. The passage describes the period after the Wakatsuki family had lost their house in Ocean Park, California, when they were forced into detention.

My own family, after three years of mess hall living,
collapsed as an integrated unit. Whatever dignity or feeling
of filial strength we may have known before December
Line   1941 was lost, and we did not recover it until many years
5   after the war, not until after Papa died and we began to
come together, trying to fill the vacuum his passing left in
all our lives.

The closing of the camps, in the fall of 1945, only aggra-
vated what had begun inside. Papa had no money then and
10   could not get work. Half of our family had already moved
to the East Coast, where jobs had opened up for them. The
rest of us were relocated into a former defense workers'
housing project in Long Beach. In that small apartment
there never was enough room for all of us to sit down for
15   a meal. We ate in shifts, and I yearned all the more for our
huge round table in Ocean Park.

Soon after we were released I wrote a paper for a
seventh-grade journalism class, describing how we used to
hunt grunion before the war. The whole family would go
20   down to Ocean Park Beach after dark, when the grunion
were running, and build a big fire on the sand. I would
watch Papa and my older brothers splash through the
moonlit surf to scoop out the fish, then we'd rush back to
the house where Mama would fry them up and set the siz-
25   zling pan on the table, with soy sauce and horseradish, for
a midnight meal. I ended the paper with this sentence: "The
reason I want to remember this is because I know we'll
never be able to do it again."

You may be asked to use personal narrative when writing your essays on the AP
English Language and Composition Exam; and you will certainly be asked to
analyze narratives that employ this rhetorical mode.

In the following passage, Booker T. Washington uses narrative to explain how his
view on education developed. Watch for changes between the first- and third-
person style of narration.

When a mere boy, I saw a young colored man, who had
spent several years in school, sitting in a common cabin in
the South, studying a French grammar. I noted the poverty,
Line   the untidiness, the want of system, and thrift that existed
5   about the cabin, notwithstanding his knowledge of French
and other academic subjects. Another time, when riding on
the outer edges of a town in the South, I heard the sound of
a piano coming from a cabin of the same kind. Contriving
some excuse, I entered and began a conversation with the
10   young colored woman who was playing, and who had
recently returned from a boarding-school, where she had
been studying instrumental music among other things.
Despite the fact that her parents were living in a rented
cabin, eating poorly cooked food, surrounded with poverty,
15   and having almost none of the conveniences of life, she had
persuaded them to rent a piano for four or five dollars per
month. Many such instances as these, in connection with
my own struggles, impressed upon me the importance of
making a study of our needs as a race, and applying the
20   remedy accordingly.

Some one may be tempted to ask, Has not the negro boy or girl as good a right to study a French grammar and instrumental music as the white youth? I answer, Yes, but in the present condition of the negro race in this country

25 there is need of something more. Perhaps I may be forgiven for the seeming egotism if I mention the expansion of my own life partly as an example of what I mean. My earliest recollection is of a small one-room log hut on a large slave plantation in Virginia. After the close of the war, while

30 working in the coal-mines of West Virginia for the support of my mother, I heard in some accidental way of the Hampton Institute.

When I learned that it was an institution where a black boy could study, could have a chance to work for his board,

35 and at the same time be taught how to work and to realize the dignity of labor, I resolved to go there. Bidding my mother good-by, I started out one morning to find my way to Hampton, though I was almost penniless and had no definite idea where Hampton was. By walking, begging

40 rides, and paying for a portion of the journey on the steam-cars, I finally succeeded in reaching the city of Richmond, Virginia. I was without money or friends. I slept under a sidewalk, and by working on a vessel next day I earned money to continue my way to the institute, where I arrived

45 with a surplus of fifty cents. At Hampton I found the opportunity—in the way of buildings, teachers, and industries provided by the generous—to get training in the class-room and by practical touch with industrial life, to learn thrift, economy, and push. I was surrounded by an atmosphere of

50 business, Christian influence, and a spirit of self-help that seemed to have awakened every faculty in me, and caused me for the first time to realize what it meant to be a man instead of a piece of property.

While there I resolved that when I had finished the course

55 of training I would go into the far South, into the Black Belt of the South, and give my life to providing the same kind of opportunity for self-reliance and self-awakening that I had found provided for me at Hampton.

Notice that in the first paragraph, the narration slips briefly into the third person—Washington is telling the story of the girl, not his own. Likewise, Washington presents the story of the boy studying French from his point of view. In these two instances, Washington switches from first- to third-person with ease, so that the transition is optimally effective and unnoticeable. The second paragraph effortlessly transitions to a personal anecdote, which is continued in the third paragraph. The final paragraph justifies the narrative: Washington's life story leads to his commitment to establish his own institute—called the Tuskegee Normal and Industrial Institute—deep in the South.

How and When to Use Narration

- When possible, structure the events in chronological order.

- Make your story complete: make sure you have a beginning, middle, and end.

- Provide a realistic setting (typically at the beginning). Notice how Booker T. Washington provides a setting in this passage with just a few details: "a young colored man," "a common cabin in the South," "the poverty, the untidiness, the want of system, and thrift that existed about the cabin."

- Whenever possible, use action verbs; for example, write "the fighters *tumbled* to the ground," rather than "there *were* fallen soldiers on the ground."

- Provide concrete and specific details.

- Show, don't tell. This is another way of saying that you should use anecdotes and examples whenever possible.

- Establish a clear point of view—if it's clear who is narrating and why, then it will be easier to choose relevant details.

- Include appropriate amounts of direct discourse (dialogue or quotations).

Sample Narration Question

"A college education is not necessary for success." Relate an experience of someone you know (directly or indirectly) that defends, challenges, or qualifies this statement. Once you've written your essay, show it to your AP teacher or tutor. You might want to show it to a fellow AP student for peer review.

Drill: Reflect on How You Could Use Narration to Address the Following Topics

Think of a personal experience (or an experience of someone you know) that pertains to the topic. Determine how you would best describe this experience. Come up with a few anecdotes or examples.

TOPIC 1: The dangers encountered when eating becomes an obsession

TOPIC 2: Hardship is a necessary part of our education

CAUSE AND EFFECT

You've read how process analysis is a useful rhetorical mode for explaining how to do things or how things were done; the rhetorical mode known as **cause and effect** explains *why things should be done* or *why things should have been done*. In a sense, cause and effect explains the processes responsible for the process.

One example of cause and effect comes from Timothy Ferriss's popular text *The 4-Hour Work Week*. In this section he describes what inspired him to quit his demanding roll as an entrepreneur and travel:

> Then a funny thing happened. In my undying quest to
> make myself miserable, I accidentally began to backpedal.
> As soon as I cut through the vague unease and ambiguous
> *Line* anxiety by defining my nightmare, the worst-case scenario,
> 5 I wasn't as worried about taking a trip. I could always
> take a temporary bartending job to pay the rent if I had
> to. I could sell some furniture and cut back on eating out.
> I could steal lunch money from the kindergarteners who
> passed by my apartment every morning. The options were
> 10 many. I realized it wouldn't be that hard to get back to
> where I was, let alone survive. None of these things would
> be fatal—not even close.
>
> I realized that on a scale of 1–10, 1 being nothing and 10
> being permanently life-changing, my so-called worst-case
> 15 scenario might have a temporary impact of 3 or 4. On the
> other hand, if I realized my best-case scenario, or even a
> probable-case scenario, it would easily have a permanent 9
> or 10 positive life-changing effect.

Here, Ferris details the logic behind why he quit his job. He identifies his fear of financial ruin and explains why this is so unlikely. He lists a number of alternate options, such as temporarily bartending or selling furniture, and even develops a 1–10 scale to rate how life-changing his trip might be. If we ask ourselves why Timothy Ferris should quit his job, the answer is clearly because "it would easily have a permanent 9 or 10 positive life-changing effect." Given this cause-and-effect relationship, quitting his job seems the obvious choice.

Another example of the cause-and-effect mode comes from Yalda Uhls, who wrote an article with the intention of soothing parental fears about growing screen time use among children. As you read, see if you can spot the cause-and-effect relationship Uhls is illustrating:

> I come bearing good news: Our teens are not growing
> into brain-dead zombies or emotionally stunted sociopaths.
> After more than a decade of research by child psycholo-
> *Line* gists like me, we have discovered that the kids are all right.
> 5 In study after study of emotional and intelligence indica-
> tors, 21st-century children use media to connect with their
> friends and learn about the world, just like those of us who
> were children of the 20th century did.
>
> But you don't have to take it from me. The proof is in
> 10 the past. Every time a new technology is introduced, it
> becomes a cultural battleground. And ultimately, we come
> to a truce. Take this one example: Near the end of the 19th
> century, a new medium was unleashed upon the world.
> Children took to it like ducks to water, and this terrified
> 15 adults. Young people everywhere spent hours on end
> immersed, while simultaneously ignoring the grown-ups
> in their lives. Understandably, parents were alarmed and
> worried that this new medium and its racy content were
> ruining young minds.

20   Change 19th to 20th, and I could be talking about the
           Internet. So what was this addictive content? Romantic
           novels.

Uhls draws a relationship between new entertainment media (romantic novels, the internet) and moral panic on the behalf of the established adult world. In other words, the upset among parents today is caused by the same factors that have been upsetting parents for generations: new media that could be corrupting the youth. By illuminating this cause-and-effect relationship, Uhls seeks to allay fears about excessive media consumption.

On this exam, the causes and effects that you choose to explore will depend on what you're asked to explain. You may have to use cause and effect in your essays, possibly in combination with one or more other rhetorical modes; you may also see a few questions in the multiple-choice section that deal with how the author uses cause and effect to make a point. When making critical decisions, writers will often consider both the immediate and the long-term effects; when analyzing an important event, writers will often examine both the immediate and the underlying causes.

When and How to Use Cause and Effect

- Do not confuse the relating of mere circumstances with a cause-and-effect relationship. For example, it is not logical to assume that socialism in Chile necessarily caused socialism in Argentina.

- Turn your causal relationships into causes and effects by using carefully chosen examples. Remember that not all causal relationships are causes and effects. However, careful use of evidence and examples can turn causal relationships into causes and effects.

- Make sure to carefully address each step in a series of causal relationships; if you don't, you risk losing your reader. Imagine the attendance secretary when she hears, "I'm sorry I'm late. We had a fire, so I had to find my cat." A better (clearer) explanation would have been as follows: "I'm sorry I'm late. This morning at 4:00 A.M. there was an electrical fire in the garage; fortunately, there was an alarm that woke my dad, who put out the fire, but when he opened the garage door, my cat ran outside. I think it was frightened so it ran up a tree. I decided to climb up the tree and get the cat but I fell, and my mother had to take me to the emergency room." Although this explanation is longer, it is far more detailed and answers any questions your reader may have.

> If you were writing about the poor average of AP English Language and Composition Exam scores at your school, you could go about it in two ways. First, you could examine some *immediate* causes: Ms. What's-Her-Name retired and was replaced by a teacher who had no experience teaching and no background in English, we didn't have a good review book for the exam, or the exam is administered in Room Z during school band practice. Alternatively, you could examine some *underlying* causes for the poor exam scores: The superintendent of schools changed hiring policies (so a terrible teacher was hired); last year, funds for buying books were diverted to buying new lockers for the football team (so we had no good review book); and the room that the school band normally practices in was flooded when a pipe broke.

Sample Cause-and-Effect Question

Write an essay in which you examine the possible causes and effects of violence in the United States today. Once you've written your essay, show it to your AP teacher or tutor. You might want to show it to a fellow AP student for peer review.

"T" It Up

One common way to compare or contrast items is with a T chart, which is basically drawing a T so that there are two columns separated by a line, with one point on the left and one on the right—in this case, causes on one side and effects on the other.

Drill: Reflect on How You Could Use Cause and Effect to Address the Following Topics

Compare the possible causes and effects of the topics below. Then for at least one topic, make sure to give examples to back up your claims.

TOPIC 1:   Academic dishonesty in high schools

TOPIC 2:   The fear of domestic terrorism in the United States

TOPIC 3:   The political affiliations of Americans

DEFINITION

You are probably familiar with definitions; you see them every time you look up a word in the dictionary. Hopefully when you write, you try to make sure your reader understands the words that you use.

> For the AP exam, we have to consider *definition* in its meaning as a rhetorical mode.

Tip:

Definition is one of the easiest and most useful rhetorical modes. If you're stuck writing one of your essays, start by defining any key terms you're using.

When writing your essays for the AP English Language and Composition Exam, if you happen to leave a key term unexplained or explained vaguely, even a carefully crafted essay will fall apart. This is especially true of very specialized terminology and obscure words. For example, if you are explaining a wonderful new tradition at your school and define it by synonym, you may write, "Basically, it's a Mexican *feis*." If your readers are Irish, this would be all right; if your readers were from just about anywhere else, you would need to define *feis* by putting it into a **category** (defining it in terms everyone will understand): "a *feis* is a competition for Irish dance, song, and instrumental music." Then, you could explain your project: "We want to do the same thing with traditional Mexican dance, song, and music."

In this case, a paragraph—or an entire essay—is devoted to the definition of a term. Here, for example, is a paragraph that defines *feis* (pronounced "fesh").

Line

5

A *feis* is a day of competition in Irish dancing, music, and song. Perhaps you were wondering where all the Irish dancers from *Lord of the Dance* came from. All first performed at a *feis* and honed their skills through competitions at various levels. A *feis* is a living legacy of Irish culture; it is where beginners, trying to remember their left from right, unknowingly dance the ancient steps of Ireland and pass this legacy on to the next generation. On the more practical side, a *feis* is to Irish performers what a soccer game is to athletes the world over. Competitions are organized by ability (Beginner, Advanced Beginner, Novice, Open, Preliminary Championships, and Championships) and by age (Under 6, Under 7, etc.). At a typical *feis*, there might be as many as 2,500 dancers.

10

The passage begins with a straightforward definition, but the definition is extended and rhetorical modes are mixed. You noted, I'm sure, the *analogy* to a soccer game; then, there is an inchoate (imperfectly formed) stab at *classification* (the divisions in the competition). You could even argue that the mention of *Lord of the Dance* serves as a kind of *example*. The rhetorical mode of *definition* can be used simply to explain a word or concept, but typically the author using it also wants to interest the reader in what's being explained.

Let's take a look at another good example of definition.

Line

5

The *Palio* is a horse race that's held twice each year in Siena, Italy: on July 2nd in honor of the Madonna of Provenzano, and on August 16th in honor of the Assumption of the Virgin. But saying that the Palio is just another horse race would be like calling the Superbowl just another football game. The Palio is not just a race. It is blood, sweat, and tears; it is part competition and part festival. According to some, it is the world's craziest horse race; according to others, it is Italy's most honored tradition. One thing is clear to everyone, however: the Palio represents the tradition, culture, and soul of Siena. The actual race lasts only about a minute, but those moments represent an entire year's worth of anticipation and preparation.

10

Again, the passage begins with a simple definition; but here, too, we have an example of another rhetorical mode—analogy (to the Super Bowl).

However, the author of this passage uses an important additional tactic, known as *definition by negation*. You should be aware of this rhetorical device and use it where appropriate. In the passage above, the negation is partial—the Palio is, indeed, a race, but it is not "just a race." Most negations work in that manner; definition by negation is usually used to impress upon the reader the importance of the item under discussion or create a distinction between the item under discussion and the item with which it is being "negatively" compared. For instance, you may write, "Madonna is not a pop singer; she's a phenomenon, a true diva, a multi-talented musical ambassador, and savvy businesswoman." Perhaps this statement is true, but she's still a pop singer.

You may be able to use definition as a mode in your free-response essays, but most likely, you will see definition used in the passages in the multiple-choice sections. For example, you may be asked to answer a question that deals with how an author uses definition to analyze a topic.

When and How to Use Definition

- Keep your reason for defining something in mind as you're writing.

- Define key terms according to what you know of your audience, in other words, the readers of the essays; you don't want to bore your reader by defining terms unnecessarily, nor do you want to perplex your reader by failing to define terms that may be obscure to your audience. Keep in mind that your readers are the AP English Language and Composition Exam graders.

- Explain the background (history) when it is relevant to your definition.

- Define by negation when appropriate.

- Combine definition with any number of other rhetorical modes when applicable.

Sample Definition Question

Write an essay in which you use definition to analyze the role of integrity in your life. Once you've written your essay, show it to your AP teacher or tutor. You might want to show it to a fellow AP student for peer review.

Drill: Reflect on How You Could Use Definition to Address the Following Topics

First define each word by category; then, define each word by negation.

WORD 1: Hip-hop

WORD 2: Success

WORD 3: Love

WORD 4: Cool

DESCRIPTION

Description can help make expository or argumentative writing lively and interesting and hold the reader's interest, which is vital, of course. Think of how many essays those test graders have to read every day; as we mentioned in the techniques chapters, a large part of scoring well on the free-response section is keeping your audience interested.

Oftentimes description serves as the primary rhetorical mode for an entire essay—or even an entire book. It's typically used to communicate a scene, a specific place, or a person to the reader. Although writers tend to concentrate most on the visual aspects of descriptions, they can be used to appeal to any of the reader's senses.

Objective:
Based on facts

Subjective:
Based on feelings or opinions

It is important to keep in mind that sometimes description can be objective; in these cases, the author is not describing something in a sentimental or otherwise subjective way—they are merely stating the facts. As an example of this, take a look at Charles Darwin's depiction of Valparaíso, the chief seaport in Chile, in *Voyage of the Beagle*.

> The town is built at the very foot of a range of hills,
> about 1,600 feet high, and rather steep. From its position, it
> consists of one long, straggling street, which runs paral-
> Line   lel to the beach, and wherever a ravine comes down, the
> 5   houses are piled up on each side of it. The rounded hills,
> being only partially protected by very scanty vegetation,
> are worn into numberless little gullies, which expose a sin-
> gularly bright red soil. From this cause, and from the low
> whitewashed houses with tile roofs, the view reminded me
> 10   of St. Cruz in Tenerife. In a northwesterly direction there
> are some fine glimpses of the Andes, but these mountains
> appear much grander when viewed from the neighboring
> hills: the great distance at which they are situated can then
> more readily be perceived.

This type of objective description tends to be drier than more subjective description. The degree of objectivity exhibited above probably doesn't thrill you—nor will it thrill the AP readers.

Fortunately, unlike most other rhetorical modes, description allows for a significant degree of subjectivity. In most descriptions, the writer attempts to communicate personal impressions of something or someone. To do so, it is necessary to draw on the powers of figurative writing; simile, metaphor, and personification are the most common.

Here is another description of a city: Nathaniel Hawthorne's impressions of Florence. The description comes not from one of Hawthorne's novels, but from one of the notebooks that he kept during his travels in Europe.

Line

5

10

15

20

25

30

35

By and by, we had a distant glimpse of Florence, showing its great dome and some of its towers out of a sidelong valley, as if we were between two great waves of the tumultuous sea of hills, while, far beyond, rose in the distance the blue peaks of three or four of the Apennines, just on the remote horizon. There being a haziness in the atmosphere, however, Florence was little more distinct to us than the Celestial City was to Christian and Hopeful, when they spied at it from the Delectable Mountains.

Florence at first struck me as having the aspect of a very new city in comparison with Rome; but, on closer acquaintance, I find that many of the buildings are antique and massive, though still the clear atmosphere, the bright sunshine, the light, cheerful hues of the stucco, and—as much as anything else, perhaps—the vivacious character of the human life in the streets, take away the sense of its being an ancient city.

As we returned home over the Arno River, crossing the Ponte di Santa Trinitá, we were struck by the beautiful scene of the broad, calm river, with the palaces along its shores repeated in it, on either side, and the neighboring bridges, too, just as perfect in the tide beneath as in the air above—a city of dream and shadow so close to the actual one. God has a meaning, no doubt, in putting this spiritual symbol continually beside us.

Along the river, on both sides, as far as we could see, there was a row of brilliant lamps, which, in the far distance, looked like a cornice of golden light; and this also shone as brightly in the river's depths. The lilies of the evening, in the quarter where the sun had gone down, were very soft and beautiful, though not so gorgeous as thousands that I have seen in America. But I believe I must fairly confess that the Italian sky, in the daytime, is bluer and brighter than our own, and that the atmosphere has a quality of showing objects to better advantage. It is more than mere daylight; the magic of moonlight is somehow mixed up with it, although it is so transparent a medium of light.

This is a much more personal vision of a city. Hawthorne uses one simile to give us a better visual image of the countryside around Florence ("as if we were between two great waves of the tumultuous sea of hills") and another to communicate the effect of the gas lamps ("like a cornice of golden light"); and he employs a metaphor ("a city of dream and shadow") to evoke his impression of the reflections in the river. In fact, virtually all of the description serves to communicate or explain Hawthorne's impressions of the city; here, the writer wishes to evoke and is not interested in scientific exactitude.

Keep in mind that this rhetorical device allows you a certain amount of freedom of language, but it also allows you certain liberties in organization. In Hawthorne's passage, for example, the author put down in writing his impressions in whatever order they came to him. In more objectively written descriptions, however, it often makes sense to think spatially when writing a visual description. You might describe a scene from left to right or front to back, for example; you might start a description of a person with the head (and end with the feet).

In the following passage, Fyodor Dostoevsky gives us both a spatial description and a barrage of sensory impressions.

> In the first place, on entering this house, one passes into
> a very bare hall, and thence along a passage to a mean
> staircase. The reception room, however, is bright, clean,
> *Line* and spacious, and is lined with redwood and metalwork.
> 5 But the scullery you would not care to see; it is greasy,
> dirty, and odoriferous, while the stairs are in rags, and
> the walls so covered with filth that the hand sticks fast
> wherever it touches them. Also, on each landing there is a
> medley of boxes, chairs, and dilapidated wardrobes; while
> 10 the windows have had most of their panes shattered, and
> everywhere stand washtubs filled with dirt, litter, eggshells,
> and fish bladders. The smell is abominable. In short, the
> house is not a nice one.
>
> As to the disposition of the rooms, I have described it to
> 15 you already. True, they are convenient enough, yet every
> one of them has an atmosphere. I do not mean that they
> smell badly so much as that each of them seems to contain
> something which gives forth a rank, sickly sweet odor. At
> first the impression is an unpleasant one, but a couple of
> 20 minutes will suffice to dissipate it, for the reason that every-
> thing here smells—people's clothes, hands, and everything
> else—and one grows accustomed to the rankness. Canaries,
> however, soon die in this house. A naval officer here has
> just bought his fifth. Birds cannot live long in such an air.
> 25 Every morning, when fish or beef is being cooked, and
> washing and scrubbing are in progress, the house is filled
> with steam. Always, too, the kitchen is full of linen hanging
> out to dry; and since my room adjoins that apartment, the
> smell from the clothes causes me not a little annoyance.
> 30 However, one can grow used to anything.

Note that Dostoevsky's description first takes us through the ground floor and leads us up the staircase. Unlike the previous passages, this one appeals to our tactile ("so covered with filth that the hand sticks") and, even more prominently, olfactory senses. Choice of detail is important, and the choice of fish bladders, for example, conveys wonderfully the disgusting sights and smell. This is great writing—not only is the description effective, it's also humorous, thanks to the short comment at the end of each paragraph.

How and When to Use Description

- When possible, call on all five senses: visual, auditory, olfactory (smell), gustatory (taste), and tactile.

- Place the most striking examples at the beginnings and ends of your paragraphs (or essay) for maximum effect.

- Show, don't tell, using anecdotes and examples.

- Use concrete nouns and adjectives; nouns, not adjectives, should dominate.

- Concentrate on details that will convey the sense you're trying to get across most effectively. (Remember the fish bladders!)

- Employ figures of speech, especially similes, metaphors, and personification, when appropriate.

- When describing people, try to focus on distinctive mannerisms; whenever possible, go beyond physical appearance.

- Direct discourse (using dialogue or quotations) can be revealing and useful.

- A brief illustrative anecdote is worth a thousand words. Instead of simply using a general statement ("My friend Kai is a very generous person"), use an example ("My friend Kai is known for his generosity; the whole school knows about the time that he spent an entire weekend volunteering at a soup kitchen").

- To the extent possible, use action verbs. You could write, "The delightful aroma of chocolate chip cookies baking in the oven *crept around the corner and filled the den* with its sweetness" instead of just "The baking chocolate chip cookies *smelled* sweet."

Sample Description Question

Write an essay in which you describe your local shopping mall. Remember that you are not limited to physical descriptions. Once you've written your essay, show it to your AP teacher or tutor. You might want to show it to a fellow AP student for peer review.

Drill: Reflect on How You Could Use Description to Address the Following Topics

First decide the general feeling you'd like to convey, and second begin to list some specifics; don't forget examples or anecdotes. When describing people, go beyond just the physical.

TOPIC 1:   A party

TOPIC 2:   Your family

TOPIC 3:   A natural disaster (experienced personally or on television)

TOPIC 4:   Your favorite place to relax

TOPIC 5:   The campus of your school

PROCESS ANALYSIS

Process analysis is a rhetorical mode that's used by writers when they want to explain either how to do something or how something was done. When your science teacher hands you instructions for a lab, she is giving you a rather dry sheet of process analysis that says, "first do this; then do that; then examine the data; then explain such-and-such." A description of the scientific method is an example of process analysis. When you write your lab report, you're also indulging in process analysis, saying, "first we did this; then we did that; then we examined the data; then we determined such-and-such." If you like to follow recipes when you cook, then you've already been exposed to process analysis. However, process analyses used in writing generally aren't as dry as recipes or how-to manuals; they usually have a few examples to spice them up a little.

Below, Under Secretary of Management Patrick F. Kennedy uses process analysis to develop his remarks given on Sri Lanka Day in 2016 before the Organization of American States, a body of the United Nations.

> 68 years ago today, Sri Lanka found itself in good company when it joined the rather exclusive club of great nations that chose the fourth day of the month to declare
> *Line* independence from the United Kingdom.
> 5   Like Sri Lankans are doing today, in a few months Americans will mark our anniversary of independence, when we will also remember the heroes and patriots of years past, and reflect on how far we've come in our long quest for a more perfect union.
> 10   And like Sri Lankans of today, Americans are still striving to address some of the very challenging problems that have long bedeviled us. Problems like poverty, discrimination, and injustice.
>   But Sri Lankans and Americans both understand that
> 15 these problems can only be solved through the use of the ballot box, the voice of a free press, the strength of a healthy civil society, and the actions of an empowered citizenry that is committed to democracy, human rights, and progress for all.

In this speech, Kennedy draws parallels between the process by which the United States and Sri Lanka obtained their independence from Great Britain. Both nations declared independence on the fourth of the month, "remember the heroes and patriots of years past," and address social problems "through the use of the ballot box." By enumerating the common stages both nations experience while obtaining independence and self governance, Kennedy emphasizes the commonalities and fraternal bonds between both nations.

A Flash of Memory

If you're having trouble remembering rhetorical modes, make some flashcards and memorize them like vocabulary words.

Another example of process analysis comes from Mary Wollstonecraft. While writing a travelogue published in 1796, she goes to great lengths to describe exactly how meals are served in continental Europe to her audience in Great Britain:

> Prelude a luncheon—then a succession of fish, flesh, and fowl for two hours, during which time the dessert—I was sorry for the strawberries and cream—rests on the
> *Line* table to be impregnated by the fumes of the viands. Coffee
> 5 immediately follows in the drawing-room, but does not preclude punch, ale, tea and cakes, raw salmon, &c. A supper brings up the rear, not forgetting the introductory luncheon, almost equalling in removes the dinner. A day of this kind you would imagine sufficient; but a tomorrow and
> 10 a to-morrow—A never-ending, still-beginning feast may be bearable, perhaps…

Wollstonecraft is so over the top in her description that it develops the humor she intends. The fact that coffee also includes "punch, ale, tea and cakes, [and] raw salmon…" gives the scene the ridiculous mood that develops the overall satire in the passage, a mood she develops explicitly by describing it as a "never-ending, still-beginning feast." Wollstonecraft is mocking the newly-developed social customs of her Swedish hosts, criticizing them for displays of wealth that lack actual sophistication.

> Remember that process analysis is a rhetorical mode that serves to organize something in a step-by-step manner, and it can serve both scientific and persuasive ends.

When and How to Use Process Analysis

- Sequence is chronological and usually fixed—think of recipes.

- When you use this device, make sure the stages of the process are clear, by using transitions (e.g., *first, next, after two days, finally*).

- Make sure your terminology is appropriate for the reader. For example, the person who will read your essays probably does not know much about the embryonic development of frogs, so you should avoid using too-specialized terms like *Spemann organizer* or *Nieuwkoop center*.

- Verify that every step is clear; an error or omission in an intermediate step may make the rest of the process analysis very confusing. Let's say you were describing how to braid hair, and wrote the following instructions: "First, comb or brush your hair so that it is untangled and manageable to work with. Next, take the far-right section of hair and put it over the middle section and under the far-left section." This could be confusing to your reader because you never said to divide the hair into three sections before starting the actual braiding process.

Sample Process Analysis Question

Write a short essay in which you describe the process of how you selected the colleges to which you applied (or are going to apply to). Once you've written your essay, show it to your AP teacher or tutor. You might want to show it to a fellow AP student for peer review.

Drill: Reflect on How You Could Use Process Analysis to Address the Following Topics

Try making a numbered list with a few examples. Make sure you have included all the necessary steps and have used appropriate language and terminology for your reader. Remember to use transition words when you write the essay.

TOPIC 1:   How decisions are made at your school

TOPIC 2:   How to get through high school successfully

TOPIC 3:   How to choose and keep close friends

INDUCTION AND DEDUCTION

You will probably find that the rhetorical modes of induction and deduction are most useful when you're writing the argument essay, although they will be helpful on the rhetorical analysis essay too.

Induction is a process in which specific examples are used to reach a general conclusion. If you took the AP European History Exam and did not like the experience, and then took the AP Calculus BC Exam and did not like the experience, you might arrive at the following general conclusion: AP exams are always an unpleasant experience. If, when you were young, you found that you didn't like broccoli, asparagus, or cabbage, your parents might have concluded that you didn't like vegetables. In both cases, the conclusion would be of questionable value because there is not enough evidence to justify the generalization.

Assume that you want to argue that your English teacher is in a bad mood every time the Boston Red Sox lose a game to the New York Yankees. You could substantiate that generalization by recalling certain tantrums that they threw and comparing those days with the dates of Red Sox losses. This would substantiate your claim but not prove it, especially if you didn't even know whether your teacher saw the games. After all, what if something else happened to coincide with the games and was the real cause of their bad temper, such as traffic jams on the way home from school?

We tend to believe in generalizations arrived at through induction, whether or not they can actually be proved. The Food and Drug Administration, for example, has to follow the inductive reasoning of scientists; just because a certain drug produced the desired results—and didn't produce an undesirable result, such as death—in

Induction:
PART to WHOLE

Deduction:
WHOLE to PART

20,000 experimental cases, this does not prove that the same results will occur when 20,000,000 people take the drug.

Deduction involves the use of a generalization to draw a conclusion about a specific case. For example, if you read in the morning paper that all schools in your county would be closed that day because of inclement weather, you could conclude that you won't have to go to school. You just used deductive reasoning.

How and When to Use Induction and Deduction

- Induction proceeds from the specific to a generalization. For example, your classmate Ricky plays on the school's football and basketball teams, and he has ice hockey posters all over his bedroom at home. You could conclude that Ricky likes all sports in general.

- Make sure you have sufficient evidence to support your claim.

- Deduction is the process of applying a generalization to a specific case. For example, your cousin Jennifer told you that she hates dancing and loud music. From this, you could safely say that she probably wouldn't want to come with you to the hot new nightclub opening this weekend.

- Make sure your generalization has sufficient credibility before applying it to specific cases. For example, it would be an unfair generalization to assume that all baseball players use or have used anabolic steroids.

Sample Induction and Deduction Question

Write a short essay in which you analyze the following statement using induction or deduction: *Contemporary films are a reflection of today's values.* Once you've written your essay, show it to your AP teacher or tutor. You might want to show it to a fellow AP student for peer review.

Drill: Reflect on How You Could Use Induction to Substantiate the Following Theses

THESIS 1: Academic honesty is alive and well.

THESIS 2: High schools don't really care about their mission to educate.

THESIS 3: Computer games have beneficial effects.

THESIS 4: Children generally demonstrate more wisdom than their parents.

SATIRE

In **satire,** something is portrayed in a way that's deliberately distorted to achieve comic effect. Implicit in most satire is the author's desire to critique what is being mocked. One example of satire comes to us from C.S. Lewis, a British author famous for novels such as *The Lion, The Witch, and the Wardrobe.* A devout Christian, Lewis wrote *The Screwtape Letters* in order to persuade his fellow British intellectual elites of the value of Christianity in their modern, 20th century world. In the fictional letters, an elderly devil advises a younger devil on the best way to corrupt humans. As you read, see if you can spot the aspects of society that Lewis satirizes.

> My dear Wormwood,
>   I am delighted to hear that your patient's age and profes-
> sion make it possible, but by no means certain, that he will
> Line be called up for military service. We want him to be in the
>   5 maximum uncertainty, so that his mind will be filled with
> contradictory pictures of the future, every one of which
> arouses hope or fear. There is nothing like suspense and
> anxiety for barricading a human's mind against the Enemy.
> He wants men to be concerned with what they do; our
>   10 business is to keep them thinking about what will happen
> to them.

Lewis's speaker, the elderly devil, is "delighted" to hear that the younger devil's "patient" is of age that makes it possible to be drafted into the military. Then, the devil gets excited about the "suspense and anxiety" that will separate the human in question from the "Enemy," or Lewis's conception of God. By feigning delight at the prospect of war, and its associated stress and worry, Lewis is mocking the greater society of Great Britain and Western Europe that made world war an available playground for the "devils" of the early 20th century. By emphasizing the immorality of social order in which they exist, Lewis draws attention to the importance of having a moral code, in this case a Christian moral code, with which to navigate it.

Most critics, however, relegate satire—and satirists—to a secondary sphere in the universe of writing; satire makes for good entertainment, but mocking others does not measure up to the conviction of cogent writing. Had Voltaire been nothing more than a satirist, he would not have been remembered as a brilliant *philosophe,* but as a clever joker—if he were remembered at all. Although Voltaire's satire in *Candide* is quite brilliant, some other examples of satire are a little easier to figure out. Let's look at a sample question based on a passage from Jonathan Swift's *Gulliver's Travels.*

The following terms are similar, but not identical. Know the differences.

Satire: A social or political criticism that relies heavily on irony, sarcasm, and often humor

Parody: Imitation for comic effect

Lampoon: Sharp ridicule of the behavior or character of a person or institution

Caricature: A ludicrous exaggeration of the defects of persons or things

For about seventy moons past there have been two
struggling parties in this empire, under the names of
Tramecksan and *Slamecksan,* from the high and low heels
Line of their shoes, by which they distinguish themselves. It is
5 alleged, indeed, that the high heels are most agreeable to
our ancient constitution; but, however this be, his majesty
has determined to make use only of low heels in the administration of the government, and all offices in the gift of the
crown, as you cannot but observe; and particularly that his
10 majesty's imperial heels are lower at least by a *drurr* than
any of his court (*drurr* is a measure about the fourteenth
part of an inch). The animosities between these two parties
run so high, that they will neither eat, nor drink, nor talk
with each other. We compute the *Tramecksan,* or high
15 heels, to exceed us in number; but the power is wholly on
our side. We apprehend his imperial highness, the heir to
the crown, to have some tendency towards the high heels;
at least we can plainly discover that one of his heels is
higher than the other, which gives him a hobble in his gait.

4. The above passage is an example of

(A) an analysis of court customs

(B) a satire of British footwear

(C) a study of British eccentricities

(D) a satire of the British court

Well, the correct answer must be either (B) or (D) because this section is all about satire. The correct answer is (D). The passage serves to satirize the Whig-Tory discord (the Whigs dominated politics during much of the 18th century) and the relationship of the "parties" (the Whigs and Tories were not really political parties as we know them today) and the king. Unless you recognize that the passage is satirical, you will not have a good grasp of what is going on—which will lead to major problems with all of the multiple-choice questions on that passage.

As you review the following elements of style and consider how they are used in context, ask yourself the following question: How does an author's use of diction, syntax, and/or figurative language develop these appeals within the text?

THE RHETORICAL FALLACY TRAP

Have you ever seen commercials or billboard ads showing a happy, carefree crowd walking on a blissful beach at a 5-star resort? Don't they always seem to be enjoying a wonderful vacation, enticing you to want to also take a vacation at that same resort?

Ads like this rely on rhetorical fallacy: a way to persuade you to buy into what they are selling. They don't explain the advantages of the resort. Instead, they promote the resort by showcasing a fun-loving couple on the beach. The people in the ad might not be anything like you; their lives might be completely different from yours. Who's to say your experience would be the same if you were to visit the same resort? This is a prime example of how rhetorical fallacy is used in everyday life.

A rhetorical fallacy is basically faulty reasoning leading to a conclusion the advertiser, author, or speaker wants you to make. They pop up often—in ads, in statements by politicians, in appeals from charities, in arguments from your own friends and family. Skilled communicators such as political speech writers use them deliberately. Others use them unconsciously—the conclusion seems so obvious to them that "everybody else has one" sounds like irrefutable evidence. You might have used rhetorical fallacies subconsciously too.

Rhetorical fallacies also pop up on the AP English Language and Composition Exam, since this test covers how language works and how it is used. A rhetorical fallacy uses (or rather, *mis*-uses) language in order to trick you into accepting the author's conclusion. This conclusion appears to be truth at first, but the evidence supporting it crumbles when your active reading or listening skills kick in. You then ask yourself, "*why* should I do or believe this?"

The AP exam will test whether you understand logical fallacies. However, you are unlikely to be tested on the exact terms for the different fallacies.

> On the test, you might find rhetorical fallacies lurking in the passages for the multiple-choice questions or in the sources provided for the synthesis and analysis essays. You need to be able to recognize them so you won't be led astray in your answers. You also need to avoid them in your own essays.

Spotting and Avoiding Rhetorical Fallacies

Think of a rhetorical fallacy as "fake evidence." It seems to support a conclusion that the author wants the reader to accept, but—on close examination—it doesn't really lead to that conclusion.

You can identify rhetorical fallacies (and avoid them in your own work) by following this process:

- Identify the conclusion. What position does the author want you to accept? What action does the author want you to take? What inference do they want you to draw?

- Identify the evidence. How does the author lead you to that conclusion? What does the author present as evidence that the conclusion is correct?

- Examine the evidence. Is it
    a. relevant to the conclusion?
    b. accurate?
    c. credible?
    d. logical?
    e. complete?

If it's not, then you've likely encountered a rhetorical fallacy.

Common Rhetorical Fallacies

Let's look at some common types of rhetorical fallacies so you can understand how they try to mislead you. The name of each specific fallacy is given, but what's most important for the exam is being able to recognize faulty reasoning when you see it, and avoiding it in the essays you write.

Emphasizing the Person

In this class of rhetorical fallacies, the evidence focuses on the person who supports a conclusion, not on the merits of the conclusion itself.

Ad Populum or "bandwagon": A certain political candidate is ahead in the polls. Since most people are going to vote for him, you should too. Otherwise you'll just be wasting your vote.

The happy crowd on the beach described at the beginning of this chapter is another instance of the "bandwagon" fallacy. All of these people are having a great vacation at this resort; you should go there, and you'll have fun too.

The conclusion is an action the author (or the advertiser) wants you to take—vote for this candidate, book a vacation at this resort. No support is provided to explain *why* the candidate is the best choice, or *why* the resort is better than others. The very thin evidence is only that others are doing it.

Argument from Authority: Dr. X recommends this medication to his patients, or well-known musician Y always drives this brand of car. Are they being paid by the manufacturers to endorse those products, or do the products have attributes that really make them superior? You'll never know. This rhetorical fallacy focuses solely on the credentials or fame of the person recommending the product, without saying anything about the product itself.

And watch those credentials—is Dr. X really a recognized specialist in the illness the medication is intended to treat? What does musician Y know about cars?

Ad Hominem: This rhetorical fallacy turns to the other side of the coin and points out negative characteristics of the person who promotes an idea or action. By implication, the action is as negative as the person who endorses it. The mayor was caught plagiarizing an essay in college and was accused of embezzlement by a former employer. Therefore, his claim that municipal taxes must increase to cover necessary road repairs has to be a lie and an attempt to steal taxpayers' money. Nothing is said about the actual condition of the roads.

Dogmatism: The conclusion must be correct because the author or speaker says it is and she can't possibly be wrong. After all, she is an internationally recognized authority on the subject, or she is the CEO of the most profitable company on the planet. She wouldn't have risen to that position if she were ever wrong. No other reasons are presented to support the conclusion, and no opposing viewpoints are even considered.

Presenting Only Part of the Truth

Equivocation: This type of fallacy leaves out facts that a reader or listener would need in order to make a thorough assessment of the conclusion. Equivocation often relies on ambiguous definitions of words.

For example, your home insurer might say that for an extra $50 premium, you'll be covered for $100,000 in water damage. Look at the "definitions" section of your policy, though, and you might see that the insurer considers "water damage" to be damage caused by a sewer backup. "Overland flooding" or "ice dams on roof" are separate categories that are not covered. You probably assumed those events would all result in "water damage," and the insurer is counting on that to lead you to the conclusion that it's worth spending the extra $50.

> In the movie *Pink Panther*, Inspector Clouseau enters a quaint European hotel and, upon spying a cute little dog, asks the owner, "Does your dog bite?" The manager responds, "No," and Clouseau attempts to pet the dog, which growls and bites him. "You told me that your dog does not bite!" exclaims Clouseau. "That's not my dog," responds the owner.

Sentimental Appeals: Charities often use this tactic when they ask for donations. Starving children living in deplorable surroundings, or clear-cut hillsides that were once covered by beautiful forests—these scenes appeal to your emotions rather than your intellect. This rhetorical fallacy omits rational explanations about why the charity deserves your donation. What has it accomplished recently to right the wrong it presents? How much of your donation is used for its programs, and how much goes into executive salaries or "team-building" events? How much is it spending in order to raise the donations it's seeking?

You're My Hero— or Not

"Argument from Authority" is really *Ad Hominem* turned upside down.

Arousing Fear

Slippery Slope: "It may seem minor now, but the end result will inevitably be a catastrophe." According to this rhetorical fallacy, if you eat at a fast-food restaurant once, pretty soon you'll never want to eat healthy, nourishing home-cooked meals again. Therefore, you can never allow yourself to eat at a fast-food restaurant, not even once. The author uses the fear of the disaster waiting at the bottom of the slippery slope to trick the reader into agreeing that the first action must not be allowed to occur.

Scare Tactics: Here the speaker or author is trying to frighten you into agreeing with him. If you don't commit to a two-year contract, your monthly rate won't be protected, and prices are going to go through the roof in the next couple of years. Who says? On what evidence does he make that prediction?

Weakening an Opposing Argument

These rhetorical fallacies present an opposing view in such a weak light that almost nobody would agree with it. Readers would, instead, accept the author's apparently stronger conclusion.

Red Herring: Instead of addressing the key issues of an opposing argument, a red herring fallacy focuses attention on an insignificant or irrelevant factor. For instance, you should avoid eating green vegetables (the conclusion) because of the risk of salmonella contamination (the red herring). This fallacy avoids the main points of the opposing argument in favor of green vegetables (such as nutritional content and health benefits).

Straw Man: The writer creates a straw man—something that's easy to knock down and tear apart—as the opposing viewpoint. The straw man could be either an over-simplification of an opponent's position, or a completely fictitious argument. In contrast, the writer's conclusion seems strong and reasonable.

For instance, suppose the mayor wants taxpayers to fund a new bridge that will lead directly to a large new subdivision. People who oppose this expense, she says, don't believe the new bridge is necessary because subdivision residents can simply spend an extra half-hour driving downtown, across the existing bridge, and back up the other side of the river to the new subdivision. That opposing viewpoint is pretty easy to knock down if you live, work, or shop in the new subdivision, so of course you favor a new bridge.

Making Inaccurate Connections

Faulty Analogy: One thing is compared with a second thing, but the comparison is exaggerated or misleading or unreasonable. Nevertheless, that comparison colors the reader's impression of the first thing. "Hiking on that trail is like descending into a dungeon of horrors from which you might never return." Perhaps it's just a challenging trail that leads through thick woods and would give you a good workout. But few people would try it after hearing the speaker's comparison.

Faulty Causality (also called *Post hoc ergo propter hoc*): This type of fallacy assumes that because one event happened shortly before another, the first event must have caused the second. (That's what the long Latin name refers to, by the way). "She wore her old Brand X runners instead of her new Brand Y runners; therefore she lost the race." Well, maybe. But perhaps she lost the race because she hadn't trained sufficiently, or because her knee was sore that day, or because others were simply faster. No evidence is presented to prove that the first event caused the second.

> ### Reverse Causation
> Causal arguments are often faulty because the reverse causation is equally plausible. For example, "Eating too much chocolate can make you depressed." Well, it's just as likely that depressed people might feel the urge to eat too much chocolate. If the author says "A caused B," ask yourself, "Is it also possible that B caused A?"

Twisting the Language

Begging the Question: In this rhetorical fallacy, an assumption which is not proven is used as evidence that the conclusion is correct. For instance, "high-altitude skiing is such a dangerous sport," (the evidence) "that no one under the age of 18 should be allowed to do it" (the conclusion). That might be a logical argument if the writer had proven—with statistics or with specific examples—that high-altitude skiing is dangerous for young people in particular. But he doesn't. He states that assumption as if it were a proven fact and then uses the assumption to prove his conclusion.

Circular Argument: This fallacy says essentially the same thing in both the conclusion and in the evidence that allegedly supports it. For example, someone might say that Sally cares about other people (the conclusion) because she is always willing to help them (the evidence). Someone who is always willing to help others obviously cares about them. Both the conclusion and the evidence describe the same idea. If the speaker had given specific examples of times when Sally helped someone else, and other actions that show she cares about others, he would have provided more credible proof for his conclusion.

Rhetorical fallacies in this category can be tough to spot, particularly when you're reading quickly under pressure. You need keen active reading skills to be able to say, "wait a minute, how do you know that piece of evidence is true?" or "didn't your evidence and your conclusion just say the same thing in different words?"

Mismatch Between Evidence and Conclusion

Missing the Point: The author offers evidence that supports a conclusion—it's just not the same conclusion that the author reaches. Imagine a presenter with gorgeous slides of meadows and grasslands in the northern plains, dense forests and subarctic tundra—the preferred habitats of grizzly bears. She cites research that reveals the grizzly population is declining and being pushed into smaller and smaller territories as humans take over the bears' habitats for their own uses. As a result, she continues, we should experiment with relocating small groups of grizzlies to see if they can adapt to habitats where they won't get so much competition from humans for use of the land. She suggests wetlands and high up on western mountains.

Her evidence does support the conclusions that we should take steps to protect the remaining grizzly population and should be more conscious of the impact our land use has on other creatures. However, it doesn't lead to a radical relocation scheme that ignores factors such as food sources, climate, and the bears' likely reaction.

Non Sequitur: This Latin term means, "it doesn't follow." In this rhetorical fallacy, the conclusion is not logically related to the evidence that preceded it. "Violent crime in this city has increased by 10 percent year over year for the past five years. Adding to the police force hasn't improved the situation. Therefore, we should build more private schools."

What do private schools have to do with the violent crime rate? Perhaps more than half of violent crimes occur around schools, private schools have the money for much better security measures, and the existing private schools all have long waiting lists. The author doesn't explain that, though; he has left serious gaps in the connection between his evidence and his conclusion.

It's easy to fall into this fallacy in your own work when the conclusion seems obvious to you. Think about your readers, though—would they need a few more steps before they could follow you to your conclusion?

Unstated Assumptions

Conclusions in this class of rhetorical fallacies rest on assumptions that the author doesn't even state, let alone prove. These, too, can be tough to spot in a pressure-cooker exam setting.

False Dichotomy: This rhetorical fallacy assumes a black-and-white world in which there is no middle ground, no other alternative. "If we don't launch a preemptive attack and destroy the enemy first, they will destroy us." No consideration is given to other possibilities, such as a diplomatic solution or a small-scale limited strike.

Hasty Generalization: Here the author or speaker assumes that a limited experience foreshadows the entire experience. The result is insufficient evidence to support the conclusion. "I could tell from the first few minutes that the movie was going to be unbearably boring, so I left rather than waste any more of my time." Maybe the director deliberately starts off slowly in order to intensify viewers' reactions to the terrifying monster that is about to appear.

You Can't Prove I'm Not Right
The absence of evidence to the contrary does not, in fact, prove anything.

Non-testable Hypothesis: In this rhetorical fallacy, anything that has not been proven false is assumed to be true; the author doesn't need to prove it's true. For example, suppose an environmental group claims that average temperatures across the entire North American continent would fall by 1° Celsius if we switched completely to renewable energy. Since we have never abandoned fossil fuels entirely, it's impossible to prove that the group's claim is false. Therefore, the argument assumes it must be true.

Drill—Catch the Rhetorical Fallacies

The following examples are similar to parts of passages you might encounter in the multiple-choice section of the AP English Language and Composition Exam, or to parts of the sources given in the essay questions. Before you read the explanation that follows each selection, try to identify how the author is misleading you into reaching the conclusion they want you to accept. Remember to look for the claim or action or belief that the author is endorsing. Then find and assess the evidence the author presents. Think about how your answer on the exam might be different depending on whether you noticed the rhetorical fallacy or not.

(Hint: One example does not contain a rhetorical fallacy. See if you can identify that one too.)

In this selection, a detective is questioning a woman in order to gather evidence about a crime he is investigating.

> "… it is on me that all this weight lies. If the police begin investigations they come close upon the fact that I went there to meet a man whom my husband has forbidden me to meet. Any little turn of evidence that involves me, any little accident that obliges me to admit it, and I am lost,"—her voice thrilled and pleaded.
>
> "It is you who are lost," he echoed dully. "I can understand how you feel. If I can ease your burden or lessen the anxiety you suffer from, you may depend upon me, Mrs. Wilder. This matter is a dark road where I, too, walk blind, not knowing the path I follow, but, at least, I can give you my word that under no circumstances shall I be led to mention your name. You can be sure of that, Mrs. Wilder. If I can add your trouble to my own burden I shall not feel its weight, …"
>
> Excerpt from *The Pointing Man: A Burmese Mystery*
> by Marjorie Douie, 1920

Now suppose a multiple-choice question asks:

> What technique does the detective use to try to gain Mrs. Wilder's confidence?
>
> (A) Deceit
> (B) Sympathy
> (C) Threats
> (D) Empathy

What conclusion is Mrs. Wilder supposed to reach?—that it's safe to answer the detective's questions. He won't tell anyone who gave him the information, so Mr. Wilder won't find out that his wife met the forbidden man. What evidence does the detective offer to support that conclusion? None. Mrs. Wilder can count on him keeping her name out of the investigation because she can depend on him (circular argument). She should believe him because he understands how she feels (non-testable hypothesis) and because he says she can (dogmatism).

Choice (C) is clearly not supported in the passage. If you didn't notice the rhetorical fallacies, though, you might be tempted to choose (D) or perhaps (B), both of which are incorrect. If you spotted the faulty evidence, you'd know the correct choice is (A). The detective's only objective is to get answers to his questions, and he'll tell this frightened woman whatever she needs to hear before she'll answer them.

This paragraph appears in "Maintenance and Safety of Hybrid and Plug-In Electric Vehicles," a resource from the U.S. Department of Energy's Vehicle Technologies Office. It is the type of source you might find in the synthesis essay question.

Safety Requirements

HEVs [hybrid electric vehicles], PHEVs [plug-in hybrid electric vehicles], and EVs [all-electric vehicles] have high-voltage electrical systems that typically range from 100 to 600 volts. Their battery packs are encased in sealed shells and meet testing standards that subject batteries to conditions such as overcharge, vibration, extreme temperatures, short circuit, humidity, fire, collision, and water immersion. Manufacturers design these vehicles with insulated high-voltage lines and safety features that deactivate the electrical system when they detect a collision or short circuit. EVs tend to have a lower center of gravity than conventional vehicles, making them more stable and less likely to roll over.

Suppose the synthesis prompt asked you to defend, challenge, or qualify the claim that electric vehicles are unsafe. How would you evaluate this excerpt when you're choosing sources for your essay? Is it a strong, reliable source, or does it contain faulty reasoning that misleads you into accepting a conclusion?

Start by identifying the conclusion: electric vehicles are safer than you might think because of the safety features designers have built into them. Now what evidence does the author give to support that conclusion? The selection lists specific examples of safety features (such as sealed cases and automatic shutoff) intended to shield people from the dangers of high voltage. It also describes a design feature (low center of gravity) that helps prevent instability and rollovers. And it acknowledges the high voltage instead of trying to hide the danger.

This author gives relevant, specific, logical evidence supporting the conclusion, and does not resort to rhetorical fallacies. This would be a good choice as one of your sources.

The following excerpt from a mobile app's End User License Agreement (EULA) illustrates the type of source you might see in the analysis essay question, for which you're asked to identify the strategies an author uses to achieve their purpose.

Bazaar Bonanza is a free, powerful, user-friendly tool to get you to the best deals on things that will make your life easier, more fulfilling and just plain more fun. Millions of users are saving money and time on products they want and need with Bazaar Bonanza. We take your privacy very seriously, and are committed to providing you with choice and transparency. We'd like you to know about the benefits you'll gain when you create an account and download our app.

In order to make sure you never miss a great deal, we track your location and maintain a database of your favorite places and the times and days you usually visit them. We also access your contacts, your messages and your emails because we know you'll want to share amazing bargains with your friends and family members. Since you'll want to return to the same shops that offered outstanding deals in the past, we track and store data about all of the purchases you make via a mobile payment service. Over time, we build a complete profile of your travel and shopping habits. So we can provide you with an ever-expanding universe of wonderful products and services at unbelievable prices, we share your profile with other companies that may be of interest to you. We also give those companies access to your reviews and endorsements so they can share them with other users who may be looking for similar deals.

What rhetorical strategies is this author using to achieve her purpose of gaining new users? Are rhetorical fallacies among those strategies?

This excerpt is full of rhetorical fallacies. First is the bandwagon ("millions of users") and then dogmatism—there's no evidence that the company values the privacy of its users or that it is offering them any choice. It's true because the company says it's true. The commitment to transparency is actually well-supported, though, in the extensive list of data the company collects and descriptions of what it does with that data. Next comes a scare tactic (missing a great deal). Then there are a few *non sequiturs*—for instance, if you want to share information about bargains with your friends, why does it follow that the app needs access to your contacts and messages? Throughout the entire excerpt is the unstated assumption that your desire to find a deal outweighs your desire to protect your personal information.

This is the type of prompt you might see in the argument essay question:

In order to save time, reduce costs, and avoid security risks, many companies are encouraging their employees to substitute technology (such as video conferencing) for business trips that can involve long absences, expensive travel, and potentially dangerous locations. In contrast, some executives and sales professionals claim there's no substitute for the personal relationships they can develop through meeting someone face to face or attending an industry event in person. Political leaders often seem to agree, traveling halfway around the world for a meeting that might last only an hour or two.

Think about the trade-off between savings and security on the one hand, and the gains that can result from an in-person meeting on the other. Then write an essay explaining your position on whether travel is worth the costs and risks. Use appropriate evidence from your reading, experience, or observations to support your argument.

Before you read the suggestions below, consider what position you would take on this question. Then think about the conclusions you'll need to persuade readers so they can follow your argument and eventually agree with it.

You could argue for using technology, for in-person travel or—most likely in this case—for a combination of the two. You might say, for example, that travel is justified for an initial meeting or two in order to establish a personal relationship, but after that, little more would be gained from the expense and potential risks of traveling to meet in person. Electronic communication or phone calls would serve the purpose.

To lead readers to agree with this argument, you'll need to get them to concede that travel is expensive, time-consuming, and depending on the destination, can be dangerous. They'll have to acknowledge the importance of saving money, saving time, and avoiding risks. They also need to accept that an in-person relationship can form a foundation that leads to a better outcome in later long-distance dealings.

Now what evidence can you use to support each of those conclusions? And how can you avoid rhetorical fallacies in presenting that evidence? This prompt is particularly vulnerable to fallacies that emphasize the person or group instead of the merits of an idea, to fallacies that arouse fear, and to mismatches between the evidence and the conclusion.

Under the time pressure of the exam, you won't have time to do a thorough assessment of your evidence for each conclusion. But as you're writing, you can ask yourself if you're really addressing the conclusion itself, or only the people who would advocate that course of action. Are you trying to frighten readers by describing the consequences that might result from not following your recommendation? Have you left any gaps in the evidence that leads to your conclusion? Are you covering the key issues and most relevant aspects of the topic?

> Don't let clever rhetorical fallacies lead you down the wrong path!

Rhetorical fallacies can be very convincing. They're also easy errors to make in your own writing, particularly when you have a strong opinion about a subject, when you're making broad claims, or when you're experiencing stress during an exam. By training yourself to think in terms of relevant, complete, logically presented evidence, you can avoid falling into the trap of believing—or creating—rhetorical fallacies.

Another Course? Of Course!

If you can't get enough AP English Language and Composition and want to review this material with an expert, we also offer an AP 5 Guarantee and an online Cram Course that you can sign up for here: www. PrincetonReview.com/ college/ap-test-prep.

Chapter 11
Style

In the context of the AP Language and Composition Exam, "style" refers to the word choices, comparisons, and syntax that a writer uses and how they contribute to the tone of the text. If you think of the zoom lens on a camera, you can consider the contents of Chapter 8, discussing the rhetorical situation, to be zoomed way out. You're considering the writer, the audience, and the overall argument presented in the text. Now, we are going to zoom way in and consider the individual words an author selects, and how that author constructs their sentences and makes use of stylistic conventions to advance their argument.

Similarly, on the free-response portion of the exam, your readers are going to want to see that you are able to strategically use diction, syntax, and stylistic conventions to advance your argument.

In this chapter, we're going to review the basics you need to know for success on the exam. We'll also review more sophisticated terminology you'll need to be familiar with to score as high as possible.

Style, Tone, and Mood

Style refers to the general manner of expression used in a text. It describes how the author uses diction, syntax, and conventions to get their point across (e.g., pedantic, scientific, or emotive).

Tone describes the speaker's attitude toward the subject. Tone describes how the author seems to be feeling (e.g., optimistic, ironic, or playful). Readers infer a writer's tone through the writer's word choice, particularly the positive or negative connotations of their diction and comparisons. Sophisticated readers will make note of shifts in a writer's tone as the writer qualifies, refines, or reconsiders their perspective on a subject over the course of a passage.

Mood describes how the text makes the audience feel.

Let's return to the excerpt from a disgruntled baseball player that we considered closely in Chapter 8.

> Our left fielder couldn't hit the floor if he fell out of bed! After striking out twice (once with the bases loaded!), he grounded into a double-play. My grandmother runs faster than he does! In the eighth inning, he misjudged a routine fly ball, which brought in the winning run. What a jerk! Why didn't the club trade him last week when it was still possible? What's wrong with you guys?

The *style* is simple, direct, unsophisticated, truculent, and even crass. The *tone* is angry, brash, emotional, and even aggressive. The *mood* is stressed and concerned. Pay close attention to the final sentence: The speaker accuses the audience directly with "you," which could make the audience feel guilty, defensive, or angry.

Now let's try a sample question with an excerpt from Fyodor Dostoevsky's *Notes from Underground*.

> The long and the short of it is, gentlemen, that it is better to do nothing! Better conscious inertia!

1. The tone of the speaker is best characterized as

    (A) ironic
    (B) nihilistic
    (C) optimistic
    (D) accusatory

Vocabulary is important for both the multiple-choice section AND the essays. Start creating flashcards: write down any unfamiliar words from this book, look up their definitions, and write them down on index cards. There is a good chance you will see many of these words on your test!

You probably immediately eliminated (C) because the passage did not sound particularly optimistic. The author is not accusatory, so eliminate (D) as well. Choice (B) may have confused you a bit; "nihilism" refers to a belief in nothing. (Again notice the importance of vocabulary!) The speaker's tone can indeed be described as more "nihilistic" (referring to nothing) than "ironic," so the correct answer is (B).

Consider the following example question:

2. The style of the explanation for question 1 can best be described as

    (A) pedantic
    (B) lyrical
    (C) terse
    (D) edifying

Don't worry. Questions on the AP English Language and Composition Exam won't refer to explanations for previous questions. Just go with it on this one.

While it's possible that none of the answers stands out to you as the correct choice, you could rule out "pedantic" if you know that it means narrowly, stodgily, and often ostentatiously learned. Likewise, the AP exam and lyricism (intense, intimate display of emotion) make for an unlikely pair, so you can use POE to get rid of that choice too. Finally, "terse" (concise, without superfluous detail) shows up regularly on this exam but probably doesn't describe the writing in this book very well. Given that the last choice can mean both enlightening and informative, (D) is the best answer.

But as you can see, if you knew none of these words, the question may as well have read as follows:

3. The style of the paragraph above can best be described as

    (A) pompom
    (B) banana
    (C) tire iron
    (D) Susan

And then which would seem like the correct answer? Obviously, vocabulary is important, so start making those flashcards.

Diction

The basic definition of **diction** is "word choice." Generally, the diction questions you'll see on the test will ask you to evaluate why an author's choice of words is particularly effective, apt, or clear. Often, the test will ask you to consider what style and/or tone an author's use of diction develops. However, as we explained in the chapters on the multiple-choice section, more often than not it is the test-writers' diction that you have to crack.

Denotation and Connotation

Denotation refers to a word's primary or literal significance, while **connotation** refers to the vast range of other meanings that a word suggests. Context (and at times, author's intent) determines which connotations may be appropriate for a word. An author will carefully pick a particular word for its connotations, knowing or hoping a reader will make an additional inference as a result. Let's look at an example.

I am looking at the sky.

The denotation of the underlined word should be as clear as a cloudless sky (the space, often blue, above the Earth's surface). However, there can be connotations associated with the word. The sky is often associated with heaven; it can also evoke the idea of freedom or vast openness. Because of connotation, one can't help but believe that the sky evokes in the writer a sense of longing for freedom from work, the computer, or the AP English Language and Composition Exam.

Syntax

Tactics for Syntax

Syntax is simply another way of talking about grammar and sentence structure.

Syntax is another language term that you should be familiar with for the AP English Language and Composition Exam. Syntax is the ordering of words in a sentence; it describes sentence structure. The term *syntax* frequently turns up on the AP English Language and Composition Exams. Don't worry: you don't need to be an expert on this subject, but you should know how manipulating syntax can enhance an author's meaning, tone, or point of view.

Before we move on to examples of syntactical analysis, let's review some basic grammatical terms you'll need to be familiar with on the exam.

First, you should be able to identify the **eight parts of speech**: verbs, nouns, adjectives, adverbs, pronouns, interjections, conjunctions, and prepositions. You should feel comfortable categorizing individual words and **phrases**, groups of words, within a sentence. Pay particular attention to adjectives and adverbs. They not only modify the things they describe, but they are important indicators of tone, conveying the writer's perspective towards that which they discuss.

You should also feel comfortable identifying **clauses** within a sentence. A clause is a group of words that contains both a subject and a verb.

- **Independent clauses** can stand alone as sentences, such as "I ate breakfast."

- **Coordinate clauses** are two independent clauses that are combined into one sentence and contain equal importance, such as "I ate breakfast, and I ate second breakfast."

- **Subordinate clauses** require an independent clause to make sense, such as "I ate breakfast because I was hungry." "Because I was hungry" is the subordinate clause in this sentence.

There is great value in being able to identify clauses. Writers use subordination and coordination to express the relationships between their ideas. Coordination reflects balance and equality; subordination reflects imbalance and inequality. Further, being able to specifically describe the elements of a passage will make analysis much easier on the free-response segment of the exam.

Lastly, make sure you're fluent with identifying and using a variety of punctuation marks (commas, colons, semicolons, dashes, hyphens, parentheses, quotation marks, and end marks). You should be able to describe how punctuation clarifies, organizes, and emphasizes content within a sentence or passage. In many cases, punctuation, and syntax as a whole, is critical to describing how a writer develops tone.

Using these tools to enhance your writing, by adding sentence variety, clarity, and emphasis, is an excellent way to enhance your score on the free-response questions. Let's look at an example from *Candide*, taken from the famous opening of Chapter 3.

> Never was anything so gallant, so well outfitted, so brilliant, and so finely disposed as the two armies. The trumpets, fifes, reeds, drums, and cannon made such harmony as never was heard in Hell.

The first sentence poses as a fairly simple sketch of a glorious battle scene. The second begins in the same fashion, but its words are arranged in a way that maximizes the effect of surprise that comes at the end of the sentence. The cannons are slipped in as the final member of a list of military musical instruments; the formation of the list creates an expectation that the final element will fit nicely into the set. It doesn't, but we don't have time to register our surprise because we're immediately distracted by a new setup with the phrase "such harmony as never was heard…." We expect harmony to be something beautiful, and we already begin to supply the final word (Earth? Heaven?) when—surprise—we are jolted by the word that Voltaire chose instead: Hell. That is the power of syntax.

Here's another slightly different example. In the following example, Candide asks about the proper etiquette for greeting the King of Eldorado through his servant and sidekick, Cacambo.

> When they drew near to the royal chamber, Cacambo asked one of the officers in what manner they were to pay their respects to His Majesty; whether it was the custom to fall upon their knees, or to prostrate themselves upon the ground; whether they were to put their hands upon their heads, or behind their backs; whether they were to lick the dust off the floor; in short, what was the usual ceremony for such occasions.

The syntax of this long sentence is very carefully constructed; Voltaire uses all of the parallel clauses that begin with "whether" to achieve great comic effect. At first, the text is fairly straightforward—after all, going down on one's knees before a king would have been fairly standard for a European reader of the 18th century; however, with each clause, the groveling etiquette becomes more extreme, and the final image—of licking the dust off the floor—pushes the concept beyond the believable. The syntax of this sentence is structured in a way that allows us to see the absurdity of *all* forms of ceremonial deference. In fact, in this story, the enlightened King of Eldorado simply embraces both Cacambo and Candide.

Note that punctuation is a critical aspect of syntax. In both of these examples, Voltaire's syntax revolves around punctuation: serial commas to create an extended list, and semicolons to unite the clauses that begin with "whether." Further, writers often use exclamation points to create an excited or emphatic tone.

COMPARISONS

As we've mentioned, you don't need to be an expert in the English language to ace the AP English Language and Composition Exam; however, you do need to have some understanding of how language works. With the exception of technical manuals (like the one that helped you assemble your entertainment center), few texts are written such that all of their language is meant to be taken literally. **Figurative language** is strictly defined as speech or writing that departs from literal meaning to achieve a special effect or meaning. Take, for example, the end of one of Abraham Lincoln's inaugural speeches.

> With malice toward none, with charity for all, with firmness in the right as God gives us to see the right, let us strive on to finish the work we are in, to bind up the nation's wounds, to care for him who shall have borne the battle and for his widow and his orphan, to do all which may achieve and cherish a just and lasting peace among ourselves and with all nations.

Are we supposed to take "to bind up the nation's wounds" literally? Of course not. Lincoln has personified our country to make the suffering of particular individuals relatable to all the people of the nation. And what about "him who shall have borne the battle"? Clearly, Lincoln is using the singular (a man) to represent the collective mass of soldiers, and when he adds "his widow and his orphan," we understand that "shall have borne the battle" really means "shall have died in battle." Lincoln personalizes the suffering of this group of people by instead speaking of individual sacrifice, which he knows is far more likely to strike a profound emotional chord in his listeners.

Despite the effectiveness of Lincoln's speech, keep in mind that many other perfectly convincing arguments and explanations are conveyed primarily through literal language. On this exam, there's no need for you to strain yourself attempting to use figurative language in the free-response section. But it will be very helpful for you to review the common terms associated with figurative language that we've listed below because you will be obliged to analyze texts that contain figurative language on this test.

The type of figurative language most important for success on the AP exam is **comparisons**. A comparison occurs anytime a writer places two different ideas next to each other for consideration. In this section, we are going to look closely at identifying and analyzing comparisons.

Imagery

For the purposes of this exam, you may consider **imagery** to be synonymous with figurative language. However, in a more restricted sense, imagery is figurative language that is used to convey a sensory perception (visual, auditory, olfactory, tactile, or gustatory).

Hyperbole

Hyperbole is overstatement or exaggeration; it is the use of figurative language that significantly exaggerates the facts for effect. In many instances, but certainly not all, hyperbole is employed for comic effect. Consider the following example.

> If you use too much figurative language in your essays, the AP readers will crucify you!

Clearly, this statement is a gross exaggeration; while the readers may give you a poor grade if you use figurative language that doesn't suit the purposes of your essay, they will not kill you.

Why use sensory imagery?

By activating one of the five senses, authors can often evoke particular emotions from their audience. For example, an author might mention the smell of salty sea air in order to garner a sense of relaxation or adventure from their audience. In other words, sensory imagery can develop pathos within an argument.

Understatement

Understatement is figurative language that presents the facts in a way that makes them appear much less significant than they really are. Understatement is almost always used for comic effect.

> After dinner, they came and took into custody Doctor Pangloss and his pupil Candide, the one for speaking his mind and the other for appearing to approve what he heard. They were conducted to separate apartments, which were extremely cool and where they were never bothered by the sun.

Taking the last sentence literally would lead you astray. The understatement in this case ("They were conducted to separate apartments, which were extremely cool and where they were never bothered by the sun") should be taken to mean that the poor men were thrown into horribly dark, dank, and cold prison cells.

Simile

Authors often use similes and metaphors to compare new information to ideas the audience is already familiar with. Depending on what is being compared, this can develop logos and/or pathos within a text. However, this consistently develops ethos: if the author uses an effective comparison, it reveals that the author understands the perspective of their audience, which can build trust and sympathy between the two.

A **simile** is a comparison between two unlike objects, in which the two parts are connected with a term such as *like* or *as*. Here's an example of a simile:

> The birds are like black arrows flying across the sky.

You can easily identify a simile—and distinguish it from a metaphor—because of the use of *like* or *as*.

Consider the way in which this comparison develops tone and mood. Arrows can be indicators of direction, suggesting positivity for forward thinking, perhaps even anticipation of the future. Arrows can also be weapons, suggesting something ominous or foreboding. The different connotations of "arrows" suggest different tones, either an optimistic or a bleak perspective on behalf of the author.

Metaphor

A **metaphor** is a simile without a connecting term such as *like* or *as*. Here's an example of a metaphor.

> The birds are black arrows flying across the sky.

Birds are not arrows, but the commonalities (both are long and sleek, and they travel swiftly through the air—and both have feathers) allow us to easily grasp the image.

Extended Metaphor

An **extended metaphor** is precisely what it sounds like—it is a metaphor that lasts for longer than just one phrase or sentence. A word of caution for the exam, however; do not use extended metaphors in your own AP essays, for many scholars (and many AP graders) believe that the extended metaphor is a poor expository or argumentative technique. Consider this example:

During the time I have voyaged on this ship, I have avoided the cabin; rather, I have remained on deck, battered by wind and rain, but able to see moonlight on the water. I do not wish to go below decks now.

As surprising as this may seem, this passage is not about nautical navigation. The ship's voyage is the central metaphor (representing the course of life); the writer extends the metaphor by relating elements of figurative language: cabin, deck, wind and rain, moonlight, water, and decks. The cabin is a safe place, but it's a place where you can't experience much; on deck, you're exposed to the elements, but you can experience beauteous sights. Having made the difficult, dangerous, but rewarding choice of staying on deck, it would be a personal defeat, a kind of surrender to wish for the safety, comfort, and limited horizons of the cabin later in life.

> **Metaphors vs. Symbols**
>
> Sometimes, it is difficult to distinguish between metaphor and symbol. Remember that a metaphor always contains an implied comparison between two elements. Recall the metaphorical image of the birds and the arrows: the birds remain birds, and the arrows remain arrows—and the metaphor serves to give us an image of the flight of the birds by suggesting a visualization of arrows. However, in the case of a symbol, the named object really doesn't count. In the example below, there is no lamb; *lamb* is merely an object that's meant to conjure up another object or element.

Symbolism

A **symbol** is a concrete object that represents an abstract idea. Here's an example:

> The Christian soldiers paused to remember the lamb.

In this case, the lamb is a symbol. The lamb is a concrete object that represents an abstract idea. In this case, the lamb symbolizes the legacy of Jesus Christ.

> Use your knowledge of denotations and connotations to analyze symbols. When you identify a symbolic object, here's how to start your analysis:
>
> **Step 1:** Denotation: Define the concrete object acting as a symbol in the text.
>
> **Step 2:** Brainstorm five connotations for the object. What does it remind you of? Are there any other well-known examples of this object?
>
> **Step 3:** Ask yourself, how do these connotations develop main ideas in the text?

Anytime you identify a simile, metaphor, or personification, you have identified a comparison between two different things that adds meaning to the text. Here's how to start your analysis:

Step 1: Identify the two things being compared. Be as specific as possible.

Step 2: Brainstorm the similarities and differences between these two things.

Step 3: Ask yourself: How do these similarities and differences develop main ideas in the text?

Personification

Personification is the figurative device in which inanimate objects or concepts are given the thoughts, feelings, or actions of a human. It can enhance our emotional response because we usually attribute more emotional significance to other humans than to things or concepts. Consider this example of personification:

He had been wrestling with lethargy for days, and every time that he thought that he was close to victory, his adversary escaped his hold.

This figurative wrestling match, in which lethargy is personified as the opponent to the author of this sentence, brings the struggle to life—human life. If you don't believe this, think about the literal alternative: he tried to stop being lethargic, but he was not successful. This doesn't sound very lively.

> **Anthropomorphism** occurs when non-human objects are given the physical shape of a human, e.g., the legs of a table, the face of a clock, the arms of a tree.

OTHER STYLISTIC DEVICES TO KNOW

Paradox

A **paradox** contains two elements which cannot both be true at the same time (although usually each one could be true on its own).

The classic example is the Cretan Liar Paradox, attributed to the 6th-century BCE philosopher and poet Epimenides. He was from Crete, and his famous paradox says, "All Cretans are liars."

Think about it. He's a Cretan; therefore (if his statement is true), he must also be a liar. But if he's a liar, he can't be making a true statement, so the statement must be false. As you can imagine, many philosophers and logicians have puzzled over how to resolve Epimenides's paradox.

Here's another ancient Greek example, this time from Socrates, the 5th-century BCE philosopher: "One thing only I know, and that is that I know nothing." Well if it's true that he knows nothing, then it can't also be true that he knows even that one thing. And if he knows that one thing, it can't be true that he knows nothing.

What's the point of putting a paradox in a piece of writing? It depends on the author's purpose and point of view—both of which you should have identified as you were reading the passage.

Perhaps the writer is describing a world—or advancing an argument—in which things are not always what they seem. A paradox is a good way to encourage readers to look at familiar things in new ways, or to question their assumptions. The writer might also be asking readers to suspend logical reasoning and use intuition or a more spiritual type of perception instead. Or, quite simply, the author might just be trying to jolt readers out of a habitual, absorption-type mode of reading—to make them think and return to reread and analyze the paradoxical statement.

Whatever the specific reason, the writer is trying to get your attention by using a paradox. It's your job to figure out why.

Rhetorical Question

A **rhetorical question** is a question whose answer is obvious; these types of questions do not need to be answered—and usually aren't. Rhetorical questions attempt to prove something without actually presenting an argument; sometimes they're used as a form of irony, in which something is stated, but its opposite is meant.

> Given how cheap the most fattening foods are, is it any wonder obesity is on the rise? (no irony)

Since it has already been determined that you agree (even if you don't), the writer need not substantiate this remark.

> Aren't AP exams great fun? (with irony)

Here, there is an assumption that you would answer in the negative, although there is no way for you to respond—unless you write a letter. Rhetorical questions allow a writer to make a point without further support, whether it's a straightforward remark or one with a touch of irony.

Irony

Generally speaking, irony refers to the relationship between the text and the audience's expectations. If the audience anticipates certain events or dialogue, and alternate events or dialogue occur, you're likely dealing with irony. Let's look at the two basic types of irony that you'll need to be familiar with for this test: verbal irony and situational irony.

Verbal Irony

Verbal irony refers to the process of stating something but *meaning* the opposite of what is stated. In cases of verbal irony, the audience can anticipate the dialogue or specific language used in a text. The author may use a common saying, situation, or emotional experience to build up the audience's expectation. For example, an author may describe an experience while shopping. When the author enters the store, the salesperson says, "Hello, how can you help me?" This would be ironic because the expectation is that the salesperson would say the opposite, "How can I help you?"

Verbal irony can refer to irony that's used in spoken language as well as in print. In spoken language, intonation is often a clue to ironic intent; however, in writing, it is not possible to imply things through intonation, so there's always a danger that the irony may be missed; in essence, the writer who employs irony risks communicating the exact opposite of what is intended. For example, let's say that you write, "This Princeton Review book is really interesting." Unless your listener or reader

Rain on Your Wedding Day

Irony is not mere misfortune. It is a set of circumstances that wind up the opposite of how the reader would expect them to turn out or how the characters had planned.

Take a minute to review the rhetorical diamond on page 138. To develop irony, the author uses the context of the text to guide the audience's expectation. The author then subverts those expectations with surprising events or dialogue.

hears your remark in context, they won't know if this is high praise for this book, or if you're bored silly and have chosen to express your sentiment more forcefully by using verbal irony.

Let's take a look at an example of verbal irony in context. In November of 1969 former Vice President Spiro Agnew gave a televised speech in which he warned about the dangers of the 24-hour news media. He says:

> Gresham's Law seems to be operating in the network news: bad news drives out good news. The irrational is more controversial than the rational. Concurrence can no longer compete with dissent…. The
> *Line* labor crisis settled at the negotiating table is nothing compared to the
> 5 confrontation that results in a strike—or better yet, violence along the picket lines. Normality has become the nemesis of the network news.
> Now the upshot of all this controversy is that a narrow and distorted picture of America often emerges from the televised news. A single, dramatic piece of the mosaic becomes in the minds of millions
> 10 the entire picture.

Initially, Agnew describes negative features of the news. That the "irrational" is more exciting than the everyday, and that "normality" is a nemesis. Then he says the "upshot" of all this is a "narrow and distorted" depiction of America. Clearly, Agnew doesn't consider the resulting "distorted picture" to be an "upshot." He is obviously very concerned! Agnew uses the word "upshot," but is actually describing a very negative side effect of the news. He's using verbal irony to underscore just how concerned he is about developments in the news.

Situational Irony

A simple example of situational irony can be found in the classic tale "The Gift of the Magi." Jim and Della are a poor couple who have no money to buy each other gifts for Christmas. Jim sells his watch to buy Della a comb for her hair. Della sells her hair to buy Jim a watch-chain. Both gifts wind up useless to their respective recipients—the ultimate in irony.

Situational Irony

Situational irony refers to a circumstance that runs contrary to what was expected.

Suppose you live in Seattle during the rainy season and plan a vacation to sunny Phoenix. While you are in Phoenix, it rains every day there, but is sunny the entire week in Seattle. This is situational irony.

Here we are at the end of the review section of the book. You are now ready to take the second practice test; depending on how you did on the first one, you may have been dreading this moment, but we know that once you begin, you'll see that you know a lot more than you think you do! If you've worked through the book up to this point and complete these practice exams, you'll certainly be ready for test day. Good luck!

Part VI
Practice Tests 2, 3, and 4

Practice Test 2

AP® English Language and Composition Exam

SECTION I: Multiple-Choice Questions

DO NOT BEGIN THE EXAM UNTIL YOU ARE TOLD TO DO SO.

DISCLAIMER: The official AP English Language and Composition Exam will be administered digitally. Instructions for the digital exam may differ from this practice test.

At a Glance

Total Time
1 hour
Number of Questions
45
Percent of Total Grade
45%

Instructions

Section I of this examination contains 45 multiple-choice questions. Choose the best answer to each question. Note: Pay particular attention to the requirements of questions that contain the words "NOT," "LEAST," or "EXCEPT."

Indicate all of your answers to the multiple-choice questions on the answer sheet. No credit will be given for anything written in this exam booklet, but you may use the booklet for notes or scratch work. After you have decided which of the suggested answers is best, completely fill in the corresponding oval on the answer sheet. Give only one answer to each question. If you change an answer, be sure that the previous mark is erased completely. Here is a sample question and answer.

Sample Question   Sample Answer

Chicago is a
(A) state
(B) city
(C) country
(D) continent

Use your time effectively, working as quickly as you can without losing accuracy. Do not spend too much time on any one question. Go on to other questions and come back to the ones you have not answered if you have time.

Many candidates wonder whether or not to guess the answers to questions about which they are not certain. Multiple-choice scores are based on the number of questions answered correctly. Points are not deducted for incorrect answers, and no points are awarded for unanswered questions. Because points are not deducted for incorrect answers, you are encouraged to answer all multiple-choice questions. On any questions you do not know the answer to, you should eliminate as many choices as you can, and then select the best answer among the remaining choices.

GO ON TO THE NEXT PAGE.

This page intentionally left blank.

ENGLISH LANGUAGE AND COMPOSITION
SECTION I
Time—1 hour

Directions: This part consists of selections from prose works and questions on their content, form, and style. After reading each passage, choose the best answer to each question and completely fill in the corresponding oval on the answer sheet.

Note: Pay particular attention to the requirement of questions that contain the words NOT, LEAST, or EXCEPT.

Questions 1–11. Read the following passage carefully before you choose your answers.

This passage is excerpted from a speech given in 1850 and published in 1855.

More than twenty years of my life were consumed in a state of slavery. My childhood was environed by the baneful peculiarities of the slave system. I grew up to manhood in the
Line presence of this hydra-headed monster—not as a master—not
5 as an idle spectator—not as the guest of the slaveholder—but as A SLAVE, eating the bread and drinking the cup of slavery with the most degraded of my brother-bondmen, and sharing with them all the painful conditions of their wretched lot. In consideration of these facts, I feel that I have a right to speak,
10 and to speak *strongly*. Yet, my friends, I feel bound to speak truly…

First of all, I will state, as well as I can, the legal and social relation of master and slave. A master is one—to speak in the vocabulary of the southern states—who claims and
15 exercises a right of property in the person of a fellow-man. This he does with the force of the law and the sanction of southern religion. The law gives the master absolute power over the slave. He may work him, flog him, hire him out, sell him, and, in certain contingencies, *kill* him, with perfect
20 impunity. The slave is a human being, divested of all rights— reduced to the level of a brute—a mere "chattel" in the eye of the law—placed beyond the circle of human brotherhood— cut off from his kind—his name, which the "recording angel" may have enrolled in heaven, among the blest, is impiously
25 inserted in a *master's ledger*, with horses, sheep, and swine. In law, the slave has no wife, no children, no country, and no home. He can own nothing, possess nothing, acquire nothing, but what must belong to another….He toils that another may reap the fruit; he is industrious that another may live in
30 idleness; he eats unbolted meal that another may eat the bread of fine flour; he labors in chains at home, under a burning sun and biting lash, that another may ride in ease and splendor abroad; he lives in ignorance that another may be educated; he is abused that another may be exalted; he rests his toil-
35 worn limbs on the cold, damp ground that another may repose on the softest pillow; he is clad in coarse and tattered raiment that another may be arrayed in purple and fine linen; he is sheltered only by the wretched hovel that a master may dwell in a magnificent mansion; and to this condition he is bound
40 down as by an arm of iron…

We are sometimes told of the contentment of the slaves, and are entertained with vivid pictures of their happiness. We are told that they often dance and sing; that their masters frequently give them wherewith to make merry; in fine, that
45 they have little of which to complain. I admit that the slave does sometimes sing, dance, and appear to be merry. But what does this prove? It only proves to my mind, that though slavery is armed with a thousand stings, it is not able entirely to kill the elastic spirit of the bondman. That spirit will rise
50 and walk abroad, despite of whips and chains, and extract from the cup of nature occasional drops of joy and gladness. No thanks to the slaveholder, nor to slavery, that the vivacious captive may sometimes dance in his chains; his very mirth in such circumstances stands before God as an accusing angel
55 against his enslaver.

1. The phrase "baneful peculiarities" functions as a euphemism for

   (A) the practices of the slavery system at large
   (B) the aspects of slavery the author found strange
   (C) the parts of the slave system the author found immoral
   (D) the features of slavery that were disagreeable to the speaker

2. The "hydra-headed monster" is a metaphor for

   (A) slave-owners
   (B) slaves
   (C) slavery
   (D) idle spectators

GO ON TO THE NEXT PAGE.

3. The function of the first paragraph is to develop

   (A) pathos: the speaker is describing his authority to speak on the subject of slavery
   (B) pathos: the speaker is trying to evoke sympathy from the audience
   (C) ethos: the speaker is trying to evoke sympathy from the audience
   (D) ethos: the speaker is describing his authority to speak on the subject of slavery

4. The speaker's attitude toward the audience can best be described as

   (A) irreverent
   (B) amicable
   (C) convivial
   (D) condescending

5. Lines 12–25 ("First of all…with horses, sheep, and swine.") serve to

   (A) explain why slavery exists
   (B) compare slaves to their masters
   (C) define the terms "master" and "slave"
   (D) analyze the nature of slavery

6. In the passage, the author provides what rationale for the legal ownership of slaves?

   (A) Legal authority
   (B) Religious authority
   (C) Legal and religious authority
   (D) Moral authority

7. The author italicizes "master's ledger" in order to emphasize

   (A) the bureaucracy of slavery
   (B) the dehumanization of slaves
   (C) the fear masters had for slaves
   (D) the hope preserved within slave communities

8. Lines 28–40 highlight the contrast between

   (A) different kinds of slaves
   (B) slaves and their owners
   (C) different kinds of slave owners
   (D) male and female slaves

9. In lines 28–40, ("He toils that another may reap the fruit…he is bound down as by an arm of iron"), the author develops his rhetorical purpose by

   (A) using repetition to emphasize the aspects of slavery the author found the most cruel
   (B) using alliteration to emphasize the poetic nature of the diction
   (C) using metaphor to illustrate the inhumanity of slavery
   (D) using parallel clause structures to list the indignities suffered by slaves

10. The third paragraph argues against which belief?

    (A) Slaves are angry.
    (B) Slaves will never revolt.
    (C) Slavery is inherent in humanity.
    (D) Slaves enjoy life.

11. The passage ends on a note of

    (A) exhausted fatigue
    (B) extreme frustration
    (C) divine retribution
    (D) dignified resignation

GO ON TO THE NEXT PAGE.

Questions 12–23. Read the following passage carefully before you choose your answers.

This passage is excerpted from a 1991 article in a popular news magazine.

As I teach, I learn a lot about our schools. Early in each session I ask my students to write about an unpleasant experience they had in school. No writers' block here! "I
Line wish someone would have had made me stop doing drugs
5 and made me study." "I liked to party and no one seemed to care." "I was a good kid and didn't cause any trouble, so they just passed me along even though I didn't read and couldn't write." And so on.

I am your basic do-gooder, and prior to teaching this
10 class I blamed the poor academic skills our kids have today on drugs, divorce and other impediments to concentration necessary for doing well in school. But, as I rediscover each time I walk into the classroom, before a teacher can expect students to concentrate, he has to get their attention, no
15 matter what distractions may be at hand. There are many ways to do this, and they have much to do with teaching style. However, if style alone won't do it, there is another way to show who holds the winning hand in the classroom. That is to reveal the trump card of failure.

20 I will never forget a teacher who played that card to get the attention of one of my children. Our youngest, a world class charmer, did little to develop his intellectual talents but always got by. Until Mrs. Stifter.

Our son was a high-school senior when he had her for
25 English. "He sits in the back of the room talking to his friends," she told me. "Why don't you move him to the front row?" I urged, believing the embarrassment would get him to settle down. Mrs. Stifter looked at me steely-eyed over her glasses." I don't move seniors," she said. "I flunk them."
30 I was flustered. Our son's academic life flashed before my eyes. No teacher had ever threatened him with that before. I regained my composure and managed to say that I thought she was right. By the time I got home I was feeling pretty good about this. It was a radical approach for these times,
35 but, well, why not? "She's going to flunk you," I told my son. I did not discuss it any further. Suddenly English became a priority in his life. He finished out the semester with an A.

I know one example doesn't make a case, but at night I see a parade of students who are angry and resentful for
40 having been passed along until they could no longer even pretend to keep up. Of average intelligence or better, they eventually quit school, concluding they were too dumb to finish. "I should have been held back," is a comment I hear frequently. Even sadder are those students who are high-
45 school graduates who say to me after a few weeks of class, "I don't know how I ever got a high-school diploma."

Passing students who have not mastered the work cheats them and the employers who expect graduates to have basic skills. We excuse this dishonest behavior by saying kids
50 can't learn if they come from terrible environments. No one seems to stop to think that—no matter what environments they come from—most kids don't put school first on their list unless they perceive something is at stake. They'd rather be sailing….

55 Flunking as a regular policy has just as much merit today as it did two generations ago. We must review the threat of flunking and see it as it really is—a positive teaching tool. It is an expression of confidence by both teachers and parents that the students have the ability to learn the material
60 presented to them. However, making it work again would take a dedicated, caring conspiracy between teachers and parents. It would mean facing the tough reality that passing kids who haven't learned the material—while it might save them grief for the short term—dooms them to longterm
65 illiteracy.

12. What purpose does the first paragraph serve?

   (A) The author relies on expert testimony to state the problem she will address in her topic.

   (B) The author uses first-hand accounts to introduce her general topic.

   (C) The author uses an anecdote to engage the reader's attention.

   (D) The author states her thesis and purpose.

13. In lines 12–19 the author draws a contrast between

   (A) addressing teaching style and letting students fail

   (B) addressing parenting style and letting students fail

   (C) addressing teacher education and letting students fail

   (D) addressing teaching style and refusing to let students fail

GO ON TO THE NEXT PAGE.

14. The function of the third paragraph is to

    (A) characterize the author
    (B) address the audience directly
    (C) begin a digression
    (D) start an anecdote

15. What purpose do lines 56–58 ("We must review the threat of flunking and see it as it really is—a positive teaching tool.") serve?

    (A) To suggest that the reader do further research
    (B) To state the author's thesis
    (C) To compare flunking to other teaching tools
    (D) To introduce another example

16. Throughout the passage, the author makes frequent use of

    (A) metaphors
    (B) similes
    (C) analogies
    (D) anecdotes

17. In paragraph 5, the author uses the phrase "I know one example doesn't make a case, ..." in order to

    (A) provide evidence for a major claim
    (B) rebut a competing claim
    (C) make an allusion
    (D) concede the limitations of a claim

18. In the second paragraph, the author

    (A) states a previously held view and an alternate option
    (B) states a previously held view and describes how it has been affirmed
    (C) describes the failure of the education system
    (D) describes herself as a teacher and mother

19. The use of the phrase "they'd rather be sailing" emphasizes

    (A) what students trapped in school would rather be doing
    (B) the preference for students to do what is easiest
    (C) how much easier it is for teachers to pass students than fail them
    (D) the preference for parents to relax instead of discipline their children

20. The passage implies that, unlike a desire to "be sailing," her son was inspired to succeed in English due to his

    (A) respect for his teacher
    (B) fear of failure
    (C) desire to go to college
    (D) fear of his teacher

21. The author is best described as

    (A) a curious individual with a question for policy makers
    (B) an exhausted teacher who is frustrated with the status quo
    (C) a former student who experienced failure
    (D) an observant individual with a suggestion for others

22. As the passage moves from the sixth to the seventh paragraph, it also moves from

    (A) pedantic to intimate
    (B) academic to personal
    (C) descriptive to political
    (D) scientific to philosophical

23. Which of the following is the purpose of the fourth paragraph?

    (A) To suggest that a teacher helped to change the work ethic of the author's son
    (B) To give an anecdote that concedes an exception to a rule
    (C) To provide a personal story that supports the main thesis
    (D) To explain why her child failed English class

GO ON TO THE NEXT PAGE.

Questions 24–31 are based on the following passage.

The passage below is a draft.

(1) One guitarist and saxophonist, Bruce Diamond, recorded nearly a hundred songs from his home in Lexington, Kentucky. (2) Recently, hundreds of these rough recordings have been re-mastered. (3) They have captured the attention of musicologists for a number of reasons.

(4) First, it is possibly apparent that Diamond's songs were influenced by many different popular artists of the day. (5) One song sounds very similar to a complicated jazz song by Charlie Parker. (6) However, another song is the opposite: the song sounds like the straightforward rock of Buddy Holly. (7) The lyrics are very similar as well, and one is led to wonder what inspired them. (8) One music critic observed that Diamond found it completely effortless to switch back and forth between very different musical genres.

(9) Diamond's recordings are noteworthy for their unique artistic voice—an interesting combination of jazz, bluegrass, and gospel styles. (10) In one piece, Diamond starts with a long soulful intro leading into an upbeat verse. (11) The verse's tempo and tone provide an interesting contrast to the mournful opening. (12) The chorus combines elements of both in an unexpected but balanced way. (13) Diamond seems to express in this song that he has overcome some emotional wounds but that he remains conflicted. (14) We have all experienced sad events and know very well what it is like to feel conflicted.

(15) Sources of music from major music towns like New Orleans, Detroit, and Nashville are abundant, little is known about Lexington's music scene because the town lacked a real recording studio. (16) Therefore, since they were recorded on two-inch tape, Diamond's songs in a city like Lexington offer music historians a rare taste of the musical culture in the 1960s.

(17) No one knows how much Diamond was affected by other musicians in Lexington, but he did perform regularly at a local blues bar and less frequently at a jazz dance hall. (18) One thing, though, is for sure: he records an interesting portfolio of songs, and he may soon be a famous saxophonist.

24. Which of the following sentences, if placed before sentence 1, would both provide relevant context and the most effective introduction to the topic of the paragraph?

   (A) Beginning around 1963, when people became able to buy cassette recorders with built-in microphones, amateur songwriters were able to record songs that had been formerly undocumented.
   (B) In 1963, musicologists were aghast when they discovered a cache of formerly undocumented songs recorded by Kentucky folk musicians.
   (C) As part of a united effort to document southern bluegrass music, many musicians in the 1960s recorded hitherto undocumented songs.
   (D) As rock and roll was gaining popularity in the 1960s, America was starting to lose touch with its musical traditions.

25. In sentence 4 (reproduced below), which of the following versions of the underlined text would most confidently establish the writer's position about the main argument of the paragraph?

   First, *it is possibly apparent that Diamond's songs were influenced by* many different popular artists of the day.

   (A) (as it is now)
   (B) Diamond's songs influenced
   (C) Diamond's songs demonstrate that he was influenced by
   (D) Diamond partnered with songwriters and

26. In sentence 7 (reproduced below), the writer wants to provide further detail about the lyrical subject matter in Diamond's songs.

   The lyrics are very similar as well, *and one is led to wonder what inspired them.*

   Which version of the underlined text best accomplishes this goal?

   (A) (as it is now)
   (B) dealing mostly with dating and automobiles.
   (C) and he mostly uses rhymed couplets and alliteration.
   (D) which are easy to understand because of Diamond's enunciation.

27. In sentence 9 (reproduced below), the writer wants an introduction to the paragraph that echoes the main point of the previous paragraph.

Diamond's recordings are noteworthy for their unique artistic voice—an interesting combination of jazz, blue-grass, and gospel styles.

Which of the following versions of the underlined text best achieves this purpose?

(A) (as it is now)
(B) voice; the beginnings of his songs often do not match the endings.
(C) voice (in spite of the opinions of many of his critics).
(D) voice—a style that has earned him a reputation for innovation.

28. In order to make the passage more concise, the writer wants to remove a sentence from the passage without losing information pertinent to the main argument. Which sentence could be removed?

(A) Sentence 5
(B) Sentence 6
(C) Sentence 7
(D) Sentence 14

29. The writer wants to the add a word or phrase to the beginning of sentence 15 (reproduced below), adjusting the capitalization as needed.

Sources of music from major music towns like New Orleans, Detroit, and Nashville are abundant, little is known about Lexington's music scene because the town lacked a real recording studio.

Which of the following would NOT be an appropriate choice?

(A) While
(B) Although
(C) Since
(D) Whereas

30. In sentence 16 (reproduced below), the writer wants to provide a clear explanation for the historical importance of Diamond's music.

Therefore, since they were recorded on two-inch tape, Diamond's songs in a city like Lexington offer music historians a rare taste of the musical culture in the 1960s.

Which version of the underlined text best accomplishes this goal?

(A) (as it is now)
(B) because a built-in microphone recorded them, Diamond's songs offer music historians in a city like Lexington a rare taste of the musical culture in the 1960s.
(C) because he played the songs into a recorder, Diamond's songs offer music historians a rare taste in a city like Lexington of the musical culture in the 1960s.
(D) Diamond's songs offer music historians a rare taste of the musical culture in a city like Lexington in the 1960s.

31. In sentence 18 (reproduced below), the writer wants to provide the best conclusion to this essay in relation to one of its main points.

One thing, though, is for sure: he records an interesting portfolio of songs, and he may soon be a famous saxophonist.

Which version of the underlined text best accomplishes this goal?

(A) (as it is now)
(B) recorded an interesting portfolio of songs, and now they provide scholars with an example of Lexington music.
(C) is recording an interesting portfolio of songs, and he probably never had to buy another cassette recorder.
(D) has recorded an interesting portfolio of songs, and he may have performed in other cities besides Lexington.

GO ON TO THE NEXT PAGE.

Questions 32–39 are based on the following passage.

The passage below is a draft.

(1) Black holes are possibly the most fascinating topic facing contemporary astronomy. (2) The concept of a black hole—a region of space with such intense gravitational pull that nothing can escape—is truly the stuff of science fiction. (3) That is what Albert Einstein believed, at least. (4) His general theory of relativity predicted their existence, but he thought of his prediction as an error to be corrected, not a predictor of one of the strangest astronomical phenomena yet discovered.

(5) Because Einstein didn't live to see it, the universe proved the accuracy of his calculations in 1970, when Cygnus X-1 was discovered about 7,000 light-years from Earth. (6) It is about 8.7 times as massive as our Sun yet has a small diameter of only about 50 km.

(7) There are several theories to explain the process. (8) The most popular hypothesis suggests that black holes are fairly common and involve the disintegration of a massive star near the end of its lifecycle. (9) At that stage, the star has nearly exhausted its hydrogen supply, consequently losing its ability to burn at a sufficiently high temperature to prevent its collapse. (10) The stars' exterior layers are blown away in a supernova, while the interior layers collapse into a highly dense core, which ultimately becomes the black hole.

(11) Other theorists suggest that black holes are the result of a galactic game of bumper cars. (12) The universe is teeming with neutron stars. (13) These are highly compact, very hot stars formed during the supernovae of smaller stars that are not sufficiently massive to create black holes. (14) On occasion these stars will actually collide with each other and together become massive enough to form a black hole.

(15) Perhaps the most bizarre observation made about these phenomena involves the existence of "micro" or "mini" black holes. (16) These peculiar items are very small, astronomically speaking. (17) They have a mass far less than that of our Sun, and, frankly, the scientific community cannot explain and articulate fully how stars with so little mass could have formed black holes at all. (18) That is a question for future generations of scientists to explore.

32. The writer wants to add a sentence after sentence 4 to emphasize that Einstein's skepticism slowed scientific inquiry into the existence of black holes. Which of the following sentences would best achieve this purpose?

(A) Despite initial skepticism, Einstein later decided that black holes did exist and encouraged the scientific community to search for them.
(B) Given the bizarre character of black holes, some leading scientists still question whether such objects could actually exist in nature.
(C) Einstein wrongly thought black holes would not form, believing that the angular momentum of collapsing particles would stabilize their motion.
(D) Sadly, for many years, Einstein's perspective persuaded those studying general relativity to dismiss all possible evidence of black holes.

33. The writer wants to replace the word at the beginning of sentence 5 (reproduced below), adjusting the capitalization as needed.

Because Einstein didn't live to see it, the universe proved the accuracy of his calculations in 1970, when Cygnus X-1 was discovered about 7,000 light-years from Earth.

Which of the following choices best accomplishes this goal?

(A) (as it is now)
(B) Although
(C) Since
(D) By contrast,

34. In the second paragraph (sentences 5–6), the writer wants to provide further detail to explain and clarify the reference to Cygnus X-1. Which of the following additions would best achieve this purpose?

(A) Clarification that Cygnus X-1 was the first discovery of something thought to be a black hole
(B) The names of those who discovered Cygnus X-1
(C) A reminder to the reader that many scientists were still skeptical about black holes even into the 1970s
(D) Clarification that, currently, better candidates for black holes are found elsewhere in the universe

GO ON TO THE NEXT PAGE.

35. The writer wants to add the following sentence to the passage to provide information that helps the reader grasp the size of black holes by presenting it in understandable terms.

    When one considers that the diameter of the Sun could accommodate over 100 Earths, it becomes clear that fitting a mass almost nine times greater than that into a space of about 31 miles is truly remarkable.

    Where would the sentence best be placed?

    (A) Before sentence 6
    (B) After sentence 6
    (C) After sentence 7
    (D) After sentence 8

36. Before sentence 7, the writer wants to add a rhetorical question which would serve as an effective introduction to the main idea of the paragraph.

    Which of the following sentences best achieves this purpose?

    (A) How do these singularities come into existence?
    (B) Why should we study black holes at all?
    (C) Is the Sun going to collapse and become a black hole?
    (D) What are the effects of such massive gravitational pull?

37. The writer wants to add a phrase at the beginning of sentence 14 (reproduced below), adjusting the capitalization as needed, to set up a comparison with the idea discussed in sentence 13.

    On occasion these stars will actually collide with each other and together become massive enough to form a black hole.

    Which of the following choices best accomplishes this goal?

    (A) Likewise,
    (B) Similarly,
    (C) In addition,
    (D) Nevertheless,

38. In the fifth paragraph (sentences 15–18), the writer wants to provide a statement to rebut the theory that "micro" black holes may pose a danger to Earth. Which of the following claims would best achieve this purpose?

    (A) Gravitational collapse is not the only process that could create black holes.
    (B) Scientists do not believe that the creation of black holes is possible on or near the Earth.
    (C) The Large Hadron Collider at The European Organization for Nuclear Research (CERN) has not successfully created a micro black hole.
    (D) Even if micro black holes could be formed near Earth, scientists expect that they would evaporate in a fraction of a second.

39. What would be the most effective title for this essay?

    (A) "Black Holes—Astronomy's Great Mystery"
    (B) "How Einstein Discovered Black Holes"
    (C) "Black Holes—Fact or Fiction?"
    (D) "The Speculative Future of Black Hole Research"

GO ON TO THE NEXT PAGE.

Questions 40–45 are based on the following passage.

The passage below is a draft.

(1) Drive through any suburb in the U.S. today, and it's hard to miss the bins that have become companions to America's trashcans. (2) Recycling has become commonplace, as people recognize the need to care for the environment. (3) Yet most people's recycling consciousness extends only as far as paper, bottles, and cans. (4) People seldom find themselves confronted with the growing phenomenon of e-waste.

(5) E-waste proliferates as the techno-fashionable constantly upgrade to the most cutting-edge devices, and the majority of them end up in landfills. (6) Activists who track such waste estimate that users discarded nearly 2 million tons of TVs, VCRs, computers, cell phones, and other electronics in 2005. (7) Unless we can find a safe alternative, this e-waste may leak into the ground and poison the water with dangerous toxins. (8) Burning the waste also dangerously contaminates the air.

(9) E-waste often contains reusable silver, gold, and other electrical conductors. (10) Recycling these materials reduces environmental impact by reducing both landfill waste and the need to mine such metals, which can destroy ecosystems.

(11) A growing number of states have adopted laws to prohibit dumping e-waste. (12) Some companies advertising safe disposal in fact merely ship the waste to third-world countries, where it still ends up in landfills.

(13) Nevertheless, the small but growing number of cities and corporations that do handle e-waste responsibly represent progress toward making the world a cleaner, better place for us all.

40. In sentence 4 (reproduced below), which of the following versions of the underlined text would most effectively begin this sentence so that it emphasizes a lack of awareness of a serious problem?

People seldom find themselves confronted with the growing phenomenon of e-waste.

(A) (as it is now)
(B) Many in our communities simply don't realize the dangers of
(C) A majority of local governments are assiduously studying
(D) Little attention is paid by the people in our neighborhoods to

41. In the second paragraph (sentences 5–8), the writer wants to add additional evidence to support a claim. Which of the following pieces of evidence would be most relevant?

(A) A government study which measured high levels of lead, mercury, and arsenic found in the groundwater around landfill sites
(B) Quotes from activists who believe that landfills have ample room to accommodate increasing volumes of waste
(C) A toxicology report which compares the relative safety and dangers of agricultural waste
(D) A scientific explanation of how toxins in groundwater can eventually contaminate the air

42. The writer wants to add a word or phrase at the beginning of sentence 9 (reproduced below), adjusting the capitalization as needed, to set up a comparison with the idea discussed in sentence 8.

E-waste often contains reusable silver, gold, and other electrical conductors.

Which of the following choices best accomplishes this goal?

(A) Consequently,
(B) Particularly,
(C) Moreover,
(D) Nevertheless,

GO ON TO THE NEXT PAGE.

43. Which of the following sentences, if placed after sentence 11, would provide a logical transition between the first and last sentences of the paragraph?

   (A) Still, less than one-quarter of this refuse will reach legitimate recycling programs.
   (B) So far, 25 states have passed legislation mandating statewide e-waste recycling.
   (C) All states except California and Utah use the Producer Responsibility approach, in which manufacturers must pay for recycling.
   (D) Let's face it: the e-waste problem is unlikely to be solved without legislative measures.

44. Which of the following sentences, if placed after sentence 12, would complete the idea expressed in sentence 12 while also supporting the author's overall claim?

   (A) Malaysia has become the world's largest importer of e-waste, receiving hundreds of millions of tons from the United States, Europe, Japan, and elsewhere.
   (B) U.S. electronics manufacturers are often unaware of where their used products and packaging end up.
   (C) These organizations hamper progress by unsafely disposing of waste in an out-of-sight, out-of-mind location.
   (D) According to activists from Greenpeace, most of that trash sits in piles for at least eight months before it is shipped overseas.

45. Which of the following sentences, if placed after sentence 13, would provide the most effective conclusion for the essay?

   (A) Today, pollution is one of the most dangerous forces threatening our environment, and the government must work to regulate its effects.
   (B) As the world's population continues to grow, the need to dramatically reduce e-waste will become ever more pressing.
   (C) Because of this, e-waste threatens to become the fastest-growing waste stream in the world.
   (D) In spite of these efforts, though, the e-waste problem may prove to be intractable.

END OF SECTION I

AP® English Language and Composition Exam

SECTION II: Free-Response Questions

DO NOT BEGIN THE EXAM UNTIL YOU ARE TOLD TO DO SO.

DISCLAIMER: The official AP English Language and Composition Exam will be administered digitally. Instructions for the digital exam may differ from this practice test.

At a Glance

Total Time
2 hours, plus a 15-minute reading period
Number of Questions
3
Percent of Total Grade
55%

Instructions

Section II of this examination requires answers in essay form. To help you use your time well, the coordinator will announce the time at which each question should be completed. If you finish any question before time is announced, you may go on to the following question. If you finish the examination in less than the time allotted, you may go back and work on any essay question you want.

Each essay will be judged on its clarity and effectiveness in dealing with the requirements of the topic assigned and on the quality of the writing. After completing each question, you should check your essay for accuracy of punctuation, spelling, and diction; you are advised, however, not to attempt many longer corrections. Remember that quality is far more important than quantity.

Write your essays with a pen, preferably in black or dark blue ink. Be sure to write CLEARLY and LEGIBLY. Cross out any errors you make.

GO ON TO THE NEXT PAGE.

**ENGLISH LANGUAGE AND COMPOSITION
SECTION II
Total Time—2 hours, 15 minutes**

Question 1

**Suggested reading and writing time—55 minutes.
It is suggested that you spend 15 minutes reading the question, analyzing and evaluating the sources,
and 40 minutes writing your response.
Note: You may begin writing your response before the reading period is over.**

(This question counts for one-third of the total essay section score.)

As the Internet and access to social media become increasingly widespread, there has been considerable debate about whether easy access to technological forms of communication is beneficial to children and teenagers. While some commentators see benefits to children from digital media, others say that "screen time" is psychologically damaging.

Carefully read the six sources, including the introductory information for each source. Write an essay that synthesizes material from at least three of the sources and develops your position on the role, if any, that digital media should play in the lives of young people.

Source A   (Mohammed)
Source B   (Grunwald report)
Source C   (Mosley)
Source D   (Uhls)
Source E   (graph)
Source F   (survey)

In your response you should do the following:

- Respond to the prompt with a thesis that presents a defensible position.

- Select and use evidence from at least 3 of the provided sources to support your line of reasoning. Indicate clearly the sources used through direct quotation, paraphrase, or summary. Sources may be cited as Source A, Source B, etc., or by using the description in parentheses.

- Explain how the evidence supports your line of reasoning.

- Use appropriate grammar and punctuation in communicating your argument.

GO ON TO THE NEXT PAGE.

> **Source A**
>
> Saro Mohammed, Ph.D., "Is technology good or bad
> for learning?", *Brookings*, May 8, 2019.

I'll bet you've read something about technology and learning recently. You may have read that device use enhances learning outcomes. Or perhaps you've read that screen time is not good for kids. Maybe you've read that there's no link between adolescents' screen time and their well-being. Or that college students' learning declines the more devices are present in their classrooms.

If ever there were a case to be made that more research can cloud rather than clarify an issue, technology use and learning seems to fit the bill. This piece covers what the research actually says, some outstanding questions, and how to approach the use of technology in learning environments to maximize opportunities for learning and minimize the risk of doing harm to students.

The Good

I have frequently cited the mixed evidence about blended learning, which strategically integrates in-person learning with technology to enable real-time data use, personalized instruction, and mastery-based progression. One thing that this nascent evidence base does show is that technology can be linked to improved learning. When technology is integrated into lessons in ways that are aligned with good in-person teaching pedagogy, learning can be better than without technology.

A 2018 meta-analysis of dozens of rigorous studies of ed tech, along with the executive summary of a forthcoming update (126 rigorous experiments), indicated that when education technology is used to individualize students' pace of learning, the results overall show "enormous promise." In other words, ed tech can improve learning when used to personalize instruction to each student's pace.

Further, this same meta-analysis, along with other large but correlational studies, also found that increased access to technology in school was associated with improved proficiency with, and increased use of, technology overall. This is important in light of the fact that access to technology outside of learning environments is still very unevenly distributed across ethnic, socio-economic, and geographic lines. Technology for learning, when deployed to all students, ensures that no student experiences a "21st-century skills and opportunity" gap.

More practically, technology has been shown to scale and sustain instructional practices that would be too resource-intensive to work in exclusively in-person learning environments, especially those with the highest needs. In multiple, large-scale studies where technology has been incorporated into the learning experiences of hundreds of students across multiple schools and school systems, they have been associated with better academic outcomes than comparable classrooms that did not include technology. Added to these larger bodies of research are dozens, if not hundreds, of smaller, more localized examples of technology being used successfully to improve students' learning experiences. Further, meta-analyses and syntheses of the research show that blended learning can produce greater learning than exclusively in-person learning.

All of the above suggest that technology, used well, can drive equity in learning opportunities. We are seeing that students and families from privileged backgrounds are able to make choices about technology use that maximize its benefits and minimize its risks, while students and families from marginalized backgrounds do not have opportunities to make the same informed choices. Intentional, thoughtful inclusion of technology in public learning environments can ensure that all students, regardless of their ethnicity, socioeconomic status, language status, special education status, or other characteristics, have the opportunity to experience learning and develop skills that allow them to fully realize their potential.

GO ON TO THE NEXT PAGE.

The Bad

On the other hand, the evidence is decidedly mixed on the neurological impact of technology use. In November 2016, the American Association of Pediatrics updated their screen time guidelines for parents, generally relaxing restrictions and increasing the recommended maximum amount of time that children in different age groups spend interacting with screens. These guidelines were revised not because of any new research, but for two far more practical reasons. First, the nuance of the existing evidence—especially the ways in which recommendations change as children get older—was not adequately captured in the previous guidelines. Second, the proliferation of technology in our lives had made the previous guidelines almost impossible to follow.

The truth is that infants, in particular, learn by interacting with our physical world and with other humans, and it is likely that very early (passive) interactions with devices—rather than humans—can disrupt or misinform neural development. As we grow older, time spent on devices often replaces time spent engaging in physical activity or socially with other people, and it can even become a substitute for emotional regulation, which is detrimental to physical, social, and emotional development.

In adolescence and young adulthood, the presence of technology in learning environments has also been associated with (but has not been shown to be the cause of) negative variables such as attention deficits or hyperactivity, feeling lonely, and lower grades.

Multitasking is not something our brains can do while learning, and technology often represents not just one more "task" to have to attend to in a learning environment, but multiple additional tasks due to the variety of apps and programs installed on and producing notifications through a single device.

The Pragmatic

The current takeaway from the research is that there are potential benefits and risks to deploying technology in learning environments. While we can't wrap this topic up with a bow just yet—there are still more questions than answers—there is evidence that technology can amplify effective teaching and learning when in the hands of good teachers. The best we can do today is understand how technology can be a valuable tool for educators to do the complex, human work that is teaching by capitalizing on the benefits while remaining fully mindful of the risks as we currently understand them.

GO ON TO THE NEXT PAGE.

> ### Source B
>
> The following is an excerpt from a private research survey entitled "What Parents Think About Mobile Devices for Early Childhood and K–12 Learning."

One in Five Children Don't Use Any Mobile or Portable Devices

- Almost one in five children (18 percent) don't use any family-owned mobile or portable devices. Younger children are most likely to be nonusers, with 29 percent of K–2 parents and 16 percent of parents of students in grades 3–5 reporting that their children don't use any family-owned mobile or portable devices. Still, 18 percent of middle school students and 9 percent of high school students are nonusers of these devices as well, their parents report.

- This doesn't mean that families of nonusers don't use any technology, or that their parents don't own portable or mobiles devices; 52 percent of parents of nonusers report that they have smartphones, and 60 percent say they have some type of mobile device in their homes.

- Parents of nonusers report mixed views about mobile devices. The majority of these parents (61 percent) completely or somewhat agree that mobiles open up learning opportunities that their child didn't have before. These parents also agree, though not as strongly as other parents, that mobile devices have the potential to provide many learning benefits. On the other hand, parents of nonusers are less likely to agree that mobile devices are a great way to engage students in the classroom. More than one in four parents of nonusers (28 percent) completely or somewhat disagree with this potential benefit, compared to 17 percent of parents overall.

- Parents of nonusers are less willing to be responsible for school-owned devices; only about one-third of parents of nonusers (31 percent) say they are willing to be responsible for school-owned devices, compared to about half of parents (51 percent) overall.

- Their parents are less likely to have a college degree and less likely to be enamored or savvy with technology.

GO ON TO THE NEXT PAGE.

Source C

Tonya Mosley, "A 'No Technology' School: The Waldorf Approach," *Seattle Refined*, September 16, 2014.

On the first day of school, Tracy Bennett and staff members at Seattle's Waldorf High School stood on the shores of Lake Washington to welcome one of its students. The high schooler had swam across the lake from his home on the eastside to class at his high school's new home in Magnuson Park.

Several other students rode in on their bicycles, and only a handful arrived by car.

"That's our students," chuckled Bennett, the head of administration at the only Waldorf high school in the state. "They're always on the move."

Educators at the Waldorf School in Seattle take a lot of pride in showing off just how handy, athletic and artistic their students are. The high school students are, after all, on the last leg of their Waldorf experience—a culmination of 12 years of education almost entirely free of television, video games, computers and smartphones.

The Waldorf philosophy is simple: Students do not benefit from using computer devices before the age of 12.

"To see a 3, 4 or 5 year old using an iPad is like giving them a steak knife," says Bennett. And she's serious. "It is potentially just as harmful and dangerous. Technology is powerful, and should be used when it is appropriate."

The Waldorf approach has been around since 1919, but in our tech-obsessed world its stance on media and electronic devices seems to resonate more than ever according to Bennett. Elementary students are discouraged from using all forms of technology, even at home. In middle school, students are introduced in controlled environments. In high school, students are encouraged to use technology as a tool for learning.

Like the middle and elementary students, the high schoolers are given breaks to play games with each other—with classes offered like woodworking, sculpture and how to make root beer and sauerkraut.

"It's the fastest growing movement in the world," says Bennett. But what may be even more surprising is the type of parents that choose this type of education. According to Bennett, a good number of them work for tech companies like Microsoft, Amazon and Google. "They want their children to be children. We are not anti-technology. We just believe it is one tool in the box."

Brenda Baker, admissions and coordinator for Waldorf continues. "It's about developing and honing the power of observation. Our students are highly curious and creative. The sensory experience gets to the heart of learning. Bringing in technology at a later age gives them the tools to discern the best times to use it."

This summer the high school moved into its new home tucked away in North Seattle's Magnuson Park. It is an unlikely location, housed just off the banks of Lake Washington and surrounded by public wetlands and sports fields. As part of the curriculum, the students will have access to many of the park's amenities. "This area fits into our curriculum nicely because our kids will have access to real life experiences."

Waldorf High School costs about $21,000 a year, and about 30 percent of the students receive financial aid. Baker says you don't have to attend Waldorf to experience the benefits of cutting down on technology.

"Maybe put the phone away during dinner with your kids. It's all about finding ways to be human and connect on a human level."

GO ON TO THE NEXT PAGE.

Source D

Yalda Uhls, "The Internet Will Not Turn Your Teen Into a Brain-Dead Zombie," Zocalo Public Square.

I come bearing good news: Our teens are not growing into brain-dead zombies or emotionally stunted sociopaths. After more than a decade of research by child psychologists like me, we have discovered that the kids are all right. In study after study of emotional and intelligence indicators, 21st-century children use media to connect with their friends and learn about the world, just like those of us who were children of the 20th century did.

But you don't have to take it from me. The proof is in the past. Every time a new technology is introduced, it becomes a cultural battleground. And ultimately, we come to a truce. Take this one example:

Near the end of the 19th century, a new medium was unleashed upon the world. Children took to it like ducks to water, and this terrified adults. Young people everywhere spent hours on end immersed, while simultaneously ignoring the grown-ups in their lives. Understandably, parents were alarmed and worried that this new medium and its racy content were ruining young minds.

Change 19th to 20th, and I could be talking about the Internet. So what was this addictive content? Romantic novels.

Example two comes from Azriel L. Eisenberg, writing in the "American Journal of Psychiatry":

This new invader of the privacy of the home has brought many a disturbing influence in its wake. Parents have become aware of a puzzling change in the behavior patterns of their children. They are bewildered by a host of new problems, and find themselves unprepared, frightened, resentful, helpless. They cannot lock out this intruder because it has gained an invincible hold of their children.

What was this dreaded intruder that Eisenberg wrote about in 1936? The radio.

Example three comes from an academic study on parents' reactions to a new media:

One mother reports that her children are aggressive and irritable as a result of over-stimulating experiences, which leads to sleepless nights and tired days.

Overstimulation and aggression? Her kids must be addicted to social media and violent video games. But this article was written in 1950. She's talking about TV.

In the second decade of the 21st century, with more information at our fingertips than any time in human history, you can find evidence of all of these old fears and trends and studies online. But we still haven't managed to assuage our concerns about kids today, who have adopted their generation's media with ardent fervor.

In a recent Pew poll, 73 percent of 13- to 17-year-olds reported they had smartphones, 52 percent said they spent time with friends playing video games, and 24 percent said they go online "almost constantly." What are we to make of these statistics? Each time I speak to adults, parents, teachers, and anyone who cares about kids, they express their worry about the "addictive" nature of digital media and mobile phones and the dangers kids are exposed to online. Meanwhile, Silicon Valley evangelists claim their new devices and apps are going to make the world a better place. Who is right, and who is wrong? The answer is somewhere in the middle: digital media are a new environment that has both positive and negative effects on our children and our society.

GO ON TO THE NEXT PAGE.

While research on the Internet and the developing brain is in the nascent stages, we can learn about our brain's ability to successfully adapt to new environments from past research. Studies show that our brains are incredibly plastic, and never more so than in early childhood and adolescence. This means our brains rapidly attune to new surroundings—whether we're moving to a new city or to a new kind of virtual environment. Moreover, we are learning that our brains adapt to new social worlds, too: As tweens and teens use the Internet and video games to connect with friends, their social brains are adapting quickly to this new environment. Remember, humans adapted and thrived in many different habitats and climates over thousands of years; as the digital natives continue to develop, so will their ability to adapt successfully to the online environment.

We may finally be at a tipping point, one we have seen with every introduction of new media. New data from respected social scientists around the world continues to demonstrate that children are adapting and sometimes thriving as they embrace 21st-century media; these small and incremental changes may be building to permanent change. Perhaps now the hysteria will finally come to an end. Encouraging signs point to a leveling out of the national conversation.

For example, the American Academy of Pediatrics just published new key messages for families regarding media and technology use. While they didn't go so far as to change their recommendations on the amount of screen time that is healthy for children, they did state that the quality of the media content is more important than time spent. They also made it clear that online relationships are essential for adolescent development. Ultimately, their message was that media is just another environment—like the playground—where children will spend time, but require careful supervision to do so safely.

Childhood is still childhood. I couldn't have put it better than K.G., a first-grade teacher whose words have become an Internet meme: "Yes, kids love technology, but they also love Legos, scented markers, handstands, books and mud puddles. It's all about balance."

It's time for adults—digital immigrants to the next generation's natives—to adapt, step in, and be that balance. Instead of focusing our energy on being "for" or "against" technology, let's guide children in how to use it wisely and safely. Let's help them make the most of this new place they love, while continuing to teach them the importance of face-time, discipline, and moderation. Judging by history, when this generation grows up, they'll be busy coping with their own fears of whatever new thing their kids are using.

GO ON TO THE NEXT PAGE.

Percentage of children ages 3 to 17 who have access to a computer at home and who use the Internet at home: Selected Years, 1984–2015

Sources: Data for 1984–2003; U.S. Census Bureau. (1988–2005). Computer and internet use in the United States: 1984–1997. Washington, DC: Author. Retrieved from https://www.census.gov/topics/population/computer-internet.html. Data for income from 2001: U.S. Department of Commerce, Economics and Statistics Administration & National Telecommunications and Information Administration. (2002). A nation online: How Americans are expanding their use of the Internet [Table 5-1]. Washington, DC: Author. Retrieved from https://www.ntia.gov/files/ntia/publications/anationonline2.pdf. Data for 2010–2015: Child Trends' original analysis of data from the Current Population Survey. Computer and Internet Use Supplement, 2010–2015.

GO ON TO THE NEXT PAGE.

Source F

The following chart was published in a report by the Pew Charitable Trust, a national research organization.

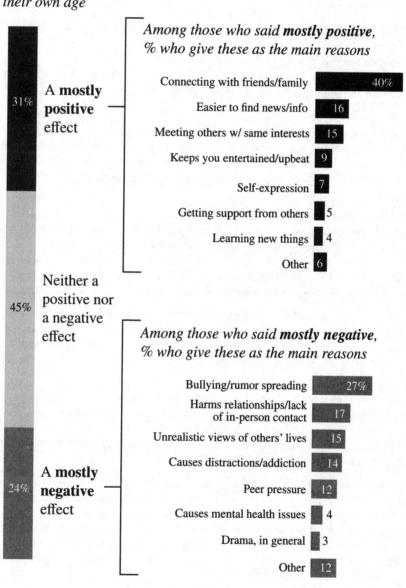

% of U.S. teens who say social media has had _____ on people their own age

A **mostly positive** effect — 31%

Neither a positive nor a negative effect — 45%

A **mostly negative** effect — 24%

*Among those who said **mostly positive**, % who give these as the main reasons*

Connecting with friends/family	40%
Easier to find news/info	16
Meeting others w/ same interests	15
Keeps you entertained/upbeat	9
Self-expression	7
Getting support from others	5
Learning new things	4
Other	6

*Among those who said **mostly negative**, % who give these as the main reasons*

Bullying/rumor spreading	27%
Harms relationships/lack of in-person contact	17
Unrealistic views of others' lives	15
Causes distractions/addiction	14
Peer pressure	12
Causes mental health issues	4
Drama, in general	3
Other	12

GO ON TO THE NEXT PAGE.

Question 2

Suggested time—40 minutes.

(This question counts for one-third of the total essay section score.)

In November 1969 former Vice President Spiro Agnew gave a speech to an audience in Des Moines, Iowa. Television networks aired the speech live, making it a nationwide address, a rarity for vice presidents. Read the speech carefully. Write an essay that analyzes the rhetorical choices Agnew makes to convey his message to his audience.

In your response, you should do the following:

- Respond to the prompt with a thesis that analyzes the writer's rhetorical choices.
- Select and use evidence to support your line of reasoning.
- Explain how the evidence supports your line of reasoning.
- Demonstrate an understanding of the rhetorical situation.
- Use appropriate grammar and punctuation in communicating your argument.

> Gresham's Law seems to be operating in the network news: bad news drives out good news. The irrational is more controversial than the rational. Concurrence can no longer compete with dissent… The labor crisis settled at the negotiating table is nothing compared to the confrontation that results in a strike—or better yet, violence along the picket lines. Normality has become the nemesis of the network news.
>
> Now the upshot of all this controversy is that a narrow and distorted picture of America often emerges from the televised news. A single, dramatic piece of the mosaic becomes in the minds of millions the entire picture. The American who relies upon television for his news might conclude that the majority of American students are embittered radicals; that the majority of black Americans feel no regard for their country; that violence and lawlessness are the rule rather than the exception on the American campus. We know that none of these conclusions is true.
>
> Perhaps the place to start looking for a credibility gap is not in the offices of the Government in Washington but in the studios of the networks in New York. Television may have destroyed the old stereotypes, but has it not created new ones in their places? What has this "passionate" pursuit of controversy done to the politics of progress through local compromise essential to the functioning of a democratic society?
>
> The members of Congress or the Senate who follow their principles and philosophy quietly in a spirit of compromise are unknown to many Americans, while the loudest and most extreme dissenters on every issue are known to every man in the street. How many marches and demonstrations would we have if the marchers did not know that the ever-faithful TV cameras would be there to record their antics for the next news show?
>
> We've heard demands that Senators and Congressmen and judges make known all their financial connections so that the public will know who and what influences their decisions and their votes. Strong arguments can be made for that view. But when a single commentator or producer, night after night, determines for millions of people how much of each side of a great issue they are going to see and hear, should he not first disclose his personal views on the issue as well? In this search for excitement and controversy, has more than equal time gone to the minority of Americans who specialize in attacking the United States—its institutions and its citizens?
>
> Tonight I've raised questions. I've made no attempt to suggest the answers. The answers must come from the media men. They are challenged to turn their critical powers on themselves, to direct their energy, their talent, and their conviction toward improving the quality and objectivity of news presentation. They are challenged to structure their own civic ethics—to relate their great feeling with the great responsibilities they hold.

GO ON TO THE NEXT PAGE.

And the people of America are challenged, too—challenged to press for responsible news presentations. The people can let the networks know that they want their news straight and objective. The people can register their complaints on bias through mail to the networks and phone calls to local stations. This is one case where the people must defend themselves, where the citizen, not the Government, must be the reformer; where the consumer can be the most effective crusader.

By way of conclusion, let me say that every elected leader in the United States depends on these men of the media. Whether what I've said to you tonight will be heard and seen at all by the nation is not my decision; it's not your decision—it's their decision.

In tomorrow's edition of the Des Moines Register, you'll be able to read a news story detailing what I said tonight. Editorial comment will be reserved for the editorial page, where it belongs. Should not the same wall of separation exist between news and comment on the nation's networks?

Now my friends, we'd never trust such power, as I've described, over public opinion in the hands of an elected Government. It's time we questioned it in the hands of a small and unelected elite. The great networks have dominated America's airwaves for decades. The people are entitled to a full accounting of their stewardship.

GO ON TO THE NEXT PAGE.

Question 3

Suggested time—40 minutes.

(This question counts for one-third of the total essay section score.)

Barry Goldwater, a former United States Senator and Presidential nominee, once warned, "Equality, rightly understood as our founding fathers understood it, leads to liberty and to the emancipation of creative differences; wrongly understood, as it has been so tragically in our time, leads first to conformity and then to despotism."

Write an essay that argues your position on Goldwater's claim that equality can lead to different outcomes depending on how it is understood.

In your response, you should do the following:

- Respond to the prompt with a thesis that may establish a line of reasoning.
- Select and use evidence to develop and support your line of reasoning.
- Explain the relationship between the evidence and your thesis.
- Demonstrate an understanding of the rhetorical situation.
- Use appropriate grammar and punctuation in communicating your argument.

STOP

END OF EXAM

Practice Test 2:
Answers and
Explanations

PRACTICE TEST 2 ANSWER KEY

1.	A		24.	A
2.	C		25.	C
3.	D		26.	B
4.	B		27.	A
5.	C		28.	D
6.	C		29.	C
7.	B		30.	D
8.	B		31.	B
9.	D		32.	D
10.	D		33.	B
11.	C		34.	A
12.	B		35.	B
13.	A		36.	A
14.	D		37.	D
15.	B		38.	D
16.	D		39.	A
17.	D		40.	B
18.	A		41.	A
19.	B		42.	D
20.	B		43.	A
21.	D		44.	C
22.	C		45.	B
23.	C			

Once you have checked your answers, remember to return to page 4 and respond to the Reflect questions.

PRACTICE TEST 2 EXPLANATIONS

SECTION I: MULTIPLE CHOICE

1. **A**   The author uses "baneful peculiarities" at the very start of the passage, after just introducing the idea of slavery in general. Therefore, (A) is the best response.

2. **C**   The "hydra-headed monster" is a metaphor for slavery. Specifically, the author refers to masters and idle spectators in the negative thereafter, so (A) and (D) can be eliminated. Choice (C) is the best answer.

3. **D**   In the first paragraph, the author describes his own experience within the slavery system. In the final sentence, he says he is speaking truthfully. Therefore, the answer is (D). Note that (A) and (C) incorrectly characterize pathos and ethos and can be immediately eliminated.

4. **B**   The speaker maintains a friendly relationship with his audience, so (A) and (D) can be eliminated. "Convivial," (C), is a celebratory, jubilant connotation and isn't appropriate to the passage. Therefore, (B) is the best answer.

5. **C**   In these lines, the author offers legal and social definitions for the terms "master" and "slave." Choice (D) is a possible trap answer, but these lines are more about legal terminology than about the nature of slavery. In fact the author states in lines 12–13 "I will state, as well as I can, the legal and social relation of master and slave," which is a statement of his purpose in these lines. Therefore, (C) is the best answer.

6. **C**   The author describes both the legal and religious justification for maintaining slavery: "This he does with the force of the law and the sanction of southern religion" (lines 16–17). By contrast, the author argues that slavery is immoral; therefore, (D) can be eliminated. Choice (C) is the best answer.

7. **B**   With the phrase "master's ledger" the author emphasizes that slaves are treated like other livestock, not like humans. Therefore, (B) is the correct answer.

8. **B**   In this sequence of sentences, the author describes a series of contrasts between "he" (the slave) and "another" (the master). Therefore, (B) is the correct answer.

9. **D**   This is an extended passage made up of clauses that use parallel syntax, (D). While (A) might describe the language of the passage, there is no assertion that one aspect of slavery is more cruel than another; therefore, (A) can be eliminated. Choice (D) is the correct answer.

10. **D**   The opening sentence of this passage describes the "vivid pictures of their happiness" that the author disagrees with. Therefore, (D) is correct.

11. **C**   The passage ends with an image of slaves experiencing joy as evidence of their humanity, condemning the actions of slave owners. Because the author talks about God as an "accusing angel," (C) is the best answer.

12. **B**   The author doesn't introduce an expert, so (A) can be eliminated. The author does give personal experience but doesn't tell a particular story, so (C) can be eliminated. There is no clear statement of thesis or purpose, so (D) can be eliminated. Choice (B) is the best answer.

13. **A**   The key to this question is identifying the transition word, "however." Prior to the transition, the author is discussing teaching strategies. After it, the author introduces the idea of student failure. Therefore, (A) is the best answer.

14. **D**   The third paragraph is a transitional paragraph the author uses to introduce a personal anecdote. Therefore, (D) is the correct answer.

15. **B**   This statement is not a comparison or an introduction; therefore, (C) and (D) can be eliminated. Similarly, there is no mention of further research (A), so (B) is the best answer.

16. **D**   Anecdotes, (D), are short stories taken from the author's own experience. In this passage, the author refers to her own teaching experiences, along with the experiences of her youngest child with Mrs. Stifter. Metaphors, (A), similes, (B), and analogies, (C), are all types of comparisons; these are not a prominent feature of the text.

17. **D**   The phrase quoted is actually an admission that the author's argument may not be universally true. Therefore, (D) is the best answer. Choices (A) and (B) are the opposite of this, and there are no allusions, (C), in this part of the text.

18. **A**   When the author says "prior to teaching this class…" she is introducing a previously held view, that poor academic performance is related to impediments to concentration. Then, she describes an alternate view: that if teaching style won't engage students, perhaps failure (an alternate option) will. Therefore, (A) is the correct answer.

19. **B**   The best strategy for approaching this question is to first identify who "they" is. Based on context, it can be understood that "they" are the students. Therefore, (C) and (D) can be eliminated. Second, "sailing" is a term meant to be taken figuratively, rather than a reference to a specific leisure activity, so (A) can be eliminated. Therefore, the answer is (B).

20. **B**   The personal anecdote provided in the story describes how the threat of failure motivated the author's son to perform better in school. Therefore, (B) is the correct answer.

21. **D**   While the author seems curious and engaged, she never questions policymakers directly, so (A) can be eliminated. Nothing suggests that the author is tired or frustrated, so (B) can be eliminated. While the speaker is a former student who has experienced failure, (C) doesn't accurately describe the passage. Therefore, the answer is (D).

22. **C**   In the sixth paragraph, the author describes what she has been detailing previously. In the seventh paragraph, she describes how failing students could be implemented as a policy. Therefore, (C) is the best answer.

23. **C** The fourth paragraph provides a story about her son who was motivated to work hard in English class by the threat of failure. The author's main thesis is that the threat of failure is beneficial to students. This story supports this thesis, which supports (C). Choice (A) is tempting, but this is one example; hard work is not necessarily an overall change in work ethic. Choice (B) is wrong because this example supports the rule. Choice (D) is incorrect because even though the child was failing, he ultimately got an A. The answer is (C).

24. **A** Paragraph 1 discusses the musician Bruce Diamond, describing his recordings as "rough" and recorded at home. Choice (A) is most relevant, since it refers to "amateur" musicians who recorded with cassette recorders. Choices (B) and (C) are not as good, since they refer to multiple musicians, which is not the subject of the essay. Choice (D) is too broad and not directly relevant to Diamond. The answer is (A).

25. **C** Choice (A) is incorrect because the question wants a *confident* tone, which is not conveyed by *possibly*. Choice (B) is wrong, since the rest of the paragraph establishes that Diamond was influenced by other artists, not the other way around. There is no evidence to say that Diamond *partnered* with anyone, (D). The answer is (C).

26. **B** Choice (B) is the only option that conveys any detail about lyrical subject matter, telling you that the lyrics to these songs involved subjects like dating and automobiles. Choice (A) is just speculation about what inspired the lyrics. Choices (C) and (D) refer to the way Diamond wrote or performed the lyrics, but they do not tell you anything about the subject matter of the lyrics. The answer is (B).

27. **A** The previous paragraph was focused on the idea that Diamond was influenced by a variety of different musical genres. Choice (A) captures this idea. Choices (B) and (C) are unknown and unsupportable by the text. Choice (D) is close, but Diamond's reputation is really not the focus of the previous paragraph, nor do we precisely know what percentage of his songs employed certain styles. The answer is (A).

28. **D** A sentence should only be in the essay if it seems to flow well with the purpose and tone of the paragraph. In this case, sentence 14 does not contribute anything new to a paragraph that has as its main theme a discussion of Diamond's unique songwriting voice. All of the other choices are directly related to Diamond and his work. The answer is (D).

29. **C** The two clauses of the sentence provide a contrast: there is abundant music knowledge about New Orleans, Detroit, and Nashville but little known about Lexington. The use of *while*, (A), indicates a contrast, as do (B) and (D). Choice (C) makes the first clause of the sentence sound as if it is the cause of the second clause, which is incorrect. The answer is (C).

30. **D** The previous sentence is a transition to begin discussing what interests musicologists about Diamond's songs. This sentence explains that there were very few other recordings from Lexington artists. Choices (A), (B), and (C) offer details about the cassette recording process that are irrelevant to the point of the sentence. The intended meaning of the sentence is that there was little known about the music culture of Lexington, Kentucky in the 1960s. The rest of the paragraph provides context to clarify that idea. Choice (D) correctly identifies the *music culture in a city like Lexington* as the topic. The answer is (D).

31. **B**   Choice (B) effectively ties the conclusion back to the intro. Since the passage deals with the present study of Diamond's work, it is not consistent to make a prediction about Diamond's future popularity as (A) does. Choices (C) and (D) offer unnecessary speculation about whether Diamond ever bought another recorder or performed in another city, neither of which were topics of discussion in the passage. The answer is (B).

32. **D**   The author's goal is to show that Einstein's skepticism slowed or stopped scientific inquiry into black holes. Only (D) correctly demonstrates this point of view. Choice (A) seems to contradict the author's goal. Choice (B) cannot be valid, since clearly research did continue, or else black holes would not have been discovered at all. Choice (C) is factually correct, but has no bearing on whether Einstein's perspective negatively affected the research community. The answer is (D).

33. **B**   The first part of the sentence highlights information that is true in spite of the second part of the sentence. Therefore, (C) is wrong, since it features a conjunction that connects two clauses as if they agree. Choice (A) is incorrect, because there is no cause-and-effect relationship indicated by the two parts of the sentence. Choice (D) may seem close, but sentence 5 is not a contrast to sentence 4. The answer is (B).

34. **A**   The second paragraph is rhetorically flawed, since it does not actually state what Cygnus X-1 is and how it is relevant to the main focus of the essay. Choice (A) is essential in order to clarify this gap in the text. All of the other choices are inadequate if the reader does not understand that Cygnus X-1 is a black hole. The answer is (A).

35. **B**   The primary purpose of the reference sentence is to demonstrate in understandable terms the extremely small size of the black hole in comparison to items of similar mass. Sentence 6 refers to the Sun, so placing this sentence after sentence 6 would clarify the significance of the Sun as a point of reference. The answer is (B).

36. **A**   Choice (A) is correct, because it is the only answer that correctly introduces the topic of how black holes are formed, which will be the focus of the rest of the passage. All the other answer choices raise interesting questions; however, none of them are actually answered by the remainder of the passage. The answer is (A).

37. **D**   This sentence needs a transition that shows a contrast from the previous sentence. Choices (A), (B), and (C) are incorrect because they all indicate that a complementary concept is being introduced. The answer is (D).

38. **D**   The writer wants to provide a statement to rebut the theory that "micro" black holes may pose a danger to Earth. Choice (A) is incorrect, since it provides evidence that black holes are possibly abundant. Choices (B) and (C) might look tempting, but we do not know whether scientists' beliefs are accurate, nor do we know whether the Large Hadron Collider is mimicking forces in nature. The best choice is (D), since it establishes that, even if micro black holes were to form near Earth, they would likely not survive long enough to pose a danger.

39. **A**   The essay focuses on the existence of black holes and theories regarding their causes. The concept of black holes is referred to as "fascinating" and "bizarre." Choices (B) and (D) are too narrow, since these things are only mentioned in passing and do not encapsulate the overall focus of the essay. Choice (C) is not the best answer, since black holes are accepted as factual by modern scientists. The answer is (A).

40. **B**   The question asks for an answer that emphasizes lack of awareness of a problem. Choices (A) and (D) say people don't often encounter or pay attention to something, not that they aren't aware of it or that it's a problem. It's a small difference, but it's a difference that means you can eliminate these two choices because (B) mentions *danger*. Choice (C) refers to governments' attempts to study it, so cross that one out too. Only (B), which matches *realize* in the answer choice with *awareness* in the question, is consistent with what you are asked to emphasize.

41. **A**   Choice (A) represents examples of toxins that could be released into the groundwater from e-waste in landfills, a claim made in sentence 7. Choice (B) is never touched on by any information in the passage, nor is it consistent with the idea that e-waste in landfills is a serious and urgent problem, so eliminate it. Choice (C) is not something relevant to the passage, since it is about agricultural waste. Choice (D) is attempting to combine two things that were not combined in the essay: groundwater pollution and air pollution. The answer is (A).

42. **D**   *Consequently* in (A) would indicate that the *reusable silver, gold, and other electrical conductors* in the motherboards were a consequence of how burning *contaminates the air*. Cross out (A) because nothing indicates that this is true; instead, the positive sentiment expressed in the first sentence of this paragraph is a marked shift from the negative sentiment at the end of the previous paragraph. Choices (B) and (C) would likewise reflect a consistent flow—so eliminate those. Choice (D), on the other hand, accurately signals the shift occurring between these two paragraphs from a problem of e-waste to a potential use of e-waste. The answer is (D).

43. **A**   Choice (A) accurately fits into the flow of this paragraph. While (B) may be true, it does not transition adequately to sentence 12, which points out that some e-waste is simply shipped off to foreign countries, thus thwarting efforts to keep it out of landfills. Choice (A) is more comprehensive and attuned to the big picture, making it a better answer than (B). Choices (C) and (D) likewise have no known relevance to sentence 12. The answer is (A).

44. **C**   Sentence 12 mentioned the practice of some companies who advertise safe disposal of e-waste simply shipping the e-waste off to foreign countries where it still sits in landfills. Only (A), (C), and (D) are relevant to sentence 12, so eliminate (B). In addition to building on sentence 12, however, we must also support the author's overall claim that e-waste in landfills is harmful to the environment. Eliminate (A) first, since it does nothing to support the author's claim. It simply establishes that foreign disposal of e-waste is happening, the same thing the author mentioned in sentence 12. Next, eliminate (D), because there is likewise no direct support for the author's overall claim. Choice (C) is preferable because it mentions the specifics of why the organizations in sentence 12 are bad. The answer is (C).

45. **B**   The passage discusses e-waste and its effect on the environment when it isn't properly recycled. It is not about pollution problems in general, so eliminate (A). Sentence 13 is optimistic in tone, pointing out positive steps in the right direction toward solving the problem of e-waste. The phrase *Because of this* in (C) would not match this sentence. Choice (D) is far too pessimistic and is, therefore, not consistent with the tone of the passage. Choice (B) sums up the author's points and is thus the best conclusion. The answer is (B).

SECTION II: FREE RESPONSE

Rubric—1 + 4 + 1 = 6 pts

A. Thesis (0–1 pts)
  ○ Responds to the prompt with a thesis that presents a defensible interpretation of the selected work.

B. Evidence and Commentary (0–4 pts)
  ○ Evidence: Provides specific evidence to support all claims in a line of reasoning.
  ○ Commentary: Consistently explains how the evidence supports a line of reasoning.
  ○ Explains how multiple literary elements or techniques in the poem contribute to its meaning.

C. Sophistication (0–1 pts)
  ○ Demonstrates sophistication of thought and/or develops a complex literary argument.

Question 1—Synthesis Essay

How to Score 6 Points
- Address the prompt with a defensible thesis.
- Present specific evidence from at least three sources and consistently explain how the evidence supports your thesis statement.
- Use style and rhetoric to persuade the reader.

Source Overview

Source A: Thoughtful inclusion of technology in the classroom is linked to positive educational outcomes. By allowing educators to "individualize a students' pace of learning," technology can drive equity in learning opportunities by expanding access to under-resourced students. However, technology use is also associated with attention disorders, loneliness, and low grades.

Source B: A recent survey presents a series of data describing mobile device use in families: Children are more likely to use devices as they grow up, and a child's cell phone use doesn't necessarily correlate with their parent's cell phone use.

Source C: The Waldorf School's curriculum features very limited technology use, with screens phased in during middle school and used as a learning tool in high school. Tuition is $21,000 per year, and the school boasts students that are "handy, athletic, and artistic."

Source D: Yalda Uhls argues that modern media is not having an adverse impact on today's youth, comparing concerns thereof to those associated with radio and television in the past. Parents and educators should guide children in using it responsibly.

Source E: This graph illustrates that home computer access and home internet use among children ages three to 17 has risen by over 50% between 1984 and 2017.

Source F: This graphic depicts the attitudes teens have toward the effect social media has had on their lives. Forty-five percent describe the effect as neutral, while 31% describe the effect as mostly positive, and 24% describe the effect as mostly negative.

Sample First Paragraph

Technology has become an intrinsic part of everyday life. What was once science fiction—using a small metal and glass rectangle to make food magically appear at one's doorstep—is now commonplace. Meanwhile, educators and parents express concern that digital media and screen time are psychologically damaging. While technology should be used with guidance and supervision, today's youth should have access to technology as both an educational and personal tool.

Question 2—Rhetorical Analysis Essay

How to Score 6 Points

Use the Rhetorical Diamond! While you're reading the prompt and the passage, imagine—and try to flesh out—a baseball diamond with the following six points:

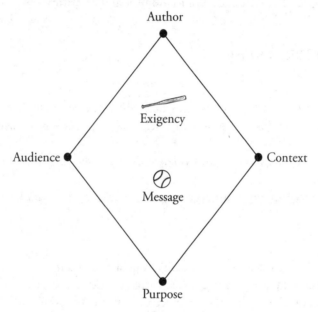

Author: Vice President Spiro Agnew
Audience: The people of Des Moines, Iowa, as well as a national televised audience
Purpose: To question the power of news media producers
Context: This speech was given by Vice President Agnew in Des Moines, Iowa. The speech was also televised live.
Exigency: To inform listeners of the power the news media holds over their perception of current events
Message: The news media is being increasingly empowered in the era of 24-hour news. People need to monitor and be critical of the news media.

Sample Rhetorical Modes and Devices

- **Allusion:** "Gresham's Law seems to be operating in the network news: bad news drives out good news. The irrational is more controversial than the rational."
- **Consonance:** "Normality has become the nemesis of the network news."
- **Verbal irony:** "Now the upshot of all this controversy is that a narrow and distorted picture of America often emerges from the televised news."

- **Rhetorical question:** "Television may have destroyed the old stereotypes, but has it not created new ones in their places? What has this "passionate" pursuit of controversy done to the politics of progress through local compromise essential to the functioning of a democratic society?"
- **Anaphora:** "And the people of America are challenged, too—challenged to press for responsible news presentations. The people can let the networks know that they want their news straight and objective. The people can register their complaints on bias through mail to the networks and phone calls to local stations."
- **Direct address:** "The answers must come from the media men.... And the people of America are challenged, too—challenged to press for responsible news presentations. The people can let the networks know that they want their news straight and objective."

Sample First Paragraph

Vice President Spiro Agnew had a unique opportunity in 1969, when he addressed an audience in Des Moines, Iowa while also having his remarks aired live nationwide. He took advantage of this opportunity to call into question the very medium that gave him such a vast audience: the cable news. Agnew used a variety of linguistic devices and direct addresses to implore the audience to monitor and be critical of the news media.

Question 3—Argument Essay

How to Score 6 Points

- Take a definite position, so no one will question where you stand on the topic of the prompt.
- Develop an argument that builds and moves forward instead of simply repeating the same point several times in different ways.
- Support the points in your argument with evidence drawn from your own knowledge, reading, experiences, and observations.
- Explain how your evidence supports your argument.

Sample Evidence

- Consider the example of a high school class schedule. Equality could mean all students have equal access to all classes. Or, equality could mean all students are forced to take the same classes.
- In terms of democracy, equality could mean one person gets one vote. However, representation in a democratic republic varies based on local election practices and institutions such as the electoral college.
- In its early years, the Soviet Union sought to enforce equality through a command economy, forcing industrialization and reallocation of resources. These practices lead to growth but widespread famine.
- Daily routines, such as eating, require a certain amount of personalization. Considering individual preferences and dietary needs such as allergies, no "equal" diet would be satisfactory, nor logistically feasible, for all members of a community.
- In the example of religious freedom, equality could mean individuals all having equal freedom to worship in their own way, or it could mean mandating one religious practice for all.

Sample First Paragraph

Equality, like many social and political ideals, is subjective. As Barry Goldwater describes, equality can for some yield "liberty" and "emancipation," and for others equality results in "conformity" and "despotism." While allowing individuals in a society equal access to resources can bring about prosperity, mandating an equal experience across diverse populations can lead to despotism and injustice.

Practice Test 3

AP® English Language and Composition Exam

SECTION I: Multiple-Choice Questions

DO NOT BEGIN THE EXAM UNTIL YOU ARE TOLD TO DO SO.

DISCLAIMER: The official AP English Language and Composition Exam will be administered digitally. Instructions for the digital exam may differ from this practice test.

At a Glance

Total Time
1 hour
Number of Questions
45
Percent of Total Grade
45%

Instructions

Section I of this examination contains 45 multiple-choice questions. Choose the best answer to each question. Note: Pay particular attention to the requirements of questions that contain the words "NOT," "LEAST," or "EXCEPT."

Indicate all of your answers to the multiple-choice questions on the answer sheet. No credit will be given for anything written in this exam booklet, but you may use the booklet for notes or scratch work. After you have decided which of the suggested answers is best, completely fill in the corresponding oval on the answer sheet. Give only one answer to each question. If you change an answer, be sure that the previous mark is erased completely. Here is a sample question and answer.

Sample Question   Sample Answer

Chicago is a
(A) state
(B) city
(C) country
(D) continent

Use your time effectively, working as quickly as you can without losing accuracy. Do not spend too much time on any one question. Go on to other questions and come back to the ones you have not answered if you have time.

About Guessing

Many candidates wonder whether or not to guess the answers to questions about which they are not certain. Multiple-choice scores are based on the number of questions answered correctly. Points are not deducted for incorrect answers, and no points are awarded for unanswered questions. Because points are not deducted for incorrect answers, you are encouraged to answer all multiple-choice questions. On any questions you do not know the answer to, you should eliminate as many choices as you can, and then select the best answer among the remaining choices.

GO ON TO THE NEXT PAGE.

This page intentionally left blank.

ENGLISH LANGUAGE AND COMPOSITION
SECTION I
Time—1 hour

Directions: This part consists of selections from prose works and questions on their content, form, and style. After reading each passage, choose the best answer to each question and completely fill in the corresponding oval on the answer sheet.

Note: Pay particular attention to the requirement of questions that contain the words NOT, LEAST, or EXCEPT.

Questions 1–13. Read the following passage carefully before you choose your answers.

This passage is excerpted from a contemporary article in a scholarly journal.

The most obvious joke in the title of Swift's *Travels into Several Remote Nations of the World* is that what purports to be a chronicle of several excursions to remote nations
Line turns out to be a satiric anatomy of specifically English
5 attitudes and values. But there is a second joke. Many of the…supposedly unfamiliar and exotic sights Gulliver sees in his sixteen years and seven months of wandering in remote nations, and even the radically altered perspectives from which he sees them (as diminutive landscapes, giant
10 people, intelligent animals, etc.), could have been seen or experienced in a few days by anyone at the tourists' sights, public entertainments, shows, spectacles, and exhibitions in the streets and at the fairs of London.

It is not surprising that *Gulliver's Travels* should be
15 filled with the shows and diversions of London. All the Scriblerians were fascinated with popular entertainments; collectively and individually, they satirized them in many of their works. Swift shared this fascination with his fellow Scriblerians, and he transforms the sights and shows of
20 London into an imaginative center of *Gulliver's Travels*.[1]

Gulliver himself senses that the wonders he sees in remote nations resemble popular entertainments back home in England when he notes that the capital city of Lilliput "looked like the painted Scene of a City in a Theatre."[1] And
25 other popular entertainments would allow Londoners to see many of the same sights Gulliver saw in Lilliput. A Londoner could experience what a miniature city looked like to the giant Gulliver by going to see the papier-mâché and clay architectural and topographical models displayed at fairs and
30 in inns, some of which were extraordinarily elaborate and detailed, such as the model of Amsterdam exhibited in 1710, which was twenty feet wide and twenty to thirty feet long, "with all the Churches, Chappels, Stadt house, Hospitals,

noble Buildings, Streets, Trees, Walks, Avenues, with the
35 Sea, Shipping, Sluices, Rivers, Canals &c., most exactly built to admiration."[2]

Miniature people, as well as miniature landscapes, could be seen in one of the most popular diversions in London, the peepshows, which were enclosed boxes containing scenes
40 made out of painted board, paper flats, and glass panels and given the illusion of depth by mirrors and magnifying glasses. All of this was seen through a hole bored in one side. Among the most popular scenes were interiors, particularly palace interiors of European royalty, and so there is a direct
45 analogy between peering in the hole of a peepshow and Gulliver's looking into the palace in Lilliput: "I applied my Face to the Windows of the middle Stories, and discovered the most splendid Apartments that can be imagined. There I saw the Empress, and the young Princes in their several
50 Lodgings. Her Imperial Majesty was pleased to smile very graciously upon me, and gave me out the window her Hand to kiss." The queen's movements could have been seen in the peepshows, too, for clockwork animating the figures was introduced early in the century. And much the same illusion
55 of a living, miniature world could be found in another popular diversion, the "moving picture," a device in which cutout figures were placed within a frame and activated by jacks and wheels. This curiosity fascinated contemporary Londoners: "The landscape looks as an ordinary picture till
60 the clock-work behind the curtain be set at work, and then the ships move and sail distinctly upon the sea till out of sight; a coach comes out of town, the motion of the horses and wheels are very distinct, and a gentleman in the coach that salutes the company; a hunter also and his dogs keep
65 their course till out of sight." Swift saw this same moving picture, or one very much like it, and was impressed.

---

1 *Gulliver's Travels*, in *The Prose Works of Jonathan Swift*, ed. Herbert Davis, 14 vols. (Oxford: B. Blackwell, 1939–68), XI:13

2 Quoted in John Ashton, *Social Life in the Reign of Queen Anne* (New York: Chatto and Windus, 1883), 219–20

GO ON TO THE NEXT PAGE.

1. The purpose of the passage is most likely to

   (A) describe the cultural landscape in *Gulliver's Travels*
   (B) draw a comparison between the fictional world Gulliver experienced and the similar imaginative elements of 18th-century London
   (C) point out the superfluous nature of entertainment in Swift's London
   (D) provide evidence that Swift's satire is derived from the natural curiosity of European royalty

2. In the passage, the author's overall attitude toward *Gulliver's Travels* can best be described as

   (A) cleverly subversive
   (B) bitingly sarcastic
   (C) generally appreciative
   (D) halfheartedly engaged

3. "Scriblerians" (line 16) refers to

   (A) book craftsmen in London
   (B) characters in Swift's novels
   (C) historians of popular entertainment
   (D) a London-based circle of English authors

4. It can be inferred from the second paragraph that Jonathan Swift was

   (A) a citizen of London
   (B) a producer of public entertainments
   (C) a member of the Scriblerians
   (D) a painter as well as an author

5. The stylistic feature most evident in the first two paragraphs (lines 1–20) is the use of

   (A) repeated syntactical patterns
   (B) shifts in tense and person
   (C) historical allusions
   (D) a series of extended metaphors

6. In describing miniature people and landscapes in the final paragraph, the author emphasizes their

   (A) obscurity
   (B) magnificence
   (C) commonness
   (D) transience

7. In the fourth paragraph, the author includes long quotes primarily in order to

   (A) refute the claims of his detractors that *Gulliver's Travels* was purely imaginative
   (B) document the connection between *Gulliver's Travels* and popular entertainments
   (C) challenge the prevailing scholarship on the miniature people and landscapes in *Gulliver's Travels*
   (D) inform the reader of the sources for the study of miniature people and landscapes in *Gulliver's Travels*

8. Which of the following best describes the relationship between the first section (lines 1–20) and the second section (lines 21–66) of the passage?

   (A) The second section answers the series of questions raised in the first section.
   (B) The second section undermines the positions of scholars introduced in the first section.
   (C) The second section expands on a technical definition introduced in the first section.
   (D) The second section provides evidence for the claims introduced in the first section.

9. Footnote 1 in line 24 indicates that

   (A) the article first appeared as an addendum to *Gulliver's Travels*
   (B) *Gulliver's Travels* was first published in 1939
   (C) the quotation "looked like the…Theater" was excerpted from *Gulliver's Travels*, part of a 14-volume set of Swift's works
   (D) the quotation "looked like the…Theater" was originally written by Herbert Davis

GO ON TO THE NEXT PAGE.

10. Footnote 2 in line 36 indicates

    (A) the quotation was taken from a professional journal
    (B) the quotation refers to a 1710 exhibit in Amsterdam
    (C) the quotation originally appeared in *Gulliver's Travels* in 1883
    (D) the quotation, describing a miniature exhibition of Amsterdam, first appeared in a book by John Ashton

11. The details in lines 46–52 suggest the scene is viewed by which of the following?

    (A) An impartial anthropologist
    (B) An intrigued visitor
    (C) A critical literary scholar
    (D) An argumentative architect

12. The speaker's tone might best be described as

    (A) emphatic and insistent
    (B) scholarly and enthusiastic
    (C) dejected but hopeful
    (D) erudite and cynical

13. In the final paragraph (lines 37–66), the writer mentions "peepshows" and "moving pictures" primarily to

    (A) illustrate the fascination that Scriblerians had with popular curiosities of the era
    (B) explain how Swift copied the literary styles and themes of his time
    (C) emphasize the influence of popular entertainment on literature
    (D) suggest that *Gulliver's Travels* was purely allegorical in its significance

GO ON TO THE NEXT PAGE.

Questions 14–25. Read the following passage carefully before you choose your answers.

This passage is from an 18th-century protofeminist work.

My own sex, I hope, will excuse me, if I treat them like rational creatures, instead of flattering their fascinating graces, and viewing them as if they were in a state of
Line perpetual childhood, unable to stand alone. I earnestly
5 wish to point out in what true dignity and human happiness consists—I wish to persuade women to endeavour to acquire strength, both of mind and body, and to convince them that the soft phrases, susceptibility of heart, delicacy of sentiment, and refinement of taste, are almost synonymous
10 with epithets of weakness, and that those beings who are only the objects of pity and that kind of love, which has been termed its sister, will soon become objects of contempt.

Dismissing then those pretty feminine phrases, which the men condescendingly use to soften our slavish dependence,
15 and despising that weak elegancy of mind, exquisite sensibility, and sweet docility of manners, supposed to be the sexual characteristics of the weaker vessel, I wish to show that elegance is inferior to virtue, that the first object of laudable ambition is to obtain a character as a human being,
20 regardless of the distinction of sex; and that secondary views should be brought to this simple touchstone.

This is a rough sketch of my plan; and should I express my conviction with the energetic emotions that I feel whenever I think of the subject, the dictates of experience
25 and reflection will be felt by some of my readers. Animated by this important object, I shall disdain to cull my phrases or polish my style;—I aim at being useful, and sincerity will render me unaffected; for, wishing rather to persuade by the force of my arguments, than dazzle by the elegance of my
30 language, I shall not waste my time in rounding periods, nor in fabricating the turgid bombast of artificial feelings, which, coming from the head, never reach the heart—I shall be employed about things, not words!—and, anxious to render my sex more respectable to members of society, I
35 shall try to avoid that flowery diction which has slided from essays into novels, and from novels into familiar letters and conversation.

These pretty nothings—these caricatures of the real beauty of sensibility, dropping glibly from the tongue, vitiate
40 the taste, and create a kind of sickly delicacy that turns away from simple unadorned truth; and a deluge of false sentiments and overstretched feelings, stifling the natural emotions of the heart, render the domestic pleasures insipid, that ought to sweeten the exercise of those severe duties,
45 which educate a rational and immortal being for a nobler field of action.

The education of women has, of late, been more attended to than formerly; yet they are still reckoned a frivolous sex, and ridiculed or pitied by the writers who endeavour by
50 satire or instruction to improve them. It is acknowledged that they spend many of the first years of their lives in acquiring a smattering of accomplishments: meanwhile strength of body and mind are sacrificed to libertine notions of beauty, to the desire of establishing themselves—the only way women
55 can rise in the world—by marriage. And this desire making mere animals of them, when they marry they act as such children may be expected to act—they dress; they paint, and nickname God's creatures—Surely these weak beings are only fit for a seraglio!—Can they govern a family, or take
60 care of the poor babes whom they bring into the world?

14. In the initial paragraph, the author employs both

   (A) apology and classification
   (B) irony and exposition
   (C) analogy and extended metaphor
   (D) flattery and epithets

15. In the initial paragraph, the author decries

   (A) traditional feminine attributes
   (B) traditional male attributes
   (C) modern sexuality
   (D) the importance of love

16. In the initial paragraph, the author suggests that

   (A) a man will never truly love a strong woman
   (B) men never respect strong women
   (C) women need emotional and physical strength
   (D) women need intellectual and physical strength

17. The author ties the second paragraph to the first by using the words

   (A) "vessel" and "touchstone"
   (B) "soften" and "inferior"
   (C) "laudable" and "sex"
   (D) "soften" and "weak"

GO ON TO THE NEXT PAGE.

18. The word "vessel" (line 17) is a metaphor for

    (A) sex
    (B) woman
    (C) man
    (D) phrase

19. The author suggests that a woman's worth may be best judged by

    (A) comparing her with a praiseworthy man
    (B) examining the elegance of her writing
    (C) evaluating the strength of her character
    (D) evaluating her physical beauty

20. The author proposes to write in a manner that is both

    (A) cogent and emotional
    (B) polished and intellectual
    (C) ornate and rhetorical
    (D) elegant and cerebral

21. The words "pretty nothings" (line 38) are a reprise of

    (A) "letters and conversation" (lines 36–37)
    (B) "essays" and "novels" (line 36)
    (C) "flowery diction" (line 35)
    (D) "rounding periods" (line 30)

22. With the phrase "dropping glibly from the tongue" (line 39) the author begins

    (A) a caricature of women
    (B) a critique of turgid bombast
    (C) a panegyric of sugary writing
    (D) an extended metaphor

23. One can infer from the passage that to become strong human beings, rather than mere children, young women need

    (A) an education different from that of young men
    (B) more understanding husbands
    (C) obliging husbands
    (D) the same education as that of young men

24. The tone of the final paragraph is

    (A) sardonic
    (B) lyrical
    (C) condescending
    (D) frivolous

25. Which of the following best describes the writer's exigence in the passage?

    (A) A low turnout rate among eligible voters in recent national elections
    (B) The trend toward violence in feminist political movements
    (C) Social inequality among men and women
    (D) Widening disparities in the socioeconomic circumstances of wealthy and poor women

GO ON TO THE NEXT PAGE.

Questions 26–33 are based on the following passage.

The passage below is a draft.

(1) Throughout her life, "Dolly" chose to speak in her native Cornish, a language that dates back to at least the early Roman occupation of Great Britain. (2) When Dolly died in 1777, she gained fame as the last fluent, native speaker of the Cornish language, which would then remain extinct for over one hundred years.

(3) Born in 1692, Dolly was one of six children born to a poor fisherman and his wife in the charmingly-named village of Mousehole in Penzance. (4) Dolly never married and lived in a shabby hut in a drab corner of Mousehole, making her living as a travelling fishwife and sometime fortune-teller. (5) By the 1760s, when the Cornish people around her had largely traded their native language for English, Dolly became known for gabbing in Cornish with whomever she could find. (6) She was especially known for singing in her language of choice.

(7) There is some controversy as to whether Dolly was, in fact, the last native speaker of Cornish. (8) Modern historians now believe that there may have been half a dozen people in the vicinity of Mousehole, all of whom died before 1800, who continued to speak Cornish after Dolly's death.

(9) What we know for sure is that Dolly Pentreath was *not* the last speaker of the Cornish language. (10) In 1904, Celtic linguist Henry Jenner published *A Handbook of the Cornish Language*.

(11) This sparked a massive revival in interest in the ancient language throughout the 20th Century. (12) Devotees taught classes, published educational materials, and coined new words. (13) It is estimated that around 600 people in Cornwall speak their ancestral tongue.

26. Which of the following sentences, if placed before sentence 1, would provide the most effective introduction to the topic of the paragraph and the passage as a whole?

(A) The eccentric Dolly Pentreath was born in 1692 in a small fishing village in Cornwall, England.

(B) According to legend, the dying words of Cornwall native Dorothy Pentreath were "*My ny vynnav kewsel Sowsnek!*" ("I don't want to speak English!")

(C) To their surprise, as part of a 1994 research project, graduate students at the University of Exeter discovered the last known speaker of the Cornish language, Dolly Pentreath.

(D) Ironically, when Dorothy Pentreath suffered brain injuries after a mining accident, she immediately started speaking English again.

27. The writer wants to add the following sentence to the second paragraph (sentences 3–6) to provide additional explanation.

She was not taught any English, since Cornish was the language of coastal Cornwall fish-traders in the 1690s.

Where would the sentence best be placed?

(A) Before sentence 3
(B) After sentence 3
(C) After sentence 5
(D) After sentence 6

28. In the third paragraph (sentences 7–8), the writer wants to expand on the controversy surrounding Dolly Pentreath. Which of the following claims would best achieve this purpose?

(A) Dolly Pentreath is not, in fact, the last speaker of Cornish, but rather its last fluent native speaker.

(B) In 1775, a fisherman in Mousehole named William Bodinar stated that he knew of five people who could speak Cornish.

(C) Dolly Pentreath was often known for cursing at people in Cornish whenever she became angry.

(D) In 1768, researcher Daines Barrington wrote of a man from Marazion named John Nancarrow who was a native speaker and survived into the 1790s.

GO ON TO THE NEXT PAGE.

29. In the third paragraph (sentences 7–8), the writer wants to provide further evidence to rebut the claim made by modern historians. Which of the following pieces of evidence would best achieve this purpose?

   (A) An interview of a modern Cornish speaker who claims Dolly Pentreath as his ancestor
   (B) A personal anecdote about the author's travels around Cornwall in the 20th century
   (C) A quote from an inscription on Dolly Pentreath's gravestone declaring her to be the last speaker of ancient Cornish
   (D) An exposé of incompetence among certain modern scholars of British languages

30. The writer wants to add more information to the fourth paragraph (sentences 9–10) to support the main argument of the paragraph. All of the following pieces of evidence help achieve this purpose EXCEPT which one?

   (A) The name of a 19th-century book written in Cornish
   (B) Census records indicating a number of Cornish speakers in Penzance in 1850
   (C) A quote from Dolly Pentreath's 18th-century diary written in Cornish
   (D) A Cornish dictionary published in 1920

31. Which one of the following true statements, if inserted after sentence 13, would provide the best evidence for the idea that the revival of Cornish was successful?

   (A) By 2010, UNESCO had removed Cornish from its list of "extinct" languages.
   (B) Many people in 1904 believed that the Cornish language was an important part of Cornish culture and heritage.
   (C) Along with Welsh and Breton, Cornish originally derived from the Brittonic language.
   (D) Most modern residents of Cornwall continue to consider English their primary language.

32. The working title of this passage is "Dolly Pentreath: The Last Speaker of Cornish?". The fourth and fifth paragraphs (sentences 9–13) answer the question posed in the title of the passage in which of the following ways?

   (A) They provide evidence that Dolly Pentreath was not historically considered the last native speaker of Cornish.
   (B) They show that, despite Dolly Pentreath's legendary status in Cornwall, the Cornish language continues to be spoken today.
   (C) They reaffirm the role that Cornish linguists and historians have played in perpetuating the Dolly Pentreath myth.
   (D) They provide evidence to finally settle the question of whether Dolly Pentreath was a real historical figure.

33. The writer wants to add a phrase at the beginning of sentence 13 (reproduced below), adjusting the capitalization as needed, to set up a continuation of the idea discussed earlier in the paragraph.

   It is estimated that around 600 people in Cornwall speak their ancestral tongue.

   Which of the following choices best accomplishes this goal?

   (A) Furthermore,
   (B) For example,
   (C) Similarly,
   (D) Today,

GO ON TO THE NEXT PAGE.

Questions 34–41 are based on the following passage.

The passage below is a draft.

(1) Sherwood Anderson saw his first novel, *Windy McPherson's Son*, published in 1916, but it was not until 1919 with the publication of his masterpiece *Winesburg, Ohio* that Anderson was pushed to the forefront of a new movement in American literature. (2) The latter book, something between a short-story collection and a novel, helped to inaugurate an age of a truly homespun American Modernism.

(3) As other writers began to supplant him in the popular imagination, Anderson continued his tireless literary experimentation until his death in 1941. (4) It takes only a few pages of *Winesburg, Ohio*, however, or many of his other short stories, articles, and novels to see that Anderson is still very much with us today and that much of what we understand about ourselves as Americans was made clear to us only by the pen of the advertising man from Ohio.

(5) Sherwood Anderson would be seen by a new generation of American writers as the first author to take a real step toward creating a type of literature that was in tune with something previously only associated with Europe. (6) Anderson was able to fuse his sense of the passing of the Industrial Age in America with a type of uniquely American expression that sought to replace previous literary conventions with more local expressions of fragmentation and alienation.

(7) With *Winesburg, Ohio*, Anderson inspired a younger group of writers, among whose ranks were Ernest Hemingway and William Faulkner, to embrace their American experiences and to express them in ways separate from those being expressed by European writers or American expatriates, as American writers living abroad were known. (8) When *Winesburg, Ohio* finally appeared in 1919, its general reception was positive, but limited to those who were able to find copies of the book.

(9) In the 1920s, Anderson wrote some direct responses to the more explicit examples of literary Modernism in Europe. (10) In the 1930s, Anderson wrote *Beyond Desire*. (11) But Anderson's most important contributions in the 1920s and 1930s are best felt indirectly through the works of the various writers he inspired. (12) Anderson was among the first to explore the troubled relationship between the city and the rural town, the direct style to which we so often apply the name, "American," and the idea that deeply intellectual concerns can be relevant to everyday people as much as they can to academics. (13) Even today, Anderson's initial treatment of these themes remains an important starting point for anyone interested in American culture.

34. The writer wants to add a sentence to create an effective transition from sentence 3 to sentence 4. Which of the following sentences, if added between sentences 3 and 4, would best achieve this purpose?

(A) In the contemporary popular imagination, Anderson's influence often appears to be diminishing.

(B) In 1912, Anderson had had a nervous breakdown that led him to abandon his business and family and to become a writer.

(C) Before he died, though, he had moved to Chicago and was eventually married four times.

(D) Even Anderson scholars often overlook the fact that *Dark Laughter*, a novel inspired by Anderson's time in New Orleans, was his only bestseller.

35. After sentence 8, the writer wants to add a sentence to provide support for the main claim made in sentence 8. Which of the following sentences best accomplishes this goal?

(A) Anderson's later books, such as *Dark Laughter*, would go on to sell many more copies.

(B) Despite the success of *Winesburg*, many critics still preferred the older European models of writing.

(C) *Winesburg, Ohio* remains one of Anderson's best-loved books.

(D) Those who did secure a copy of *Winesburg, Ohio* felt that it inaugurated a new age in American literature.

36. For the sake of the logic and coherence of this essay, the second paragraph (sentences 3–4) should be placed:

(A) Before the first paragraph (sentences 1–2)
(B) After the third paragraph (sentences 5–6)
(C) After the fourth paragraph (sentences 7–8)
(D) After the fifth paragraph (sentences 9–13)

GO ON TO THE NEXT PAGE.

37. At the end of sentence 10 (reproduced below), the writer wants to provide clear and effective support for the claim made in sentence 4, adjusting punctuation as needed.

    In the 1930s, Anderson wrote Beyond Desire.

    Which of the following additions to the end of sentence 10 best achieves this purpose?

    (A) which addressed social questions that only social scientists and propagandists dared touch.
    (B) which was heavily influenced by the literature of the Southern Populist movement.
    (C) which has been named by many literary critics as a highlight from Anderson's later work.
    (D) which was not as highly revered as *Winesburg, Ohio*.

38. The writer wants to provide additional detail to clarify information that is crucial to the overall topic but may be unfamiliar to the average reader. Which of the following additions would be most effective?

    (A) A definition of literary Modernism in the first paragraph (sentences 1–2)
    (B) More detail about Anderson's advertising career in the second paragraph (sentences 3–4)
    (C) An expanded discussion of the Industrial Age in the third paragraph (sentences 5–6)
    (D) A list of the major works of Hemingway and Faulkner in the fourth paragraph (sentences 7–8)

39. How does the writer's purpose in the first paragraph (sentences 1–2) compare to the writer's purpose in the fifth paragraph (sentences 9–13)?

    (A) The first paragraph is expository, while the fifth paragraph is analytical.
    (B) The first paragraph provides evidence for the conclusion drawn in the fifth paragraph.
    (C) The fifth paragraph provides additional detail about a general claim made in the first paragraph.
    (D) The first paragraph provides objective analysis, while the fifth paragraph provides subjective advice.

40. The writer is considering adding the following quote from literature scholar Daniel Mark Fogel:

    "Instead of emphasizing plot and action, Anderson used a simple, precise, unsentimental style to reveal the frustration, loneliness, and longing in the lives of his characters. These characters are stunted by the narrowness of Midwestern small-town life and by their own limitations."

    Where would be the most effective place to add this quote?

    (A) After sentence 2
    (B) After sentence 4
    (C) After sentence 6
    (D) After sentence 8

41. All of the following sentences help to establish the writer's main argument EXCEPT

    (A) sentence 1
    (B) sentence 2
    (C) sentence 7
    (D) sentence 10

GO ON TO THE NEXT PAGE.

Questions 42–45 are based on the following passage.

The passage below is a draft.

(1) Siena is an old, picturesque city located in the hills of Tuscany. (2) Many historical markers from as far back as medieval Italy still remain throughout the city. (3) Another remnant from Siena's rich history that still plays a very prominent role today is the tradition of *Il Palio*.

(4) *Il Palio di Siena* is held twice a year: once in July and once in August. (5) A field of ten bareback horses races three laps, each with two dreaded right-angle turns, around a dangerously steep track circling the city's central plaza, the *Piazza del Campo*. (6) Even though *Il Palio* lasts only about 90 seconds, its importance in Siena goes far beyond the race itself.

(7) Members are fiercely committed emotionally, socially, and financially to their own *contrada*. (8) They voluntarily tax themselves to support their own *contrada* and to invest in a good horse and jockey for the biannual race. (9) Jockey salaries for a single race often exceed 250,000 euros! (10) This is, however, a small price to pay to achieve victory at *Il Palio*. (11) Seeing the colors and arms of their *contrada* in the winner's circle is the most glorious event—even more so than getting married—for many Sienese citizens. (12) Old men weep openly out of sheer joy, and elated adults and children parade throughout the city with their newly won silk banner, also called the *palio*.

(13) The brief race is a spectacular culmination of an entire way of life in Siena. (14) Every citizen belongs to one of seventeen city districts, collectively known as the *Contrade*. (15) *Contrada* is the term for a single district that has its own color and arms, such as the *Aquila* (the eagle) or *Bruco* (the caterpillar). (16) A *contrada* is the source of so much local patriotism that every important event, from baptisms to food festivals, is celebrated only within one's own contrada and fellow members, who become more like family.

(17) After the actual race day, the *Palio* festivities continue for a minimum of two weeks. (18) Thousands of visitors from around the world travel to Siena during the summer, not only to witness the exciting race but also to attend the after-parties thrown by the locals. (19) While the *Palio* is not important to outsiders who do not live in Siena, the race and the festivities that follow are a spectacular experience.

42. The writer wants to add a phrase at the beginning of sentence 2 (reproduced below), adjusting the capitalization as needed, to set up a contrast within the paragraph.

    Many historical markers from as far back as medieval Italy still remain throughout the city.

    Which of the following choices best accomplishes this goal?

    (A) In contrast to cities in nearby Greece,
    (B) As examples of modernity,
    (C) Even though its inhabitants live modern lives,
    (D) Despite what many may assume,

43. Which of the following true statements, if inserted after sentence 2, would best connect the first part of the first paragraph with the last part while illustrating the main idea of this paragraph?

    (A) Like most Italian cities, Siena is very serious about soccer, a modern sport codified in England in the 1800s.
    (B) Cobblestone streets and Gothic architecture are blended with modern sidewalk cafes and trendy designer stores.
    (C) The city of Siena is certainly a mixture of ancient and contemporary practices.
    (D) Siena is famous among culinary enthusiasts for its delicious cuisine.

44. For the sake of the logic and coherence of this essay, what would be the best placement for the third paragraph (sentences 7–12)?

    (A) (where it is now)
    (B) Before the first paragraph (sentences 1–3)
    (C) Before the second paragraph (sentences 4–6)
    (D) Before the fifth paragraph (sentences 17–19)

GO ON TO THE NEXT PAGE.

45. In sentence 19 (reproduced below), which of the following versions of the underlined text best establishes the writer's position on the main argument of the passage?

While the Palio is not important to outsiders who do not live in Siena, the race and the festivities that follow are a spectacular experience.

(A) (as it is now)
(B) It is no wonder:
(C) Although the Sienese have often been suspicious of outsiders,
(D) Despite outside efforts to stop the *Il Palio,*

END OF SECTION I

AP® English Language and Composition Exam

SECTION II: Free-Response Questions

DO NOT BEGIN THE EXAM UNTIL YOU ARE TOLD TO DO SO.

DISCLAIMER: The official AP English Language and Composition Exam will be administered digitally. Instructions for the digital exam may differ from this practice test.

<table>
<tr><td>

At a Glance

Total Time
2 hours, plus a 15-minute reading period

Number of Questions
3

Percent of Total Grade
55%

</td><td>

Instructions

Section II of this examination requires answers in essay form. To help you use your time well, the coordinator will announce the time at which each question should be completed. If you finish any question before time is announced, you may go on to the following question. If you finish the examination in less than the time allotted, you may go back and work on any essay question you want.

Each essay will be judged on its clarity and effectiveness in dealing with the requirements of the topic assigned and on the quality of the writing. After completing each question, you should check your essay for accuracy of punctuation, spelling, and diction; you are advised, however, not to attempt many longer corrections. Remember that quality is far more important than quantity.

Write your essays with a pen, preferably in black or dark blue ink. Be sure to write CLEARLY and LEGIBLY. Cross out any errors you make.

</td></tr>
</table>

GO ON TO THE NEXT PAGE.

ENGLISH LANGUAGE AND COMPOSITION
SECTION II
Total Time—2 hours, 15 minutes

Question 1

Suggested reading and writing time—55 minutes.
It is suggested that you spend 15 minutes reading the question, analyzing and evaluating the sources,
and 40 minutes writing your response.
Note: You may begin writing your response before the reading period is over.

(This question counts for one-third of the total essay section score.)

Throughout much of history, humans have defined themselves as members of their tribe. With the growth of civilization in the Neolithic period, humans began to define themselves by their village or state. By the 19th century, humans were defining themselves by their nation. Today, in the 21st century, humans are being asked to define themselves as citizens of the world.

Carefully read the following seven sources, including the introductory information for each source. Then synthesize the information from at least three of the sources and incorporate it into a coherent, well-developed essay that argues a clear position on the extent to which people are able to define themselves as global citizens.

Source A   (Hassanpour)
Source B   (graph)
Source C   (Symons)
Source D   (Kennedy)
Source E   (Pirie)
Source F   (Yeo)
Source G   (map)

In your response you should do the following:

- Respond to the prompt with a thesis that presents a defensible position.

- Select and use evidence from at least 3 of the provided sources to support your line of reasoning. Indicate clearly the sources used through direct quotation, paraphrase, or summary. Sources may be cited as Source A, Source B, etc., or by using the description in parentheses.

- Explain how the evidence supports your line of reasoning.

- Use appropriate grammar and punctuation in communicating your argument.

GO ON TO THE NEXT PAGE.

Source A

Hassanpour, Amir. "The Kurdish Experience." *MERIP*
189. Middle East Research and Information
Project. July 1994. Web. 31 Jan. 2017.

The following is excerpted from an article on a website that provides analysis and information on the Middle East.

Numbering over 22 million, the Kurds are one of the largest non-state nations in the world. Their homeland, Kurdistan, has been forcibly divided and lies mostly within the present-day borders of Turkey, Iraq and Iran, with smaller parts in Syria, Armenia and Azerbaijan. The greatest number of Kurds today still live in Kurdistan, though a large Kurdish diaspora has developed in this century, especially in the main cities of Turkey and Iran and more recently in Europe as well. Between 10 and 12 million Kurds live in Turkey, where they comprise about 20 percent of the population. Between 5 and 6 million live in Iran, accounting for close to 10 percent of the population. Kurds in Iraq number more than 4 million, and comprise about 23 percent of the population.

In the modern era, the Kurdish nation, with its distinctive society and culture, has had to confront in all of the "host" states centralizing, ethnically-based nationalist regimes—Turkish, Arab and Persian—with little or no tolerance for expressions of national autonomy within their borders. While the modes and scale of oppression have varied in time and by place, the conditions of Kurds share some important features. First, the Kurdish areas overlap nation-state borders: They thus acquire significance for "national security" and are vulnerable to interference and manipulation by regional and international powers. Second, the Kurdish regions of these countries are usually the poorest, least developed areas, systematically marginalized by the centers of economic power. Third, the dynamics of assimilation, repression and Kurdish resistance in each country have affected the direction and outcome of the Kurdish struggles in the neighboring countries. A fourth shared feature is that these Kurdish societies are themselves internally complex, and fraught with differences of politics and ideology, social class, dialect and, still in a few places, clan.

In spite of a long history of struggle, Kurdish nationalism has not succeeded in achieving its goal of independence or even enduring autonomy. Do recent events require us to change this assessment? In 1992, a Regional Government of Iraqi Kurdistan was established, but it is economically besieged and functions very much at the sufferance of a Western military umbrella. In Turkey, a ten-year-old armed struggle has effectively defied the unrestrained efforts of the Turkish state to impose a military solution, but a political solution acceptable to the Kurds does not appear imminent. The Kurdish movement, in contrast to many other national liberation movements, has experienced a persistent contradiction between its traditional leadership and the relatively developed society it seeks to liberate. Only to the extent that this may be changing does the future hold some promise for Kurdish aspirations. Today, about half the population lives in urban centers, and feudal relations of production in rural areas have almost disappeared. Yet the politics and ideology of much of the leadership can hardly be distinguished from the worldview of landed notables of the past.

GO ON TO THE NEXT PAGE.

The following is a graphic depicting the value of the British pound sterling on June 24, 2016, the day that England voted to leave the European Union.

Source C

Symons, Emma-Kate. "Marine Le Pen's New York
Times op-ed is a knife in the back for France."
Qz.com. 19 Jan. 2015. Web. 31 Jan. 2017.

The following is excerpted from an article taking exception with The New York Times' *publication of an op-ed by Marine Le Pen, the leader of the French far-right political party Front National.*

Since 17 people were murdered in the Paris terror attacks that started with a massacre of cartoonists, staff, and police at Charlie Hebdo magazine, *The New York Times* has not deemed fit to print even one caricature by the French satirical weekly, citing Muslim sensitivities.

But today the *Times* opened up her August op-ed pages to France's extreme right Front National (FN) party president, Marine Le Pen, the chief Gallic spokesperson for Islamophobia and racism.

We must explain who Le Pen is here because the *Times* did not include even a phrase qualifying its op-ed contributor as a far right party boss, nor explaining her movement's long history of Muslim-baiting, incitement to racial hatred, Holocaust denial, and generalized anti-foreigner bile stretching back to the grimmest days of World War II collaborationist Vichy France.

The deliberately divisive FN leader is less Pat Buchanan, the renegade Republican, as she is white supremacist David Duke, and it is highly doubtful the *Times* would give an op-ed to either, especially on the Martin Luther King Jr. holiday weekend.

The daughter of party founder Jean-Marie Le Pen, an avowed Algerian war-torturer, she appropriated the legacy of Albert Camus and Georges Clemenceau, then purported to speak for "The French people," "French values," and the national value of "laïcité," secularism built upon the strict separation of church and state.

In 2010, to cite one notorious example among many, Le Pen compared Muslims praying in French streets (for lack of mosques) to an "occupying force" akin to the Nazis, though such outrages were airbrushed from her carefully-worded *Times* screed.

Her op-ed, littered with half-truths and lies, distorts the position of the French government, which strongly condemned the Charlie Hebdo attacks, the murder of police, and the attack on a Kosher market as terrorism, driven by Islamism, and as fundamentally anti-Semitic.

Of course Le Pen did not dare mention anti-Semitism, and she conveniently neglected to detail that her party promises to end all immigration, send migrants "home," strip non-white French people arbitrarily of citizenship, close mosques and prayer halls, deport Roma peoples, close France's borders and Europe's free movement of peoples, leave the euro zone, and install the "national preference" for only "real" French i.e., white, nationals, thus forcing out millions of French people with dual nationality.

Le Pen is hoping to having a real shot at the French presidency in the 2017 elections, and her popularity is soaring, with more than one third of French agreeing with her views. Her success would mean a hijacking of French democracy as we know it.

The FN's DNA is firmly fascist and Le Pen has never renounced the core of her father's ideology; she has just presented a more acceptable face, refocused the hatred on Muslims, and calibrated her incoherent economic "platform" to sound like far-left anti-globalization populism.

But the leopard has not changed its spots. The FN remains what it always has been. It is a fascist-derived front party that capitalizes on hatred of the other, chiefly immigrants, and today, especially Muslims. Its platform espouses a monocultural white France, and its supporters are among France's most virulently anti-Semitic voters.

Le Pen's values are an insult to French values—the Front National abhors the legacy of the French revolution, and the universalist notion of French citizenship, as something that is not tied to race, but tied to republican French values of liberty, equality and fraternity.

GO ON TO THE NEXT PAGE.

Source D

Kennedy, Patrick F. Statement on Sri Lanka Day.
4 Feb. 2016.

The following are remarks given on Sri Lanka Day in 2016 from the Under Secretary of Management, Organization of American States, U.S. Department of State.

Thank you, Ambassador Kariyawasam, for that kind introduction, and the honor of your invitation. And I must say that I'm incredibly excited to visit your beautiful country later this month and see the progress already made on our new embassy complex.

68 years ago today, Sri Lanka found itself in good company when it joined the rather exclusive club of great nations that chose the fourth day of the month to declare independence from the United Kingdom.

Like Sri Lankans are doing today, in a few months Americans will mark our anniversary of independence, when we will also remember the heroes and patriots of years past, and reflect on how far we've come in our long quest for a more perfect union.

And like Sri Lankans of today, Americans are still striving to address some of the very challenging problems that have long bedeviled us. Problems like poverty, discrimination, and injustice.

But Sri Lankans and Americans both understand that these problems can only be solved through the use of the ballot box, the voice of a free press, the strength of a healthy civil society, and the actions of an empowered citizenry that is committed to democracy, human rights, and progress for all.

Yes, our nations share many interests in global affairs, and that makes us strong partners. We also have many of the same core values, and face many of the same hard problems. And that, I believe, makes us strong friends. For, in the words of the Roman poet Sallust, "to like and dislike the same things, that is indeed true friendship."

We love to see our friends succeed, and the accomplishments of the Sri Lankan people and their government over the past year have made all of us rightly proud.

GO ON TO THE NEXT PAGE.

Source E

Pirie, Dr. Madsen. "Ten Very Good Things: 9.
Globalization." *AdamSmith.org*. 12 Oct. 2012. Web.
31 Jan. 2017.

The following is excerpted from a blog of a nonprofit organization dedicated to economic policy.

Over the course of decades globalization is turning the world into an integrated economy instead of what it has been for most of its history, a series of relatively isolated economies. The more trading that takes place, the more wealth is created, and global trade across international frontiers has created more wealth than ever before in human history, and has helped lift more people out of mere subsistence than ever before.

To poorer countries, globalization brings the chance to sell their relatively low cost labour onto world markets. It brings the investment that creates jobs, and although those jobs pay less than their counterparts in rich economies, they represent a step up for people in recipient countries because they usually pay more than do the more traditional jobs available there.

To people in richer countries, globalization brings lower cost goods from abroad, which leaves them with spending power to spare and a higher standard of living. It also brings opportunities for productive investment in high growth industries in developing countries.

Those adversely affected by the global exchanges are the people in rich countries whose output is now undercut by the cheaper alternatives from abroad. They often need to find new jobs or to be retrained to do work that adds higher value. The extra wealth generated by globalization has brought an increase in service sector employment, which provides many of the new jobs needed.

Competition from abroad forces firms to become more efficient and to use resources more efficiently. Often they choose to go upmarket, seeking higher added value products that face less competition from relatively unskilled labour. Thus firms which once sold cheap textiles move into fashion and design, and find customers among the rising middle classes in developing countries.

The integration of the world economy has brought with it an interdependence. As countries co-operate in trade with each other, they get to know each other and grow into the habit of resolving disputes by negotiation and agreement instead of by armed conflict. The 19th century French economist Frederic Bastiat expressed this pithily: "Where goods do not cross frontiers, armies will."

GO ON TO THE NEXT PAGE.

Source F

Yeo, Sophie. "China Air Pollution Blankets U.S. West Coast." *ClimateChangeNews.com.* 21 Jan. 2014. Web. 31 Jan. 2017.

The following is excerpted from an article on a website devoted to matters of climate change.

Air pollution in China is blowing over the Pacific Ocean and settling on the west coast of America, causing at least one extra day of dangerous smog in Los Angeles every year.

This is a case of getting what you pay for, according to a new study led by researchers from Peking University in Beijing.

They have calculated that approximately one quarter of the sulphate pollutants that cross into the US are tied to products created within China but destined for American consumers.

"We've outsourced our manufacturing and much of our pollution, but some of it is blowing back across the Pacific to haunt us," said co-author Steve Davis from the University of California Irvine.

"Given the complaints about how Chinese pollution is corrupting other countries' air, this paper shows that there may be plenty of blame to go around."

One of the drivers of the economic boom in China over the past ten years has been the demand for its exports. Between 2000 and 2007, the volume of Chinese exports grew by 390%.

At the same time, discontent over hazardous levels of air pollution in cities such as Beijing has been growing. Today, the governor of Hebei, the province surrounding Beijing, threatened to fire any officials who add new steel capacity, and thus increase the amount of coal being burnt.

GO ON TO THE NEXT PAGE.

Source G

"International Space Station Operation and Management." *NASA.gov.* Web. 31 Jan. 2017.

The following map shows the various international facilities that support the operation and management of the International Space Station, launched in 1998.

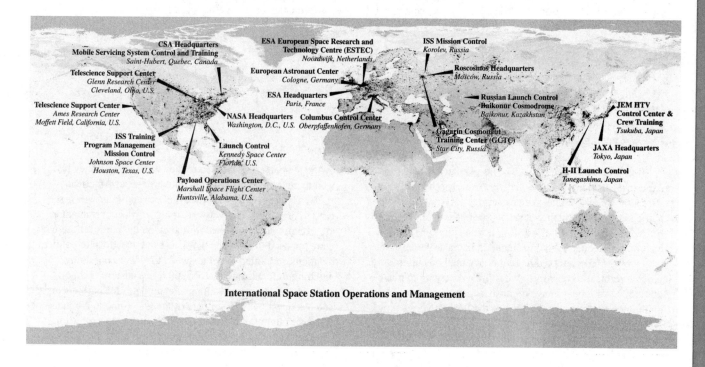

International Space Station Operations and Management

GO ON TO THE NEXT PAGE.

Question 2

Suggested time—40 minutes.

(This question counts for one-third of the total essay section score.)

The passage that follows is an excerpt from Emmeline Pankhurst's "Freedom or Death" speech, delivered in Hartford, Connecticut, on November 13, 1913. Pankhurst was a British political activist and leader of the women's suffrage movement in Britain who was widely criticized for her militancy. The following speech addresses her critics and defends the tactics of the suffragettes. Read the passage carefully. Then, in a well-developed essay, analyze the rhetorical strategies Pankhurst uses to convey her message.

In your response, you should do the following:

- Respond to the prompt with a thesis that analyzes the writer's rhetorical choices.
- Select and use evidence to support your line of reasoning.
- Explain how the evidence supports your line of reasoning.
- Demonstrate an understanding of the rhetorical situation.
- Use appropriate grammar and punctuation in communicating your argument.

Tonight I am not here to advocate woman suffrage. American suffragists can do that very well for themselves.

Line 5   I am here as a soldier who has temporarily left the field of battle in order to explain—it seems strange it should have to be explained—what civil war is like when civil war is waged by women….Since I am a woman it is necessary to explain why women have adopted revolutionary methods in order to win the rights of citizenship. We women, in trying to make our case clear, always have to make as part of our argument,

10   and urge upon men in our audience the fact—a very simple fact—that women are human beings.

Suppose the men of Hartford had a grievance, and they laid that grievance before their legislature, and the legislature obstinately refused to listen to them, or to remove their

15   grievance, what would be the proper and the constitutional and the practical way of getting their grievance removed? Well, it is perfectly obvious at the next general election the men of Hartford would turn out that legislature and elect a new one.

20   But let the men of Hartford imagine that they were not in the position of being voters at all, that they were governed without their consent being obtained, that the legislature turned an absolutely deaf ear to their demands, what would the men of Hartford do then? They couldn't vote

25   the legislature out. They would have to choose; they would have to make a choice of two evils: they would either have to submit indefinitely to an unjust state of affairs, or they would have to rise up and adopt some of the antiquated means by which men in the past got their grievances remedied.

30   Your forefathers decided that they must have representation for taxation, many, many years ago. When they felt they couldn't wait any longer, when they laid all the arguments before an obstinate British government that they could think of, and when their arguments were absolutely

35   disregarded, when every other means had failed, they began

by the tea party at Boston, and they went on until they had won the independence of the United States of America.

It is about eight years since the word *militant* was first used to describe what we were doing. It was not militant at all, except that it provoked militancy on the part of those who

40   were opposed to it. When women asked questions in political meetings and failed to get answers, they were not doing anything militant. In Great Britain it is a custom, a time-honored one, to ask questions of candidates for parliament

45   and ask questions of members of the government. No man was ever put out of a public meeting for asking a question. The first people who were put out of a political meeting for asking questions were women; they were brutally ill-used; they found themselves in jail before 24 hours had expired.

50   We were called militant, and we were quite willing to accept the name. We were determined to press this question of the enfranchisement of women to the point where we were no longer to be ignored by the politicians.

You have two babies very hungry and wanting to be fed.

55   One baby is a patient baby, and waits indefinitely until its mother is ready to feed it. The other baby is an impatient baby and cries lustily, screams and kicks and makes everybody unpleasant until it is fed. Well, we know perfectly well which baby is attended to first. That is the whole history of politics.

60   You have to make more noise than anybody else, you have to make yourself more obtrusive than anybody else, you have to fill all the papers more than anybody else, in fact you have to be there all the time and see that they do not snow you under.

When you have warfare things happen; people suffer; the

65   noncombatants suffer as well as the combatants. And so it happens in civil war. When your forefathers threw the tea into Boston Harbor, a good many women had to go without their tea. It has always seemed to me an extraordinary thing that you did not follow it up by throwing the whiskey overboard;

70   you sacrificed the women; and there is a good deal of warfare

GO ON TO THE NEXT PAGE.

for which men take a great deal of glorification which has involved more practical sacrifice on women than it has on any man. It always has been so. The grievances of those who have got power, the influence of those who have got power
75 commands a great deal of attention; but the wrongs and the grievances of those people who have no power at all are apt to be absolutely ignored. That is the history of humanity right from the beginning.

Well, in our civil war people have suffered, but you cannot
80 make omelettes without breaking eggs; you cannot have civil war without damage to something. The great thing is to see that no more damage is done than is absolutely necessary, that you do just as much as will arouse enough feeling to bring about peace, to bring about an honorable peace for the combatants;
85 and that is what we have been doing.

We entirely prevented stockbrokers in London from telegraphing to stockbrokers in Glasgow and vice versa: for one whole day telegraphic communication was entirely stopped. I am not going to tell you how it was done. I am not
90 going to tell you how the women got to the mains and cut the wires; but it was done. It was done, and it was proved to the authorities that weak women, suffrage women, as we are supposed to be, had enough ingenuity to create a situation of that kind. Now, I ask you, if women can do that, is there
95 any limit to what we can do except the limit we put upon ourselves?

GO ON TO THE NEXT PAGE.

Question 3

Suggested time—40 minutes.

(This question counts for one-third of the total essay section score.)

In response to the issue of racial imbalance, a sociologist argued, "Neutrality in our society is supposed to be the great equalizer because we believe that, if we don't favor any one group, things will work themselves out and become more equal. But the thing is this: neutrality has this effect only if there is no previous social or historical context. But that's not how the real world is. There is, in fact, a social and historical context for every situation. So if I were being "neutral" and viewing everyone as being the same, ignoring personal contexts, I wouldn't be promoting equality because I would be ignoring the differences that exist and allowing the inequalities to continue to exist, given that I wouldn't do anything to help change them. Identifying problems and actively promoting solutions are necessary to effect useful change; being neutral is consenting to the status quo."

In a well-written essay, develop your position on whether a "neutral" stand on race perpetuates racial imbalance today. Use appropriate evidence from your reading, experience, or observations to support your argument.

In your response, you should do the following:

- Respond to the prompt with a thesis that may establish a line of reasoning.
- Select and use evidence to develop and support your line of reasoning.
- Explain the relationship between the evidence and your thesis.
- Demonstrate an understanding of the rhetorical situation.
- Use appropriate grammar and punctuation in communicating your argument.

STOP

END OF EXAM

Practice Test 3:
Answers and
Explanations

PRACTICE TEST 3 ANSWER KEY

1.	B		24.	A	
2.	C		25.	C	
3.	D		26.	B	
4.	C		27.	B	
5.	A		28.	D	
6.	C		29.	C	
7.	B		30.	C	
8.	D		31.	A	
9.	C		32.	B	
10.	D		33.	D	
11.	B		34.	A	
12.	B		35.	D	
13.	A		36.	D	
14.	B		37.	A	
15.	A		38.	A	
16.	D		39.	C	
17.	D		40.	C	
18.	A		41.	D	
19.	C		42.	C	
20.	A		43.	B	
21.	C		44.	D	
22.	D		45.	B	
23.	D				

Once you have checked your answers, remember to return to page 4 and respond to the Reflect questions.

PRACTICE TEST 3 EXPLANATIONS

SECTION I: MULTIPLE CHOICE

1. **B**   To answer this question, think in terms of main idea. This is a fairly straightforward question that asks you to consider the type of material you are reading and what the author is saying within that context. In this piece of literary criticism, the author is making a connection between what Gulliver experienced and what an 18th-century Londoner might have seen exhibited in the streets and fairs. This is best summarized in (B).

2. **C**   The author describes Swift's achievement in *Gulliver's Travels* in generally positive terms, so (C) is correct. If the author were *cleverly subversive*, he would have attempted to undercut his generally positive portrayal of Swift in some way, but he never does; eliminate (A). Authors on the AP exam are rarely only *halfheartedly engaged*, so (D) can also be eliminated. Choice (B) is wrong and cannot be substantiated in the passage.

3. **D**   This is a challenging question because the author provides no explicit definition for the *Scriblerians* in the passage. You know that they were *fascinated with popular entertainments* (line 16) and that they *satirized them in many of their works* (lines 17–18), which means they are authors, not book craftsmen, (A), or literary characters, (B). There is no evidence that they worked as historians, so eliminate (C).

4. **C**   In lines 18–19, you learn that Swift *shared this fascination with his fellow Scriblerians*, which makes him a member of the circle. Therefore, (C) is correct. While he does have a distinct interest in public entertainments, he is not necessarily a *producer* of them himself, so (B) can be eliminated. There is simply no evidence in the passage for any of the other answer choices.

5. **A**   The first two paragraphs maintain a consistent tense and person, so (B) can be eliminated. The author does not invest time in drawing historical allusions or extended metaphors, so (C) and (D) can also be eliminated. The correct answer is (A) because the author uses a parallel, consistent syntactical structure throughout these paragraphs.

6. **C**   The author wants readers to see the connection between miniature people and landscapes in *Gulliver's Travels* and the common public entertainments of Swift's London. Thus, he emphasizes their *commonness*, (C), over other features. This directly contradicts *obscurity* in (A), which can be eliminated. *Transience*, (D), which emphasizes their fleeting nature, is not discussed in the final paragraph; neither is *magnificence*, (B), so both answer choices can be ruled out.

7. **B**   The series of quotes in the final paragraph substantiate the author's claim that *Gulliver's Travels* was at least somewhat based on the kinds of popular entertainments that people often saw in London. Therefore, (B) is the correct answer. The author does not really aim his argument at other scholars or at claims that *Gulliver's Travels was purely imaginative*, so eliminate (A) and (C). While he certainly does include information from other sources, his primary purpose is not to *inform the reader of the sources*, so eliminate (D).

8. **D** The first section of the essay introduces readers to the connection between *Gulliver's Travels* and popular entertainments, while the second section provides evidence to support that claim. Thus, (D) is correct. There really are no *series of questions*, (A), *positions of scholars*, (B), or *a technical definition*, (C), so those choices can be eliminated.

9. **C** Footnote questions were added to the test in response to concerns raised by colleges and universities. In these days of easy access to information via the Internet, colleges are becoming increasingly concerned that students do not take seriously the intellectual property of authors and end up plagiarizing, knowingly or not. Footnotes give information about authorship and publication place and date and can also provide hints as to the purpose of a piece of writing or its context. This particular footnote simply indicates that the quote about Lilliput does indeed come from *Gulliver's Travels*, part of a 14-volume set of works by Swift, making the correct answer (C).

10. **D** This question asks you to analyze the citation in the footnote to assess the source of the cited information. Given the author, title, publisher and page numbers in the footnote, this was a book-length text written by John Ashton. The correct answer is (D).

11. **B** By paying attention to the title, author, subject matter, and footnotes, you can use POE to eliminate (D). And while the subject matter of this essay might be of interest to an *anthropologist*, (A), the writer is not impartial. Further, the content and format are inconsistent with literary criticism, (C). The correct answer is (B).

12. **B** The tone of this passage is scholarly and generally positive, which is somewhat more difficult to detect than more overtly negative tones. Therefore, (B) is correct. He does support his claims, but not frantically, so (A) is incorrect. He is not *dejected* (i.e., sad), so (C) is also incorrect. And while this passage certainly is *erudite* (i.e., learned), he does not show any signs of cynicism, so (D) is incorrect.

13. **A** In the first two paragraphs, the author establishes that Jonathan Swift was a Scriblerian and that *All the Scriblerians were fascinated with popular entertainments; collectively and individually, they satirized them in many of their works.* Peepshows and moving pictures would be examples of this. Choice (C) may seem close, but since the passage is mainly about Swift and *Gulliver's Travels*, this choice is too broad.

14. **B** POE is the best way to approach this question. Choices (A), (C), and (D) are all partially wrong (and therefore completely wrong). Take a look at (B). The author is being ironic when she says in the first line, *My own sex, I hope, will excuse me, if I treat them like rational creatures*. The second part of (B), *exposition*, is defined as *a setting forth of meaning or intent*, and that is exactly what the author is doing in this first paragraph. Choice (B) is correct. Note that in this context, *apology* has nothing to do with being sorry; it most nearly means *defense of an idea*.

15. **A** The author addresses women directly and pretends to excuse herself for addressing them as strong, confident people, instead of the weak, overly sentimental creatures that society wants (and expects) them to be. The correct answer is (A).

16. **D** Since men aren't mentioned anywhere in the first paragraph, your choice should boil down to (C) and (D). When the author says, *I wish to persuade women to endeavour to acquire strength, both of mind and body*, she means intellectual and physical strength, (D). Had she wanted to stress emotional strength, she would have replaced *mind* with *heart*.

17. **D** The roots *soft* and *weak* appear in both paragraphs and are used in both their adjective and verb forms. The connotations of these terms, and their use to describe negative stereotypes of women, unite the two paragraphs. The correct answer is (D).

18. **A** Narrow down your choices to (A) and (B). The best way to approach this type of question is to substitute each of the answer choices for the original word to see which one makes the most sense. Try (A): *supposed to be the sexual characteristics of the weaker sex.* This seems great, but try (B) too, just in case: *supposed to be the sexual characteristics of the weaker woman.* Not as good. Naturally, in this case, the weaker sex is woman, but you are asked to find the meaning for *vessel* only. Choice (A) is the best answer.

19. **C** Using Process of Elimination, get rid of (B) and (D). Now you're down to (A) and (C). The author states that *the first object of laudable ambition is to obtain a character as a human being, regardless of the distinction of sex.* Thus, you should eliminate (A) because she is not suggesting that a comparison be made between a man and woman. This leaves (C) as the answer.

20. **A** The author wishes to convince the reader by the force of her cogent arguments and the sincerity of her emotions, so the answer is (A). If *cogent* is not on your vocabulary list, add it now. It means appealing to the intellect or powers of reasoning or convincing. You can eliminate the other choices because the author states unequivocally that she does not wish to polish her style, to employ the bombast and periodic sentences of a rhetorical style, to write elegantly, or to use flowery diction.

21. **C** The author points out that the *flowery* diction expected of women relegated them to a world outside that of men. The difference in the social level of men and women was reflected in the way they used language. Only men could use the crude words that attempt to express the harsh realities of life. Women were not supposed to know those same harsh realities and, therefore, could not use the crude words that fit with those realities. The correct answer is (C).

22. **D** The sugary diction becomes associated with the taste of a cloyingly sweet delicacy. This is an extended metaphor, (D), so Process of Elimination allows you to eliminate (A) and (B); this is not a caricature of women, nor is it a critique of bombast (pompous speech or writing). If you do not know the meaning of *panegyric*, then add it to your list of vocabulary. A panegyric is a statement of high praise. It should be clear that the author does not sing the praises of *sugary writing*, so (C) can be eliminated. The correct answer is (D).

23. **D** In this passage, the author suggests that women have the capacity to be independent equals of men. She states this most plainly at the end of the second paragraph: *the first object of laudable ambition is to obtain a character as a human being, regardless of the distinction of sex.* Therefore, she is most likely to agree that if women were educated in the same manner as men, they would be more likely to be viewed as equal with men in the eyes of the world. The correct answer is (D).

24. **A** Use Process of Elimination, especially if you don't know what *sardonic* means (harsh, bitter, or caustic). *Lyrical* is far too positive, so rule out (B). *Frivolous*, (D), is a trap: the women are perceived as frivolous, but that is not the author's tone. *Condescending*, (C), is a trap as well; lines 55–59 seem to convey this mood, but it directly contradicts the message of line 2 (*rational creatures*) as well as the main idea of the passage as a whole. The last line of the passage betrays the author's true purpose: to point out the illogic of assuming that women are helpless, useless creatures unfit for positions of responsibility. The correct answer is (A).

25. **C**   The writer's *exigence* is the motivation for the writer's effort in creating a piece of work. Here, the author is a feminist who wishes to argue that women should not be viewed as beings with inferior skills or rights in society. She must have been motivated by the observation that women were not viewed as equals in her era. Therefore, the answer is (C).

26. **B**   The passage as a whole explores the legend that Dolly Pentreath was the last fluent, native speaker of Cornish before it went temporarily extinct. Choice (A) is lacking any reference to her language choices. Choice (C) cannot be true, since Dolly died in 1777. Choice (D) is out of sequence and seems to contradict sentence 1. Sentence 1 states that Dolly *chose* to speak in Cornish, which implies that she rejected English. Choice (B) would establish this idea, as well as provide Dolly's full name, along with an entertaining start to the topic. Therefore, the answer is (B).

27. **B**   The given sentence discusses her education. Look at the sequence of events in the paragraph. Since sentence 3 is about Dolly's birth, that should start the paragraph. Eliminate (A). It doesn't make sense to insert this sentence after any mention of her adult life (sentences 4–6). Eliminate (C) and (D). The answer is (B).

28. **D**   The controversy in the third paragraph is about whether Dolly Pentreath was, in fact, the last fluent native speaker of Cornish before the language went extinct. No one claims that she was the last speaker in *any* era, (A), since the last paragraph mentions the revival of Cornish in the 20th century. Choice (B) would not necessarily exacerbate the controversy since Dolly died in 1777, and it's possible that the people William Bodinar knew were deceased before then. Choice (C) is irrelevant to the controversy. Choice (D) mentions a native speaker who survived after Dolly's death. This expands on the controversy, so the answer is (D).

29. **C**   The claim made by modern historians in the third paragraph is that Dolly Pentreath was *not* the last fluent speaker of Cornish. To rebut them, the author needs some additional evidence. Choices (A) and (B) are both irrelevant to the issue of the last fluent speaker. Choice (D) may look tempting, but you do not know whether the incompetent scholars are the ones making the claim in question. Choice (C) provides evidence that the people in Dolly's time believed her to be the last speaker of Cornish; it does not prove the historians wrong, but it weakens their case. The answer is (C).

30. **C**   The main argument made in the fourth paragraph is that people who lived after Dolly Pentreath died did, in fact, speak some Cornish. Choice (C) is irrelevant to this claim, since this evidence would come from Dolly's own life. All the other choices provide evidence that there was interest in Cornish *after* the 18th century. The answer is (C).

31. **A**   Choice (B) may show that there was an interest in Cornish, but does not prove that, in fact, people were actively speaking the language. Choice (C) does not support any particular argument, while (D) tends to weaken the author's argument. Choice (A) says that UNESCO does not consider Cornish to be an extinct language. If that is the case, then modern people must be speaking it, thus providing evidence of a successful revival. The answer is (A).

32. **B**   Although Dolly is famous for being the "last" speaker of Cornish, the fourth and fifth paragraphs establish that there was a resurgence of interest in the language in the 20th century, and it is now spoken by around 600 people. Choice (A) is incorrect. Although her status as the last speaker of Cornish is disputable, it is how she was historically known. Choice (C) is incorrect based on statements made about historians in sentence 8. Choice (D) is incorrect because the question of whether she was a real historical figure is not posed. The correct answer is (B).

33. **D**   Sentences 11 and 12 are written with past tense verbs (*sparked, taught, published, coined*), but sentence 13 is written in the present tense (*speak*). The transition, therefore, must indicate this time shift. There is no example, so (B) is incorrect. Choices (A) and (C) are close, but do not communicate the time shift. The answer is (D).

34. **A**   Sentence 4 mentions that *Anderson is still very much with us today* and contains the word *however*, so the sentence we insert before it must represent a contrasting idea. Choices (B) and (C) contain details about Anderson's life and death that are irrelevant to any contrast in the perception of his work. Choice (D) may seem tempting, but it is not as effective as (A) since it merely refers to his past career and not his present influence. Only (A) represents the needed contrast, since it states that Anderson's influence often *appears* to be diminishing. The answer is (A).

35. **D**   The claim made in sentence 8 is that *Winesburg, Ohio* was well-received by the reading public, but apparently it was difficult to obtain. Choice (C) is not effective since it does not establish that the book was difficult to obtain. Choices (A) and (B) detract from the claim in sentence 8 by pointing out weaknesses in *Winesburg*'s success. Choice (D) adds detail to directly support both that it was well-received and that it was difficult to obtain. The answer is (D).

36. **D**   Pay close attention to the years discussed in each of these paragraphs. The second paragraph discusses Anderson's death in *1941* and his influence *today*. It should be logically placed after the paragraph discussing the time period most directly before that. The fifth paragraph discusses the 1920s and the 1930s, the periods closest to 1941 in this passage. Therefore, the second paragraph would be best placed after the fifth paragraph. The other choices would put the timeline out of sequence. The answer is (D).

37. **A**   This question asks you to identify something which harmonizes with the claim in sentence 4, which states that *much of what we understand about ourselves as Americans was made clear to us* by Sherwood Anderson. Choice (B) suggests that *Beyond Desire* had other influences and does not say whether Anderson was the first to incorporate these influences. Choices (C) and (D) discuss the reactions of critics and readers to the book, not the book itself. Choice (A) supports the idea that Anderson addressed an understanding of American culture that hadn't been written about by novelists previously. The answer is (A).

38. **A**   The first paragraph states that Sherwood Anderson *helped to inaugurate an age of a truly homespun American Modernism* but never really explains what Modernism is or how Anderson made it *homespun* or *American*. Modernism is likewise referred to in the third and fifth paragraphs, so it is a major theme within the passage. All the other answers except for (A) mention things that are merely passing details in the passage, not crucial themes, so (A) is correct.

39. **C**   The first paragraph makes the claim that Sherwood Anderson was part of a *new movement* in American literature and *helped to inaugurate an age of a truly homespun American Modernism*. The fifth paragraph provides much more detail about his role in Modernism and how his innovative style influenced other writers. Choice (B) gets this backward. Only (C) describes this relationship, so the answer is (C).

40. **C**   Sentence 6 mentions *fragmentation and alienation* in Anderson's *uniquely American* characters. This is a good match for Fogel's quote, which mentions *frustration, loneliness, and longing* in *Midwestern small-town life*. Sentences 2, 4, and 8 don't have the same clear connection, so the answer is (C).

41. **D** The main claims made in the essay are that a) Sherwood Anderson was part of a new literary movement, American Modernism, and that b) he influenced other writers. Choices (A), (B), and (C) all refer to sentences that support these ideas. Sentence 10 is not directly connected to these claims, since we're actually told nothing about *Beyond Desire* other than its time of publication, so the answer is (D).

42. **C** Choice (B) does not set up a contrast and, therefore, can be eliminated. Choice (A) and (D) do introduce contrasts but ones that are not supported by anything in the paragraph. Eliminate (A) and (D). Choice (C) is the best since it uses *Even though* to introduce two contrasting ideas.

43. **B** The best connecting statement should continue the previous idea that Siena has medieval elements, eliminating (A) and (D). The following sentence begins with *Another remnant*, which means the inserted sentence should already list specific examples and makes (B) better than (C). The answer is (B).

44. **D** Because the fourth paragraph introduces and defines the *contrada* discussed in sentence 7, the third paragraph cannot come before the fourth. Eliminate (A), (B), and (C). The best location for the third paragraph is before the fifth paragraph, so (D) is correct.

45. **B** The main argument of the passage is that the Palio horse race is a significant tradition in the lives of the Sienese and remarkable for its long-lived popularity. Three of the answers mention *outsiders*, but the author's main argument is not that those who do not live in Siena do not care about the race, (A), are suspicious to the Sienese, (C), or have tried to stop the tradition, (D). Choice (B) is the best answer.

SECTION II: FREE RESPONSE

Rubric—1 + 4 + 1 = 6 pts

A. Thesis (0–1 pts)
   ○ Responds to the prompt with a thesis that presents a defensible interpretation of the selected work.

B. Evidence and Commentary (0–4 pts)
   ○ Evidence: Provides specific evidence to support all claims in a line of reasoning.
   ○ Commentary: Consistently explains how the evidence supports a line of reasoning.
   ○ Explains how multiple literary elements or techniques in the poem contribute to its meaning.

C. Sophistication (0–1 pts)
   ○ Demonstrates sophistication of thought and/or develops a complex literary argument.

Question 1—Synthesis Essay

How to Score 6 Points
- Address the prompt with a defensible thesis.
- Present specific evidence from at least three sources and consistently explain how the evidence supports your thesis statement.
- Use style and rhetoric to persuade the reader.

Source Overview

Source A: Kurdistan was divided between other nations in the Middle East, leaving over 22 million Kurds stateless. Perceived as a security threat within their new political boundaries, Kurds are generally economically disenfranchised and culturally oppressed. Leadership within the Kurdish community also remains rife with conflict.

Source B: The value of the British pound dropped 8.4% on the day that England voted to leave the European Union.

Source C: Written in response to Marine Le Pen's op-ed published by *The New York Times*, the author describes Le Pen's political ideology as fascist, white-supremacist, anti-semitic, and antithetical to the values of the French Revolution. According to the author, more than one-third of French people agree with Le Pen's views.

Source D: To celebrate Sri Lankan independence from the United Kingdom, Patrick F. Kennedy, a representative of the U.S. Department of State, drew parallels between Sri Lanka and the U.S., saying that both nations face similar challenges such as poverty, discrimination, and injustice. He ends by saying Sri Lankan success has made the U.S. proud.

Source E: Dr. Madsen Pirie argues that globalization has greatly benefited humanity, creating more wealth than ever and lifting people out of poverty. Those living in poor nations earn wages in the global marketplace, and those in wealthy countries enjoy increased buying power from less expensive goods. Further, trade between nations prevents military conflict.

Source F: Increasing pollution in China, caused in large part by American demand for Chinese goods, is blowing across the Pacific Ocean and impacting the western United States.

Source G: This map reflects the international cooperation underway to support the International Space Station, with participating facilities across the Northern Hemisphere, in North America, Europe, and Asia.

Sample First Paragraph

In some of the most persistent myths depicting the human experience, from Odysseus's journey homeward to the life of Jesus depicted in the New Testament, there is an inherent paradox in how humans relate to each other: Humans can be kindred spirits in a shared community; Or, humans notice divisions between themselves, seeking to always define friend from foe. While humans are certainly able to see themselves as global citizens, there remain political entities that seek to capitalize on divisions among us for their own gain.

Question 2—Rhetorical Analysis Essay

How to Score 6 Points

Use the Rhetorical Diamond! While you're reading the prompt and the passage, imagine—and try to flesh out—a baseball diamond with the following six points:

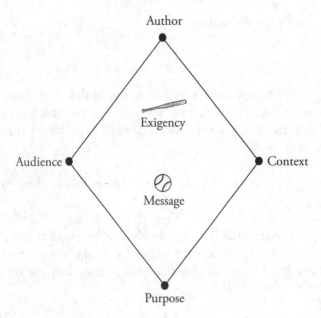

Author: Emmeline Pankhurst
Audience: Critics and supporters of women's suffrage in New England
Purpose: To address the critics and defend the tactics of the suffragettes
Context: Written in 1913 by a lead suffragette known for her militancy and delivered in the geographical region that sparked the American Revolution
Exigency: To explain why women have adopted "military tactics" in order to "win the rights of citizenship"
Message: Like the oppression of the colonists prior to the American Revolution, the oppression of women merits revolutionary, militant tactics.

Sample Rhetorical Modes and Devices

- **Analogy:** "I am here as a soldier who has temporarily left the field of battle in order to explain…"
- **Hypothetical situation:** "Suppose the men of Hartford have a grievance…Let the men of Hartford imagine…"
- **Historical allusion:** "Your forefathers decided that they must have representation for taxation, many, many years ago. When they felt they couldn't wait any longer, when they laid all the arguments before an obstinate British government that they could think of, and when their arguments were absolutely disregarded, when every other means had failed, they began by the tea party at Boston, and they went on until they had won the independence of the United States of America."
- **Analogy:** "You have two babies very hungry and wanting to be fed. One baby is a patient baby, and waits indefinitely until its mother is ready to feed it. The other baby is an impatient baby and cries lustily, screams and kicks and makes everybody unpleasant until it is fed. Well, we know perfectly well which baby is attended to first. That is the whole history of politics. You have to make more noise than anybody

else, you have to make yourself more obtrusive than anybody else, you have to fill all the papers more than anybody else, in fact you have to be there all the time and see that they do not snow you under."

- **Rhetorical question:** Now, I ask you, if women can do that, is there any limit to what we can do except the limit we put upon ourselves?

Sample First Paragraph

As women fought for their rights to vote in the early 20th century, British activist Emmeline Pankhurst was accused of being militaristic, or overly aggressive. On November 13, 1913, Pankhurst gave a speech addressing her critics in Hartford, Connecticut. By invoking the men in her audience directly and walking them through a series of familiar analogies and historical allusions, Pankhurst argues that British and American suffragettes are justified in their use of "militant" strategies to advocate for voting rights for women.

Question 3—Argument Essay

How to Score 6 Points

- Take a definite position, so no one will question where you stand on the topic of the prompt.
- Develop an argument that builds and moves forward instead of simply repeating the same point several times in different ways.
- Support the points in your argument with evidence drawn from your own knowledge, reading, experiences, and observations.
- Explain how your evidence supports your argument.

Sample Evidence

- In *To Kill a Mockingbird*, Tom Robinson is falsely accused of sexual assault. A Black man living during the Great Depression in Alabama, Robinson was economically and legally disenfranchised. Though he was ultimately wrongfully convicted, if Atticus Finch hadn't defended him, Finch himself would have been perpetuating the social injustice around him as opposed to fighting it.
- On the hit show *I Love Lucy*, Lucille Ball, the lead actress, had to advocate for her Cuban American spouse Desi Arnaz to act the lead male part. Had she remained neutral, the show's producers would have gone ahead and cast a white actor, perpetuating limited representation in television.
- In his *Letters from Birmingham*, Dr. Martin Luther King, Jr. explains that mobilizing white moderates is a key facet in advancing civil rights.
- In the context of the American Civil War, remaining neutral would have meant allowing the Southern states to secede from the union and continue enslaving Black Americans.
- President Kennedy called for "affirmative action" to reduce the impacts of systemic racism in the United States. While affirmative action, as applied to secondary education, has been imperfect, it has consistently resulted in more diverse student populations where it has been applied.

Sample First Paragraph

The sociologist in question argues that, when it comes to racial justice today, there is no such thing as an innocent bystander. Due to the systemic injustice embedded into the American political and social system, a "neutral" stance on race does in fact perpetuate racial imbalance in the United States.

Practice Test 4

AP® English Language and Composition Exam

SECTION I: Multiple-Choice Questions

DO NOT BEGIN THE EXAM UNTIL YOU ARE TOLD TO DO SO.

DISCLAIMER: The official AP English Language and Composition Exam will be administered digitally. Instructions for the digital exam may differ from this practice test.

At a Glance

Total Time
1 hour
Number of Questions
45
Percent of Total Grade
45%

Instructions

Section I of this examination contains 45 multiple-choice questions. Choose the best answer to each question. Note: Pay particular attention to the requirements of questions that contain the words "NOT," "LEAST," or "EXCEPT."

Indicate all of your answers to the multiple-choice questions on the answer sheet. No credit will be given for anything written in this exam booklet, but you may use the booklet for notes or scratch work. After you have decided which of the suggested answers is best, completely fill in the corresponding oval on the answer sheet. Give only one answer to each question. If you change an answer, be sure that the previous mark is erased completely. Here is a sample question and answer.

Sample Question   Sample Answer

Chicago is a
(A) state
(B) city
(C) country
(D) continent

Use your time effectively, working as quickly as you can without losing accuracy. Do not spend too much time on any one question. Go on to other questions and come back to the ones you have not answered if you have time.

About Guessing

Many candidates wonder whether or not to guess the answers to questions about which they are not certain. Multiple-choice scores are based on the number of questions answered correctly. Points are not deducted for incorrect answers, and no points are awarded for unanswered questions. Because points are not deducted for incorrect answers, you are encouraged to answer all multiple-choice questions. On any questions you do not know the answer to, you should eliminate as many choices as you can, and then select the best answer among the remaining choices.

GO ON TO THE NEXT PAGE.

This page intentionally left blank.

ENGLISH LANGUAGE AND COMPOSITION
SECTION I
Time—1 hour

Directions: This part consists of selections from prose works and questions on their content, form, and style. After reading each passage, choose the best answer to each question and completely fill in the corresponding oval on the answer sheet.

Note: Pay particular attention to the requirement of questions that contain the words NOT, LEAST, or EXCEPT.

Questions 1–11. Read the following passage carefully before you choose your answers.

This is from the Lincoln-Douglas Debates of 1858.

Now, I hold that Illinois had a right to abolish and
prohibit slavery as she did, and I hold that Kentucky has
the same right to continue and protect slavery that Illinois
Line had to abolish it. I hold that New York had as much right to
5 abolish slavery as Virginia has to continue it, and that each
and every State of this Union is a sovereign power, with the
right to do as it pleases upon this question of slavery, and
upon all its domestic institutions. Slavery is not the only
question which comes up in this controversy. There is a far
10 more important one to you, and that is, what shall be done
with the free negro? We have settled the slavery question
as far as we are concerned; we have prohibited it in Illinois
forever, and in doing so, I think we have done wisely, and
there is no man in the State who would be more strenuous in
15 his opposition to the introduction of slavery than I would; but
when we settled it for ourselves, we exhausted all our power
over that subject. We have done our whole duty, and can do
no more. We must leave each and every other State to decide
for itself the same question. In relation to the policy to be
20 pursued toward the free negroes, we have said that they shall
not vote; whilst Maine, on the other hand, has said that they
shall vote. Maine is a sovereign State, and has the power to
regulate the qualifications of voters within her limits. I would
never consent to confer the right of voting and of citizenship
25 upon a negro, but still I am not going to quarrel with Maine
for differing from me in opinion. Let Maine take care of her
own negroes, and fix the qualifications of her own voters to
suit herself, without interfering with Illinois, and Illinois will
not interfere with Maine. So with the State of New York. She
30 allows the negro to vote provided he owns two hundred and
fifty dollars' worth of property, but not otherwise. While I
would not make any distinction whatever between a negro
who held property and one who did not, yet if the sovereign
State of New York chooses to make that distinction it is her
35 business and not mine, and I will not quarrel with her for
it. She can do as she pleases on this question if she minds
her own business, and we will do the same thing. Now, my
friends, if we will only act conscientiously and rigidly upon
this great principle of popular sovereignty, which guarantees
40 to each State and Territory the right to do as it pleases on all
things, local and domestic, instead of Congress interfering,

we will continue at peace one with another. Why should
Illinois be at war with Missouri, or Kentucky with Ohio, or
Virginia, with New York, merely because their institutions
45 differ? Our fathers intended that our institutions should differ.
They knew that the North and the South, having different
climates, productions, and interests, required different
institutions. This doctrine of Mr. Lincoln, of uniformity
among the institutions of the different States, is a new
50 doctrine, never dreamed of by Washington, Madison, or the
framers of this government. Mr. Lincoln and the Republican
party set themselves up as wiser than these men who made
this government, which has flourished for seventy years
under the principle of popular sovereignty, recognizing the
55 right of each State to do as it pleased. Under that principle,
we have grown from a nation of three or four millions to a
nation of about thirty millions of people; we have crossed
the Allegheny mountains and filled up the whole Northwest,
turning the prairie into a garden, and building up churches
60 and schools, thus spreading civilization and Christianity
where before there was nothing but savage barbarism. Under
that principle we have become, from a feeble nation, the
most powerful on the face of the earth, and if we only adhere
to that principle, we can go forward increasing in territory,
65 in power, in strength, and in glory until the Republic of
America shall be the north star that shall guide the friend of
freedom throughout the civilized world. And why can we
not adhere to the great principle of self-government upon
which our institutions were originally based? I believe that
70 this new doctrine preached by Mr. Lincoln and his party will
dissolve the Union if it succeeds. They are trying to array all
the Northern States in one body against the South, to excite a
sectional war between the free States and the slave States, in
order that the one or the other may be driven to the wall.

GO ON TO THE NEXT PAGE.

1. In this passage the speaker's purpose is to

   (A) analyze the causes of slavery
   (B) argue in favor of states' rights
   (C) criticize individual states
   (D) describe the advantages of a federal government

2. Which of the following best describes the tone of the passage?

   (A) Mock enthusiasm
   (B) Bitter indignation
   (C) Formal polemic
   (D) Outraged accusation

3. In the first two sentences (lines 1–8), the speaker grounds his central idea on which of the following rhetorical strategies?

   (A) Inductive reasoning
   (B) Deductive reasoning
   (C) Description
   (D) Classification

4. In line 36, the word "it" most closely refers to

   (A) "property" (line 33)
   (B) "citizenship" (line 24)
   (C) "distinction" (line 34)
   (D) "business" (line 35)

5. The sentence that begins "Now, my friends, if we will..." (lines 37–42) contains all of the following EXCEPT

   (A) a classification
   (B) a call to action
   (C) a definition
   (D) an accusation

6. The author suggests that which of the following is true of Maine, Illinois, and New York?

   (A) They have relatively liberal policies toward "negroes."
   (B) They prove that popular sovereignty has been generally successful.
   (C) They exemplify the principle of popular sovereignty.
   (D) They create inconsistent laws for both "negroes" and citizens.

7. The speaker substantiates his central idea with

   (A) clever anecdotes
   (B) innovative symbols
   (C) extended metaphors
   (D) appeal to authority

8. From the passage, it appears that the speaker's personal view is that African Americans

   (A) should be slaves and should not be allowed to hold property
   (B) should not be slaves and should be allowed to vote
   (C) should not be free but should be allowed to hold some property
   (D) should be free but not allowed to vote

9. The author implies that Abraham Lincoln's policies would have all of the following potential negative effects EXCEPT

   (A) consolidating power
   (B) hindering westward expansion
   (C) dissolving the Union
   (D) hindering population growth

10. In the final lines of the passage, the speaker attempts to win over his audience by

    (A) inspiring confidence
    (B) shifting blame
    (C) instilling fear
    (D) reconciling differences

11. The development of the passage can best be described as the

    (A) argument for a particular solution to a political problem
    (B) rebuttal of those who challenge the authority of Congress
    (C) explanation of the failings of a political opponent
    (D) exploration of the various meanings of a universal principle

GO ON TO THE NEXT PAGE.

Questions 12–23. Read the following passage carefully before you choose your answers.

This passage is excerpted from a recent work that examines popular conceptions of the history of medieval Spain.

If you have read anything about medieval Spain, then you probably know about *convivencia*—the peaceful "coexistence" of Muslims, Christians, and Jews for nearly
Line eight hundred years on the Iberian peninsula. The story
5 is invariably told in the same way: "once upon a time,"[1] after the Muslim invasion of the Iberian peninsula in 711, a "culture of tolerance"[2] was created among Muslims, Christians, and Jews. Tolerant adherents of these three Abrahamic faiths shared philosophical and scientific
10 learning, translating previously unknown sources (especially the works of Aristotle) for the rest of Europe. "But," the author or narrator intones in his gravest voice, "this world too quickly vanished. Greed, fear, and intolerance swept it away. Puritanical judgments and absolutism snuffed out the
15 light of learning." Then the author or narrator laments the loss of this vanished world: "it was truly a bright light in what was largely a dark and ignorant medieval landscape. Its loss is one of the great tragedies in history."[3] This is almost always followed by a didactic—and dramatic—moral
20 about the relevance of medieval Spain for contemporary problems: "Humanity has never completely found the way back. Medieval Spain might help point the way."[4] This is a fairy tale for adults who, like children, know nothing about the actual (medieval) world it attempts to describe. The story
25 of *convivencia* fulfills the requirements of the genre, replete as it is with exotic journeys in faraway lands and epic battles between noble heroes and depraved villains. And like all fairy tales, this story of *convivencia* tells us much more about the world of storytelling in which it was created than about
30 the historical past or objective reality, on which it is only loosely based.

While some of the recent books on *convivencia* have gestured in the direction of scholarly discourse, more often than not, they cannot resist the temptation to indulge our
35 basest tendencies of exoticism. In nearly every popular recounting of *convivencia,* images of an Islamic *locus amoenus* abound: we hear of gardens, bath-houses, exotic fruits, and enchanting mosques. Chris Lowney, in *A Vanished World,* emphasized that "daily life was transformed as exotic
40 new species like cotton, figs, spinach, and watermelon burgeoned in fields nourished by new irrigation techniques." The "luxury and sophistication" of the Islamic city of Cordoba "undoubtedly surpassed anything found elsewhere in Europe." Maria Rosa Menocal's syrupy confection, *The*
45 *Ornament of the World,* simmers under a thick layer of

[Asian stereotypes]. Some of her chapter titles themselves suffice to prove the point, "The Palaces of Memory," "The Mosque and the Palm Tree," "A Grand Vizier, A Grand City," "The Gardens of Memory," and "Sailing Away, Riding
50 Away." And when these authors describe Islam, it is with the wonderment and delight of a tourist. We, their audience, are supposed to share in their surprise—and in the delicious irony—that Islam was a peaceful, tolerant religion, while Christianity was persecutory, cruel, and violent.

12. One purpose of the first paragraph is to

(A) discount the importance of medieval history
(B) reinforce a popular perception of medieval Spain
(C) suggest that historical research will need to explore new sources
(D) define *convivencia* for non-specialists

13. The primary purpose of the quotes in the first paragraph is to

(A) emphasize the author's bewilderment with the narrative of medieval history offered by most historians of medieval Spain
(B) reinforce the author's position that proponents of *convivencia* misinterpret their evidence by quoting directly from their works
(C) suggest an alternate interpretation of the historical record
(D) recount the conventional narrative of *convivencia* in the words of its historians

14. The footnotes serve to

(A) demonstrate the range of sources he cites
(B) reveal that all the quotes are from the same source
(C) provide documentation for the sources of his quotes
(D) impress the reader with the technical expertise of the author

---

1 Maria Rosa Menocal, *Ornament of the World: How Muslims, Christians, and Jews Created a Culture of Tolerance in Medieval Spain* (New York: Little, Brown, 2002), 5.
2 The subtitle of Menocal's *Ornament of the World,* 7.
3 Chris Lowney, *A Vanished World: Muslims, Christians, and Jews in Medieval Spain* (Oxford: Oxford University Press, 2005), 18.
4 Lowney, *A Vanished World,* 14.

GO ON TO THE NEXT PAGE.

15. The content of the second footnote

    (A) undermines the claims made by Maria Rosa Menocal
    (B) provides a citation for more information about the subject
    (C) introduces information that will turn out to be essential to the main argument
    (D) clarifies the source of the expression used in the text

16. In line 25, the word "genre" refers to

    (A) "fairy tale" (line 23)
    (B) "*convivencia*" (line 25)
    (C) "children" (line 23)
    (D) "it" (line 26)

17. Which one of the following characteristics of the scholarship on *convivencia* is most troublesome to the author?

    (A) Its inherent lack of documentary evidence
    (B) Its misleading emphasis on the importance of religion
    (C) Its lack of methodological rigor or complexity
    (D) Its tendency to exaggerate historical reality

18. All of the following accurately describe the tone of the second paragraph EXCEPT

    (A) emphatic
    (B) acerbic
    (C) relieved
    (D) comic

19. Which of the following sentences best represents the author's main point in the passage?

    (A) "If you have read anything about medieval Spain, then you probably know about *convivencia*—the peaceful 'coexistence' of Muslims, Christians, and Jews for nearly eight hundred years on the Iberian peninsula." (lines 1–4)
    (B) "And like all fairy tales, this story of *convivencia* tells us much more about the world of storytelling in which it was created than about the historical past or objective reality, on which it is only loosely based." (lines 27–31)
    (C) "While some of the recent books on *convivencia* have gestured in the direction of scholarly discourse, more often than not, they cannot resist the temptation to indulge our basest tendencies to exoticism." (lines 32–35)
    (D) "And when these authors describe Islam, it is with the wonderment and delight of a tourist." (lines 50–51)

20. The author's observation about Maria Rosa Menocal's *The Ornament of the World* (lines 44–46) is best described as an example of which of the following?

    (A) Alliteration
    (B) Metaphor
    (C) Allegory
    (D) Linguistic paradox

21. The speaker mentions the chapter titles in lines 47–50 as examples of which of the following?

    (A) Islamic history
    (B) Poetic imagery
    (C) Hyperbolic language
    (D) Stereotypically Asian excess

22. Which of the following best describes the rhetorical function of the phrase "and in the delicious irony" (lines 52–53)?

    (A) It raises a question the author answered at the beginning of the second paragraph.
    (B) It alludes to a contention made in the first paragraph.
    (C) It reiterates the thesis of the passage as stated in the first paragraph.
    (D) It extends the metaphorical language of the second paragraph.

23. The passage as a whole is best characterized as

    (A) a treatise on history
    (B) an ironic attack
    (C) a qualified dismissal
    (D) an analysis of historical evidence

GO ON TO THE NEXT PAGE.

Questions 24–32 are based on the following passage.

The passage below is a draft.

(1) Cities around the United States have been put into a tenuous situation due to the practice of offering stadium subsidies. (2) Stadium subsidies refer to funds given by city municipalities to fund professional sports stadiums and have real budgetary consequences.

(3) The impact that stadiums have had on cities such as Detroit, which subsidized a hockey arena for its hockey team in 2014 by decreasing pensions, and Oakland, which chopped its police department by 18% to continue funding the Oakland Coliseum, make it clear that the practice of building new stadiums must come to an end. (4) Four-fifths of all stadiums constructed since the turn of the century have benefited from tax-free bonds, leaving taxpayers to foot a total bill exceeding three billion dollars.

(5) Why, then, does this practice persist? (6) Some feel that stadiums bring economic benefits that outweigh the costs of the stadiums, though this claim has been categorically denied by economists. (7) The few studies that support the use of stadium subsidies are funded by sports franchises and cannot be used as serious evidence.

(8) While stadium subsidies make little economic sense, they do occur under some significant pressure: cities pass new budgets annually and must meet the needs of a multitude of interests. (9) The monopoly held by the major sports leagues lead municipalities to feel that they must cower to the demands of their local teams, lest they lose their beloved franchise to a city that will pay the subsidy. (10) Therefore, cities with professional sports teams will likely face this quandary for the foreseeable future.

24. Which of the following sentences, if placed before sentence 1, would both capture the audience's interest and provide the most effective introduction to the topic of the paragraph?

   (A) Professional sports teams have long brought a sense of civic pride to American cities.
   (B) Even though professional sports teams are large revenue generators, they can be a financial drain on local resources.
   (C) The Las Vegas football franchise, Arlington baseball team, and Detroit's hockey organization are all sports franchises that have been rewarded with expensive stadiums in recent years.
   (D) In 2018, Las Vegas celebrated its acquisition of a professional football team, but the joy may have been overshadowed by a steep budgetary hit to the tune of $750 million in tax-free municipal bonds.

25. In sentence 2 (reproduced below), the writer wants an effective transition from the introductory paragraph to the main idea of the passage.

   Stadium subsidies refer to funds given by city municipalities to fund professional sports stadiums and have real budgetary consequences.

   Which of the following versions of the underlined text best achieves this purpose?

   (A) (as it is now)
   (B) are important to attracting professional sports teams to a city.
   (C) can exceed hundreds of millions of dollars.
   (D) are heavily supported by local politicians as well as several powerful interest groups.

26. In sentence 3 (reproduced below), which of the following versions of the underlined text best establishes the writer's position on the main argument of the passage?

   The impact that stadiums have had on cities such as Detroit, which subsidized a hockey arena for its hockey team in 2014 by decreasing pensions, and Oakland, which chopped its police department by 18% to continue funding the Oakland Coliseum, make it clear that the practice of building new stadiums must come to an end.

   (A) (as it is now)
   (B) using public land to build stadiums
   (C) offering tax-payer funded subsidies for new stadiums
   (D) allowing the public to privately donate to developing sports venues

27. The writer wants to add a phrase at the beginning of sentence 7 (reproduced below), adjusting the capitalization as needed, to set up a relationship with the idea discussed in sentence 6.

   The few studies that support the use of stadium subsidies are funded by sports franchises and cannot be used as serious evidence.

   Which of the following choices best accomplishes this goal?

   (A) However,
   (B) By contrast,
   (C) Nevertheless,
   (D) Furthermore,

GO ON TO THE NEXT PAGE.

28. In sentence 8 (reproduced below), the writer wants to provide a convincing explanation for why cities feel they must give in to the demands of sports franchises.

    While stadium subsidies make little economic sense, they do occur under some significant pressure: cities pass new budgets annually and must meet the needs of a multitude of interests.

    Which version of the underlined text best accomplishes this goal?

    (A) (as it is now)
    (B) a limited number of sports teams in each league make cities feel that they could ill-afford to lose their teams.
    (C) cities have large surpluses and are more than willing to move the extra money to vanity projects, allowing the public to privately donate to developing sports venues.
    (D) sports is only part of the interests of city residents, and politicians do not want to alienate potential voters by supporting stadium subsidies.

29. The writer wants to add the following sentence to the third paragraph (sentences 5–7) to provide additional explanation.

    Whatever the case, the process for generating and approving stadium subsidies is generally quite byzantine and hidden from public view.

    Where would the sentence best be placed?

    (A) Before sentence 5
    (B) After sentence 5
    (C) After sentence 6
    (D) After sentence 7

30. The writer wants to add more information to the third paragraph (sentences 5–7) to support the main argument of the passage. All of the following pieces of evidence help achieve this purpose EXCEPT which one?

    (A) A quote from an economist who has studied the detrimental impacts of stadium subsidies
    (B) An explanation of the methodological flaws of the studies funded by sports franchises
    (C) A short overview of why the economic benefits of stadium subsidies do not outweigh the costs
    (D) Statistics that support the number of jobs created by the development of a new stadium

31. In the fourth paragraph (sentences 8–10), the writer wants to expand on the claim that a sports franchise can be offered a stadium subsidy simply by threatening to leave its current city. Which of the following claims would best achieve this purpose?

    (A) San Diego lost its football team to Los Angeles when residents of San Diego refused to fund a new stadium for the team.
    (B) The city of St. Louis was left paying for its stadium even after its football team moved away.
    (C) Teams have been leaving their cities for newer locations ever since Major League Baseball began to try to expand its market westward.
    (D) Finding public funds for a stadium does not always prevent a team from moving to another city.

32. In the fourth paragraph (sentences 8–10), the writer wants to conclude with a statement that best calls for an action supportive of the essay's central claim. Which of the following sentences would best achieve this purpose?

    (A) (as it is now)
    (B) However, for the sake of local budgets, lawmakers must find a way to prevent teams from demanding free state-of-the-art facilities at the expense of taxpayers.
    (C) Accordingly, stadium subsidies should be avoided at all costs.
    (D) Consequently, the stranglehold that professional sports teams maintain over their home cities will remain a budget killer for years to come.

GO ON TO THE NEXT PAGE.

Questions 33–40 are based on the following passage.

The passage below is a draft.

(1) As America's healthcare system becomes more complex and doctors more specialized, consumers of healthcare may wonder how to evaluate the quality of their physicians. (2) Surely one may consult the subjective "gut feeling" that a patient may feel about a physician: that they have a good rapport with their doctor. (3) In recent years, insurance companies, hospitals, and professional medical societies have posited a variety of "objective" metrics to inform patients of doctor quality.

(4) One such metric is patient evaluations, which can only be conducted in large healthcare systems. (5) In the pursuit of maximizing the patient experience, interested parties consult patients with a post-visit survey. (6) The physician and the facilities are therefore rated from the patient's perspective. (7) Another approach to quantifying doctor quality is examining outcomes. (8) For instance, when a patient visits a hospital for a surgery, they may be contacted for follow-up information on how the patient has recovered in the short, medium, and long terms.

(9) But these types of standardized approaches that aim to measure physician quality are flawed and unfair. (10) The patient experience may not accurately reflect the quality of healthcare the patient received. (11) Physicians could boost these ratings by simply decreasing waiting room time or offering more comfortable exam tables, regardless of the quality of medical attention offered. (12) Further, attributing patient outcomes solely to the performance of a doctor, with no regard to patient lifestyle (diet and tobacco use, for instance) will certainly push physicians away from treating the most vulnerable patients, such as those who suffer from obesity, poverty, and congenital diseases.

(13) Nobody wants to choose a doctor primarily based on the accoutrements of the waiting room. (14) Further, it would not be desirable to potentially leave the most vulnerable patients to fend for themselves. (15) Perhaps the best approach would be a system that allows doctors to be evaluated by experts in their field—their peers. (16) Medical professionals can look at data and outcomes within their proper context in order to best communicate essential information about a physician's quality to America's health care consumers.

33. After sentence 1, the writer wants to provide a convincing explanation for why it is important for healthcare consumers to learn more about physicians. Which sentence below best accomplishes this goal?

(A) Specialists are largely similar due to the nature of their work, so the most important factor in finding a doctor is a convenient schedule.
(B) No two doctors are alike, and quality healthcare stems from factors as diverse as a physician's experience to the physician's relationship with patients.
(C) The complexity of the healthcare system has made it nearly impossible to learn anything about a doctor before going in for a visit.
(D) Recent trends in medicine towards team-oriented healthcare have made doctors interchangeable with one another.

34. The writer wants to add a phrase at the beginning of sentence 3 (reproduced below), adjusting the capitalization as needed, to set up a relationship with the idea discussed in sentence 2.

In recent years, insurance companies, hospitals, and professional medical societies have posited a variety of metrics to inform patients of doctor quality.

Which of the following choices best accomplishes this goal?

(A) In other words,
(B) Similarly,
(C) For example,
(D) However,

35. The writer wants to add more information to the second paragraph (sentences 4–8) to further develop the examples in the paragraph. All of the following pieces of evidence help achieve this purpose EXCEPT which one?

(A) Information about the types of questions posed on patient surveys
(B) How patient feedback is translated into a doctor rating
(C) The types of illnesses that bring patients into a doctor's office
(D) Factors that are measured in the follow-up patient visits

GO ON TO THE NEXT PAGE.

36. In sentence 4 (reproduced below), the writer wants an effective transition from the topic sentence to the main idea of the paragraph.

   One such metric is patient evaluations, which <u>can only be conducted in large healthcare systems.</u>

   Which of the following versions of the underlined text best achieves this purpose?

   (A) (as it is now)
   (B) create a consumer-based assessment of the healthcare experience.
   (C) look toward the medical community's perspective for feedback on a physician.
   (D) are typically flawed approaches to understanding a doctor's effectiveness.

37. In the third paragraph (sentences 9–12), the writer wants to provide further evidence that the current systems of evaluation are unfair. Which of the following pieces of evidence would best achieve this purpose?

   (A) Patient feedback that typically aligns directly with other types of doctor evaluations
   (B) Patients who do not always have the knowledge about what kind of medical care is optimal for a particular ailment
   (C) Data that suggests that measuring long-term patient outcomes is a more effective method than patient surveys for evaluating physician quality
   (D) A quote from a health-consumer advocacy organization

38. In the third paragraph (sentences 9–12), the writer wants to expand upon the idea that attributing patient outcomes solely to the performance of the doctor could be harmful to certain patients. Which of the following claims would best achieve this purpose?

   (A) The most effective physicians will continue to gravitate toward treating patients who suffer from congenital diseases.
   (B) The systems of doctor evaluation currently proposed will incorporate consideration of patient lifestyle when evaluating physician performance.
   (C) Studies suggest that smokers evaluate their physicians most harshly.
   (D) People who live in poverty are more susceptible to adverse long-term health conditions regardless of the quality of their physicians.

39. The writer wants to add the following sentence to the fourth paragraph (sentences 13–16) to provide additional explanation.

   The aforementioned approaches put both healthcare providers and consumers in an undesirable situation.

   Where would the sentence best be placed?

   (A) Before sentence 13
   (B) After sentence 13
   (C) After sentence 14
   (D) After sentence 15

40. In sentence 16 (reproduced below), which of the following versions of the underlined text best establishes the writer's position on the main argument of the passage?

   Medical professionals can look at data and outcomes within their proper context in order to <u>best communicate essential information about a physician's quality to America's health care consumers.</u>

   (A) (as it is now)
   (B) remove patients from the process of evaluating physicians.
   (C) ensure that patients afflicted by poverty, obesity, and congenital diseases continue to receive quality healthcare.
   (D) best enhance the patient experience during visits to doctors' offices and hospitals.

GO ON TO THE NEXT PAGE.

Questions 41–45 are based on the following passage.

The passage below is a draft.

(1) Zoos are the subject of controversy due to a fundamental misunderstanding of their role in the survival of various species. (2) The moral imperative of keeping some animals in captivity has unfortunately been clouded by less humane practices from a century ago. (3) In reality, most modern zoos provide necessary joy and entertainment to their thousands of annual visitors.

(4) Climate change has resulted in threats to nearly half of all small mammals and a quarter of the world's bird population. (5) However, repopulation programs hosted by zoos have shown only moderate effects in recent decades. (6) Even larger animals, such as wild horses, which were considered extinct a half century ago, have benefited from repopulation programs at zoos: the 12 horses in captivity at the time of extinction have now increased to over 2,000, with a significant number being reintroduced to the wild.

(7) While there have been questions about the effects of zoos on the health of animals due to small enclosures, there is a net benefit stemming from captivity due to the amount of scientific research that is possible. (8) One outcome of such research arises when zoo veterinarians use a comparison of disease surveillance in the wild with their own animals in captivity and can warn the public about possible outbreaks that are forthcoming.

(9) Zoos of the twenty-first century are a far cry from the circus sideshows that have informed our popular perception of zoos as inhumane animal prisons. (10) Nowadays, all it takes is a single visit to make it clear that park goers are primarily on an educational journey focused on the conservation of some of the planet's most threatened species. (11) The challenging living conditions are just an unfortunate side effect of a system that benefits humans as well as animals.

41. In sentence 3 (reproduced below), which of the following versions of the underlined text best establishes the writer's position on the main argument of the passage?

In reality, most modern zoos provide <u>necessary joy and entertainment to their thousands of annual visitors.</u>

(A) (as it is now)
(B) unjust and inhumane living quarters for their inhabitants.
(C) animals with an adequate habitat.
(D) an indispensable service in promoting public education and the survival of threatened species.

42. In sentence 5 (reproduced below), the writer wants to provide a convincing explanation for why zoos provide a necessary service.

However, repopulation programs hosted by zoos have <u>shown only moderate outcomes in recent decades.</u>

Which version of the underlined text best accomplishes this goal?

(A) (as it is now)
(B) had dramatic effects in recent decades.
(C) failed to accomplish their goals.
(D) attracted large crowds.

43. The writer wants to add more information to the second paragraph (sentences 4–6) to support the main argument of the passage. All of the following pieces of evidence help achieve this purpose EXCEPT which one?

(A) American zoos have invested more than $25 million in research during a single year.
(B) Zoos have used their resources to help minority students access STEM training and careers.
(C) Conservation efforts in California zoos have helped increase the population of California condors from nine to over four hundred during a period of thirty years.
(D) Polar bears in captivity were found to have an infant mortality rate of 65%.

GO ON TO THE NEXT PAGE.

44. The writer wants to add a phrase at the beginning of sentence 8 (reproduced below), adjusting the capitalization as needed, to set up a relationship with the idea discussed in sentence 7.

One outcome of such research arises when zoo veterinarians use a comparison of disease surveillance in the wild with their own animals in captivity and can warn the public about possible outbreaks that are forthcoming.

Which of the following choices best accomplishes this goal?

(A) On the other hand,
(B) However,
(C) In fact,
(D) By contrast,

45. In the fourth paragraph (sentences 9–11), the writer wants to conclude with a statement that supports the essay's central claim. Which of the following sentences would best achieve this purpose?

(A) (as it is now)
(B) However, the controversy surrounding zoos will not disappear anytime soon.
(C) With any luck, animals caged in zoos will one day find the freedom they deserve.
(D) We must therefore continue to support America's zoos on their path toward helping a wide array of species.

END OF SECTION I

AP® English Language and Composition Exam

SECTION II: Free-Response Questions

DO NOT BEGIN THE EXAM UNTIL YOU ARE TOLD TO DO SO.

DISCLAIMER: The official AP English Language and Composition Exam will be administered digitally. Instructions for the digital exam may differ from this practice test.

At a Glance

Total Time
2 hours, plus a 15-minute reading period
Number of Questions
3
Percent of Total Grade
55%

Instructions

Section II of this examination requires answers in essay form. To help you use your time well, the coordinator will announce the time at which each question should be completed. If you finish any question before time is announced, you may go on to the following question. If you finish the examination in less than the time allotted, you may go back and work on any essay question you want.

Each essay will be judged on its clarity and effectiveness in dealing with the requirements of the topic assigned and on the quality of the writing. After completing each question, you should check your essay for accuracy of punctuation, spelling, and diction; you are advised, however, not to attempt many longer corrections. Remember that quality is far more important than quantity.

Write your essays with a pen, preferably in black or dark blue ink. Be sure to write CLEARLY and LEGIBLY. Cross out any errors you make.

GO ON TO THE NEXT PAGE.

ENGLISH LANGUAGE AND COMPOSITION
SECTION II
Total Time—2 hours, 15 minutes

Question 1

Suggested reading and writing time—55 minutes.
It is suggested that you spend 15 minutes reading the question, analyzing and evaluating the sources,
and 40 minutes writing your response.
Note: You may begin writing your response before the reading period is over.

(This question counts for one-third of the total essay section score.)

Individuals have argued the concept of what it means to live a good life for thousands of years. Many have posited that happiness is an internal choice, a question of free will, and that it is something that can be reached every moment of every day. Others have pointed to external factors such as the slow accumulation of wealth and the construction of solid relationships—both of which require time and long-term strategy—as the primary drivers of a "life well-lived." More recently, some have even pointed to the role of genes in determining life satisfaction.

Carefully read the following seven sources, including the introductory information for each source. Then synthesize the information from at least three of the sources and incorporate it into a coherent, well-developed essay that argues a clear position on whether life satisfaction is better achieved by living in the moment or by working toward long-term goals.

Source A	(National Institute on Drug Abuse)
Source B	(Dixit)
Source C	(map)
Source D	(Helliwell, Layard, and Sachs)
Source E	(chart)
Source F	(Ferriss)
Source G	(Department of Labor)

In your response you should do the following:

- Respond to the prompt with a thesis that presents a defensible position.

- Select and use evidence from at least 3 of the provided sources to support your line of reasoning. Indicate clearly the sources used through direct quotation, paraphrase, or summary. Sources may be cited as Source A, Source B, etc., or by using the description in parentheses.

- Explain how the evidence supports your line of reasoning.

- Use appropriate grammar and punctuation in communicating your argument.

GO ON TO THE NEXT PAGE.

Source A

"Drugs, Brains, and Behavior: The Science of Addiction." National Institute on Drug Abuse. 2014. Web. 2 Feb. 2017.

The following is excerpted from an article on the National Institute of Health's website.

How do drugs work in the brain to produce pleasure?

Most drugs of abuse directly or indirectly target the brain's reward system by flooding the circuit with dopamine. Dopamine is a neurotransmitter present in regions of the brain that regulate movement, emotion, motivation, and feelings of pleasure. When activated at normal levels, this system rewards our natural behaviors. Overstimulating the system with drugs, however, produces euphoric effects, which strongly reinforce the behavior of drug use—teaching the user to repeat it.

How does stimulation of the brain's pleasure circuit teach us to keep taking drugs?

Our brains are wired to ensure that we will repeat life-sustaining activities by associating those activities with pleasure or reward. Whenever this reward circuit is activated, the brain notes that something important is happening that needs to be remembered, and teaches us to do it again and again without thinking about it. Because drugs of abuse stimulate the same circuit, we learn to abuse drugs in the same way.

Why are drugs more addictive than natural rewards?

When some drugs of abuse are taken, they can release 2 to 10 times the amount of dopamine that natural rewards such as eating do. In some cases, this occurs almost immediately (as when drugs are smoked or injected), and the effects can last much longer than those produced by natural rewards. The resulting effects on the brain's pleasure circuit dwarf those produced by naturally rewarding behaviors. The effect of such a powerful reward strongly motivates people to take drugs again and again. This is why scientists sometimes say that drug abuse is something we learn to do very, very well.

What happens to your brain if you keep taking drugs?

For the brain, the difference between normal rewards and drug rewards can be described as the difference between someone whispering into your ear and someone shouting into a microphone. Just as we turn down the volume on a radio that is too loud, the brain adjusts to the overwhelming surges in dopamine (and other neurotransmitters) by producing less dopamine or by reducing the number of receptors that can receive signals. As a result, dopamine's impact on the reward circuit of the brain of someone who abuses drugs can become abnormally low, and that person's ability to experience *any* pleasure is reduced.

This is why a person who abuses drugs eventually feels flat, lifeless, and depressed, and is unable to enjoy things that were once pleasurable. Now, the person needs to keep taking drugs again and again just to try and bring his or her dopamine function back up to normal—which only makes the problem worse, like a vicious cycle. Also, the person will often need to take larger amounts of the drug to produce the familiar dopamine high—an effect known as tolerance.

GO ON TO THE NEXT PAGE.

*The following is excerpted from an article published by a website dedicated to current psychology
topics and research.*

Life unfolds in the present. But so often, we let the present slip away, allowing time to rush past
unobserved and unseized, and squandering the precious seconds of our lives as we worry about the
future and ruminate about what's past.

When we're at work, we fantasize about being on vacation; on vacation, we worry about the work
piling up on our desks. We dwell on intrusive memories of the past or fret about what may or may not
happen in the future. We don't appreciate the living present because our "monkey minds," as Buddhists
call them, vault from thought to thought like monkeys swinging from tree to tree.

Most of us don't undertake our thoughts in awareness. Rather, our thoughts control us. "Ordinary
thoughts course through our mind like a deafening waterfall," writes Jon Kabat-Zinn, the biomedical
scientist who introduced meditation into mainstream medicine. In order to feel more in control of our
minds and our lives, to find the sense of balance that eludes us, we need to step out of this current, to
pause, and, as Kabat-Zinn puts it, to "rest in stillness—to stop doing and focus on just being."

We need to live more in the moment. Living in the moment—also called mindfulness—is a state of
active, open, intentional attention on the present. When you become mindful, you realize that you are
not your thoughts; you become an observer of your thoughts from moment to moment without judging
them. Mindfulness involves being with your thoughts as they are, neither grasping at them nor pushing
them away. Instead of letting your life go by without living it, you awaken to experience.

Cultivating a nonjudgmental awareness of the present bestows a host of benefits. Mindfulness reduces
stress, boosts immune functioning, reduces chronic pain, lowers blood pressure, and helps patients
cope with cancer. By alleviating stress, spending a few minutes a day actively focusing on living in the
moment reduces the risk of heart disease. Mindfulness may even slow the progression of HIV.

Mindful people are happier, more exuberant, more empathetic, and more secure. They have higher
self-esteem and are more accepting of their own weaknesses. Anchoring awareness in the here and now
reduces the kinds of impulsivity and reactivity that underlie depression, binge eating, and attention
problems. Mindful people can hear negative feedback without feeling threatened. They fight less with
their romantic partners and are more accommodating and less defensive. As a result, mindful couples
have more satisfying relationships.

Mindfulness is at the root of Buddhism, Taoism, and many Native-American traditions, not to mention
yoga. It's why Thoreau went to Walden Pond; it's what Emerson and Whitman wrote about in their
essays and poems.

"Everyone agrees it's important to live in the moment, but the problem is how," says Ellen Langer, a
psychologist at Harvard and author of *Mindfulness*. "When people are not in the moment, they're not
there to know that they're not there." Overriding the distraction reflex and awakening to the present
takes intentionality and practice.

Living in the moment involves a profound paradox: You can't pursue it for its benefits. That's because
the expectation of reward launches a future-oriented mindset, which subverts the entire process.
Instead, you just have to trust that the rewards will come.

GO ON TO THE NEXT PAGE.

Source C

Esteban Ortiz-Ospina and Max Roser. (2019). "Happiness and Life Satisfaction." *Published online at OurWorldInData.org.* Retrieved from: 'https:// ourworldindata.org/happiness-and-life-satisfaction.'

Self-reported Life Satisfaction, 2018

Life satisfaction is self-reported as the answer to the following question: "Please imagine a ladder, with steps numbered from 0 at the bottom to 10 at the top. The top of the ladder represents the best possible life for you and the bottom of the ladder represents the worst possible life for you. On which step of the ladder would you say you personally feel you stand at this time?"

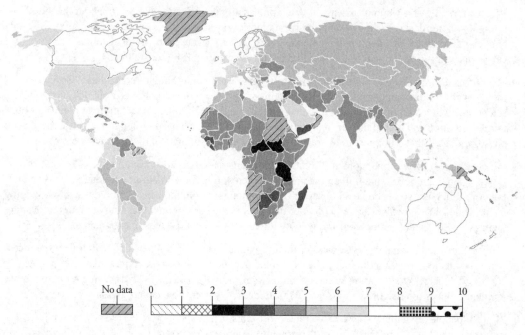

GO ON TO THE NEXT PAGE.

Source D

Helliwell, J., Layard, R., & Sachs, J. (2018). World Happiness Report 2018, New York: Sustainable Development Solutions Network.

The World Happiness Report is a landmark survey of the state of global happiness. The World Happiness Report 2018, ranks 156 countries by their happiness levels, and 117 countries by the happiness of their immigrants. [...]

The overall rankings of country happiness are based on the pooled results from Gallup World Poll surveys from 2015–2017, and show both change and stability. There is a new top ranking country, Finland, but the top ten positions are held by the same countries as in the last two years, although with some swapping of places. Four different countries have held top spot in the four most recent reports-Denmark, Switzerland, Norway and now Finland.

All the top countries tend to have high values for all six of the key variables that have been found to support well-being: income, healthy life expectancy, social support, freedom, trust and generosity. Among the top countries, differences are small enough that that year-to-year changes in the rankings are to be expected.

The analysis of happiness changes from 2008–2010 to 2015–2015 shows Togo as the biggest gainer, moving up 17 places in the overall rankings from the last place position it held as recently as in the 2015 rankings. The biggest loser is Venezuela, down 2.2 points on the 0 to 10 scale. [...]

The importance of social factors in the happiness of all populations, whether migrant or not, is emphasized in Chapter 6, where the happiness bulge in Latin America is found to depend on the greater warmth of family and other social relationships there, and to the greater importance that people there attach to these relationships.

The Report ends on a different tack, with a focus on three emerging health problems that threaten happiness: obesity, the opioid crisis, and depression. Although set in a global context, most of the evidence and discussion are focused on the United States, where the prevalence of all three problems has been growing faster and further than in most other countries.

GO ON TO THE NEXT PAGE.

Source E

"8-channel model of flow," a concept in psychology based on the research of psychologist Mihály Csíkszentmihályi.

In positive psychology, flow, also known as the zone, is the mental state of operation in which a person performing an activity is fully immersed in a feeling of energized focus, full involvement, and enjoyment in the process of the activity. The chart below describes the balance that a person encounters, when doing an activity, between how much challenge the task presents and how much skill that person already possesses for the activity. Experts such as Mihály Csíkszentmihályi have suggested that happiness can be found by entering the upper right quadrant of this chart.

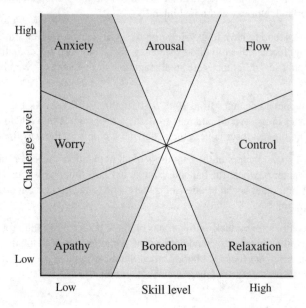

Source F

Ferriss, Timothy. *The 4-Hour Work Week.* 2007.

The following is excerpted from a book about redesigning your lifestyle in order to work less and increase your income.

To do or not to do? To try or not to try? Most people will vote no, whether they consider themselves brave or not. Uncertainty and the prospect of failure can be very scary noises in the shadows. Most people will choose unhappiness over uncertainty. For years, I set goals, made resolutions to change direction, and nothing came of either. I was just as insecure and scared as the rest of the world.

The simple solution came to me accidentally four years ago. At that time, I had more money than I knew what to do with—I was making $70K or so per month—and I was completely miserable, worse than ever. I had no time and was working myself to death. I had started my own company, only to realize it would be nearly impossible to sell.

Critical mistakes in its infancy would never let me sell it. I could hire magic elves and connect my brain to a supercomputer—it didn't matter. My little baby had some serious birth defects. The question then became, How do I free myself from this Frankenstein while making it self-sustaining? How do I pry myself from the tentacles of workaholism and the fear that it would fall to pieces without my 15-hour days? How do I escape this self-made prison? A trip, I decided. A sabbatical year around the world.

So I took the trip, right? First, I felt it prudent to dance around with my shame, embarrassment, and anger for six months, all the while playing an endless loop of reasons why my cop-out fantasy trip could never work. One of my more productive periods, for sure.

Then a funny thing happened. In my undying quest to make myself miserable, I accidentally began to backpedal. As soon as I cut through the vague unease and ambiguous anxiety by defining my nightmare, the worst-case scenario, I wasn't as worried about taking a trip. I could always take a temporary bartending job to pay the rent if I had to. I could sell some furniture and cut back on eating out. I could steal lunch money from the kindergarteners who passed by my apartment every morning. The options were many. I realized it wouldn't be that hard to get back to where I was, let alone survive. None of these things would be fatal—not even close.

I realized that on a scale of 1–10, 1 being nothing and 10 being permanently life-changing, my so-called worst-case scenario might have a temporary impact of 3 or 4. On the other hand, if I realized my best-case scenario, or even a probable-case scenario, it would easily have a permanent 9 or 10 positive life-changing effect.

In other words, I was risking an unlikely and temporary 3 or 4 for a probable and permanent 9 or 10, and I could easily recover my baseline workaholic prison with a bit of extra work if I wanted to. This all equated to a significant realization: There was practically no risk, only huge life-changing upside potential.

That is when I made the decision to take the trip and bought a one-way ticket to Europe. I started planning my adventures and eliminating my physical and psychological baggage. None of my disasters came to pass, and my life has been a near fairy tale since.

GO ON TO THE NEXT PAGE.

Source G

"Top 10 Ways to Prepare for Retirement." *Employee Benefits Security Administration/United States Department of Labor.* Web. 2 Feb. 2017.

The following is excerpted from a pamphlet on retirement savings.

Fewer than half of Americans have calculated how much they need to save for retirement.

In 2014, 30 percent of private industry workers with access to a defined contribution plan (such as a 401(k) plan) did not participate.

The average American spends roughly 20 years in retirement. Putting money away for retirement is a habit we can all live with. Remember…saving matters!

Start saving, keep saving, and stick to your goals. If you are already saving, whether for retirement or another goal, keep going! You know that saving is a rewarding habit. If you're not saving, it's time to get started. Start small if you have to and try to increase the amount you save each month. The sooner you start saving, the more time your money has to grow. Make saving for retirement a priority. Devise a plan, stick to it, and set goals. Remember, it's never too early or too late to start saving.

Know your retirement needs. Retirement is expensive. Experts estimate that you will need at least 70 percent of your preretirement income—lower earners, 90 percent or more—to maintain your standard of living when you stop working. Take charge of your financial future. The key to a secure retirement is to plan ahead.

Contribute to your employer's retirement savings plan. If your employer offers a retirement savings plan, such as a 401(k) plan, sign up and contribute all you can. Your taxes will be lower, your company may kick in more, and automatic deductions make it easy. Over time, compound interest and tax deferrals make a big difference in the amount you will accumulate. Find out about your plan. For example, how much would you need to contribute to get the full employer contribution and how long would you need to stay in the plan to get that money?

Learn about your employer's pension plan. If your employer has a traditional pension plan, check to see if you are covered by the plan and understand how it works. Ask for an individual benefit statement to see what your benefit is worth. Before you change jobs, find out what will happen to your pension benefit. Learn what benefits you may have from a previous employer. Find out if you will be entitled to benefits from your spouse's plan.

Consider basic investment principles. How you save can be as important as how much you save. Inflation and the type of investments you make play important roles in how much you'll have saved at retirement. Know how your savings or pension plan is invested. Learn about your plan's investment options and ask questions. Put your savings in different types of investments. By diversifying this way, you are more likely to reduce risks and improve return. Your investment mix may change over time depending on a number of factors such as your age, goals, and financial circumstances. Financial security and knowledge go hand in hand.

Don't touch your retirement savings. If you withdraw your retirement savings now, you'll lose principal and interest and you may lose tax benefits or have to pay withdrawal penalties. If you change jobs, leave your savings invested in your current retirement plan, or roll them over to an IRA or your new employer's plan.

GO ON TO THE NEXT PAGE.

Question 2

Suggested time—40 minutes.

(This question counts for one-third of the total essay section score.)

The passage that follows is an excerpt from C.S. Lewis' *The Screwtape Letters*, a fictional series of letters from an elderly devil to a younger devil advising him on the best way to corrupt humans. C.S. Lewis (1898–1963) was a devout Christian who was widely credited for bringing religious ideas to an audience of intellectual religious skeptics. Read the passage carefully. Then, in a well-developed essay, analyze the rhetorical strategies that Lewis uses to convey his message.

In your response, you should do the following:

- Respond to the prompt with a thesis that analyzes the writer's rhetorical choices.
- Select and use evidence to support your line of reasoning.
- Explain how the evidence supports your line of reasoning.
- Demonstrate an understanding of the rhetorical situation.
- Use appropriate grammar and punctuation in communicating your argument.

My dear Wormwood,

I am delighted to hear that your patient's age and profession make it possible, but by no means certain, that
Line he will be called up for military service. We want him to be
5 in the maximum uncertainty, so that his mind will be filled with contradictory pictures of the future, every one of which arouses hope or fear. There is nothing like suspense and anxiety for barricading a human's mind against the Enemy. He wants men to be concerned with what they do; our
10 business is to keep them thinking about what will happen to them.

Your patient will, of course, have picked up the notion that he must submit with patience to the Enemy's will. What the Enemy means by this is primarily that he should accept
15 with patience the tribulation which has actually been dealt out to him—the present anxiety and suspense. It is about *this* that he is to say "Thy will be done," and for the daily task of bearing this that the daily bread will be provided. It is your business to see that the patient never thinks of the present
20 fear as his appointed cross, but only of the things he is afraid of. Let him regard them as his crosses: let him forget that, since they are incompatible, they cannot all happen to him, and let him try to practice fortitude and patience to them all in advance. For real resignation, at the same moment, to a
25 dozen different and hypothetical fates, is almost impossible, and the Enemy does not greatly assist those who are trying to attain it: resignation to present and actual suffering, even where that suffering consists of fear, is far easier, and is usually helped by this direct action....
30 One can therefore formulate the general rule: In all activities of mind which favour our cause, encourage the patient to be un-selfconscious and to concentrate on the object, but in all activities favourable to the Enemy bend

his mind back on itself. Let an insult or a woman's body
35 so fix his attention outward that he does not reflect "I am now entering into the state called Anger—or the state called Lust." Contrariwise let the reflection "My feelings are now growing more devout, or more charitable," so fix his attention inward that he no longer looks beyond himself to see our
40 Enemy or his own neighbours.

Do what you will, there is going to be some benevolence, as well as some malice, in your patient's soul. The great thing is to direct the malice to his immediate neighbours whom he meets every day and to thrust his benevolence out
45 to the remote circumference, to people he does not know. The malice thus becomes wholly real and the benevolence largely imaginary. There is no good at all in inflaming his hatred of Germans if, at the same time, a pernicious habit of charity is growing up between him and his mother, his
50 employer, and the man he meets in the train. Think of your man as a series of concentric circles, his will being the innermost, his intellect coming next and finally his fantasy. You can hardly hope, at once, to exclude from all the circles everything that smells of the Enemy; but you must keep on
55 shoving all the virtues outward till they are finally located in the circle of fantasy, and all the desirable qualities inward into the Will....

GO ON TO THE NEXT PAGE.

Question 3

Suggested time—40 minutes.

(This question counts for one-third of the total essay section score.)

The French Enlightenment writer Voltaire wrote, "It is dangerous to be right in matters about which the established authorities are wrong."

In a well-written essay, develop your position on Voltaire's claim. Use appropriate evidence from your reading, experience, or observations to support your argument.

In your response, you should do the following:

- Respond to the prompt with a thesis that may establish a line of reasoning.
- Select and use evidence to develop and support your line of reasoning.
- Explain the relationship between the evidence and your thesis.
- Demonstrate an understanding of the rhetorical situation.
- Use appropriate grammar and punctuation in communicating your argument.

STOP

END OF EXAM

_____

Practice Test 4:
Answers and
Explanations

PRACTICE TEST 4 ANSWER KEY

1.	B	24.	D
2.	C	25.	A
3.	A	26.	C
4.	C	27.	D
5.	A	28.	B
6.	C	29.	D
7.	D	30.	D
8.	D	31.	A
9.	D	32.	B
10.	C	33.	B
11.	A	34.	D
12.	D	35.	C
13.	D	36.	B
14.	C	37.	B
15.	D	38.	D
16.	A	39.	A
17.	D	40.	A
18.	C	41.	D
19.	B	42.	B
20.	B	43.	D
21.	D	44.	C
22.	D	45.	D
23.	B		

Once you have checked your answers, remember to return to page 4 and respond to the Reflect questions.

PRACTICE TEST 4 EXPLANATIONS

SECTION I: MULTIPLE CHOICE

1. **B**   This passage is from one of the famous Lincoln-Douglas debates; here, Douglas argues in favor of states' rights. You should note that it is possible to eliminate several of the choices based on the verb *used*. The speaker presents an argument; he does not *analyze*, (A), *criticize*, (C), or *describe*, (D). Douglas says directly that he is vehemently opposed to the idea of slavery in his home state of Illinois; he argues in favor of letting each state decide the issue for itself and goes on to claim that the greatness of the country rests on the sovereignty of the states to do so, which is expressed in (B).

2. **C**   You might not agree with what Douglas is saying in this passage, but he controls his tone carefully; remember, he is engaged in a debate at a time when people turned out in droves, expecting not colossal home runs, spectacular slam-dunks, hockey fights, or touchdown passes, but brilliantly conceived, expertly delivered rhetoric. If you use POE, you can narrow it down to three choices by eliminating (A). Choice (D) may be tempting, but be careful not to apply a 21st-century point of view to 19th-century reality. While we would see Douglas's defense of states' rights of slavery as outrageous, the question is about the tone of the author. There is no evidence that the author expresses outrage. The tone is best described as the tone of a debate; in other words, a formal discussion of the major issue of the day. Also, remember that a polemic is a controversial argument. The correct answer is (C).

3. **A**   The speaker uses inductive reasoning (reasoning derived from detailed facts to form general principles) that goes something like this: you all agree that it was right for Illinois to vote as it chose and abolish slavery; thus, every state should be able to make its own choice on this issue. Moreover, every state should be able to make its own choices on just about everything. The correct answer is (A).

4. **C**   In this instance, the word *it* is referring to the choice of New York to make the distinction between *a negro who held property and one who did not* (lines 32–33), so (C) is the best answer. Each of the other answer choices points to a different antecedent and is therefore not correct.

5. **A**   The long sentence in lines 37–42 accomplishes many of Douglas's goals at once. It defines the term (lines 39–41), accuses Congress of *interfering* (line 41), and encourages his readers to *act conscientiously and rigidly* (line 38). Thus, (A) is the correct answer because this question highlights the word EXCEPT in capital letters. There is no evidence of a classification taking place in this sentence.

6. **C**   Check lines 18–37. The author shows that Maine and New York have very different laws regarding African Americans, and that Maine and Illinois are not interfering with each other. Lines 40–41 define popular sovereignty as a guarantee *to each State and Territory the right to do as it pleases on all things, local and domestic*. This supports either (B) or (C). Choice (B) is too strong, since it uses the word *prove*, and the author has not necessarily shown that the laws are *successful*. Therefore, (C) is the best answer.

7. **D** The correct answer may not have been readily apparent, but using POE allows you to eliminate (A) through (C). Douglas uses no anecdotes, much less clever ones; likewise, there are no symbols or metaphors. The authorities in this case are not only the other states (meaning the voters in the other states), but also the founding fathers: *Washington, Madison, or the framers of this government.* The correct answer is (D).

8. **D** Douglas states his own opinion on slavery (his official opinion, at least) at the beginning of the passage (*there is no man in the State who would be more strenuous in his opposition to the introduction of slavery than I would*). Douglas also presents a clear position on voting: *I would never consent to confer the right of voting and of citizenship upon a negro.* Finally, there is a clear position on property: *I would not make any distinction whatever between a negro who held property and one who did not.* Of course, this implies that he would allow African Americans to have property, but he states that, propertied or not, they should not be able to vote. With this information, it is possible to answer the question with certainty; the correct answer is (D).

9. **D** Use POE! The last paragraph claims that Abraham Lincoln's policies will bring about the end of America's greatness and plunge the nation into Civil War. The *new doctrine* (line 70) is in opposition to *popular sovereignty* (line 54) and thus would lead to a consolidation of power, (A). Westward expansion, (B), is suggested in lines 57–59, and the author states that popular sovereignty enabled such expansion (line 64), so Lincoln's *new doctrine* may hinder that. Choice (C) is explicitly stated in line 71. Population, (D), is mentioned in lines 56–57, but there is no direct link between Lincoln's policies and population growth.

10. **C** Here Douglas uses a scare tactic by saying that Lincoln and his party are deliberately infringing on states' rights to incite a civil war, making (C) the correct answer. Hopefully you were not fooled by (B). While it is true that Douglas is blaming the war (that hadn't yet begun) on Lincoln and his political party, he is not shifting any blame; nowhere does he imply that anyone was blaming or accusing Douglas and his party of trying to provoke a war, and to shift blame, Douglas would have to have had blame at some point.

11. **A** In this passage, Douglas is arguing for the application of the doctrine of *popular sovereignty* against the claims of Abraham Lincoln, which is why (A) is correct. He does not spend his time talking at length about Lincoln's failings, so (C) is incorrect. Douglas offers a nuanced argument, but he does not spend his time exploring *the various meanings of a universal principle*, so (D) is out as well. Because Douglas actively criticizes Congress (in lines 41–42, for example), (B) can also not be correct.

12. **D** The first paragraph lays out the definition of *convivencia* ("coexistence" among Muslims, Christians, and Jews in medieval Spain), so (D) is correct. Choices (A) and (B) are incorrect because the author does not want to say that medieval history is unimportant, just that it is portrayed incorrectly in popular histories, which he hardly wants to *reinforce*. Notice the way the test-writers used words and phrases that sounded correct (*discount the importance of* and *the popular perception of*), but were not part of complete, correct answer choices. Remember that if an answer is slightly wrong, it is entirely wrong. Choice (C) doesn't appear in the passage, which does not discuss historical sources.

13. **D**   The author strings together quotes from various authors in order to retell the traditional *fairy tale* of medieval *convivencia*, which he then goes on to attack. This is why (D) is correct. While the author is frustrated with the *narrative of medieval history offered by most historians of medieval Spain*, he is not confused by the narrative, so eliminate (A). Though the author criticizes the works of others, he does not offer his own interpretation in this excerpt, so eliminate (C). Choice (B) is also incorrect; although the author is interested in how the *proponents of convivencia misinterpret* history, he is less concerned with their understanding of evidence. Besides, that's not the primary reason he used quotes in this paragraph.

14. **C**   The primary purpose of the footnotes in the first paragraph is to document the sources for the expressions in quotes, so (C) is correct. While footnotes can *demonstrate the range of sources* in a work or *reveal that all the quotes are from the same source*, neither is the case here (there are two sources), so (A) and (B) can be eliminated. Choice (D) is not likely to be true because that is a relatively shallow reason for including footnotes and not one that can be easily detected.

15. **D**   The second footnote clarifies that the expression *culture of tolerance* originates in the subtitle of Maria Rosa Menocal's book, making (D) correct. While the author is interested in undermining the claims of Menocal, (A) is not correct. Neither are the other choices, which do not accurately portray the author's purposes for including this information here.

16. **A**   *Genre* refers in this case directly to *fairy tale*, so (A) is correct. The AP exam writers love to embed these grammatical/vocabulary questions into the multiple-choice section. Remember to take your time rereading a few lines above and a few lines below the sentence in which the word "genre" appears. Then, eliminate every word that you know does not relate to *genre* directly, such as *children*, (C).

17. **D**   The author does not mention documentary evidence or methodology, so eliminate (A) and (C) right away. He does claim that some scholars have distorted the relationship between Islam and Christianity during this period, but he does not do so in terms of (B), which is not precise. The author believes that *convivencia* exaggerates historical reality and distorts the history of medieval Spain into a fairy tale, so (D) is the correct answer.

18. **C**   Don't forget the word EXCEPT (printed entirely in capital letters) or you will have trouble with this kind of question. Four of these answer choices will be accurate in describing the tone of the second paragraph and one will not. The author shifts his tone between sharp criticism of academic works and elaborate metaphors and humorous insults. He certainly does insist on some of his claims, so (A) is accurate and can be eliminated. *Acerbic*, (B), means sharp or bitter, and accurately describes much of this paragraph, so it can also be eliminated. At no point does the author express a distinct feeling of relief, so (C) must be correct.

19. **B**   This question asks you to identify the author's main point in this passage, which is that the proponents of *convivencia* have encouraged people to believe a *fairy tale* about medieval Spain rather than its real history. Choice (A) is merely the author's introduction of the concept of *convivencia*, while (D) is more like an aside than the main point. While (C) is appealing, it is making a specific point about Asian stereotypes that the author sustains throughout the second paragraph, not the entire passage. Choice (B) emphasizes the disconnect the author identifies between *convivencia* as a myth and the historical record, which he does not believe supports this view of *convivencia*. The answer is (B).

20. **B** By calling *The Ornament of the World a syrupy confection* that *simmers under a thick layer of* [Asian stereotypes], the author uses a metaphor built around food imagery to attack the book as unserious. Thus, (B) is correct. Remember that alliteration, (A), is the repetition of the same sound at the beginning of a word; and allegory, (C), is an extended series of symbols in a story. There is not a directly paradoxical (contradictory) claim in the sentence, so eliminate (D).

21. **D** As you saw in the previous question, the author directly states that the chapter titles of *The Ornament of the World* emphasize the extent to which the book *simmers under a thick layer of* [Asian stereotypes], so (D) is correct. While the titles do refer to Islamic history, (A), and use poetic images, (B), the titles are not included to demonstrate either of these features. The author makes many accusations in this excerpt, but he does not accuse Menocal of hyperbole, so eliminate (C).

22. **D** This is a challenging question. The author inserts *and in the delicious irony* as an aside in the final sentence of the second paragraph. Throughout the paragraph, he alluded to sickly sweet food products in the overly dramatic characterizations of *convivencia*: he criticizes *Menocal's syrupy confection* and says that it *simmers under a thick layer of* [Asian stereotypes]. This metaphorical language is extended by his choice of the word *delicious* here, so (D) is correct. The phrase is too short and too unimportant to do any of the tasks mentioned in the other three answer choices.

23. **B** This is a critique of a particular historical perspective, but it is hardly comprehensive or complete enough to be considered a treatise, so eliminate (A). And while the author is certainly writing a *dismissal*, he is not qualifying it in the sense of limiting or restricting a critique, so eliminate (C) because it is only partially correct. (Remember that when *qualified* appears on the exam, it rarely refers to qualifications or credentials.) Because there is no *analysis* of evidence at work in the passage, (D) can be eliminated as well. Choice (B) is correct because the author sustains an aggressive attack on a position while employing humor and irony throughout.

24. **D** You have two tasks on this question: ensure that the statement relates to the topic of the paragraph and make sure it is engaging (has a hook). The topic of this paragraph, much like the main idea of the entire passage, is that stadium subsidies are harmful to cities. Choices (A) and (C) can be eliminated because they do not convey the downside of building a new stadium. Choice (D) engages the audience with a real-world example of a city that is experiencing the consequences of stadium subsidies, while the statement in (B) is a bit general. Eliminate (B). Choice (D) is correct.

25. **A** The main idea of the passage is that stadium subsidies have a serious downside in terms of a municipality's budget. Keep (A) because it directly references budgetary consequences. Choices (B) and (D) can be eliminated because they have nothing to do with local budgets. Choice (C) may seem tempting, but the main idea is about the consequences, which are not referred to in (C). Eliminate it. Choice (A) is correct.

26. **C** The author's main point is that the benefits of a new professional sports stadium do not justify using local bonds to fund them. While (A), (B), and (D) are about constructing new stadiums, they do not tie in the idea of using local funds. Eliminate them. Choice (C) is correct.

27. **D** Sentence 6 shows how an oppositional perspective can be dismissed. Sentence 7 does the same thing with another possible piece of oppositional evidence. Since these sentences are doing the same thing, you need a transitional word that shows agreement. Choices (A), (B), and (C) can be eliminated because they all should be used when one sentence shows a contrast to another. *Furthermore* provides the necessary agreement transition, so (D) is correct.

28. **B** For this question, you want to keep the focus on what might justify a city making a poor financial choice. Further, that decision should be due to pressure from a sports franchise. Use POE. Choice (A) is incorrect because it relates neither to making a poor financial choice nor pressure from a sports team. Eliminate it. Choice (C) references a poor financial decision, but there is no evidence that it is under the pressure from a professional sports franchise. Eliminate it. Choice (D) is about decision makers not supporting the use of stadium subsidies, so it can be eliminated. Choice (B) indicates that cities cave to pressure from sports teams because they do not want to lose their local team to another city. This accomplishes the goal, so the correct answer is (B).

29. **D** The proposed sentence starts with the phrase *whatever the case*, which implies that it comes after the discussion of more than one potential reason. Choices (A), (B), and (C) can all be eliminated because they occur before the discussion on potential reasons has concluded. The sentence should go at the end of the paragraph, which delves into the question of why cities might offer stadium subsidies. Choice (D) is correct.

30. **D** Since this is an EXCEPT question, you want to find the one answer choice that stands apart from the rest. Choices (A), (B), and (C) are all supportive of the author's claim that tax-payer funded stadium subsidies are bad for cities. Choice (D), however, looks into the benefits of building a new stadium. This would contradict the author's main purpose. Choice (D) is, therefore, correct.

31. **A** For this question, you want to find evidence of a team actually leaving a city because it did not get a subsidy to build a new stadium. Choice (A) is an example that perfectly fits this scenario. Keep it. Choices (B) and (C) are irrelevant to the issue at hand. Eliminate them. Choice (D) does discuss stadium subsidies, but takes a left turn by mentioning a team may leave even after getting what it wants. This is not as directly aligned with the claim as (A), so eliminate (D). Choice (A) is correct.

32. **B** Since the question mentions a *call to action*, look for an answer choice that references a remedy, or at least doing *something*, to combat the practice of offering stadium subsidies. Choice (A) does not do this, but rather states that the practice will be an inevitability for years to come. Eliminate (A). Choice (B) is at least solution-oriented (*lawmakers must find a way*), so that is worth keeping. Choice (C) is incorrect because, while it opposes stadium subsidies, it is certainly not solution-oriented. Choice (D), like (A), is more a statement of inevitability, bereft of any semblance of a solution. Eliminate (D). The only choice remaining is (B), which is the correct answer.

33. **B** For this question, you want to find an answer choice that touches on both the patients' healthcare needs and their lack of information on the topic (and therefore the need to learn more). Choice (A) contradicts much of the passage because it suggests that a patient's convenience is more important than receiving proper medical treatment from a quality doctor. Eliminate it. Choice (B) is plausible because it focuses on the complexity of the healthcare system (*no two doctors are alike, diverse factors*), in which patients would need to be advised as to which doctor is most appropriate for their

needs. Choice (C) is extreme and contradicted by the rest of the passage, which focuses on ways patients can learn about their doctors. Eliminate it. Choice (D) is incorrect because the idea of interchangeable doctors would undermine the need to evaluate them, which contradicts the main idea of the passage. Choice (B) is correct.

34. **D**   Sentence 2 is concerned with subjective evaluations of doctors, while sentence 3 looks at newer "*objective*" ways to measure doctor quality. Since you are looking for a contrast, find an answer choice that provides a contrast. Choice (D) is the only transition word that contrasts. Choices (A), (B), and (C) are incorrect because they all signal transitions to similar ideas rather than contrasting ones. Choice (D) is correct.

35. **C**   Since this is an EXCEPT question, you want to find the one answer choice that stands out from the rest. Choices (A), (B), and (D) all deal with methods of evaluating physicians. Choice (C) is the one choice that is irrelevant to the evaluation process, so it is the correct answer.

36. **B**   The main idea of the paragraph is that the new trend in doctor evaluations comes from the perspective of patient satisfaction and health outcomes. Therefore, it is from the perspective of the health-care consumer. Choice (A) is irrelevant to the rest of the paragraph. Eliminate it. Furthermore, eliminate (C) because it focuses on feedback from the medical community, rather than from patients, which is the focus of this paragraph. Choice (D) is tempting because the author goes on to explain that these are flawed approaches, but that does not occur until the third paragraph, and it is therefore not connected to the main idea of the second paragraph. Eliminate (D). Choice (B) indicates that the assessment is from the perspective of the consumer, so (B) is correct.

37. **B**   Use POE on this question. If an answer choice does not give evidence of an unfair system, eliminate it. Choice (A) suggests that what patients say in their feedback is consistent with other types of evaluations, which would indicate that patients are accurate and therefore, fair evaluators of physicians. Eliminate it. Choice (B) states that patients are not necessarily qualified to evaluate physician quality. If they are in a position to do so, then this would be evidence of an unfair system. Keep (B). Choice (C) should be eliminated because it suggests that one of the forms of evaluation currently in use (measuring long-term patient outcomes) is relatively effective (at least more so than patient surveys). Choice (D) is incorrect because a quote from a health-consumer advocate would likely argue that patients provide relevant, effective feedback and should be considered for evaluation. In other words, this type of evidence would defend the fairness of the current system. Choice (B) is correct.

38. **D**   In the third paragraph, the writer claims that some patient populations could be harmed by the current system of evaluation because it would disincentivize doctors from taking on patients with conditions that are more chronic (obesity, congenital diseases) because the effects of those conditions will likely persist despite medical intervention. Therefore, some doctors may not want to take on these patients because their health circumstances would reflect poorly on their physicians. This is the opposite of (A), so eliminate it. Choice (B) is something that would make the system fairer to doctors, but it does not explain why some patients could be avoided by physicians. This answer, along with (C), is irrelevant. Eliminate both. Choice (D) is correct because it best describes the disincentive system that is created by tracking patient outcomes.

39. **A**   The fourth paragraph describes the problems with the current system of physician evaluation. Therefore, this sentence would make a great topic sentence as it gives a general claim about the all-around flaws of doctor evaluation. Choices (B), (C), and (D) are incorrect as they would awkwardly misplace a topic sentence into the middle or end of a paragraph it was intended to introduce. Choice (A) would place this as a topic sentence, and thus is correct.

40. **A**   The main argument of the passage can be found in the first paragraph: patients need a fair way to know which doctors are most effective. This purpose is reflected in (A), which is the correct answer. Choice (B) is incorrect because it goes too far: patient input does not need to be completely removed from the process, but there are flaws in relying solely on patient input. Choice (C) is incorrect because it focuses on one detail from the third paragraph, rather than the passage as a whole. Eliminate (D) because the passage states that measuring the patient experience is a flawed method for evaluating physicians.

41. **D**   The main argument of the passage is that zoos have many benefits that outweigh the problems of keeping animals in captivity. Choice (A) is incorrect because the author does not tout the entertainment quality of zoos. Choice (B) articulates an oppositional argument. Eliminate it. Choice (C) does not relate to the benefits the author goes on to mention (research, education, conservation), so it is incorrect. Choice (D) does the best job conveying the author's central claim and is therefore correct.

42. **B**   For this question, look for an answer choice that conveys how successful zoos have been in repopulating animal species. Choice (C) can be eliminated because it indicates failure. Choice (D) is incorrect because it is irrelevant to explaining how the zoos have provided a necessary service. Although both (A) and (B) describe success, (A) is too measured, indicating only moderate outcomes. Eliminate (A). Choice (B) is correct because it notes that the programs have had dramatic effects (successes) recently.

43. **D**   Since this is an EXCEPT question, use POE. The answer to this question should be an answer choice that makes zoos look bad, while the incorrect choices are all supportive of the author's defense of zoos. Choices (A), (B), and (C) all support zoos and can be eliminated. Choice (D) shows a problem with zoos, and is therefore the correct answer.

44. **C**   Sentence 8 builds directly from sentence 7: both sentences argue that some important research comes out of zoos. Therefore, look for a transition that shows agreement between ideas. Choices (A), (B), and (D) are incorrect because they are all transitions to be used when showing contrast. Choice (C), *In fact*, shows agreement, so the answer is (C).

45. **D**   For this question, locate an answer choice that sees zoos as beneficial. Choice (A) is incorrect because the current sentence does not provide closure and conveys a troubling tone if not followed up with a more solution-oriented sentence. Choice (B) is incorrect because its matter-of-fact content is not the author's central claim. Choice (C) is the opposite of the author's claim about the benefits of zoos, so it should be eliminated. Choice (D) is correct as it is consistent with the central claim and the author's tone.

SECTION II: FREE RESPONSE

Rubric—1 + 4 + 1 = 6 pts

A. Thesis (0–1 pts)
   ○ Responds to the prompt with a thesis that presents a defensible interpretation of the selected work.

B. Evidence and Commentary (0–4 pts)
   ○ Evidence: Provides specific evidence to support all claims in a line of reasoning.
   ○ Commentary: Consistently explains how the evidence supports a line of reasoning.
   ○ Explains how multiple literary elements or techniques in the poem contribute to its meaning.

C. Sophistication (0–1 pts)
   ○ Demonstrates sophistication of thought and/or develops a complex literary argument.

Question 1—Synthesis Essay

How to Score 6 Points

- Address the prompt with a defensible thesis.
- Present specific evidence from at least three sources and consistently explain how the evidence supports your thesis statement.
- Use style and rhetoric to persuade the reader.

Source Overview

Source A: Drugs of addiction function by flooding a person's nervous system with dopamine, causing a euphoric experience. Overtime, drug users build tolerance, resulting in a depressive state without drugs and a need for a higher quantity of drugs to experience the same initial high.

Source B: Many people are unable to experience happiness because they are worried about the future. Mindfulness, the practice of bringing one's attention to the present moment through meditation, allows individuals to enjoy the present. Mindfulness benefits one's health and the quality of one's relationships.

Source C: This map depicts average, self-reported happiness from different nations across the world. Measured on a scale from one to ten, where ten represents one's best possible life. Much of the Eurasian continent responded with levels between five and seven; North America, South America, Western Europe, and Australia responded with levels between six and eight; nations in Africa responded with levels between two and six.

Source D: The world happiness survey seeks to measure happiness by nation based on six variables: income, healthy life expectancy, social support, freedom, trust, and generosity. Denmark, Switzerland, Norway, and Finland have held the top rank in recent years. Obesity, the opioid crisis, and depression threaten happiness in the United States.

Source E: Some psychologists suggest that happiness can be found when the mind is engaged in flow. Flow occurs when individuals are presented with significant challenges for which they are highly skilled.

Source F: Timothy Ferriss describes making $70,000 per month and feeling exhausted due to workaholism. Leaving his work to travel was a risk but offered huge rewards, and his life has been a "near fairy tale" ever since.

Source G: The average American spends roughly 20 years in retirement, and lifestyle costs can be between 70% and 90% of those that one incurs while working. Individuals need to prepare for their retirement finances by taking advantage of their employer's retirement benefits, maximizing personal investments, and letting investment monies accrue over time.

Sample First Paragraph

There can be as many definitions of happiness as there are people on Earth. For some, personal satisfaction can mean finding ease and peace in the present moment; For others, happiness is knowing they have a family to go home to or that they won't be a burden on others when they're no longer able to provide for themselves. Life satisfaction is best achieved by striking a personal balance between living in the moment and preparing for the future.

Question 2—Rhetorical Analysis Essay

How to Score 6 Points

Use the Rhetorical Diamond! While you're reading the prompt and the passage, imagine—and try to flesh out—a baseball diamond with the following six points:

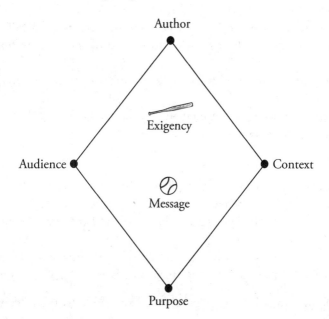

Author: C.S. Lewis
Audience: Intellectual British skeptics
Purpose: To convey the value of Christianity to intellectual British skeptics
Context: Written in the early 20th century for a predominantly British, academic audience
Exigency: C.S. Lewis's desire for intellectual discourse and/or the presence of potential military conflict presents a need for religion.
Message: As life inevitably includes fear, anxiety, and selfishness, Christianity provides opportunities to show compassion and love to fellow humans.

Sample Rhetorical Modes and Devices
- **Epistolary structure:** "My dear Wormwood…."
- **Personification:** The fictional author ("I") is an elderly devil writing to "Wormwood," whom is also referred to as "you."
- **Personification:** The letter refers to the "Enemy," the Christian conception of a personified deity.

- **Allegory:** "It is your business to see that the patient never thinks of the present fear as his appointed cross, but only of the things he is afraid of. Let him regard them as his crosses…"
- **Definition:** "Your patient will, of course, have picked up the notion that he must submit with patience to the Enemy's will. What the Enemy means by this is primarily that he should accept with patience the tribulation which has actually been dealt out to him—the present anxiety and suspense."

Sample First Paragraph

Faith is commonly considered to be belief in the absence of evidence. C.S. Lewis took on a great challenge in trying to convince the intellectual religious skeptics of his day to appreciate the value of Christianity. To do so, Lewis wrote *The Screwtape Letters*, fictitious letters from an elderly devil to a younger "Wormwood" advising him on how to best corrupt humans. By taking advantage of the epistolary structure, personification, and allegory, Lewis posits that Christianity provides opportunities for love and compassion amid a life that is troubled by anxiety, temptation, and selfishness.

Question 3—Argument Essay

How to Score 6 Points

- Take a definite position, so no one will question where you stand on the topic of the prompt.
- Develop an argument that builds and moves forward instead of simply repeating the same point several times in different ways.
- Support the points in your argument with evidence drawn from your own knowledge, reading, experiences, and observations.
- Explain how your evidence supports your argument.

Sample Evidence

- Galileo contradicted the Catholic Church by arguing against the idea that the Earth was the center of the solar system. He was prosecuted as a heretic and spent much of his life under house arrest.
- During World War II, those caught fighting for the Jewish resistance were sent to concentration camps and/or executed.
- The U.S. Supreme Court provides a peaceful means of protesting laws one finds unjust. State laws upholding segregation and banning gay marriage have both been successfully overturned.
- Mahatma Gandhi was shot by a Hindu religious extremist while working to unify Muslim and Hindu factions in India.
- Martin Luther King, Jr. was assassinated by an escaped fugitive. The assassin confessed, but rumors of a government conspiracy to eliminate King have persisted.

Sample First Paragraph

Galileo, Mahatma Gandhi, Martin Luther King, Jr, and even Voltaire himself suffered the dangers of being "right in matters about which the established authorities are wrong." While history is filled with countless examples of individuals who suffered great dangers for challenging the established authorities of their time, there are institutions today that provide both a means for peaceful protest and hope for the further progress of human society.

Part VII
Practice Test 5

- Practice Test 5
- Practice Test 5: Answers and Explanations

Practice Test 5

AP® English Language and Composition Exam

SECTION I: Multiple-Choice Questions

DO NOT BEGIN THE EXAM UNTIL YOU ARE TOLD TO DO SO.

DISCLAIMER: The official AP English Language and Composition Exam will be administered digitally. Instructions for the digital exam may differ from this practice test.

At a Glance

Total Time
1 hour
Number of Questions
45
Percent of Total Grade
45%

Instructions

Section I of this examination contains 45 multiple-choice questions. Choose the best answer to each question. Note: Pay particular attention to the requirements of questions that contain the words "NOT," "LEAST," or "EXCEPT."

Indicate all of your answers to the multiple-choice questions on the answer sheet. No credit will be given for anything written in this exam booklet, but you may use the booklet for notes or scratch work. After you have decided which of the suggested answers is best, completely fill in the corresponding oval on the answer sheet. Give only one answer to each question. If you change an answer, be sure that the previous mark is erased completely. Here is a sample question and answer.

Sample Question   Sample Answer

Chicago is a   (A) ● (C) (D)
(A) state
(B) city
(C) country
(D) continent

Use your time effectively, working as quickly as you can without losing accuracy. Do not spend too much time on any one question. Go on to other questions and come back to the ones you have not answered if you have time.

About Guessing

Many candidates wonder whether or not to guess the answers to questions about which they are not certain. Multiple-choice scores are based on the number of questions answered correctly. Points are not deducted for incorrect answers, and no points are awarded for unanswered questions. Because points are not deducted for incorrect answers, you are encouraged to answer all multiple-choice questions. On any questions you do not know the answer to, you should eliminate as many choices as you can, and then select the best answer among the remaining choices.

GO ON TO THE NEXT PAGE.

This page intentionally left blank.

ENGLISH LANGUAGE AND COMPOSITION
SECTION I
Time—1 hour

Directions: This part consists of selections from prose works and questions on their content, form, and style. After reading each passage, choose the best answer to each question and completely fill in the corresponding oval on the answer sheet.

Note: Pay particular attention to the requirement of questions that contain the words NOT, LEAST, or EXCEPT.

Questions 1–12. Read the following passage carefully before you choose your answers.

The following is an excerpt from *The Poetry of Science*, an 1848 book by British mineralogist Robert Hunt.

In contemplating works of nature, we cannot but regard, with feelings of religious admiration, the infinite variety of forms under which matter is presented to our senses. On
Line every hand, the utmost diversity is exhibited; through all
5 things we trace the most perfect order; and overall is diffused the charm of beauty. It is the uneducated or depraved alone, who find deformities in the creations by which we are surrounded.

The three conditions of matter are, the solid, the fluid,
10 and the aeriform; and these belong equally to the organic and inorganic world.

In organic nature we have an almost infinite variety of animal form, presenting developments widely different from each other; yet in every case suited to the conditions required
15 by the position which the creature occupies in the scale of being. Through the entire series, from the Polype to the higher order of animals, even to man, we find a uniformity in the progress towards perfection, and a continuity in the series, which betrays the great secret, that the mystery of life
20 is the same in all—a pervading spiritual essence associated with matter, and modifying it by the master-mechanism of an Infinite mind.

In the vegetable clothing of the surface of the earth, which fits it for the abode of man and animals—from the
25 confervae[1] of a stagnant pool, or the lichen of the wind-beaten rock, to the lordly oak or towering palm—a singularly beautiful chain of being, and of gradual elevation in the scale of organization, presents itself to the contemplative mind.

In the inorganic world, where the great phenomena of
30 life are wanting, we have constantly exhibited the working of powers of a strangely complicated kind. The symmetrical arrangement of crystals—the diversified characters of mineral formations—the systematic aggregation of particles to form masses possessing properties of a peculiar and
35 striking nature—all prove that agencies, which science with all its refinements has not detected, are unceasingly at work....

_____
1 A genus of filamentous green algae.

The naturalist searches the earth, the waters, and the air, for their living things; and the diversity of form, the variety
40 of condition, and the perfection of organization which he discovers as belonging to this our epoch—differing from, indeed bearing but a slight relation to, those which mark the earth's mutations—exhibit in a most striking view the endless variety of characters which matter can assume.

45 We are so accustomed to all these phenomena of matter, that it is with some difficulty we can bend ourselves to the study of the more simple conditions in which it exists....

To nature alone belongs the mysterious power of transmutation. The enthusiastic alchemist, by the agency of
50 physical power, dissipates a metal in vapour; but it remains a metal, and the same metal still. By the Hermetic art, he breaks up the combinations of masses; but he cannot alter the principles of any one of the elements which formed the mass upon which his skill is tried.

55 Every atom is invested with properties peculiar to all of its class; and each one possesses powers, to which in mute obedience it is compelled, by which these properties are modified, and the character of matter varied. What are those properties? Do we know anything of those powers?

1. According to lines 23–28 ("In the vegetable clothing… contemplative mind"), Hunt's primary point about organic life is that it

   (A) offers immense variety
   (B) features the coexistence of humans and animals
   (C) is systematically arranged
   (D) can only be understood through meditation

2. The passage implies that there is nothing in nature that

   (A) can be positively labeled
   (B) exists separate from other things
   (C) does not mutate
   (D) changes between the three conditions of matter

GO ON TO THE NEXT PAGE.

3. The organization of this passage can best be described as

   (A) presentation of empirical data followed by rigorous analysis
   (B) personal experience followed by self-doubt
   (C) ironic evasion followed by a serious statement of intent
   (D) categorization followed by an exploration of general underlying conditions

4. What is the relationship between the sixth and seventh paragraphs of the passage?

   (A) The sixth describes the overall task of a naturalist, while the seventh prepares the reader for a change of topic.
   (B) The sixth underlines the difficulty of categorizing nature, while the seventh reminds us of conditions in which it exists.
   (C) The sixth considers Hunt's primary focus upon the present, while the seventh considers the future.
   (D) The sixth details the search for natural perfection, while the seventh reveals in which situation that perfection is found.

5. The "Polype" (line 16) represents

   (A) a higher class of angels
   (B) a multitude of organisms
   (C) a lower order of earthly life
   (D) a Greek goddess of the underworld

6. The effect of using long periodic sentences such as the one in lines 12–22 is to

   (A) emphasize the author's educational level
   (B) imply that complexity grants intellectual validity
   (C) suggest a complex thinking pattern
   (D) ignore the needs of the average reader of the time

7. Which of the following lines in the passage does NOT support the author's belief in the interconnectedness of nature?

   (A) Lines 16–17 ("through…order")
   (B) Lines 14–16 ("yet in every case…scale of being")
   (C) Lines 26–28 ("a singularly beautiful…contemplative mind")
   (D) Lines 49–51 ("The enthusiastic alchemist…the same metal still")

8. The author's attitude towards nature can best be described as

   (A) infinite
   (B) analytical
   (C) mystical
   (D) methodical

9. The word "it" in the ninth paragraph refers to which of the following?

   (A) "properties"
   (B) "powers"
   (C) "obedience"
   (D) "atom"

10. What purpose does the seventh paragraph ("We are…it exists…") serve?

    (A) An explanation of an ambiguous concept
    (B) A transition to a related topic
    (C) A redefinition of a controversial term
    (D) An amplification of a previous idea

11. In the fourth paragraph (lines 25–26), the author mentions "confervae" and "towering palm" primarily to

    (A) differentiate between the two animal kingdoms
    (B) suggest the linkages in nature are more extensive than most believe
    (C) emphasize the beauty of nature available to those willing to contemplate it
    (D) illustrate the wide variety of plants that are connected in the great chain of being

12. One can infer from the fifth paragraph (lines 29–37) that the author believes in

    (A) an innate sense of order underlying all of creation
    (B) an undetectable system of organization
    (C) a constant mineralization of all living things
    (D) a chaos that is kept controlled by a watchful overspirit

GO ON TO THE NEXT PAGE.

Questions 13–23. Read the following passage carefully before you choose your answers.

The following is an excerpt from the 2015 San Diego County Medical Examiner's Report.

Medico-legal investigations are completed in a professional, ethical and timely manner and they are geared to assist in the determination of the cause and manner
Line of death. This is accomplished through the continued
5 cooperation between law enforcement agencies, health care professionals, and the public.

The initial phase of the process typically starts with a report of death. In 2015, investigators processed 8,717 reports of death. In 5,721 (66 percent) of those cases, after
10 undergoing a methodical and structured process of review to ensure they did not fall under the criteria of California Government Code 27491 requiring further investigation, we waived jurisdiction to the treating physician so he or she could attest the death certificate. Medical Examiner's
15 Jurisdiction was invoked in the other 2,996 (34 percent) of those reports.

Investigators physically respond to the majority of the death scenes falling into the Medical Examiner jurisdiction. In 2015, we responded to 2,022 scenes (67 percent). An
20 initial body and scene assessment is completed at the place of death, which can be virtually anywhere in the 4,261 square miles of San Diego County. Photographs are taken and relevant evidence is collected in order to assist in the investigation. The evidence may include weapons, biological
25 specimens, medications, drugs, and drug paraphernalia. All the investigations are completed with a methodical and systematic approach and all the findings are documented in a comprehensive investigative report.

Medical Examiner's investigators have the difficult task
30 of notifying the next of kin of the death. This process starts with the identification of the decedent –one of the most important duties of our office. Methods for identification include fingerprint and dental comparison, unique skeletal features, DNA analysis, visual comparison, or even
35 serial numbers on implanted medical devices. This is a multidisciplinary approach which involves other county agencies. The process continues with a diligent search for the decedent's family, with which the Medical Examiner's Office has a high rate of success. (See John/Jane Doe Center for
40 more information.)

Those who die suddenly or unexpectedly often die with valuables—both monetary and sentimental—in their possession. It is extremely important that we ensure that these items make their way to the next of kin. Often, the
45 retention of the decedent's personal property is of the utmost importance to the family. We take this responsibility seriously, accurately tracking and recording the chain of custody until the property is returned to the family.

When a death occurs at home, that person may leave
50 behind many medications, many of which are often

controlled substances. As part of our investigation, we collect and inventory all of the decedent's prescription medications at the scene. This task serves three functions. First, by inventorying the remaining medications, including
55 dosage and dates, we can gain an understanding as to whether there was medication overuse or non-compliance. Second, medications can give clues to an individual's medical or social history, and provide names of prescribing physicians who may know critical information about the
60 person's history. Lastly, we remove medications from the home, eliminating the possibility of inappropriate use by other members of the household (especially children), as well as the possibility that the medications will become part of illegal trafficking. Medication disposal occurs at regular
65 intervals after a period of secure storage at our offices.

Medical Examiner investigators also discuss the circumstances of the death with the decedent's family; conduct interviews at the scene; and obtain additional statements from witnesses, the treating physician and
70 responding emergency personnel. They also offer the family free support through our Bereavement Center. Follow-up investigation is required in many cases, and may involve reviewing medical records, police reports and traffic accident reports.
75 Medical Examiner investigators are the front line for our office—the eyes and ears of the Medical Examiner. Their caring attitudes, compassion, professionalism, and objectivity allow our office to conduct thorough, balanced and accurate death investigations while at the same time helping ease the
80 difficulties the family will have during their time of grief.

13. The gravity of the subject matter is best reflected in the authors' use of which of the following phrases?

(A) "ethical and timely manner"
(B) "a multidisciplinary approach"
(C) "extremely important" and "utmost importance"
(D) "controlled substances"

14. The second and third paragraphs primarily utilize which of the following rhetorical strategies?

(A) Classification
(B) Compare and contrast
(C) Bandwagon appeal
(D) Factual reporting

GO ON TO THE NEXT PAGE.

15. The purpose of the passage is

(A) to analyze the efficiency of the processes already in place
(B) to explain how the office conducts its investigations
(C) to refute objections to the office's methods
(D) to briefly summarize all the tasks of the office

16. In the third paragraph, passive verbs such as "evidence is collected" and "investigations are completed" indicate a writing style that is

(A) removed from the individual
(B) understated for effect
(C) cold and merciless
(D) indicative of a strong authorial point of view

17. The authors develop the passage primarily through

(A) narrating events
(B) defining terms
(C) extended analogy
(D) process analysis

18. All of the following phrases reflect the overall tone of the medical examiner's investigations EXCEPT

(A) "a methodical and structured process of review"
(B) "a methodical and systematic approach"
(C) "a comprehensive investigative report"
(D) "helping ease the difficulties"

19. In contrast with the rest of the passage, the tone of the final paragraph is

(A) curious and interested
(B) emotional and reassuring
(C) cautious and reflective
(D) caustic and vituperative

20. It can be inferred from the sixth paragraph that

(A) investigators take inventory of medications when they enter any person's home
(B) medications sometimes play a role in deaths that occur at home
(C) the medical examiner's office had failed previous investigations into deaths at home
(D) the role of medications in deaths at home is unknown

21. In lines 76–77, the author's use of "Their caring attitudes, compassion, professionalism, and objectivity" is an example of which of the following rhetorical appeals?

(A) Caricature
(B) Pathos
(C) Ethos
(D) Proverb

22. The phrase "eyes and ears" in the final paragraph is an example of

(A) diversion
(B) a metaphor
(C) parody
(D) analogy

23. The authors use all of the following EXCEPT

(A) scientific description
(B) quantifiable evidence
(C) connotations
(D) formal diction

GO ON TO THE NEXT PAGE.

Questions 24–31 are based on the following passage.

The passage below is a draft.

(1) But the nation has also long suffered a perhaps unfair reputation for urban violence. (2) It's true that for one year, in 1991, Medellín, Colombia was the most dangerous city in the world—even more dangerous than Beirut—with a murder rate of nearly 400 per 100,000. (3) It was said that the most dangerous job in the world was to be a law enforcement officer in Medellín at that time. (4) And it's also true that there were so many young men killed during this time that it altered the male-female ratio of the region for an entire generation. (5) One reason for this is because of the lingering perception of lack of security.

(6) The instigator for this extreme violence was Pablo Escobar, the leader of the Medellín cartel, who was making so many millions of dollars selling cocaine that he was burying money in the ground and letting it rot in the nineteen nineties because he forgot about it, which is an amazing thing for anybody to do. (7) His war against law enforcement was essentially a civil war, and it tore the country apart.

(8) You can argue with statistics, but they are often the only way of judging phenomena. (9) In 2016, the murder rate in Medellín was down to 22 per 100,000 people, and murders are often measured against a six-figure number. (10) In that same year, the murder rate in Chicago was about 16 per 100,000 people. (11) The difference between the two is statistically insignificant, and so it means that they are just as safe as one another, violently. (12) The murder rate in Cali, Colombia, however, is consistently higher than in other cities, with about 60 per 100,000 people.

(13) Other cities of the United States have suffered similarly unfair derogation. (14) Detroit, for instance, also carries the reputation of a dangerous and violent city, even if that reputation doesn't reflect reality any longer. (15) They even have a saying, *dar la papaya* ("to give the papaya"), which in essence means that when something of value is left unattended, a person has the unspoken right to steal it. (16) Given the growth of the middle class and reduced violence, visitors to Colombia may discover that the biggest problem they encounter is a backpack that quietly gets up and walks away.

24. Which of the following sentences, if placed before sentence 1, would both appeal to the senses and provide a contrast with the rest of the paragraph?

(A) The smell of diesel fumes and the aggressive screech of horns blaring are part of urban life.
(B) Those who attempt to describe Colombia often paint pictures of idyllic rural life.
(C) Yellow plantains, red coffee beans, tall green wax palms, clear waterfalls tumbling from misty mountains—this is typical rural life in Colombia.
(D) The blood stains on the cement, the tear-stained cheeks of mourning family members—the horror of violence is a constant in Colombia.

25. To improve coherence, the author would like to move sentence 5 (reproduced below) to a better place in the passage.

One reason for this is because of the lingering perception of lack of security.

Where would the sentence be best placed?

(A) Before sentence 2
(B) Before sentence 3
(C) Before sentence 4
(D) After sentence 8

26. In sentence 8 (reproduced below), the author wants an effective transition from the preceding paragraph to the new paragraph.

You can argue with statistics, but they are often the only way of judging phenomena.

Which of the following versions of sentence 8 best achieves this goal?

(A) (as it is now)
(B) Statistics reveal an incomplete picture of the change.
(C) Depending on the source, statistics are sometimes trustworthy, sometimes not.
(D) Look to statistics to see this story told in data.

GO ON TO THE NEXT PAGE.

27. The author would like to move or delete sentence 12 (reproduced below).

    The murder rate in Cali, Colombia, however, is consistently higher than in other cities, with about 60 per 100,000 people.

    Which choice most effectively improves the coherence of the paragraph?

    (A) Move it after sentence 9.
    (B) Move it after sentence 10.
    (C) Move it after sentence 13.
    (D) Delete it completely.

28. In sentence 14 (reproduced below), the author would like to rewrite the underlined portion to provide more evidence of Detroit's historical success and subsequent decline.

    Detroit, for instance, <u>also carries the reputation of a dangerous and violent city, even if that reputation doesn't reflect reality any longer.</u>

    Which version of the underlined text best supports this goal?

    (A) a working-class industrial city known as "the arsenal of democracy," has failed to make the transition to modern digital hub, and faces an uphill battle in rehabilitating its reputation.
    (B) still carries the reputation of a dangerous and violent city; however, this ignores the present reality, which is that Detroit currently enjoys a 99% rental occupancy rate and record low unemployment.
    (C) a place that used to be the fourth-largest city in the nation, has one problem: its reputation no longer reflects reality.
    (D) which used to be the fourth-largest city in the nation but whose population has dropped by almost seventy percent in the last generation, is still unjustly regarded as a dangerous city.

29. Which of the following sentences, if inserted before sentence 15, would provide the most effective introduction to the final paragraph?

    (A) Even with dropping nonviolent crime rates, the violent crime rates are still on the rise.
    (B) Today, Colombia has seen an increase in nonviolent crime, such as robbery and theft.
    (C) Compared with violent crime, such as robbery and theft, nonviolent crime has been rising in Colombia.
    (D) Whether violent or nonviolent, a society such as Colombia will always have to deal with the criminal side of life.

30. In the fourth paragraph, the author would like to conclude with a sentence that reinforces the increasingly global nature of the topic under discussion. Which of the following sentences would best achieve this purpose?

    (A) This phenomenon isn't limited to the Western Hemisphere—municipal governments on every continent employ public relations teams to polish their public images.
    (B) These days, social media isn't limited to only the developed Western world; many developing countries in Asia and Africa use messaging platforms for many purposes, including commerce.
    (C) While public image is a definite concern across the world, it has taken on special importance in developed Western cities.
    (D) One has to wonder at what point, if ever, the necessity of such public rehabilitation will be finally addressed in violent cities across the globe.

31. The author would like to edit sentence 15 (reproduced below) for syntactic clarity.

    <u>They even have a saying,</u> dar la papaya ("to give the papaya"), which in essence means that when something of value is left unattended, a person has the unspoken right to steal it.

    Which version of the underlined text best accomplishes this goal?

    (A) (as it is now)
    (B) They use a common expression,
    (C) There is a saying of the people of Colombia,
    (D) The people of Colombia even have a saying,

GO ON TO THE NEXT PAGE.

Questions 32–40 are based on the following passage.

The passage below is a draft.

(1) The huge explosion of self-publishing has changed life irrevocably for a whole mess of authors. (2) In the past, being a self-published author carried a fairly serious stigma. (3) This was because a self-published author usually had published with a vanity press, in which the author pays for the production of the books. (4) The introduction of the Amazon Kindle in 2007 began a slow transformation of the industry.

(5) While electronic readers had existed before—Sony had brought the first to market several years earlier—Amazon's Kindle was the first to be adopted en masse. (6) Significantly, this meant the end of the traditional publishing gatekeepers, as they were beginning to lose market share.

(7) This, predictably, caused a gold rush mentality. (8) The ranks of self-publishers swelled like a river after a spring melt, with hundreds publishing books every day. (9) Some hit it big with one title, made a few tens of thousands of dollars, and disappeared. (10) Others saw slower, steadier success.

(11) There are both advantages and disadvantages to self-publishing. (12) One, the author becomes the publisher, with total control over price, cover design, book design, marketing, and promotions. (13) For another, the revenue percentage is much greater as well, generally seventy percent of list price. (14) Traditionally published authors only receive approximately fourteen percent and have zero control.

(15) Most importantly, self-published authors retain total control of their copyright, unlike traditionally published authors, who are forced to either give away all rights permanently, or for a set period of years, usually either 7, 15, or 20. (16) It's a tantalizing future, because there, given the rapidly changing publishing landscape when everyone is carrying reading devices around in their pockets, where audiobooks have become king, anything can happen.

32. In sentence 1 (reproduced below), the writer wants to establish a more formal tone.

The huge explosion of self-publishing has changed life irrevocably for a whole mess of authors.

Which of the following versions of the sentence best achieves this purpose?

(A) (as it is now)
(B) The explosion of self-publishing has changed life irrevocably for a group of authors.
(C) When self-publishing arose, the rapid increase of authors participating in it changed their lives like crazy.
(D) The rapid rise of self-publishing as a viable career option has changed the lives of many authors.

33. In paragraph 1, the author wants to add the following sentence to provide additional explanation.

The result was usually a garage filled with stacks of unsold titles that were sure to be pulped.

Where would the sentence best be placed?

(A) Before sentence 1
(B) After sentence 1
(C) After sentence 2
(D) After sentence 3

34. In sentence 4 (reproduced below), which of the following versions of the underlined text best explains the writer's perspective on the main idea of the passage?

The introduction of the Amazon Kindle in 2007 <u>began a slow transformation of the industry.</u>

(A) (as it is now)
(B) concluded an unhappy decade in publishing history.
(C) finally began a long overdue transformation of the publishing industry—in favor of the writer.
(D) underscored the continued need for new ways of reaching readers.

GO ON TO THE NEXT PAGE.

35. In sentence 6 (reproduced below), the author wants to provide convincing evidence that Amazon democratized book publishing.

    Significantly, this meant the end of the traditional publishing gatekeepers, as they were beginning to lose market share.

    Which version of the underlined text best achieves this goal?

    (A) (as it is)
    (B) gatekeepers; through CreateSpace, Amazon's extended distribution network, as well as Amazon's own Kindle store, a self-published author could now sell a paper or electronic book in almost any bookstore in the world (except for big-box retailers such as Walmart or Costco).
    (C) gatekeepers; in fact, the monetary advances offered to authors by traditional publishing houses have decreased in size since the Kindle's arrival.
    (D) gatekeepers: because of the electronic revolution, agents report fewer submissions and fewer sales to traditional publishing houses.

36. The writer would like to combine sentences 9 and 10 (reproduced below).

    Some hit it big with one title, made a few tens of thousands of dollars, and disappeared. Others saw slower, steadier success.

    Which version of the underlined text best achieves this goal?

    (A) disappeared, while others
    (B) disappeared, and others
    (C) disappeared; furthermore, others
    (D) disappeared—so others

37. The writer would like to add another sentence to the end of the third paragraph (sentences 7–10) to support the main idea of the paragraph. Which of the following pieces of evidence would best achieve this purpose?

    (A) Nobody really lost in this equation—except, perhaps, bookshelf manufacturers.
    (B) As a result of this growth, though traditionally published bestselling authors saw their overall sales decrease, the public was buying more books than ever before.
    (C) The long tail theory was in effect.
    (D) In response, hand-wringing about falling literacy rates grew in intensity.

38. The author would like to rewrite sentence 11 (reproduced below) to better reflect the ideas in the fourth paragraph.

    There are both advantages and disadvantages to self-publishing.

    Which of the following versions of that sentence best accomplishes this?

    (A) (as it is now)
    (B) Those individuals with a sixth sense for business are the only ones who will benefit from this new self-publishing landscape.
    (C) The disadvantages of self-publishing aren't worth discussion, since the benefits of self-publishing outweigh them so heavily.
    (D) Self-publishing books requires more responsibility for authors but is accompanied by potentially greater rewards.

GO ON TO THE NEXT PAGE.

39. What is the best way to combine sentences 13 and 14 (reproduced below)?

    For another, the revenue percentage is much greater as well, generally seventy percent of list price. Traditionally published authors only receive fourteen percent and have zero control.

    Which version of the underlined portion of the sentences best achieves this task?

    (A) price, for traditionally published authors
    (B) price, while traditionally published authors
    (C) price, and traditionally published authors
    (D) price—traditionally published authors

40. The author wants to rewrite sentence 16 (reproduced below) for clarity and conciseness.

    It's a tantalizing future, because there, given the rapidly changing publishing landscape when everyone is carrying reading devices around in their pockets, where audiobooks have become king, anything can happen.

    Which of the following versions of the sentence would accomplish this?

    (A) (as it is now)
    (B) Audiobooks having become king, electronic books being read on mobile phones—the future will be a tantalizing place for readers.
    (C) The rapidly changing publishing landscape will include the future consumption of electronic books, audiobooks, and mobile phones.
    (D) The publishing landscape of the future may have already arrived, since mobile phones serve as devices for consuming both electronic books and audiobooks.

GO ON TO THE NEXT PAGE.

Questions 41–45 are based on the following passage.

The passage below is a draft.

(1) Driverless cars may be the future, but ironically nobody really knows what they should look like—and it's because nobody has tried to make anything like them before. (2) Ford Motor Company chose as its new CEO the former president of a furniture company. (3) That may seem like an unusual choice, but it was an effort by America's original auto companies to secure its place in the future. (4) His emphasis on design thinking—ergonomic, the human experience with automobile design—is evidently seen as the key to the future.

(5) People under age 35 are avoiding auto ownership in record numbers; for this reason, a growing percentage of the automakers' sales are coming from the Far East, particularly China. (6) To attract young Westerners, auto manufacturers have made attempts at car-sharing programs, such as the Mercedes car2go program. (7) In these programs, fleets of cars sit on city streets, waiting to be unlocked by an app on subscribers' phones. (8) It's a good idea, but unreliable: such programs aren't monitored very much by city governments. (9) Furthermore, many people in urban environments argue that it's simply easier and cheaper to request a Lyft or an Uber.

(10) Whatever happens, the auto industry is in for a wrenching change. (11) Driverless cars are part of that future—but how big a part they play has yet to be determined.

41. The writer wants to expand the first paragraph. Which of the following would best amplify the ideas already present in sentence 1?

(A) An explanation of automobile manufacturers' tradition of ignoring previous designs

(B) A list of automotive ideas for the future that have not come to fruition

(C) An analysis of rejected ideas for the design of driverless automobiles

(D) A quote from an automobile design expert describing the specific aspects of the automobile that must be rethought

42. The writer would like to add a transition at the beginning of sentence 2 (reproduced below) to reflect the idea that the upcoming changes are new.

Ford Motor Company chose as its new CEO the former president of a furniture company.

Which of the following would best accomplish this goal?

(A) For example,

(B) Plus,

(C) Recently, however,

(D) In fact,

43. Which of the following sentences, if placed before sentence 5, would provide the most effective introduction to the topic of the paragraph?

(A) One consistent trend in automobile ownership is the fact that people purchase more automobiles, and more expensive ones, as they grow older.

(B) There is some evidence, however, that ride-sharing is uncomfortable for younger people, who were reared in a society filled with private automobile ownership.

(C) Older citizens who are accustomed to private automobile ownership are sitting on the sidelines, waiting for their voices to be heard.

(D) The view of private automobile ownership is changing based upon a number of other factors, particularly generational ones.

GO ON TO THE NEXT PAGE.

44. In sentence 8 (reproduced below), the writer wants to better explain the danger of excessive reliance upon auto companies.

    It's a good idea, but <u>unreliable: such programs aren't monitored very much by city governments.</u>

    Which version of the underlined text best accomplishes this goal?

    (A) (as it is now)
    (B) unreliable: the Mercedes program recently shut down its North American operations, which left many frequent users without transportation—one major hazard of depending upon private companies for public transportation.
    (C) unreliable: the Mercedes program, which was lauded by various publications when it launched, has failed to expand to many major markets, such as Asia.
    (D) unreliable: since many competing programs have arisen to compete with Mercedes, competition and tax rebates keep everything affordable.

45. The writer wants to add the following sentence to the third paragraph (sentences 5 to 9) to unite the ideas.

    Regardless, full automobile ownership plays almost no role in these rapidly multiplying urban transportation options.

    Where would the sentence best be placed?

    (A) Before sentence 5
    (B) After sentence 5
    (C) After sentence 6
    (D) After sentence 9

END OF SECTION I

AP® English Language and Composition Exam

SECTION II: Free-Response Questions

DO NOT BEGIN THE EXAM UNTIL YOU ARE TOLD TO DO SO.

DISCLAIMER: The official AP English Language and Composition Exam will be administered digitally. Instructions for the digital exam may differ from this practice test.

At a Glance

Total Time
2 hours, plus a 15-minute reading period

Number of Questions
3

Percent of Total Grade
55%

Instructions

Section II of this examination requires answers in essay form. To help you use your time well, the coordinator will announce the time at which each question should be completed. If you finish any question before time is announced, you may go on to the following question. If you finish the examination in less than the time allotted, you may go back and work on any essay question you want.

Each essay will be judged on its clarity and effectiveness in dealing with the requirements of the topic assigned and on the quality of the writing. After completing each question, you should check your essay for accuracy of punctuation, spelling, and diction; you are advised, however, not to attempt many longer corrections. Remember that quality is far more important than quantity.

Write your essays with a pen, preferably in black or dark blue ink. Be sure to write CLEARLY and LEGIBLY. Cross out any errors you make.

GO ON TO THE NEXT PAGE.

ENGLISH LANGUAGE AND COMPOSITION
SECTION II
Total Time—2 hours, 15 minutes

Question 1

Suggested reading and writing time—55 minutes.
It is suggested that you spend 15 minutes reading the question, analyzing and evaluating the sources,
and 40 minutes writing your response.
Note: You may begin writing your response before the reading period is over.

(This question counts for one-third of the total essay section score.)

In recent decades, the difference in conditions between the poorest and the wealthiest Americans—often referred to as "the wealth gap"—has grown larger and more visible. Some believe that this stratification will ultimately cause severe damage to our nation, while others argue that inequality is a natural part of any society. Some of the causes of this trend can be ascribed to technological changes, while other causes can be seen in specific policy actions.

Carefully read the following six sources, including the introductory information for each. Then synthesize the information from at least three of the sources and incorporate it into a coherent, well-developed essay that discusses the extent to which the size of the wealth gap affects the health of a society.

Your argument should be the focus of your essay. Use the sources to develop your argument and explain the reasoning for it. Avoid merely summarizing the sources. Indicate clearly which sources you are drawing from, whether through direct quotation, paraphrase, or summary. You may cite the sources as Source A, Source B, and so forth, or by using the descriptions in parentheses.

Source A   (Congressional Budget Office)
Source B   (Pew Research Center)
Source C   (Brady)
Source D   (Smith)
Source E   (Roosevelt)
Source F   (Chicago Labor)

GO ON TO THE NEXT PAGE.

The following chart was released by the Congressional Budget Office.

Holdings of Family Wealth

Trillions of 2013 Dollars

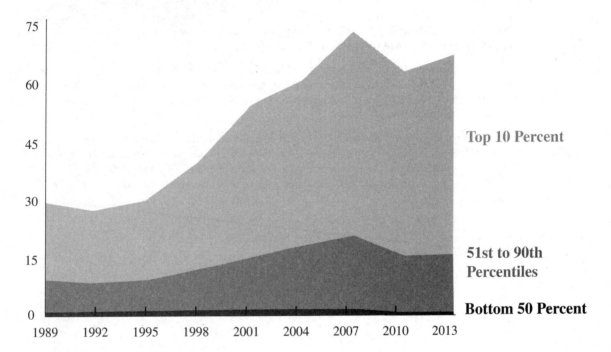

The Great Recession of 2007-2009 triggered a sharp, prolonged decline in the wealth of American families, and an already large wealth gap between white households and black and Hispanic households widened further in its immediate aftermath. But the racial and ethnic wealth gap has evolved differently for families at different income levels, according to a new Pew Research Center analysis of data from the Federal Reserve Board's Survey of Consumer Finances.

Among lower-income families, the gap between white households and their black and Hispanic counterparts *shrank* by about half from 2007 to 2016. But among middle-class families, it increased and shows no sign of retreating. (There are an insufficient number of observations in the SCF data to report on upper-income black and Hispanic families separately.)…

Among upper-income families, white households had a median net worth of $971,500 in 2016, notably higher than the overall median for this income tier. Moreover, the median wealth of upper-income white families in 2016 was 25% greater than its pre-recession level, an increase greater than for all upper-income families combined.

There is also a growing separation in wealth among white households by income tier. In 2016, upper-income white families had six times as much wealth as middle-income white families, compared with four times as much prior to the recession. Upper-income white families also had 42 times the wealth of lower-income white families in 2016, compared with 18 times the wealth in 2007.

GO ON TO THE NEXT PAGE.

Source C

Opening statement of Hon. Kevin Brady, Chairman, a U.S. representative from Texas. *Income inequality in the United States: A hearing before the Joint Economic Committee, Congress of the United States, One Hundred Thirtieth Congress, second session, January 16, 2014.*

We are not all blessed with the same talents, but in America we should all have an equal chance to climb the ladder of success—driven upward by our personal initiative, and not burdened by the deadweight of a bloated government....

Economic mobility is very much alive. In America today the children of the poorest are more likely to climb up the ladder of success than the children of the wealthy are likely to stay where they are.

Through hard work, today one in three American families live an upper-middle class lifestyle or better, more than double what it was just 40 years ago.

Astoundingly, better than one in five Americans are likely to rise to the top two percent of earners sometime during their lifetime. The American Dream is very much alive....

The real challenge we face today is too many Americans no longer believe the ladder of success is available to them. They have lost hope that if they work hard and play by the rules tomorrow will be better than today....

So finally, how should the government act to help restore Americans' belief in opportunity? We can heed the advice of President Lincoln, perhaps the greatest "equalizer" to inhabit the White House. In his message to Congress on July 4, 1861, he made clear the proper role of government in promoting economic opportunity is, quote, "to elevate men—to lift artificial weights from all shoulders—to clear the paths of laudable pursuit for all—to afford all, an unfettered start and a fair chance, in the race of life." End quote.

We must do more to "lift the artificial weights" off our poorest families and get Washington out of the way so that every American truly has "an unfettered start and a fair chance in the race of life."

I yield back, Vice Chair.

GO ON TO THE NEXT PAGE.

Source D

An Inquiry into the Nature and Causes of the Wealth of Nations, Adam Smith. March 9, 1776.

The following is an excerpt from Chapter XI of An Inquiry into the Nature and Causes of the Wealth of Nations, *by Scottish economist Adam Smith.*

The whole annual produce of the land and labour of every country, or, what comes to the same thing, the whole price of that annual produce, naturally divides itself, it has already been observed, into three parts; the rent of land, the wages of labour, and the profits of stock; and constitutes a revenue to three different orders of people; to those who live by rent, to those who live by wages, and to those who live by profit…

The interest of the first of those three great orders, it appears from what has been just now said, is strictly and inseparably connected with the general interest of the society. Whatever either promotes or obstructs the one, necessarily promotes or obstructs the other…They are the only one of the three orders whose revenue costs them neither labour nor care, but comes to them, as it were, of its own accord, and independent of any plan or project of their own. That indolence which is the natural effect of the ease and security of their situation, renders them too often, not only ignorant, but incapable of that application of mind, which is necessary in order to foresee and understand the consequence of any public regulation.

The interest of the second order, that of those who live by wages, is as strictly connected with the interest of the society as that of the first. The wages of the labourer, it has already been shewn, are never so high as when the demand for labour is continually rising, or when the quantity employed is every year increasing considerably. When this real wealth of the society becomes stationary, his wages are soon reduced to what is barely enough to enable him to bring up a family, or to continue the race of labourers. When the society declines, they fall even below this. The order of proprietors may perhaps gain more by the prosperity of the society than that of labourers; but there is no order that suffers so cruelly from its decline. But though the interest of the labourer is strictly connected with that of the society, he is incapable either of comprehending that interest, or of understanding its connexion with his own. His condition leaves him no time to receive the necessary information, and his education and habits are commonly such as to render him unfit to judge, even though he was fully informed. In the public deliberations, therefore, his voice is little heard, and less regarded; except upon particular occasions, when his clamour is animated, set on, and supported by his employers, not for his, but their own particular purposes.

His employers constitute the third order, that of those who live by profit. It is the stock that is employed for the sake of profit, which puts into motion the greater part of the useful labour of every society. The plans and projects of the employers of stock regulate and direct all the most important operation of labour, and profit is the end proposed by all those plans and projects. But the rate of profit does not, like rent and wages, rise with the prosperity, and fall with the declension of the society. On the contrary, it is naturally low in rich, and high in poor countries, and it is always highest in the countries which are going fastest to ruin. The interest of this third order, therefore, has not the same connexion with the general interest of the society, as that of the other two… To widen the market, and to narrow the competition, is always the interest of the dealers. To widen the market may frequently be agreeable enough to the interest of the public; but to narrow the competition must always be against it, and can only serve to enable the dealers, by raising their profits above what they naturally would be, to levy, for their own benefit, an absurd tax upon the rest of their fellow-citizens.

GO ON TO THE NEXT PAGE.

Source E

Theodore Roosevelt, "Address of President Roosevelt at the laying of the corner stone of the office building of the House of Representatives (The Man with the Muck Rake)" (14 April, 1906).

It is important to this people to grapple with the problems connected with the amassing of enormous fortunes, and the use of those fortunes, both corporate and individual, in business. We should discriminate in the sharpest way between fortunes well-won and fortunes ill-won; between those gained as an incident to performing great services to the community as a whole, and those gained in evil fashion by keeping just within the limits of mere law-honesty. Of course no amount of charity in spending such fortunes in any way compensates for misconduct in making them. As a matter of personal conviction, and without pretending to discuss the details or formulate the system, I feel that we shall ultimately have to consider the adoption of some such scheme as that of a progressive tax on all fortunes, beyond a certain amount either given in life or devised or bequeathed upon death to any individual—a tax so framed as to put it out of the power of the owner of one of these enormous fortunes to hand on more than a certain amount to any one individual; the tax, of course, to be imposed by the National and not the State government. Such taxation should, of course, be aimed merely at the inheritance or transmission in their entirety of those fortunes swollen beyond all healthy limits.

GO ON TO THE NEXT PAGE.

Source F

"The Condition of the Laboring Man at Pullman,"
Chicago Labor. July 7, 1894.

The following cartoon appeared in the Chicago Labor *newspaper on July 7, 1894.*

THE CONDITION OF THE LABORING MAN AT PULLMAN. —

GO ON TO THE NEXT PAGE.

Question 2

Suggested time—40 minutes.

(This question counts for one-third of the total essay section score.)

The passage that follows is an excerpt from *From Letters Written in Sweden, Norway, and Denmark*, a travelogue published in 1796 by British proto-feminist author Mary Wollstonecraft. Composed two years after her masterwork, *A Vindication of the Rights of Woman*, this series of twenty-five letters was inspired by a three-month journey to Scandinavia that she undertook after a suicide attempt. Read the passage carefully. Then, in a well-developed essay, analyze the rhetorical strategies that Wollstonecraft uses to both fulfill and transcend the travel narrative genre.

In your response, you should do the following:

- Respond to the prompt with a thesis that analyzes the writer's rhetorical choices.
- Select and use evidence to support your line of reasoning.
- Explain how the evidence supports your line of reasoning.
- Demonstrate an understanding of the rhetorical situation.
- Use appropriate grammar and punctuation in communicating your argument.

LETTER II.

Gothenburg is a clean airy town, and, having been built by the Dutch, has canals running through each street; and in some of them there are rows of trees that would render it very pleasant were it not for the pavement, which is intolerably bad.

There are several rich commercial houses—Scotch, French, and Swedish; but the Scotch, I believe, have been the most successful. The commerce and commission business with France since the war has been very lucrative, and enriched the merchants I am afraid at the expense of the other inhabitants, by raising the price of the necessaries of life.

As all the men of consequence—I mean men of the largest fortune—are merchants, their principal enjoyment is a relaxation from business at the table, which is spread at, I think, too early an hour (between one and two) for men who have letters to write and accounts to settle after paying due respect to the bottle.

However, when numerous circles are to be brought together, and when neither literature nor public amusements furnish topics for conversation, a good dinner appears to be the only centre to rally round, especially as scandal, the zest of more select parties, can only be whispered. As for politics, I have seldom found it a subject of continual discussion in a country town in any part of the world. The politics of the place, being on a smaller scale, suits better with the size of their faculties; for, generally speaking, the sphere of observation determines the extent of the mind.

The more I see of the world, the more I am convinced that civilisation is a blessing not sufficiently estimated by those who have not traced its progress; for it not only refines our enjoyments, but produces a variety which enables us to retain the primitive delicacy of our sensations. Without the aid of the imagination all the pleasures of the senses must sink into grossness, unless continual novelty serve as a substitute for the imagination, which, being impossible, it was to this weariness, I suppose, that Solomon alluded when he declared that there was nothing new under the sun!—nothing for the common sensations excited by the senses. Yet who will deny that the imagination and understanding have made many, very many discoveries since those days, which only seem harbingers of others still more noble and beneficial? I never met with much imagination amongst people who had not acquired a habit of reflection; and in that state of society in which the judgment and taste are not called forth, and formed by the cultivation of the arts and sciences, little of that delicacy of feeling and thinking is to be found characterised by the word sentiment. The want of scientific pursuits perhaps accounts for the hospitality, as well as for the cordial reception which strangers receive from the inhabitants of small towns.

GO ON TO THE NEXT PAGE.

Hospitality has, I think, been too much praised by travellers as a proof of goodness of heart, when, in my opinion, indiscriminate hospitality is rather a criterion by which you may form a tolerable estimate of the indolence or vacancy of a head; or, in other words, a fondness for social pleasures in which the mind not having its proportion of exercise, the bottle must be pushed about.

These remarks are equally applicable to Dublin, the most hospitable city I ever passed through. But I will try to confine my observations more particularly to Sweden.

It is true I have only had a glance over a small part of it; yet of its present state of manners and acquirements I think I have formed a distinct idea, without having visited the capital—where, in fact, less of a national character is to be found than in the remote parts of the country.

The Swedes pique themselves on their politeness; but far from being the polish of a cultivated mind, it consists merely of tiresome forms and ceremonies. So far, indeed, from entering immediately into your character, and making you feel instantly at your ease, like the well-bred French, their over-acted civility is a continual restraint on all your actions. The sort of superiority which a fortune gives when there is no superiority of education, excepting what consists in the observance of senseless forms, has a contrary effect than what is intended; so that I could not help reckoning the peasantry the politest people of Sweden, who, only aiming at pleasing you, never think of being admired for their behaviour.

Their tables, like their compliments, seem equally a caricature of the French. The dishes are composed, as well as theirs, of a variety of mixtures to destroy the native taste of the food without being as relishing. Spices and sugar are put into everything, even into the bread; and the only way I can account for their partiality to high-seasoned dishes is the constant use of salted provisions. Necessity obliges them to lay up a store of dried fish and salted meat for the winter; and in summer, fresh meat and fish taste insipid after them. To which may be added the constant use of spirits. Every day, before dinner and supper, even whilst the dishes are cooling on the table, men and women repair to a side-table; and to obtain an appetite eat bread-and-butter, cheese, raw salmon, or anchovies, drinking a glass of brandy. Salt fish or meat then immediately follows, to give a further whet to the stomach. As the dinner advances, pardon me for taking up a few minutes to describe what, alas! has detained me two or three hours on the stretch observing, dish after dish is changed, in endless rotation, and handed round with solemn pace to each guest; but should you happen not to like the first dishes, which was often my case, it is a gross breach of politeness to ask for part of any other till its turn comes. But have patience, and there will be eating enough. Allow me to run over the acts of a visiting day, not overlooking the interludes.

Prelude a luncheon—then a succession of fish, flesh, and fowl for two hours, during which time the dessert—I was sorry for the strawberries and cream—rests on the table to be impregnated by the fumes of the viands. Coffee immediately follows in the drawing-room, but does not preclude punch, ale, tea and cakes, raw salmon, &c. A supper brings up the rear, not forgetting the introductory luncheon, almost equalling in removes the dinner. A day of this kind you would imagine sufficient; but a to-morrow and a to-morrow—A never-ending, still-beginning feast may be bearable, perhaps, when stern winter frowns, shaking with chilling aspect his hoary locks; but during a summer, sweet as fleeting, let me, my kind strangers, escape sometimes into your fir groves, wander on the margin of your beautiful lakes, or climb your rocks, to view still others in endless perspective, which, piled by more than giant's hand, scale the heavens to intercept its rays, or to receive the parting tinge of lingering day—day that, scarcely softened unto twilight, allows the freshening breeze to wake, and the moon to burst forth in all her glory to glide with solemn elegance through the azure expanse.

The cow's bell has ceased to tinkle the herd to rest; they have all paced across the heath. Is not this the witching time of night? The waters murmur, and fall with more than mortal music, and spirits of peace walk abroad to calm the agitated breast. Eternity is in these moments. Worldly cares melt into the airy stuff that dreams are made of, and reveries, mild and enchanting as the first hopes of love or the recollection of lost enjoyment, carry the hapless wight into futurity, who in bustling life has vainly strove to throw off the grief which lies heavy at the heart. Good night! A crescent hangs out in the vault before, which woos me to stray abroad. It is not a silvery reflection of the sun, but glows with all its golden splendour. Who fears the fallen dew? It only makes the mown grass smell more fragrant. Adieu!

GO ON TO THE NEXT PAGE.

Question 3

Suggested time—40 minutes.

(This question counts for one-third of the total essay section score.)

British Prime Minister Winston Churchill (1874–1965) is remembered primarily for his stalwart leadership in the darkest days of World War II. When asked for his opinion of courage, he stated, "Courage is what it takes to stand up and speak. Courage is also what it takes to sit down and listen."

Write a carefully reasoned persuasive essay that defends, challenges, or qualifies Churchill's assertion. Use evidence from your observation, experience, or reading to develop your position.

In your response, you should do the following:

- Respond to the prompt with a thesis that may establish a line of reasoning.
- Select and use evidence to develop and support your line of reasoning.
- Explain the relationship between the evidence and your thesis.
- Demonstrate an understanding of the rhetorical situation.
- Use appropriate grammar and punctuation in communicating your argument.

STOP

END OF EXAM

_____

Practice Test 5:
Answers and
Explanations

PRACTICE TEST 5 ANSWER KEY

1.	C		24.	C
2.	B		25.	A
3.	D		26.	D
4.	A		27.	D
5.	C		28.	D
6.	C		29.	B
7.	D		30.	A
8.	C		31.	D
9.	D		32.	D
10.	B		33.	D
11.	D		34.	C
12.	A		35.	B
13.	C		36.	A
14.	D		37.	B
15.	B		38.	D
16.	A		39.	B
17.	D		40.	D
18.	D		41.	D
19.	B		42.	C
20.	B		43.	D
21.	C		44.	B
22.	B		45.	D
23.	C			

Once you have checked your answers, remember to return to page 4 and respond to the Reflect questions.

PRACTICE TEST 5 EXPLANATIONS

SECTION I: MULTIPLE CHOICE

1. **C** The stated text notes the existence of "a singularly beautiful chain of being" as well as a "scale of organization." This would suggest some type of systematic ordering of nature. While immense variety, (A), and the coexistence of humans and animals, (B), are present in nature, neither is the primary point of these lines. The text does mention "the contemplative mind" but does not indicate that contemplation is the *only* way to understand organic life, (D). Choice (C) is correct.

2. **B** First be sure to note the negative in the question, which states "*nothing* in nature." The key word in the correct answer is *separate*. Throughout the text, you can find many references to a web of connections that exists between the many disparate parts of nature—"the most perfect order" (paragraph 1), a "uniformity" and "a continuity in the series" (paragraph 3), "a singularly beautiful chain of being" (paragraph 4), "the perfection of organization" (paragraph 6), and others. None of the other answer choices reflects this idea nearly as well. Choice (B) is correct.

3. **D** The second paragraph is a single sentence that divides all matter into three categories. There follows a description of two kinds of matter (a different distinction), followed by another short paragraph—the seventh—that notes that *we can bend ourselves to the study of the more simple conditions.* The author then pulls back into an extremely abstract look at life at the atomic level. There is no empirical data or personal experience presented in the passage, so eliminate (A) and (B). Likewise, there is nothing ironic about the passage, so eliminate (C). Choice (D) is correct.

4. **A** The sixth paragraph begins with *The naturalist searches the earth, the waters, and the air, for their living things.* This is obviously a naturalist's purpose, or task. The seventh paragraph, meanwhile, states that *it is with some difficulty we can bend ourselves to the study of the more simple conditions in which it exists.* This is a little tough to interpret, but reading the next paragraphs should at least demonstrate that categories of matter are no longer being discussed. The topic has changed. Choice (B) should be eliminated because the variety of living things is discussed, but not *the difficulty of categorizing* that variety; the mention of difficulty actually occurs in the seventh paragraph. Eliminate (C) because the passage of time is out of scope. Eliminate (D) because the seventh paragraph never mentions the discovery of perfection. Choice (A) is correct.

5. **C** Context is key here. The sentence reads *Through the entire series, from the Polype to the higher order of animals....* This implies that the Polype are a lower order of animals, since the author is moving through a series, from low to high. Choice (D) is a trap for anybody who recognizes Polype as a Greek goddess; though it mentions both the underworld and the word Greek, it is severely off topic. Choice (C) is correct.

6. **C** A periodic sentence is defined as a sentence that is not grammatically complete before the final clause. In other words, it gets to the point not at the beginning, but at the end. It tends to be quite long, because it's stuffed with many dependent clauses and phrases before finally arriving at the independent clause. You can't conclude very much on inference questions; all we really know is that anybody who uses complex sentences probably has complex thoughts. No other inferences are safer than that. It's possible to achieve complex thought without a high educational level, so eliminate

(A). Intellectual validity is a vague concept—who grants it? do you need a license?—so eliminate (B). Also, you don't know the needs of the average reader in the 19th century, and whatever those needs may have been, they're outside the scope of the question, so eliminate (D). Choice (C) is correct.

7. **D** In (D), the author describes the way that *an alchemist…dissipates a metal in vapour*, then notes that *it remains a metal, and the same metal still.* This describes the tendency of matter to retain its original identity. It does not relate to the *interconnectedness of nature* mentioned in the question, which the other three answers do. Choice (D) is correct.

8. **C** The first sentence notes the *feelings of religious admiration* that we experience when we look at nature. Likewise, the third paragraph discusses *the mystery of life, a pervading spiritual essence*, and *an Infinite mind.* This indicates a mystical outlook. While there is a case to be made for *methodical*, (D), note the title of the book: *The Poetry of Science.* Choice (C) is correct.

9. **D** This one is a little tricky, because *it* refers to *each one*, at the beginning of that independent clause. However, *each one* isn't an answer choice, so find the antecedent. *Each one* refers to *every atom* at the beginning of the sentence. At the very least, recognize that *it* is singular, so immediately eliminate (A) and (B), since they're plural nouns. Choice (D) is correct.

10. **B** The single sentence that forms the seventh paragraph signals an end to the categorizing of classes of matter discussed in the sixth paragraph. At the same time, it signals a switch to a more abstract topic—*the more simple conditions* in which matter exists, namely a laughably antiquated discussion of atomic theory, one that includes alchemy, in the eighth paragraph. (Hey, it was 1848.) Eliminate (D) because the author is describing the conditions in which the conditions of the previous paragraph occur, which is not amplification. The syntactic structure of *so…that…*doesn't indicate a redefinition, so eliminate (C). While the paragraph is definitely ambiguous, there is no single concept being addressed, and certainly not being explained. So eliminate (A). Choice (B) is correct.

11. **D** Between the dashes the author makes a list of four different types of plants: *confervae* (algae), *lichen, lordly oak,* and *towering palm.* The first two are small; the last two are large, made even bigger by their accompanying adjectives. Therefore, the purpose of this list of words is to illustrate the scale of plants in the natural world. The other answers have all been misinterpreted to varying degrees, or are out of scope.

12. **A** The text discusses a *symmetrical arrangement*, a *systematic aggregation*, and *powers of a strangely complicated kind.* These phrases point towards (A), *an innate sense of order underlying all of creation.* Choice (B) is a trap; while the passage does note that *science with all its refinements has not detected the agencies* that order the universe, the passage does not state that those agencies are *undetectable.* Likewise, though the paragraph does discuss minerals, it is never implied that living things become mineralized, so eliminate (C). No chaos is ever mentioned or suggested, nor is a watchful overspirit; eliminate (D). Choice (A) is correct.

13. **C** The word *gravity*, found in the question, is a synonym of *importance*—and that word is used in two different forms in the same paragraph (paragraph 5). Doing things in an *ethical and timely manner* is irrelevant to the gravity of the situation, so eliminate (A). So are *a multidisciplinary approach* and *controlled substances*, so eliminate (B) and (D). Choice (C) is correct.

14. **D**   The second and third paragraphs contain mostly statistics and statements of fact about the medical examiner's process of responding to deaths. There is little else offered except facts, not even conclusions. On the whole, this is what might be called "dry" reading. It's also close to *logos*, or logical reasoning, which Aristotle ranked as the least effective appeal out of the main trio of *ethos, pathos,* and *logos.* Choice (D) is correct.

15. **B**   This passage is fairly simple in its aim: The authors describe for the reader how the medical examiner's office goes about investigating deaths in San Diego County. In that sense, there is no argument being made here—it's a simple description of a process, using a fair amount of detail. There is no analysis of *efficiency* or *objections*, so eliminate (A) and (C). The article does not claim to cover all of the office's tasks (too extreme), so eliminate (D). Choice (B) is correct.

16. **A**   The passive tense is used when the tasks being completed are the focus of the writing, rather than the people who are performing them. The information presented doesn't involve much emphasis on the individuals performing these tasks, so (A) is correct.

17. **D**   Process analysis is the mode of this essay. The authors are describing the medical examiners' office's process of investigating deaths at home. There is simply no narration, (A), definition of terminology, (B), or analogies of any kind, (C). Choice (D) is correct.

18. **D**   The tone of this piece is structured, disciplined, cautious, and quantitative. Answer choices with words such as *methodical, structured, systematic, investigative,* and *comprehensive* all reflect that tone. However, the tone is unemotional and detached, which rules out *helping ease the difficulties.* Choice (D) is correct.

19. **B**   Most of this passage strikes a serious, patient tone, which is appropriate given that it was written by and about a group of professional investigators. However, the final paragraph changes that tone. The authors remind us that these investigators have *caring attitudes* and *compassion.* These are the first emotional words used in the entire passage. Choice (B) is correct.

20. **B**   Infer and imply questions are touchy, and the best answers are the safest, smallest conclusions that can be drawn from the paragraph. In this case, the safest conclusion is that *medications sometimes play a role in deaths that occur at home.* Choice (A) is too large of a conclusion, because it says *any person's home* rather than just the home of a deceased person. There is no evidence in the passage to support (C) or (D). Choice (B) is correct.

21. **C**   *Ethos* is a rhetorical appeal using the speaker's ethical character. It is noted by Aristotle as being the most effective of the trio of rhetorical appeals: *ethos, pathos,* and *logos.* In this case, the authors' testimony to the positive characteristics of the investigators is a rather obvious instance of *ethos.* Choice (C) is correct.

22. **B**   The investigators are not serving as literal eyes and ears of the medical examiner; that person presumably has a pair of eyes and ears of their own. Therefore, their service as the eyes and ears of the medical examiner must be metaphorical. The trap answer, (D), can be eliminated because there is no analogy being drawn. Instead, it's a piece of figurative language. Choice (B) is correct.

23. **C**   A *denotation* is a first definition of a word. A *connotation* is a secondary or tertiary definition of a word, often something more obscure that not everybody can grasp. However, the purpose of this report is not to obscure meaning—its purpose is to be quite clear and transparent. The words used in this passage do not carry secondary meanings; they are clear and unmistakable denotations, as befits a report by and about scientific investigators. Eliminate (A) because the fourth paragraph is full of scientific description; eliminate (B) because the second and third paragraphs are filled with statistics, e.g., quantifiable evidence. Terms such as *decedent* and *bereavement* and *inappropriate* indicate formal syntax, so eliminate (D). Choice (C) is correct.

24. **C**   Only (C) contains both sensory language—*Yellow plantains, red coffee beans, tall green wax palms, clear waterfalls tumbling from misty mountains*—and a contrast with the violence of city life. Some choices, such as (A) and (D), contain sensory language but no contrast. Choice (B) contrasts with the following sentences but does not contain sensory language. The answer is (C).

25. **A**   Watch for referent words such as *this* and *such*—these words often provide the linguistic hook to an idea expressed in a previous sentence. In this case, *this* refers to *an unfair reputation for violence* described in sentence 1. Therefore, the best placement of the sentence should be immediately following sentence 1, or *before sentence 2*, which is (A).

26. **D**   Because the paragraph illustrates with numbers the story of Colombia's decreasing levels of violence, select a transition sentence that simply eases us from anecdotal to statistical evidence. Choice (A) features the pronoun *you*—among other problems—so eliminate it. Choice (B) is tempting, but the point of the paragraph is not to highlight the *incomplete* nature of the evidence, so eliminate that too. Choice (C) introduces doubt as to the trustworthiness of the statistics, eliminate it. The answer is (D).

27. **D**   Consider sentence 13, the following sentence, when making your decision: *Other cities of the United States have suffered similarly unfair derogation.* This indicates that the previous sentence, sentence 12, should describe some type of criticism of U.S. cities. The current sentence discusses the city of Cali, Colombia. Because of that, either moving or deleting sentence 13 would work best. Unfortunately, however, because the entire paragraph is structured as a compare-and-contrast between Medellín and Chicago, there is little thematic room for information about a third city. The sentence should be deleted, so the answer is (D).

28. **D**   Read the question carefully; it asks for an answer choice that reflects *Detroit's historical success and subsequent decline.* Choice (D) mentions Detroit's former status as *the fourth-largest city in the nation* (historical success) as well as the fact that its *population has dropped by almost seventy percent* (subsequent decline). The other choices are missing one or both of these requirements.

29. **B**   Sentences 15 and 16 return to discussing Colombia and describe the rise of theft, which is a nonviolent crime. Therefore, the inserted sentence needs to mention Colombia and pivot away from violent crime—the focus of the previous paragraphs—to nonviolent crime. Eliminate (A). Choice (B) does this directly and succinctly, while the other answer choices all compare violent and nonviolent crime.

30. **A** Only (A) accurately depicts the idea that public rehabilitation of cities' images is growing across the world. Choice (D) does have a global scope but refers to the nonexistence of this phenomenon; eliminate it. Choice (C) implies that this phenomenon is more important in Western cities than globally, which is a misinterpretation of the question stem; eliminate it as well. And while (B) does display an appropriate discussion of the increasingly global nature of something, that something is the wrong topic, social networking, so eliminate this too. The answer is (A).

31. **D** The problem with the underlined portion is that *they* has an unclear antecedent, since no plural noun exists in the prior sentence. Eliminate (A) and (B). Starting any sentence with *There is*, while not incorrect, is by nature weaker than using a concrete noun as the subject, so eliminate (C). The answer is (D).

32. **D** In the original sentence, there are three terms that contribute to an informal tone—*huge, irrevocably*, and *whole mess*. The correct answer will change all three of those, so eliminate (A). Choice (B) keeps the word *irrevocably*, which is a word of exaggeration and should be removed; eliminate (B). Choice (C) successfully changes or deletes all three terms, but the new phrase *like crazy* is still informal; eliminate (C). Choice (D) eliminates all three terms, changes one of them to *rapid rise*, and then inserts the formal phrase *as a viable career option*. The answer is (D).

33. **D** Ask yourself what could've resulted in *a garage filled with stacks of unsold titles that were sure to be pulped*. It isn't normal to begin an essay with a discussion of a result without first mentioning the cause, so eliminate (A). Likewise, these unsold titles could be related to the huge explosion of self-publishing, but there is no specific evidence of that; eliminate (B). Choice (C) may look a bit more promising, but placing the sentence here separates the stigma of self-published books from the reason for the stigma. However, once sentence 3 discusses how the self-published author *pays for the production of the books*, it is then safe to discuss a logical outcome of that—the possibility that they may not be able to sell them. Choice (D) is correct.

34. **C** Since the question asks about the main idea of the passage, it might be a good idea to save it for last. In the remainder of the passage, the writer clearly views self-publishing as a tremendous gift for writers. Therefore, this sentence should reflect that same point-of-view. Only (C) uses language of that type—the *long overdue* transformation, and especially *in favor of the writer*. The other answer choices are not necessarily incorrect, either in fact or in bias, but none of them reflects the writer-centric quality of the new publishing landscape that Amazon created.

35. **B** Remember that the question is asking for *convincing evidence that Amazon democratized book publishing*. This is different from providing evidence that traditional publishing is suffering. Proving an opposing argument wrong is different from proving your argument to be right. Choices (C) and (D), while offering decent evidence of a decline in traditional publishing, don't directly support the notion that *Amazon democratized book publishing*. (They do indirectly imply the idea, however.) Eliminate both. Only (B) provides specific evidence to support this claim.

36. **A** The original sentence discusses opposing ideas—fast success versus slow success—so the correct answer will feature connective words that show contrast. For this reason, eliminate (B), (C), and (D), since *and, furthermore*, and *so* are all transition words showing continuity. Choice (A) is correct.

37.   **B**   The main idea of the paragraph is that a torrent of self-published titles made their way into the book marketplace. Choice (A) is a humorous aside that doesn't support the main idea, since some of these independently published books were in fact made of paper; eliminate it. Choice (C) can be eliminated because it mentions the long tail theory without explaining anything about it, even though that concept would be germane here. Choice (D) supports the opposite idea from that of the paragraph, eliminate it. The answer is (B).

38.   **D**   Read the sentences that follow. Sentence 12 discusses the added business responsibilities that self-published authors must shoulder, while sentence 13 discusses the possible financial windfall that comes to self-published authors as a result of making seventy percent of list price (instead of a paltry fourteen percent). The sentence that addresses both of those ideas, to an appropriate degree, and with different language, is (D). Choice (B) does address both of those ideas as well, but the word *only* is extreme and inaccurate, since the writer never states that only business-minded writers make profits. The other three answers are more general and fail to address either idea directly. The answer is (D).

39.   **B**   Remember the two simplest options for transitions—ideas that move in the same direction, or ideas that move in opposite directions. These two sentences are set in opposition to one another. Therefore, eliminate any answer choice that uses transition words indicating continuity of thought. Since (A) and (C) use *for* and *and*, eliminate both. Likewise, a dash is typically used to express continuity of expression, so eliminate (D). To show contrast, do not rely on implied or vague contrast; select answers with clear and explicit contrast words such as *but, yet, while, though,* and *however.* The answer is (B).

40.   **D**   Keep in mind conciseness and clarity: the correct answer must create both. The original sentence is neither concise nor clear and can be eliminated. Choice (B) is concise, but it vaguely implies that electronic books will be read on mobile phones in the future, when in fact that is already happening. Eliminate (B). Choice (C) attempts to clarify the sentence by creating parallelism using *1, 2, and 3 structure,* but unfortunately the third item—mobile phones—aren't consumed in the same way that the first two items are. Eliminate (C). The answer is (D).

41.   **D**   Sentence 1 states that *nobody really knows what [a driverless car] should look like.* Therefore, a better explanation of what that entails would naturally follow, which (D) provides—and it carries even more weight when coming from the mouth of an expert. Choice (A) would support the idea of constant innovation, which is the opposite of what's implied, so eliminate it. Choice (B) is outside the scope of driverless cars, so eliminate it. Choice (C) is the trap answer, because while it's close to being on topic, there is no need to understand why certain designs were rejected without knowing what aspects of driverless automobile design need to be changed to begin with. The answer is (D).

42.   **C**   This is a straightforward transition question. *Recently* tells us that something is a new development, and *however* indicates that there's a contrast with the idea in the previous paragraph. No other answer describes anything new. The answer is (C).

43. **D** Because the paragraph discusses many other aspects of transportation that affect consumer behavior—such as generational changes and ride-sharing apps—the topic sentence should mention *a number of other factors*, which (D) does. The additional phrase *particularly generational ones* sets up sentence 5 perfectly. The other answers do address generational issues in car ownership, such as (A), (B), and (C), but they've all slightly misinterpreted the meaning of the paragraph. The answer is (D).

44. **B** The sentence is supposed to transmit *the danger of excessive reliance upon auto companies*. Choice (B) illustrates the way that Mercedes pulled the rug out from beneath its users by closing all of its North American operations, leaving many without a method of getting to work. Mercedes' failure to expand the program to Asia doesn't indicate any lack of reliability, so eliminate (C). Choice (D) discusses affordability, which is not the purpose of the question; eliminate it. The answer is (B).

45. **D** The reference to *these rapidly multiplying urban transportation options* implies that the previous sentences would feature discussions of those options. Since most of the paragraph concerns those options, this sentence is best placed at or near the end; eliminate (A), (B), and (C). The answer is (D).

SECTION II: FREE RESPONSE

Rubric—1 + 4 + 1 = 6 pts

A. Thesis (0–1 pts)
   - Responds to the prompt with a thesis that presents a defensible interpretation of the selected work.

B. Evidence and Commentary (0–4 pts)
   - Evidence: Provides specific evidence to support all claims in a line of reasoning.
   - Commentary: Consistently explains how the evidence supports a line of reasoning.
   - Explains how multiple literary elements or techniques in the poem contribute to its meaning.

C. Sophistication (0–1 pts)
   - Demonstrates sophistication of thought and/or develops a complex literary argument.

Question 1—Synthesis Essay

How to Score 6 Points
- Address the prompt with a defensible thesis.
- Present specific evidence from at least three sources and consistently explain how the evidence supports your thesis statement.
- Use style and rhetoric to persuade the reader.

Source Overview

Source A: The Congressional Budget Office reports that wealth held by the top 10% of families has radically increased between 1989 and 2013.

Source B: While the income gap by race among low-income Americans shrank in the wake of the Great Recession, the wealth gap held by upper-income white families dramatically increased and continues to do so.

Source C: According to Hon. Kevin Brady, a U.S. representative from Texas, the American Dream of social mobility is still accessible in the U.S. today. The government must remove unnecessary burdens to economic success.

Source D: Adam Smith divides society into three groups: landowners, workers, and business owners. Landowners earn passively, and their income is tied to the overall success of society; workers earn well when demand for labor is high, but they suffer when economic growth stalls; business owners increase their profits to the detriment of others in society.

Source E: According to Theodore Roosevelt, it's problematic for an individual to amass a large fortune. There ought to be a progressive inheritance tax to redistribute wealth among the population.

Source F: This cartoon depicts a leader of industry abusing workers with simultaneous high rents and low wages.

Sample First Paragraph

There are many ways to measure the health of a society: lifespan, access to education and opportunity, individual wealth, or even gross domestic product. One such measure is the "wealth gap," or the difference in conditions between the poorest and wealthiest Americans. While absolute economic equality may be unattainable, and perhaps even undesirable, recent evidence suggests that as the wealth gap increases, it does so to the detriment of society overall.

Question 2—Rhetorical Analysis Essay

How to Score 6 Points

Use the Rhetorical Diamond! While you're reading the prompt and the passage, imagine—and try to flesh out—a baseball diamond with the following six points:

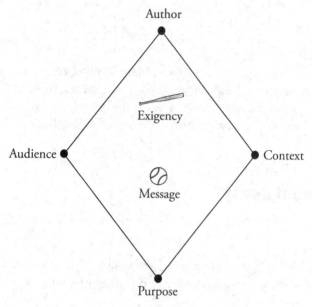

Author: Mary Wollstonecraft
Audience: British readers curious about life abroad
Purpose: As a travelogue, to amuse, entertain, perhaps inspire
Context: Written in 1796 by an author known for social criticism
Exigency: Wollstonecraft's timely travels ("since the war") and cultural observations
Message: The influx of wealth in the Swedish merchant-class has led to an absurd caricature of sophistication.

Sample Rhetorical Modes and Devices

- **Cause and effect:** "There are several rich commercial houses—Scotch, French, and Swedish; but the Scotch, I believe, have been the most successful. The commerce and commission business with France since the war has been very lucrative, and enriched the merchants I am afraid at the expense of the other inhabitants, by raising the price of the necessaries of life."
- **Definition:** "As all the men of consequence—I mean men of the largest fortune—are merchants, their principal enjoyment is a relaxation from business at the table, which is spread at, I think, too early an hour (between one and two) for men who have letters to write and accounts to settle after paying due respect to the bottle."
- **Definition:** "Hospitality has, I think, been too much praised by travellers as a proof of goodness of heart, when, in my opinion, indiscriminate hospitality is rather a criterion by which you may form a tolerable estimate of the indolence or vacancy of a head; or, in other words, a fondness for social pleasures in which the mind not having its proportion of exercise, the bottle must be pushed about."

- **Situational irony:** "The sort of superiority which a fortune gives when there is no superiority of education, excepting what consists in the observance of senseless forms, has a contrary effect than what is intended; so that I could not help reckoning the peasantry the politest people of Sweden, who, only aiming at pleasing you, never think of being admired for their behaviour."
- **Situational irony:** "Prelude a luncheon—then a succession of fish, flesh, and fowl for two hours, during which time the dessert—I was sorry for the strawberries and cream—rests on the table to be impregnated by the fumes of the viands. Coffee immediately follows in the drawing-room, but does not preclude punch, ale, tea and cakes, raw salmon, &c."

Sample First Paragraph

Traveling on the continent in the wake of a European war, Mary Wollstonecraft, an author known for social criticism, turns her lens away from her native England and toward the Swedish town of Gothenburg. Wollstonecraft uses a combination of definition and situational irony to describe the impact that an influx of capital has had on the Swedes, portraying the merchant class as an absurd caricature of sophistication.

Question 3—Argument Essay

How to Score 6 Points

- Take a definite position, so no one will question where you stand on the topic of the prompt.
- Develop an argument that builds and moves forward instead of simply repeating the same point several times in different ways.
- Support the points in your argument with evidence drawn from your own knowledge, reading, experiences, and observations.
- Explain how your evidence supports your argument.

Sample Evidence

- Receiving any type of criticism takes courage. Rehearsing for a play, turning in the first draft of an essay, or submitting a photograph to be critiqued. Being vulnerable to the opinions of others is scary.
- In *Oedipus Rex*, Oedipus has the courage to face the sphinx, but doesn't have the courage to accept the truth Tiresias tries to tell him about his own identity.
- Prime Minister Churchill and President Roosevelt collaborated with Premier Joseph Stalin of Russia to end World War II.
- I was terrified of my Biology teacher in ninth grade, but pointed out an error she made in grading my final exam anyway.

Sample First Paragraph

Known for both his wit and steadfast leadership against German aggression in World War II, British Prime Minister Winston Churchill described courage as "what it takes to stand up and speak," as well as "what it takes to sit down and listen." While courage is certainly required to speak out against a perceived threat, humility is a far more critical characteristic required to consider an opposing point of view.

Completely darken bubbles with a No. 2 pencil. If you make a mistake, be sure to erase mark completely. Erase all stray marks.

1. YOUR NAME:
(Print)
Last   First   M.I.

SIGNATURE: DATE: /   /

HOME ADDRESS:
(Print)
    Number and Street

    City   State   Zip Code

PHONE NO. :
(Print)

5. YOUR NAME

First 4 letters of last name					FIRST INIT	MID INIT

(A)(A)(A)(A)   (A)(A)
(B)(B)(B)(B)   (B)(B)
(C)(C)(C)(C)   (C)(C)
(D)(D)(D)(D)   (D)(D)
(E)(E)(E)(E)   (E)(E)
(F)(F)(F)(F)   (F)(F)
(G)(G)(G)(G)   (G)(G)
(H)(H)(H)(H)   (H)(H)
(I)(I)(I)(I)   (I)(I)
(J)(J)(J)(J)   (J)(J)
(K)(K)(K)(K)   (K)(K)
(L)(L)(L)(L)   (L)(L)
(M)(M)(M)(M)   (M)(M)
(N)(N)(N)(N)   (N)(N)
(O)(O)(O)(O)   (O)(O)
(P)(P)(P)(P)   (P)(P)
(Q)(Q)(Q)(Q)   (Q)(Q)
(R)(R)(R)(R)   (R)(R)
(S)(S)(S)(S)   (S)(S)
(T)(T)(T)(T)   (T)(T)
(U)(U)(U)(U)   (U)(U)
(V)(V)(V)(V)   (V)(V)
(W)(W)(W)(W)   (W)(W)
(X)(X)(X)(X)   (X)(X)
(Y)(Y)(Y)(Y)   (Y)(Y)
(Z)(Z)(Z)(Z)   (Z)(Z)

IMPORTANT: Please fill in these boxes exactly as shown on the back cover of your test book.

2. TEST FORM

3. TEST CODE

4. REGISTRATION NUMBER

6. DATE OF BIRTH

Month	Day	Year

JAN
FEB
MAR
APR
MAY
JUN
JUL
AUG
SEP
OCT
NOV
DEC

(0)(0)(0)(0)
(1)(1)(1)(1)
(2)(2)(2)(2)
(3)(3)(3)(3)
(4)(4)(4)
(5)(5)(5)
(6)(6)(6)
(7)(7)(7)
(8)(8)(8)
(9)(9)(9)

Test Code column:
(0)(A)(0)(0)(0)   (0)(0)(0)(0)(0)(0)
(1)(B)(1)(1)(1)   (1)(1)(1)(1)(1)(1)
(2)(C)(2)(2)(2)   (2)(2)(2)(2)(2)(2)
(3)(D)(3)(3)(3)   (3)(3)(3)(3)(3)(3)
(4)(E)(4)(4)(4)   (4)(4)(4)(4)(4)(4)
(5)(F)(5)(5)(5)   (5)(5)(5)(5)(5)(5)
(6)(G)(6)(6)(6)   (6)(6)(6)(6)(6)(6)
(7)(7)(7)   (7)(7)(7)(7)(7)(7)
(8)(8)(8)   (8)(8)(8)(8)(8)(8)
(9)(9)(9)   (9)(9)(9)(9)(9)(9)

The **Princeton Review**®

Section ①   Start with number 1 for each new section.
If a section has fewer questions than answer spaces, leave the extra answer spaces blank.

1. (A) (B) (C) (D) (E)
2. (A) (B) (C) (D) (E)
3. (A) (B) (C) (D) (E)
4. (A) (B) (C) (D) (E)
5. (A) (B) (C) (D) (E)
6. (A) (B) (C) (D) (E)
7. (A) (B) (C) (D) (E)
8. (A) (B) (C) (D) (E)
9. (A) (B) (C) (D) (E)
10. (A) (B) (C) (D) (E)
11. (A) (B) (C) (D) (E)
12. (A) (B) (C) (D) (E)

13. (A) (B) (C) (D) (E)
14. (A) (B) (C) (D) (E)
15. (A) (B) (C) (D) (E)
16. (A) (B) (C) (D) (E)
17. (A) (B) (C) (D) (E)
18. (A) (B) (C) (D) (E)
19. (A) (B) (C) (D) (E)
20. (A) (B) (C) (D) (E)
21. (A) (B) (C) (D) (E)
22. (A) (B) (C) (D) (E)
23. (A) (B) (C) (D) (E)
24. (A) (B) (C) (D) (E)

25. (A) (B) (C) (D) (E)
26. (A) (B) (C) (D) (E)
27. (A) (B) (C) (D) (E)
28. (A) (B) (C) (D) (E)
29. (A) (B) (C) (D) (E)
30. (A) (B) (C) (D) (E)
31. (A) (B) (C) (D) (E)
32. (A) (B) (C) (D) (E)
33. (A) (B) (C) (D) (E)
34. (A) (B) (C) (D) (E)
35. (A) (B) (C) (D) (E)
36. (A) (B) (C) (D) (E)

37. (A) (B) (C) (D) (E)
38. (A) (B) (C) (D) (E)
39. (A) (B) (C) (D) (E)
40. (A) (B) (C) (D) (E)
41. (A) (B) (C) (D) (E)
42. (A) (B) (C) (D) (E)
43. (A) (B) (C) (D) (E)
44. (A) (B) (C) (D) (E)
45. (A) (B) (C) (D) (E)

NOTES

The **Princeton Review**®

Completely darken bubbles with a No. 2 pencil. If you make a mistake, be sure to erase mark completely. Erase all stray marks.

1. YOUR NAME:
(Print)
Last   First   M.I.

SIGNATURE: _____ DATE: ____ / ____ / ____

HOME ADDRESS: _____
(Print)
Number and Street

_____
City   State   Zip Code

PHONE NO. : _____
(Print)

IMPORTANT: Please fill in these boxes exactly as shown on the back cover of your test book.

2. TEST FORM

3. TEST CODE

4. REGISTRATION NUMBER

6. DATE OF BIRTH

Month		Day		Year	
◯ JAN					
◯ FEB					
◯ MAR	⓪	⓪	⓪	⓪	
◯ APR	①	①	①	①	
◯ MAY	②	②	②	②	
◯ JUN	③	③	③	③	
◯ JUL		④	④	④	
◯ AUG		⑤	⑤	⑤	
◯ SEP		⑥	⑥	⑥	
◯ OCT		⑦	⑦	⑦	
◯ NOV		⑧	⑧	⑧	
◯ DEC		⑨	⑨	⑨	

5. YOUR NAME

First 4 letters of last name   FIRST INIT   MID INIT

The **Princeton Review**®

Section ① Start with number 1 for each new section.
If a section has fewer questions than answer spaces, leave the extra answer spaces blank.

1. Ⓐ Ⓑ Ⓒ Ⓓ Ⓔ
2. Ⓐ Ⓑ Ⓒ Ⓓ Ⓔ
3. Ⓐ Ⓑ Ⓒ Ⓓ Ⓔ
4. Ⓐ Ⓑ Ⓒ Ⓓ Ⓔ
5. Ⓐ Ⓑ Ⓒ Ⓓ Ⓔ
6. Ⓐ Ⓑ Ⓒ Ⓓ Ⓔ
7. Ⓐ Ⓑ Ⓒ Ⓓ Ⓔ
8. Ⓐ Ⓑ Ⓒ Ⓓ Ⓔ
9. Ⓐ Ⓑ Ⓒ Ⓓ Ⓔ
10. Ⓐ Ⓑ Ⓒ Ⓓ Ⓔ
11. Ⓐ Ⓑ Ⓒ Ⓓ Ⓔ
12. Ⓐ Ⓑ Ⓒ Ⓓ Ⓔ

13. Ⓐ Ⓑ Ⓒ Ⓓ Ⓔ
14. Ⓐ Ⓑ Ⓒ Ⓓ Ⓔ
15. Ⓐ Ⓑ Ⓒ Ⓓ Ⓔ
16. Ⓐ Ⓑ Ⓒ Ⓓ Ⓔ
17. Ⓐ Ⓑ Ⓒ Ⓓ Ⓔ
18. Ⓐ Ⓑ Ⓒ Ⓓ Ⓔ
19. Ⓐ Ⓑ Ⓒ Ⓓ Ⓔ
20. Ⓐ Ⓑ Ⓒ Ⓓ Ⓔ
21. Ⓐ Ⓑ Ⓒ Ⓓ Ⓔ
22. Ⓐ Ⓑ Ⓒ Ⓓ Ⓔ
23. Ⓐ Ⓑ Ⓒ Ⓓ Ⓔ
24. Ⓐ Ⓑ Ⓒ Ⓓ Ⓔ

25. Ⓐ Ⓑ Ⓒ Ⓓ Ⓔ
26. Ⓐ Ⓑ Ⓒ Ⓓ Ⓔ
27. Ⓐ Ⓑ Ⓒ Ⓓ Ⓔ
28. Ⓐ Ⓑ Ⓒ Ⓓ Ⓔ
29. Ⓐ Ⓑ Ⓒ Ⓓ Ⓔ
30. Ⓐ Ⓑ Ⓒ Ⓓ Ⓔ
31. Ⓐ Ⓑ Ⓒ Ⓓ Ⓔ
32. Ⓐ Ⓑ Ⓒ Ⓓ Ⓔ
33. Ⓐ Ⓑ Ⓒ Ⓓ Ⓔ
34. Ⓐ Ⓑ Ⓒ Ⓓ Ⓔ
35. Ⓐ Ⓑ Ⓒ Ⓓ Ⓔ
36. Ⓐ Ⓑ Ⓒ Ⓓ Ⓔ

37. Ⓐ Ⓑ Ⓒ Ⓓ Ⓔ
38. Ⓐ Ⓑ Ⓒ Ⓓ Ⓔ
39. Ⓐ Ⓑ Ⓒ Ⓓ Ⓔ
40. Ⓐ Ⓑ Ⓒ Ⓓ Ⓔ
41. Ⓐ Ⓑ Ⓒ Ⓓ Ⓔ
42. Ⓐ Ⓑ Ⓒ Ⓓ Ⓔ
43. Ⓐ Ⓑ Ⓒ Ⓓ Ⓔ
44. Ⓐ Ⓑ Ⓒ Ⓓ Ⓔ
45. Ⓐ Ⓑ Ⓒ Ⓓ Ⓔ

NOTES

Completely darken bubbles with a No. 2 pencil. If you make a mistake, be sure to erase mark completely. Erase all stray marks.

1. YOUR NAME:
(Print) _____ Last _____ First _____ M.I.
SIGNATURE: _____ DATE: ___ / ___ / ___

HOME ADDRESS: _____
(Print) _____ Number and Street
_____ City _____ State _____ Zip Code

PHONE NO. : _____
(Print)

IMPORTANT: Please fill in these boxes exactly as shown on the back cover of your test book.

2. TEST FORM
_____
_____

6. DATE OF BIRTH

Month		Day		Year	
○ JAN					
○ FEB					
○ MAR	⓪	⓪	⓪	⓪	
○ APR	①	①	①	①	
○ MAY	②	②	②	②	
○ JUN	③	③	③	③	
○ JUL		④	④	④	
○ AUG		⑤	⑤	⑤	
○ SEP		⑥	⑥	⑥	
○ OCT		⑦	⑦	⑦	
○ NOV		⑧	⑧	⑧	
○ DEC		⑨	⑨	⑨	

3. TEST CODE   **4. REGISTRATION NUMBER**

⓪	Ⓐ	⓪	⓪	⓪	⓪	⓪	⓪	⓪	⓪	⓪
①	Ⓑ	①	①	①	①	①	①	①	①	①
②	Ⓒ	②	②	②	②	②	②	②	②	②
③	Ⓓ	③	③	③	③	③	③	③	③	③
④	Ⓔ	④	④	④	④	④	④	④	④	④
⑤	Ⓕ	⑤	⑤	⑤	⑤	⑤	⑤	⑤	⑤	⑤
⑥	Ⓖ	⑥	⑥	⑥	⑥	⑥	⑥	⑥	⑥	⑥
⑦		⑦	⑦	⑦	⑦	⑦	⑦	⑦	⑦	⑦
⑧		⑧	⑧	⑧	⑧	⑧	⑧	⑧	⑧	⑧
⑨		⑨	⑨	⑨	⑨	⑨	⑨	⑨	⑨	⑨

The **Princeton Review**®

5. YOUR NAME

First 4 letters of last name					FIRST INIT	MID INIT
Ⓐ	Ⓐ	Ⓐ	Ⓐ		Ⓐ	Ⓐ
Ⓑ	Ⓑ	Ⓑ	Ⓑ		Ⓑ	Ⓑ
Ⓒ	Ⓒ	Ⓒ	Ⓒ		Ⓒ	Ⓒ
Ⓓ	Ⓓ	Ⓓ	Ⓓ		Ⓓ	Ⓓ
Ⓔ	Ⓔ	Ⓔ	Ⓔ		Ⓔ	Ⓔ
Ⓕ	Ⓕ	Ⓕ	Ⓕ		Ⓕ	Ⓕ
Ⓖ	Ⓖ	Ⓖ	Ⓖ		Ⓖ	Ⓖ
Ⓗ	Ⓗ	Ⓗ	Ⓗ		Ⓗ	Ⓗ
Ⓘ	Ⓘ	Ⓘ	Ⓘ		Ⓘ	Ⓘ
Ⓙ	Ⓙ	Ⓙ	Ⓙ		Ⓙ	Ⓙ
Ⓚ	Ⓚ	Ⓚ	Ⓚ		Ⓚ	Ⓚ
Ⓛ	Ⓛ	Ⓛ	Ⓛ		Ⓛ	Ⓛ
Ⓜ	Ⓜ	Ⓜ	Ⓜ		Ⓜ	Ⓜ
Ⓝ	Ⓝ	Ⓝ	Ⓝ		Ⓝ	Ⓝ
Ⓞ	Ⓞ	Ⓞ	Ⓞ		Ⓞ	Ⓞ
Ⓟ	Ⓟ	Ⓟ	Ⓟ		Ⓟ	Ⓟ
Ⓠ	Ⓠ	Ⓠ	Ⓠ		Ⓠ	Ⓠ
Ⓡ	Ⓡ	Ⓡ	Ⓡ		Ⓡ	Ⓡ
Ⓢ	Ⓢ	Ⓢ	Ⓢ		Ⓢ	Ⓢ
Ⓣ	Ⓣ	Ⓣ	Ⓣ		Ⓣ	Ⓣ
Ⓤ	Ⓤ	Ⓤ	Ⓤ		Ⓤ	Ⓤ
Ⓥ	Ⓥ	Ⓥ	Ⓥ		Ⓥ	Ⓥ
Ⓦ	Ⓦ	Ⓦ	Ⓦ		Ⓦ	Ⓦ
Ⓧ	Ⓧ	Ⓧ	Ⓧ		Ⓧ	Ⓧ
Ⓨ	Ⓨ	Ⓨ	Ⓨ		Ⓨ	Ⓨ
Ⓩ	Ⓩ	Ⓩ	Ⓩ		Ⓩ	Ⓩ

Section ①

Start with number 1 for each new section.
If a section has fewer questions than answer spaces, leave the extra answer spaces blank.

1. Ⓐ Ⓑ Ⓒ Ⓓ Ⓔ
2. Ⓐ Ⓑ Ⓒ Ⓓ Ⓔ
3. Ⓐ Ⓑ Ⓒ Ⓓ Ⓔ
4. Ⓐ Ⓑ Ⓒ Ⓓ Ⓔ
5. Ⓐ Ⓑ Ⓒ Ⓓ Ⓔ
6. Ⓐ Ⓑ Ⓒ Ⓓ Ⓔ
7. Ⓐ Ⓑ Ⓒ Ⓓ Ⓔ
8. Ⓐ Ⓑ Ⓒ Ⓓ Ⓔ
9. Ⓐ Ⓑ Ⓒ Ⓓ Ⓔ
10. Ⓐ Ⓑ Ⓒ Ⓓ Ⓔ
11. Ⓐ Ⓑ Ⓒ Ⓓ Ⓔ
12. Ⓐ Ⓑ Ⓒ Ⓓ Ⓔ

13. Ⓐ Ⓑ Ⓒ Ⓓ Ⓔ
14. Ⓐ Ⓑ Ⓒ Ⓓ Ⓔ
15. Ⓐ Ⓑ Ⓒ Ⓓ Ⓔ
16. Ⓐ Ⓑ Ⓒ Ⓓ Ⓔ
17. Ⓐ Ⓑ Ⓒ Ⓓ Ⓔ
18. Ⓐ Ⓑ Ⓒ Ⓓ Ⓔ
19. Ⓐ Ⓑ Ⓒ Ⓓ Ⓔ
20. Ⓐ Ⓑ Ⓒ Ⓓ Ⓔ
21. Ⓐ Ⓑ Ⓒ Ⓓ Ⓔ
22. Ⓐ Ⓑ Ⓒ Ⓓ Ⓔ
23. Ⓐ Ⓑ Ⓒ Ⓓ Ⓔ
24. Ⓐ Ⓑ Ⓒ Ⓓ Ⓔ

25. Ⓐ Ⓑ Ⓒ Ⓓ Ⓔ
26. Ⓐ Ⓑ Ⓒ Ⓓ Ⓔ
27. Ⓐ Ⓑ Ⓒ Ⓓ Ⓔ
28. Ⓐ Ⓑ Ⓒ Ⓓ Ⓔ
29. Ⓐ Ⓑ Ⓒ Ⓓ Ⓔ
30. Ⓐ Ⓑ Ⓒ Ⓓ Ⓔ
31. Ⓐ Ⓑ Ⓒ Ⓓ Ⓔ
32. Ⓐ Ⓑ Ⓒ Ⓓ Ⓔ
33. Ⓐ Ⓑ Ⓒ Ⓓ Ⓔ
34. Ⓐ Ⓑ Ⓒ Ⓓ Ⓔ
35. Ⓐ Ⓑ Ⓒ Ⓓ Ⓔ
36. Ⓐ Ⓑ Ⓒ Ⓓ Ⓔ

37. Ⓐ Ⓑ Ⓒ Ⓓ Ⓔ
38. Ⓐ Ⓑ Ⓒ Ⓓ Ⓔ
39. Ⓐ Ⓑ Ⓒ Ⓓ Ⓔ
40. Ⓐ Ⓑ Ⓒ Ⓓ Ⓔ
41. Ⓐ Ⓑ Ⓒ Ⓓ Ⓔ
42. Ⓐ Ⓑ Ⓒ Ⓓ Ⓔ
43. Ⓐ Ⓑ Ⓒ Ⓓ Ⓔ
44. Ⓐ Ⓑ Ⓒ Ⓓ Ⓔ
45. Ⓐ Ⓑ Ⓒ Ⓓ Ⓔ

NOTES

The **Princeton Review**®

Completely darken bubbles with a No. 2 pencil. If you make a mistake, be sure to erase mark completely. Erase all stray marks.

1. YOUR NAME:
(Print) _____ Last _____ First _____ M.I.

SIGNATURE: _____ DATE: ___/___/___

HOME ADDRESS: _____
(Print) _____ Number and Street

_____
City _____ State _____ Zip Code

PHONE NO. : _____
(Print)

IMPORTANT: Please fill in these boxes exactly as shown on the back cover of your test book.

2. TEST FORM
_____

3. TEST CODE

4. REGISTRATION NUMBER

5. YOUR NAME

First 4 letters of last name | FIRST INIT | MID INIT

6. DATE OF BIRTH

Month	Day	Year
⃝ JAN		
⃝ FEB		
⃝ MAR	⓪ ⓪ ⓪ ⓪	
⃝ APR	① ① ① ①	
⃝ MAY	② ② ② ②	
⃝ JUN	③ ③ ③ ③	
⃝ JUL	④ ④ ④	
⃝ AUG	⑤ ⑤ ⑤	
⃝ SEP	⑥ ⑥ ⑥	
⃝ OCT	⑦ ⑦ ⑦	
⃝ NOV	⑧ ⑧ ⑧	
⃝ DEC	⑨ ⑨ ⑨	

The **Princeton Review**®

Section   1

Start with number 1 for each new section.
If a section has fewer questions than answer spaces, leave the extra answer spaces blank.

1. Ⓐ Ⓑ Ⓒ Ⓓ Ⓔ
2. Ⓐ Ⓑ Ⓒ Ⓓ Ⓔ
3. Ⓐ Ⓑ Ⓒ Ⓓ Ⓔ
4. Ⓐ Ⓑ Ⓒ Ⓓ Ⓔ
5. Ⓐ Ⓑ Ⓒ Ⓓ Ⓔ
6. Ⓐ Ⓑ Ⓒ Ⓓ Ⓔ
7. Ⓐ Ⓑ Ⓒ Ⓓ Ⓔ
8. Ⓐ Ⓑ Ⓒ Ⓓ Ⓔ
9. Ⓐ Ⓑ Ⓒ Ⓓ Ⓔ
10. Ⓐ Ⓑ Ⓒ Ⓓ Ⓔ
11. Ⓐ Ⓑ Ⓒ Ⓓ Ⓔ
12. Ⓐ Ⓑ Ⓒ Ⓓ Ⓔ

13. Ⓐ Ⓑ Ⓒ Ⓓ Ⓔ
14. Ⓐ Ⓑ Ⓒ Ⓓ Ⓔ
15. Ⓐ Ⓑ Ⓒ Ⓓ Ⓔ
16. Ⓐ Ⓑ Ⓒ Ⓓ Ⓔ
17. Ⓐ Ⓑ Ⓒ Ⓓ Ⓔ
18. Ⓐ Ⓑ Ⓒ Ⓓ Ⓔ
19. Ⓐ Ⓑ Ⓒ Ⓓ Ⓔ
20. Ⓐ Ⓑ Ⓒ Ⓓ Ⓔ
21. Ⓐ Ⓑ Ⓒ Ⓓ Ⓔ
22. Ⓐ Ⓑ Ⓒ Ⓓ Ⓔ
23. Ⓐ Ⓑ Ⓒ Ⓓ Ⓔ
24. Ⓐ Ⓑ Ⓒ Ⓓ Ⓔ

25. Ⓐ Ⓑ Ⓒ Ⓓ Ⓔ
26. Ⓐ Ⓑ Ⓒ Ⓓ Ⓔ
27. Ⓐ Ⓑ Ⓒ Ⓓ Ⓔ
28. Ⓐ Ⓑ Ⓒ Ⓓ Ⓔ
29. Ⓐ Ⓑ Ⓒ Ⓓ Ⓔ
30. Ⓐ Ⓑ Ⓒ Ⓓ Ⓔ
31. Ⓐ Ⓑ Ⓒ Ⓓ Ⓔ
32. Ⓐ Ⓑ Ⓒ Ⓓ Ⓔ
33. Ⓐ Ⓑ Ⓒ Ⓓ Ⓔ
34. Ⓐ Ⓑ Ⓒ Ⓓ Ⓔ
35. Ⓐ Ⓑ Ⓒ Ⓓ Ⓔ
36. Ⓐ Ⓑ Ⓒ Ⓓ Ⓔ

37. Ⓐ Ⓑ Ⓒ Ⓓ Ⓔ
38. Ⓐ Ⓑ Ⓒ Ⓓ Ⓔ
39. Ⓐ Ⓑ Ⓒ Ⓓ Ⓔ
40. Ⓐ Ⓑ Ⓒ Ⓓ Ⓔ
41. Ⓐ Ⓑ Ⓒ Ⓓ Ⓔ
42. Ⓐ Ⓑ Ⓒ Ⓓ Ⓔ
43. Ⓐ Ⓑ Ⓒ Ⓓ Ⓔ
44. Ⓐ Ⓑ Ⓒ Ⓓ Ⓔ
45. Ⓐ Ⓑ Ⓒ Ⓓ Ⓔ

NOTES

The Princeton Review®

Completely darken bubbles with a No. 2 pencil. If you make a mistake, be sure to erase mark completely. Erase all stray marks.

1. YOUR NAME:
(Print) _____ Last _____ First _____ M.I.

SIGNATURE: _____ DATE: ___ / ___ / ___

HOME ADDRESS: _____
(Print) _____ Number and Street

_____ City _____ State _____ Zip Code

PHONE NO. : _____
(Print)

IMPORTANT: Please fill in these boxes exactly as shown on the back cover of your test book.

2. TEST FORM

_____

3. TEST CODE

4. REGISTRATION NUMBER

5. YOUR NAME

First 4 letters of last name | FIRST INIT | MID INIT

6. DATE OF BIRTH

Month	Day		Year	

JAN, FEB, MAR, APR, MAY, JUN, JUL, AUG, SEP, OCT, NOV, DEC

The Princeton Review®

Section ①

Start with number 1 for each new section.
If a section has fewer questions than answer spaces, leave the extra answer spaces blank.

1. Ⓐ Ⓑ Ⓒ Ⓓ Ⓔ   13. Ⓐ Ⓑ Ⓒ Ⓓ Ⓔ   25. Ⓐ Ⓑ Ⓒ Ⓓ Ⓔ   37. Ⓐ Ⓑ Ⓒ Ⓓ Ⓔ
2. Ⓐ Ⓑ Ⓒ Ⓓ Ⓔ   14. Ⓐ Ⓑ Ⓒ Ⓓ Ⓔ   26. Ⓐ Ⓑ Ⓒ Ⓓ Ⓔ   38. Ⓐ Ⓑ Ⓒ Ⓓ Ⓔ
3. Ⓐ Ⓑ Ⓒ Ⓓ Ⓔ   15. Ⓐ Ⓑ Ⓒ Ⓓ Ⓔ   27. Ⓐ Ⓑ Ⓒ Ⓓ Ⓔ   39. Ⓐ Ⓑ Ⓒ Ⓓ Ⓔ
4. Ⓐ Ⓑ Ⓒ Ⓓ Ⓔ   16. Ⓐ Ⓑ Ⓒ Ⓓ Ⓔ   28. Ⓐ Ⓑ Ⓒ Ⓓ Ⓔ   40. Ⓐ Ⓑ Ⓒ Ⓓ Ⓔ
5. Ⓐ Ⓑ Ⓒ Ⓓ Ⓔ   17. Ⓐ Ⓑ Ⓒ Ⓓ Ⓔ   29. Ⓐ Ⓑ Ⓒ Ⓓ Ⓔ   41. Ⓐ Ⓑ Ⓒ Ⓓ Ⓔ
6. Ⓐ Ⓑ Ⓒ Ⓓ Ⓔ   18. Ⓐ Ⓑ Ⓒ Ⓓ Ⓔ   30. Ⓐ Ⓑ Ⓒ Ⓓ Ⓔ   42. Ⓐ Ⓑ Ⓒ Ⓓ Ⓔ
7. Ⓐ Ⓑ Ⓒ Ⓓ Ⓔ   19. Ⓐ Ⓑ Ⓒ Ⓓ Ⓔ   31. Ⓐ Ⓑ Ⓒ Ⓓ Ⓔ   43. Ⓐ Ⓑ Ⓒ Ⓓ Ⓔ
8. Ⓐ Ⓑ Ⓒ Ⓓ Ⓔ   20. Ⓐ Ⓑ Ⓒ Ⓓ Ⓔ   32. Ⓐ Ⓑ Ⓒ Ⓓ Ⓔ   44. Ⓐ Ⓑ Ⓒ Ⓓ Ⓔ
9. Ⓐ Ⓑ Ⓒ Ⓓ Ⓔ   21. Ⓐ Ⓑ Ⓒ Ⓓ Ⓔ   33. Ⓐ Ⓑ Ⓒ Ⓓ Ⓔ   45. Ⓐ Ⓑ Ⓒ Ⓓ Ⓔ
10. Ⓐ Ⓑ Ⓒ Ⓓ Ⓔ   22. Ⓐ Ⓑ Ⓒ Ⓓ Ⓔ   34. Ⓐ Ⓑ Ⓒ Ⓓ Ⓔ
11. Ⓐ Ⓑ Ⓒ Ⓓ Ⓔ   23. Ⓐ Ⓑ Ⓒ Ⓓ Ⓔ   35. Ⓐ Ⓑ Ⓒ Ⓓ Ⓔ
12. Ⓐ Ⓑ Ⓒ Ⓓ Ⓔ   24. Ⓐ Ⓑ Ⓒ Ⓓ Ⓔ   36. Ⓐ Ⓑ Ⓒ Ⓓ Ⓔ

NOTES